To Stephanie Molin
with warm welcome to
esv and best wishes...

David M. Furrer

October 31, 2013

CHOICE AGAINST CHOICE

CHOICE AGAINST CHOICE

Constructing a Policy-Assessing Sociology for Social Development

David M. Freeman

UNIVERSITY PRESS OF COLORADO

Copyright © 1992 by the University Press of Colorado
P.O. Box 849
Niwot, Colorado 80544

10 9 8 7 6 5 4 3 2 1

The University Press of Colorado is a cooperative publishing enterprise
supported, in part, by Adams State College, Colorado State University, Fort
Lewis College, Mesa State College, Metropolitan State College of Denver,
University of Colorado, University of Northern Colorado, University of
Southern Colorado, and Western State College.

Library of Congress Cataloging-in-Publication Data

Freeman, David M.
   Choice against choice: constructing a policy-assessing sociology for
social development / David M. Freeman.
       p.   cm.
   Includes index.
   ISBN 0-87081-237-8 (alk. paper)
   1. Social policy — Valuation. 2. Social values. 3. Social choice.
4. Technology assessment. I. Title.
HN28.F68 1992
361.6'1 — dc20   91-40379
                                                                              CIP

The paper used in this publication meets the minimum requirements of the
American National Standard for Information Sciences—Permanence of
Paper for Printed Library Materials. ANSI Z39.48–1984

∞

To Sandra

"For, having such a blessing in his lady,
He finds the joys of heaven here on earth."

William Shakespeare
Merchant of Venice
Act III, Scene V

CONTENTS

Contents

Contents

Contents

Contents

TABLES

FIGURES

Figures

PREFACE

Technology creates potential to do work; technological potentials must be disciplined by information about values. Values are criteria for choice that harness and direct technological potential, but judgments of value cannot be directly deduced from scientific statements of "what is," and value preferences of diverse publics are typically mutually incompatible. Given that technological alternatives will differentially hurt and help people, promote and retard incompatible choices, or advance and extinguish components of the ecosystem, welfare is always transferred from group to group, time to time, and place to place. Policy assessment in the service of a vision of societal development focuses on the question: What is to be preferred and why? Which values serving which interests should guide collective choices from among technological and natural resource options?

It is impossible to distinguish between better and worse technological policies except in the context of value criteria that define what is meant by social progress or development. Concern with the idea of social development has dominated social science for well over two hundred years, but the meaning of the concept has been subject to much debate, confusion, and polemic — a situation that gives pause to anyone contemplating policy assessment for technology or anything else. The objective of this book is to show that a policy-assessing sociology can be constructed in a defensible manner so as to serve a coherent conception of social development. Concepts and procedures will be illustrated by examples drawn from the United States and South Asia.

The reader is advised that this book does not address policy formulation — the traditional domain of the political scientist and political sociologist. Nor does this effort focus on policy execution or implementation — so dear to students of public administration and complex organization. The task of designing appropriate institutional frameworks for pursuit of social development is not addressed here. Those seeking to learn techniques of policy evaluation, for determining whether announced program goals have been achieved by a given set of policy-implementing organizational units, will find no discussion of quasi-experimental or experimental designs for evaluational research.

This effort is focused on the problem of policy assessment — assessment of alternative policy proposals in terms of defensible value criteria organized to serve a viable conception of social development. Many policies may well be proposed in the policy formulation processes emergent out of the interaction among politicians, the judiciary, administrators, and conflicting and cooperating publics. After policies have been assessed, questions of implementation and evaluation arise. This is not to hold that policies flow in simple linear fashion from formulation, assessment, and implementation to evaluation and ultimately back to reformulation. This is only to say that, given complex and subtle interaction among these activities, valuation for policy assessment must occur, however well or poorly.

The thesis is that policy assessment can be approached in a logically sound manner and that sociologists can usefully contribute to it while remaining sensitive to cultural diversity, without falling into ethnocentrism or incommensurable subjective assertion. Sociology has witnessed long and bitter debate about inserting values into scientific analysis; this argument holds forth a logically viable method for reasoning about policy "oughts," informed by empirical "facts," using generalizable nomothetic principles that can be employed in particular settings and to which sociology makes a central but not exclusive contribution. The assessment of policy alternatives to ascertain which best serve a defensible conception of social development is a task that must draw upon insights of those in many disciplines — philosophers, political scientists, economists, ecologists, engineers, agriculturalists, and those representing the several natural sciences. Nothing advanced in this argument should be taken as denigrating the crucial contributions of other disciplines to questions raised here. It is only to assert that sociologists can advance an analysis to inform developmental policy choice in interdisciplinary and cross-cultural contexts.

Chapter 1 states the terms of the policy-assessment challenge by addressing four interrelated problems. First, agents of the public household must possess logically defensible value criteria for choosing among policy options in a world in which each alternative would impose a combination of benefit and harm. Second, a case is made that technology does not impact society evenly. Struggle over technology and natural resources policy revolves around the clash of opposing values where each alternative has its desirable side, but advantages come at serious cost. The problem of public policy choice for societal development must come to grips with its tragic dimension — choice in the public household is all too rarely one between "good" and "bad" consequences but is typically between "good-good" or, more accurately, between the "good-bad" associated with policy X as compared to the mix of "good-bad" entrained by Y. The twin questions become, then:

1. What logic(s) of empirical fact can be advanced for examining what "is" or "will be" under policy X? This speaks to the questions: "Good" and "bad" for whom? For how long?

2. What logic(s) of value can be advanced for selecting a preferred set of "goods" and "bads" associated with policy X and for rejecting the profile of advantage and disadvantage associated with Y? This speaks to the question: What defensible grounds can be advanced for justifying the imposition of a particular profile of benefit and harm to the advantage of some and detriment of others in the name of social development?

Within the framework of a technologically dynamic society and its transfers of welfare, an important part of the policy-assessment challenge has to do with the limits of theory — any scientific theory. Can theoretical propositions, in either the realm of fact or value, abstracted from a richer whole, and parsimoniously characterizing aspects of the whole, inform and guide policy that must impact the whole? Or how can the abstract, general, and parsimonious direct the concrete, specific, and complex? This is grist for the third section. The fourth section of the first chapter addresses a final question: Is it possible to recognize a humanly constructed value-relativistic world and still assert value judgments defining societal development that are rooted in defensible logics and applicable to various cultural meaning systems without falling into ethnocentrism?

Chapter 2 briefly traces the historical response to this challenge. Beginning by noting the breakdown of the supranatural medieval value synthesis, the discussion proceeds to the aspirations of the Enlightenment thinkers who avidly, but naively, trusted that reason would lead to formulation of value criteria for guiding technology in society for the welfare of all. Early naturalist value thought was destroyed by David Hume, just as later nineteenth-century evolutionary value thought was destroyed by G. E. Moore, the cultural relativism of the English anthropologists, and the sharp attacks of Max Weber.

Nevertheless, sociology was established by nineteenth-century disciples of evolutionism with the express purpose of bringing Enlightenment science to bear on social policy assessment for the purpose of advancing social development. Sociology, the queen of the sciences, was to provide guiding rationality to insure that society advanced to its greatest developmental potentials. The twentieth-century story has been one of retreat and disappointment; the discipline has not sufficiently come to grips with the policy-assessment question within a coherent developmental vision. Sociology's failure to fulfill the Enlightenment development project, to the satisfaction of even a minority of its practitioners, is associated with much contemporary unrest and unease within the discipline and among its several audiences.

By the 1920s, troubled sociologists became embroiled in bitter disputes and formed mutually hostile camps from which they have yet to extract themselves. In one corner are the value-free scientists, for whom values are left to citizens, and scientists functioning only as citizens for whom sociology cannot perform valid policy assessment. In an opposing corner are applied researchers who admit to making value judgments in the choice of problems, variables, and clients, but for whom the basic value premises are fundamentally based on subjective preference and trust in the benign disposition of power within their particular society. In a third position, and rejecting both of the above, are value-critical theorists who embrace value judgment as central to their efforts to construct a science capable of performing a liberating function, but for whom logically justified value assessments have posed as much a problem as for pure and applied scientists. Critical theorists have, whatever their critics may say, kept alive in the late twentieth century the much beleaguered notion of a cross-culturally viable conception of social development.

Chapter 3 comes to grips with the fact that economics has provided the dominant valuational logic for defining social development and doing policy assessment. But economic valuational logics break down for at least five interrelated reasons — concentrations of power, technological externalities, public-goods problems, the tyranny of small decisions, and difficulties associated with social stratification and resource distributions. Calls for socialization of production and elimination of marketplaces are badly misplaced because such remedies lack adequate valuational analysis that would insure that market deficiencies would not be replaced by assessment mechanisms as defective as those associated with blind trust in markets. The troubles of Eastern European, Soviet, and Chinese political economies provide ample testimony with respect to deficiencies of twentieth-century to-talitarian socialist experiments in controlling markets. Finally, Chapter 3 notes that the sociology of development literature, insofar as there is admission that analysis of societal development must involve a normative enterprise, also fails to generate workable policy-assessment muscle.

Chapter 4, in its first part, explores the major value criteria extant in contemporary policy-assessment literature — economic, sociological, political, and philosophical. Each criterion is found to be deficient in important respects. It is no coincidence, given problems found, that the dispute between the sociological camps identified in Chapter 2 has been so bitter, so polemical, so arid. Chapter 4, in its second part, reviews the consequent fragmentation of the sociological policy-assessment enterprise — broken into disparate domains of social problems, social indicators and quality of life research, technology assessment, social impact assessment, public involvement, and the appropriate technology movement. All of this is to document the twentieth-century confusion and fragmentation of the nineteenth-century policy-assessment and development vision. Attacked by cultural relativists, denied by the logical positivists, hidden by many applied sociologists, and polemicized by the radicals, the idea of a developmental sociology relevant to policy assessment barely breathes in the final decades of the twentieth century.

Chapter 5 responds to the challenge articulated in Chapter 1 and traced in Chapters 2, 3, and 4. The argument demonstrates that it is possible to construct a logically justifiable, cross-culturally viable method for conducting normative "ought" policy assessments in the context of empirically established "is" conditions. Three normative questions are addressed: (1) what reasoned criteria are appropriate for determining the adequacy of value criteria for public policy assessment (this is a question of defining meta-criteria); (2) what substantive value criteria can be proposed, and so arranged, as to best fulfill the meta-tests; and (3) what rationale undergirds the value criteria proposed for defining social development and for doing the analytical work of policy assessment? The value logic advanced makes no claim to prescribe individual life plans. It accepts that private ends do not require ranking or harmonizing while at the same time it holds forth an explicit set of value criteria — connected with empirically determined analysis of fact — with which to resolve policy conflicts arising out of patterns of private action.

The logics of fact and value advanced do not pretend to completeness. They are intended to give defensible meaning to the idea of social development, but the analysis cannot be comprehensive, tidy, and rounded off so as to pretend to finality. Rather, the work presented here is necessarily tentative and partial; it comes packaged with an invitation to improve and extend these logics of fact and value and thereby make the idea of development increasingly robust. Most specifically, the logics of fact and value put forth in this effort are designed to focus on matters of technology and natural resources. It may well be that some of the analysis will be suggestive for policy assessment in other domains.

The argument in Chapter 5 finds that it is possible to construct a policy-assessment language centered on the measurement of specific social structural phenomena. The neglected message of concepts having to do with the breakdown of faith in markets — externality, public goods, the tyranny of small decisions, concentrated power, and problematic resource distributions — is the primacy of publicly sanctioned social structures within which people make their private and public lives and conduct market exchange. I seek, and find, a set of concepts for the investigation of the "is" and the "ought" that focuses attention on the shape of social structures within which individuals operate. How is a developmental policy assessment possible? To this philosophical and social science question, a social structural sociological answer is constructed. It is possible by examining the impact of proposed policies on specific and measurable properties of social structures, each of which is abstracted from a richer, more complete whole, none of which can pretend to adequately describe that whole, but each of which represents a key parameter upon which life in the whole is strategically conditioned.

Chapters 6, 7, and 8 each operationalize, apply, and illustrate one structural sociological dimension of policy assessment summarized in Chapter 5. Natural resource policy problems encountered in the western United States and South Asia provide grist for the analytical mills.

Chapter 9 examines implications of the argument for the open liberal society and for the kind of policy-assessing social science required to serve that society. A sociology that conducts authentically critical policy assessment, in the service of a coherent conception of developmental change, is found to be a viable enterprise.

DAVID M. FREEMAN

ACKNOWLEDGMENTS

Great poets are said to judge their critics. That audacious soul who critiques Shakespeare runs the risk of revealing his or her own inadequacies more clearly than those of the subject. That is the case here. Enduring issues of technology and society, fact and value, change and development, public policy and its assessment must humble anyone so impertinent as to attempt to bring to these domains useful analytical order of even a most modest nature. In confronting this task, I have been the beneficiary of much help deserving of warm acknowledgement.

Many colleagues have provided constructive reaction to the manuscript: Keith Warner of Brigham Young University, Robert Hunt of Brandeis University, R. Scott Frey of Kansas State University, Dora Lodwick of Miami University (Ohio), and Edward Knop, David Crocker, Holmes Rolston III, Edward Sparling, and Frank Santopolo of Colorado State University. To each I express my warmest appreciation. David Hittle rendered most useful assistance with the conflict analysis in Chapter 6. In addition, deeply felt thanks are expressed to Peter Ashton and Coryell Ohlander of the U.S. Forest Service, who contributed so much to the early field testing of the analytical procedures advanced in Chapters 6, 7, and 8. Vicki Duneman has attended to many details of manuscript preparation — an effort that has earned my lasting gratitude. Jody Berman of the University Press of Colorado and Libby Barstow deserve special mention for their editorial talent and effort, which have done much to improve this presentation. Those unnamed students who have galvanized probing dialogue in graduate seminars on developmental change deserve special acknowledgment, for they have provided the opportunity to address the critical issues. Finally, I have benefited from support rendered by the United States Agency for International Development under its Title XII program administered through Colorado State University's Office of International Programs. Dr. James Meiman, director of that office, and Betty Eckert, who has so ably assisted him, are to be warmly acknowledged for their administrative support.

Acknowledgments

This effort represents a gentle protest against the view that insists that specialists stick to their niches. It may well be thought that what follows is an impertinent crashing of guild boundaries. But there is an issue to be addressed that requires it, however clumsily done and with whatever risk to one's reputation — the problem of harnessing, in a cross-culturally defensible vision of social development, logics of empirical factual "is" statements and those of normative "oughts." It is only fair to note that the impertinence of this effort cannot be attributed to any of the above named individuals. Although I hope that mistakes have been minimized, errors are those of the author alone. I proceed in the spirit of Clarence S. Darrow's affirmation: "Chase after the truth like all hell and you will free yourself, even though you never touch its coattails."

D.M.F.

CHOICE AGAINST CHOICE

I

The Challenge of Policy Assessment

The survival of mankind is threatened by overpopulation, waste of resources, by voluntary weapons of nuclear war and the involuntary ones of pollution. The forces of enlightened rationality seem to have turned against their best purpose. The justice of man's social institutions is threatened, too, by the uncontrolled power of organizations and firms and bureaucracies. . . . And the solutions offered by some for these problems make matters worse: The authoritarianism of a small elite which is supposed to assure survival along with law and order, the egalitarianism of a tyrannic majority for which justice has come to mean that no man must have to do anything which is different. — Ralf Dahrendorf[1]

What is needed in order to make . . . [value] judgments is a new paradigm which will encompass the man technology natural environment interdependencies more effectively than any currently available. — Nathan Rosenberg[2]

At the time of the discovery of the Americas, some thinking people in western Europe believed that their troubled world faced impending disaster. *The Nuremberg Chronicle* dwelt on "the calamity of our time . . . in which inequity and evil have increased to the highest pitch. . . ." Readers were given six blank pages to record events from 1493 to the end of the world.[3] Every age is considered, by at least some of its contemporaries, to be an age of crisis. In our time, crises associated with matters of technology and natural resources are the stuff of daily news — the international debt crises; the energy and water crises; the degradation of urban and rural environments in both rich and poor countries associated with maldistribution of natural, economic, and political resources; the crises associated with toxic wastes, destruction of tropical forests, acid rain, ozone depletion, ocean pollution, and extinction of species; and the bundle of crises associated with local terrorism, illicit drugs, and the global diffusion of weaponry.

1

The idea of crisis has almost become banal, but beneath the daily headlines many contemporary thinkers sense crisis in a deeper sense — a sense that public institutions in both capitalist and socialist societies have been exposed as lacking capacity to allocate resources to values in legitimate ways informed by a defensible collective vision of social development. Western culture has been built upon the idea of progress rooted in the power of human intellect, rationality, science, and technological advancement. The idea of progress, in turn, has been embodied in the concept of social development. Whereas the verb to change means simply that something has been altered and to grow means to change in the direction of increased scale, to develop means to effect a transformation from some state of affairs defined as inferior to some new condition thought to be superior.

A commonsense post–eighteenth-century Enlightenment view has been that history represents progress, a march upward as humanity employs ever more sophisticated science, technology, and forms of social organization to develop more choices for human beings to exercise in domination of each other and the environment. The general value, giving meaning to social development in the twentieth century, has been economic growth in the service of a continuous expansion of choices in the aggregate. The idea of development has, in most quarters, been reduced to little more than a function of the advancement and diffusion of more efficacious technological means to produce growth of old choices at less cost and whole new orders of choice. In the course of all this, our collective civic capacity to undertake reasoned valuative discussion about technological and natural resource policy options and, thereby, about the structural shape of a "better" or more "socially developed" society has fragmented and faltered.

Social development has to do with advancement and diffusion of new structures of choice opportunities that fulfill reasoned value criteria. More choice per se does not necessarily imply social development, but more choice that fulfills logically defensible value standards does. But what value standards, cross-culturally defensible, can be asserted to define the meaning of development? Social development must be embedded with specific logics of fact and value that will provide analytical policy assessment muscle.

A simple assertion that more choice is better cannot constitute a defensible value criterion. Such a notion connotes an absence of values. To advance choice X, choice Y must be sacrificed. Some justifiable value standard must do the work of sorting out benefits and burdens of options X and Y. Simple-minded dedication to "more choice" overlooks the real valuational issues and can be of interest only to an isolate trapped on a desert island or to utopians who envision a world without scarcity, without limits, without the negative spillovers that associate with the exercise of some choices to the detriment of others. Agents of the public household must deny choice to some in order to open choice to others. Value criteria must include coherent justification for advancing some choices and extinguishing others — and that justification must be open to the inspection of reason by citizens.

Growth, especially economic growth, has become the secular moral foundation for the twentieth-century state — capitalist and socialist — and the central component of the idea of social development. Although strictly speaking growth is not a value-laden concept, it has become intertwined with valuational matters: Growth in employment, per capita income, and gross national product has been seen by virtually all twentieth-century regimes as "good" because it promises to make resources available to fulfill dreams of social development however defined and however open to serious question.[4] Concern with the meaning and measurement of social development has been a central feature of social analysis at least since the eighteenth-century Enlightenment, but the meaning of that concept remains confused.[5]

In the mid-1980s, when Mikhail Gorbachev gave tacit approval to changes in Poland wrought by Solidarity's extended struggle, he sent a signal to people in Eastern Europe that the U.S.S.R. would permit reform in their political economies. When reform came in the late 1980s, it came fast. The old totalitarian systems were so lacking in performance — especially in delivering economic growth fitted for a consumer society so long promised and so obviously available across the borders — that once Soviet support for the old order vanished, the systems collapsed in the "revolution of 1989" for lack of legitimacy in front of a euphoric citizenry and an incredulous outside world. In less than two years, in August 1991, the Communist Party of the Soviet Union was swept from its centralized perch in the aftermath of a failed coup d'etat conducted in its name, an event that pushed Gorbachev straight into the grasp of those demanding fundamental liberal reforms. The larger meaning of these Eastern European and Soviet events will be studied and debated for centuries, but the immediate effect has been to permit the bubbling-up of political pluralism, elections, and greater scope for markets. A central purpose in all this is, of course, to get on with the business of generating greater economic growth.

3

Yet as the ideological Holy War has been called off, or at least placed on temporary hold, there is little to celebrate. A turn to free enterprise in pursuit of social development defined as growth in supersaturated material abundance, blind to the shape of society within which markets function, has already led to a ravaged environment, mountains of trash and streams of toxic wastes, neglect of human resources, and explosive increases in inequality between rich and poor.

By the 1970s and 1980s, in most Western nations, economic growth was associated less and less with progress and increasingly with problems of dual societies, injustice, and environmental destruction. In addition, the very idea of social development fell upon hard times as any attempt to define "better" for society came under hostile fire by those who pointed out that a "solution" for some was a "problem" for others depending on position in social structure. The idea of secular human progress has therefore fallen into disrepute among the knowledgeable and into disuse among those scrambling for immediate political and economic advantage. What we are left with is a general commitment to more "growth" so somehow more people can experience more things generated by growth. Henry Teune has clearly stated the problem: "An individually based secular morality cannot accept a world without growth. What can be the basis for judging what and how much growth is good or bad in order to make collective decisions to help the good things and relationships grow and to retard the growth of the bad? Secular answers have to be found. . . ."[6]

On the one hand, a secular vision of social progress rooted in ever greater consumption of products of economic growth cannot accept a world without ever more growth; on the other hand, such a crippled vision of societal development cannot address the issues surrounding the need to put reason about desirable structural shapes of society in control of economic growth. What composition of economic growth fulfills reasoned normative standards and therefore should be pursued in the name of social development? What composition of growth does not? Why not? How can we know? In a world racing past the old nineteenth-century ideologies, secular reasoned answers must be found and sociology must be part of the hunt.

As we set aside our cold war ideological prisms, we must pick up new lenses capable of focusing on more adequate conceptions of collective social progress. We need visions that can guide technology in the construction of more developed societies conceived in terms other than continued value-blind economic growth at 4 percent per year forever — the ideology of the cancer cell.

The desperate mix of progress and despair that marks our age is rooted in the fact that advancing technologies have created new capacities for action; new options for production, consumption, and destruction; and thereby new ways to interfere with each other over wide space and extended time unmatched by advancement of value standards for guiding technological applications toward some coherent vision of social development. Policy selection in the face of scarcity brings into focus alternative values, and the criteria chosen for guiding policy in the public household are the means by which a society defines itself. There must be a legitimate sense of what is better and worse, developmental and nondevelopmental, for the public household within which gains and losses can be allocated and claims of equity versus equity can be adjudicated. The foundation of any society is the capacity of agencies in the public household to constrain and compromise private ends for public purposes to protect neighbor from neighbor, entrepreneur from entrepreneur, the next generation from depredations of contemporaries. But an insufficiency of policy-assessment value criteria threatens the viability of the civitas. Public exchanges become quiet, cynical deals by which the powerful benefit at the expense of the weak, or interests become so polarized that the civic process of public household choice becomes laced with destructive conflict. It is in this fundamental sense that one speaks of a crisis in the public household and asserts that it is without logics of "good reasons" for making important policy choices in the service of a viable conception of social development.

It is the purpose of the remainder of this chapter to clarify the terms of the challenge. Discussion will proceed in four parts: (1) first, by addressing the concept of the public household, agents of which are responsible for the shape of society within which people make their lives; (2) second, by noting that technological change transfers welfare and illfare in multiple ways, thereby establishing demand for assessment; (3) third, by acknowledging the problem of employing abstract general nomothetic knowledge in a theory-defying complex world; and (4) by recognizing the problem of bringing reason and logic to normative questions in a socially constructed value-relativistic world.

SOCIAL DEVELOPMENT POLICY AND THE PUBLIC HOUSEHOLD

A policy consists of a settled course of action that is applied to numerous individual decisions. In a specific instance, a farmer may decide to burn, or not to burn, weeds out of an irrigation ditch; in such an instance no policy question is addressed. However, if public authorities settle on a course of action prohibiting outdoor burning in the name of preserving community air quality, a policy has been established that transcends the interests of any particular farmer in the name of social progress. Many specific cases will then be decided in the light of the general policy. Public policy formulation, assessment, and implementation consist of deliberate attempts to shape collective futures. Alternative shapes of choice structures may be viewed as being more or less socially developmental depending upon the extent to which policy-affected choice structures fulfill values defining development for the collectivity.

Distinction between the policy affairs of the public household and private life has not always been a part of the common sense of the community. Medieval European thought saw all mankind as constituting a God-ordained earthly community within which both sacred and secular authority could interfere in aspects of life people would later call private. For centuries, European and Oriental despots made common practice of coupling private with public funds and purposes. In the West, the concept of secular public and private spheres did not fully develop until the church was relegated to a narrower role under the control of the secular state associated with increased toleration of religious dissent and autonomy of religious groups.[7]

The distinction between affairs of the private and public households remains complex. *Public* does not necessarily mean government controlled, and *private* does not mean free of regulation by public authorities. The source of funding is not necessarily a useful indicator of the spheres because private organizations are often publicly subsidized, and public authorities can be recipient of private largess. Furthermore, the difference cannot neatly be determined by services performed, as it is well known that many private organizations provide public services for profit — package delivery, refuse collection and treatment, education, health care — and much public output goes to private consumers — for example, social security checks, coal leases, timber sale authorizations.

Policies are public because they have a broad effect on the social structure of choice opportunities. More specifically, issues between

6

individuals, groups, and organizations become public because primary, secondary, or higher-order effects of decision X impact other actors in ways that require public negotiation and resolution. It is the unkind rub of one group's choice upon another's that generates demand for a public policy to address matters for the impacted parties and for future generations. When public authorities specify policy in the name of collective well-being, they reshape social networks in ways impacting social life far beyond the interests of the original decision-making organization that generated the initial spillover effect. Public policies, therefore, emerge out of collisions in private spheres, and they, in turn, shape the very structure of social networks within which private choices are made.

For Aristotle collective discourse about matters of the polis was the essence of citizenship. Those outside the polis — slaves and barbarians — were deprived of the essential feature of the good life. Persons who lived only a private life — who were not permitted to enter the public realm (slaves) or who had not yet established such a realm (barbarians) were not fully human. During the Peloponnesian War the Greek dead were brought home to be honored by Pericles, who in his funeral oration spelled out overarching civic values for which the ultimate sacrifice had been made; there was a clear sense of larger community purpose to be promoted by public authorities. The Athenian Republic had produced, at least in a limited sense, a set of collective values stressing equality of citizen participation, equality before the law, equality of opportunity, and a minimum floor of social status below which no citizen could be allowed to fall.

Later, the civic orders of Rome, the Italian Renaissance cities, the urban centers of the Hanseatic League, and the commercial bourgeoisie of the eighteenth century drew upon and expanded the ancient legacy. As commercial interests continued to struggle for their place under the political sun, they produced an Adam Smith who was not naive in the matter of the importance of good public household policy. His analysis of social development began in Book 1, Chapter 1 of his *Wealth of Nations* (1776) by recognizing that it could only occur ". . . in a well governed society." Smith knew well that public authorities and the citizenry must manage to shape certain desired social structures for the collectivity as a whole within which markets could function to produce healthy forms of economic growth. He saw clearly that markets must operate within an encompassing social structure that would work against coercion, dishonesty, false measurement, and incivility.

Long before Smith, many in the English tradition were steeped in the idea of "commonwealth" derived directly from the old words common and weal. Its original meaning suggested common well-being, the general good of the community as distinguished from the interest of any particular member, and came to be associated with ideas of civic-mindedness and participation. By the eighteenth century, commonwealth conveyed the notion of free citizens conducting public life through representative and responsive government. It comprehended the fundamental notion that what best served the interest of any given individual, or segment of society, did not necessarily best serve the community as a whole. The idea of the commonwealth has developed in several traditions of social thought.[8] No comprehensive survey can be undertaken here, but several lines of thinking require at least cursory mention.

In the lively classical economic tradition of Adam Smith and David Ricardo, two realms of economic activity — the domestic household and the market economy — functioned within a larger social framework established by the state.[9] The domestic household is taken to consist of family-based social units whose production is valued for local consumption. The central organizing principle in this realm is production for use and self-sufficiency with distribution to family members according to need. The market economy, on the other hand, consists of specialized firms exchanging goods and services on an impersonal market. The controlling principle is efficiency in the service of private demand.

In the classical liberal tradition, therefore, there has always been a tension between the desire for lives of self-interest and general community moral and civic responsibility. The very idea of liberal individualism is itself a collective achievement, a product of a particular variety of carefully structured social order that can produce the individually rational decision-maker who seeks advantage in market exchange but who must also be a civically active collectively rational citizen of the encompassing community. The liberal idea of citizenship is unintelligible apart from some sense of participation in an overarching commonwealth.[10] The problems of fitting individualistic liberalism exalting the supremacy of private self-interest with an awareness that individualism could only operate in a social structure that attended to collective facts of interdependency forced a recognition of the need for discourse about the public household and what it could and should do for social development. It was no accident that the inventors of liberal thought also invented "political economy," the

8

"political" part of which was seen to promote the general welfare in ways beyond the capacity of markets alone.

Alexis de Tocqueville pursued this point as he published the first of two volumes entitled *Democracy In America* (1835). De Tocqueville developed an analysis of the normative tradition of a public household rooted in religion and local civic organizational commitments that constrained private pursuit of self-interest. People required public goods that required local organizations to provide and manage them. Furthermore, people required community protection from damaging spillovers — negative externalities in our parlance — induced by unbridled seeking of self-interest in markets. Private market exchange was supplemented by local social and political organization that guided markets according to nonmarket values. This mix of local organization and markets was seen by de Tocqueville to be a fundamental source of national strength and engine of progress in the United States.

Almost a century later, in the 1920s, German and Austrian social-economists, dealing with problems of public finance, commonly used the term *public household* for the set of public agencies required to resolve public conflicts emergent out of mutually incompatible private activities and to satisfy public needs as against private wants. Many have held that the marketplace failed automatically to increase societal welfare in the absence of discipline from an active public household.[11] This strain of thought has culminated in recognition of the need for civic regulation of economic enterprises by popular discourse conducted through planning and coordinating mechanisms fitted to the needs of a liberal open society.[12]

American sociology, emergent around nineteenth-century problems of industrialization and urbanization, was constructed by analysts committed to a conception of secular rationality providing service to a liberal state that would advance the interests of the commonweal. Those founding members of the discipline envisioned a sociology that would, like all callings, serve a conception of the public good, and to that end sociologists sought to contribute to the solution of social problems on terms that served a broad conception of progress for the civil community.[13] "Sociology, standing above both religion and radicalism, was to become an ethical science of social reconstruction."[14] The idea of a public household, to be served by reason in the social sciences, has deep roots in the earliest aspirations of the discipline.

At about the same time that the Austrian social-economists were advancing the idea of public household, a group of European thinkers founded the Institute for Social Research at Weimar, Germany. Elaborating upon the Marxian tradition, Theodore Adorno, Max Horkheimer, and Herbert Marcuse began developing a critique of the structure of opportunity for authentic public discourse in modern technologically advanced societies. Although each had a unique agenda, a fundamental theme for all was investigation of the conditions under which the eighteenth-century Enlightenment project of bringing "practical reason" to social policy assessment had fallen apart under the pressures of modern fascism, capitalism, and communism.[15] Jürgen Habermas, the leading contemporary champion of this line of critical inquiry, has stressed the importance of critical rational public moral discourse capable of guiding policy assessment to steer society toward desirable collective ends.[16] Building on the insights of both Max Weber and Karl Marx, Habermas has pointed to the inadequacies of instrumental (means-oriented) technological rationalities that tend to dominate policy assessment, and he calls for a polis in which the very shape of society itself can be meaningfully examined in the best lights of rational dialogue. Habermas advocates a public household in which people "practice," among other things, policy assessment. Cultivation of that capacity must occur in contexts below and above the level of the nation-state so as to be fitted to the needs of affected people. Habermas wishes to avoid policy assessment situations in which either (1) politicians are ultimate authorities making arbitrary policy choices while employing technical expertise only in selection of instrumental means, or (2) politicians are dependent on scientific-technical elites that establish policy agendas and manipulate discussion of options. He advocates authentic civic dialogue mediating between technocrats and politicians, and with all segments of the citizenry free from domination and contributing to "unconstrained communication," he envisions reasoned discourse on matters of collective action. This tradition has produced another ardent exponent of strengthened practical reason for the public household. Fred R. Dallmayr, in *Polis and Praxis* (1984), fights against the retreat of philosophy and the social sciences into political subjectivism and advances a view of active citizens shaping societies through civil participation in their respective public households by employing reasoned value standards.

Thinkers other than those associated with the tradition of critical theory have also focused on the quality of public policy assessment and have lamented the weakness of public household institutions capable of sustaining it. Most notably among mid-twentieth-century intellectuals, Hannah Arendt (*Origins of Totalitarianism*, 1951) and William J. Kornhauser (*The Politics of Mass Society*, 1959) each succeeded in rendering an analysis of the breakdown of the civic community occurring as social conditions produced by modern technology pulverized citizen capacity for both individual thought and meaningful policy discourse in mass society — a society wherein people were ripped from community traditions, atomized, and stripped of the capacity to engage in rational discussion of alternative developmental directions.

Theodore J. Lowi won wide attention for a rather different but compelling critique of the institutions of modern liberal society as presented in *The End of Liberalism: Ideology, Policy and the Crisis of Public Authority* (1969). Lowi provided a penetrating examination of the weaknesses of interest-group liberalism in conducting the affairs of the public household in the United States. He concluded that the liberal state could not properly and justifiably allocate values among competing interests because it was bereft of the capacity to advance rationally a value position from which incompatible demands of competing interests could be appraised. Lowi found the institutions of the contemporary liberal state to be in a condition of virtual valuational bankruptcy.

The year 1969 marked a sea change in social sciences in the United States for another reason, as it was then that David Easton, addressing the American Political Science Association as its newly installed president, spoke of a "post-behavioral" revolution channeling energies toward the solution of major social and political problems.[17] Easton signaled a reallocation of priorities, a move to a more policy-conscious social science. The new policy sciences were to address description and explanation of causes and consequences of public policy generally. This effort was not necessarily seen to be equivalent to assessing which policies "ought" to win merit in public household decision-making, however, and some wished to avoid the normative implications of the enterprise by denying any attempt to engage in "prescription."[18] But others were prepared to confront directly the fact that policy proposals were supposed to enhance well-being of the commonwealth by some potentially defensible standard.[19]

Broadly paralleling the work of Habermas and building upon renewed policy-assessment interest in U.S. social science, Duncan MacRae, in 1976, advanced the view in his landmark *The Social Function of Social Science* that students of social life could not limit themselves to empirical investigations of the "facts" but had to probe

11

normative questions and be guided by a conception of social science that was placed in the service of some defensible set of public values.[20] Scientific inquiry, for MacRae, is to be wielded to rational valuation for social policy. MacRae systematically went about the task of explicating value standards implicit in the several social sciences. He then contended that the values of science could inform conduct of valuational discourse for the public household. Analysts working in the redirected tradition of the postbehavioral revolution were beginning to valuationally prepare themselves.

During the late 1970s and throughout the 1980s, observers witnessed a surge of interest in diagnosing the aridity of public discourse on valuation and noted continued calls for explicit advancement of public developmental values. Part of the recent critique has lamented the retreat from public commitment and involvement to personal subjective self-absorption, as diagnosed by Christopher Lasch in *The Culture of Narcissism* (1979), *Robert Bellah* et al. in *Habits of the Heart* (1985), and Robert Nisbet in *The Present Age: Progress and Anarchy in Modern America* (1988), where the subjectivist threat to meaningful dialogue about the shape of society is forcefully put:

> The great fallacy, ultimately the evil, of subjectivism is that from it one comes to be convinced that what lies within consciousness, within one person's consciousness, has more reality, more value, perhaps even more truth, than what lies outside the person in the world of external events and change. The objective, the dispassionate, even as ideals, are derided by the subjectivist, who even binds the school to the belief that what pupils know, or think they know, about their feelings, natural impulses, likes and dislikes, is more important than what might be taught them about the external world.[21]

People handicapped by lack of tools to probe, discuss, and valuate alternative shapes of social structures above and beyond their internal subjective realities are deprived of the essential capacity to participate in public household discourse about developmental directions for society. Alasdair MacIntyre (*After Virtue*, 1981; *Whose Justice? Which Rationality?* 1988) has provided a compelling history of breakdowns and discontinuities of public valuational logics in Western philosophic thought, breakdowns and discontinuities that are especially problematic under social conditions of technologically advanced and socially differentiated societies. Given the serious problems identified by

MacIntyre, there is little surprise that many analysts of the contemporary scene in the West observe and lament a continuing decline of public discourse in advanced political economies, as revealed in Daniel Bell's *The Cultural Contradictions of Capitalism* (1976), Richard Sennett's, *Fall of Public Man* (1978), Neil Postman's *Amusing Ourselves to Death: Public Discourse in the Age of Show Business (1986)*, and Murray Bookchin's *Rise of Urbanization and Decline of Citizenship* (1987).

Across the political spectrum, therefore, analysts have been pointing to a deep crisis in the civic culture of the Western world. Liberals, conservatives, and leftists have been disturbed by the social and political drift that has accompanied our collective failure to work out a development vision for steering society according to something more than value-blind economic growthmanship.

Some have ventured preliminary formulations of civic developmental values with which citizens might counter the tendency of social development to disintegrate into little more than tawdry pursuit of aggregate economic growth to the detriment of both society and environment. Explorers include Robert A. Dahl, in his *Dilemmas Of Pluralist Democracy* (1982); Amitai Etzioni, in *The Moral Dimension: Toward A New Economics* (1988); Ralf Dahrendorf, in his *Life Chances* (1979) and *The Modern Social Conflict* (1988); John S. Dryzek, in *Rational Ecology* (1987); Barry Hindess, in his *Choice, Rationality and Social Theory* (1987); Elise Boulding, in her *Building a Global Civic Culture* (1988); Nancy L. Schwartz, in *The Blue Guitar: Political Representation and Community* (1988); William M. Sullivan, in his *Reconstructing Public Philosophy* (1986); John Friedmann, in *Planning in the Public Domain* (1987); Russell Hardin, in *Morality Within the Limits of Reason* (1988); and Alan Wolfe, in his *Whose Keeper? Social Science and Moral Obligation* (1989). Although they represent a diverse array of traditions and would likely dispute assumptions, units, variables, and theoretical propositions, all recognize that careful reasoning over fact and value must somehow be employed to assess policy in the public household and that the social sciences must be viewed as central contributors. All question the positivistic article of faith that investigation of collective values must be beyond reason, that we must be limited to analyzing instrumental means. They each press for improved collective means for shaping a conception of social progress.

13

TECHNOLOGICAL CHANGE
AND THE PROBLEM OF WELFARE TRANSFER

Technological projects, programs, and policies transfer social welfare from group to group, time to time, and place to place. For example, when the Bureau of Reclamation promotes itself as a force for social development when it propagates the following story: The small town in decline, served by bad schools, poor streets, and nonexistent health care facilities and economically exhausted, is transformed into a thriving population center by a Bureau dam. The Fish and Wildlife Service, on the other hand, defines its mission by the number of dam projects blocked so as to preserve amenities of naturally flowing streams for present and future generations. Is social development better served by the dam or by the free-flowing water? Each option represents a very different, and incompatible, mix of welfare and illfare.

Technology creates the capacity to pursue alternative courses of action, and each proposed alternative promises to distribute disadvantage and advantage differently — economically, ecologically, politically, and socially.[22] Technological capacities make possible the building of alternative behavioral bridges representing new freedom to choose but at a cost to incompatible choice opportunities. Which technological bridges to new choices should be erected and crossed?

Technology is usefully defined as consisting of sets of standardized operations that regularly yield predetermined results.[23] It is typically the case that we take technology to be physical objects or hardware such as dams, computers, automobiles, and the wide array of appliances to which we have been accustomed. But to think of technology as individual units of machinery is to misunderstand it. Machines are visible and easily comprehended, but they are only some of the components in highly organized systems. Technology encompasses the organizational "software" that operates the physical "hardware." Each technological system of social rules, roles, and physical tools has somebody's values built into it — values defining somebody's conception of "problems" and somebody's idea of "solutions." Yet solutions for some represent problems for others.

Technology lies at the heart of economic and ecological aspects of public development policy because it is axiomatic that resources do not exist independently of technology. Orthodox definitions of resources found in the economic literature emphasize that resources are those things useful for production.[24] The level of technological operations — the quality of the physical and organizational know-how — determines the extent to which materials available in the environment can be ferreted out and shaped up so as to be useful in the production of goods and services. Mother Nature may provide a waterfall, but the energy of the falling water is not a resource until the technology of the waterwheel — physical and organizational — is applied to it. Technological operations, applied to available raw materials so as to create resources for production, determine (1) the range of the goods and services that can be exchanged in the economy, the private household, and in the public sector; (2) the productivity of human effort (technological advance makes more output available from a given amount of resource input); and (3) the variety of ways to employ human labor.[25] In an ecological sense, it is also axiomatic that as technological operations capture energy to do work in the production of wealth and choice, some energy must be degraded, a fact that makes for anti-wealth or pollution. When residuals from production and consumption processes are discharged into ecological and social networks, the results can sometimes be such highly negative effects as killing fish, creating public health problems, causing buildings and works of art to deteriorate, fouling the air and water, and disturbing solitude.

Technology is also central to life as experienced politically. It rarely confers benefits either equally or equitably among diverse and conflicting social groups. Much political coalition-building and decision-making center on efforts to organize the favorable distribution of advantage associated with technological programs and policies. In addition, technological capacity to act, to deliver and withhold resources, is a major source of political power. If power is the capacity to compel compliance to one's wishes by virtue of the threat of sanctions — rewards or punishments — technology can be viewed as a central political resource.[26] To control a given technology is to control material resources that become currency in political exchange among allies and adversaries. For instance, as the technology of commercial aviation and interstate long-haul truckers advanced, so did the power of these social interests vis-à-vis those founded on railway technology.[27] In another setting, as farm mechanization proceeds, the sociopolitical power base of many tenant farmers in South Asia erodes. In the United States new computerized and automated technologies of newspaper production have directly threatened control of the production process by typesetters' and printers' unions, who have felt slippage in their grasp of resources with which they could threaten sanctions to preserve their positions.

Standardized procedures at the center of any given technology specify role behavior, and therein lies a significant sociological implication. The essence of role theory is that the great variety of unique human personalities is harnessed into structures of role expectations such that roughly similar and predictable social behavior is delivered by role players with greatly different personality inclinations.[28] Unique personalities "harnessed" into the role of assembly line worker in a factory deliver commonly expected behavior even though it is the case that there is a wide range of commitment to the product and of affection for the shop supervisor. Role expectations, emergent above and beyond any individual person and sustained in continuous symbolic interaction, insure that common behavioral outputs will be delivered by diverse personalities. Roles are not "things"; they are sets of social expectations maintained in the process of social interaction. Social structure is event structure — patterned relationships — in which a most basic social process is that of "role taking" in webs of group affiliation.

Many socially important roles consist of patterned expectations prescribed by technological procedures. Accountants play job roles according to detailed and highly sophisticated technical operations for bookkeeping and for data manipulation and transfer. Examine the behavior of a medical doctor and bear witness to the manner in which his or her professional role is prescribed by technologies associated with diagnosis, prescription, and surgery. An artist's creative spirit finds expression through the mastery of standardized operations for managing line, space, and color or those specified by the rich technology of the piano, oboe, or violin. Investigate the world of the recreationist and note the manner in which the physical and organizational components of technologies for playing tennis or for camping, snowmobiling, skiing, and hunting define role behavior. One can be a truck driver, aircraft pilot, logger, or mathematician only to the extent that technologically standardized operations for yielding predetermined results in these domains of activity have been advanced and diffused.[29]

Yet roles exist not in isolation but in complementary and interdependent sets. A role-set is a complement of roles, any one of which contributes to the performance of the others. Aircraft technologies specify not only the roles of pilot but also those of the cockpit and cabin crew. Ground controllers, maintenance technicians, baggage handlers, and ticket sales people all work in their respective role-sets coordinated by still other specialists in the technologies of management. Single technologies are combined into complexes with other technologies to fly a plane, extract coal, generate electricity, farm a parcel of land, or transport commodities; likewise, roles are combined into role-sets, organizations, and sets of organizations. Roles are the building blocks of role-sets, which in turn are the component parts of organizations, and clusters of mutually interdependent organizations constitute organization-sets that, in their interaction, generate the structured shape of organized society.[30]

As complexes of technology associated with commercial sailing ships became obsolete, old role-sets disappeared, and many organization-sets were fundamentally altered as their component technologies fell by the wayside. The new steamships required revised sets of expectations for sailors; changes in the role components of shipboard organization and onshore management came to reflect the new technologically induced realities. To give another example: As the land grant college system has generated new technologies, some of which have shifted profits and power to the advantage of large-scale corporate agriculture, small farmers and small town businesspeople have witnessed a withering of their local communities. Entire role- and organization-sets have been destroyed by movement away from the kinds of agricultural technology upon which the small communities were based and toward centralized corporate farming technology, the management of which is centered in metropolitan areas.[31]

All this is not to propound a crude technological determinism; it is only to hold that technological operations yield predictable results when human beings appropriately enact specified role requirements within ranges tolerated by the procedures. Human beings, in turn, change and modify technologies and, thereby, their social webs. Technology is part and parcel of social role structures — it is not a nonsocial, or socially neutral, outside impinging force.[32] Technology is a medium of procedures for obtaining predetermined results within which human beings live and from which they construct much social and cultural meaning. To change technologies is to change roles, role-sets, organizations, organization-sets, communities, and societies.

As one witnesses the complex shift of welfare from group to group, time to time, place to place, it is the unpleasant duty of the economist to remind us that everything has a price tag. Each new technology exacts its cost in choices not pursued while resources are committed elsewhere. Ecologists point out that ecosystems have evolved their particular dynamics out of eons of subtle experience processing solar energy through complex chains of energy exchange among living plants and animals and that these chains have limited capacity to absorb residual anti-wealth of production and consumption. The political analyst hastens to inform us that choices among policy mixes for guiding technology are made by conflicting, competing, compromising coalitions of actors who struggle for immediate advantage and that each alternative sociotechnical policy package represents a mix of opportunities for advancement and destruction of political interest. The sociologist notes that the rise and fall of technologies create and destroy social roles around which much personal identity is constructed, promote and undermine social organizations, and expand and retard communities and entire sectors of activity.

Technology, therefore, is at the center of the contemporary problem of social development. We are compelled to make choices — choices between competing uses of natural resources and of the land and water base upon which society is constructed. A fundamental challenge for policy assessment is to incorporate a view of technology that comprehends that it shifts welfare in several dimensions simultaneously: economic, ecological, political, and social.

THE PROBLEM OF KNOWING WHAT "IS" — NOMOTHETIC THEORY IN AN IDIOGRAPHIC WORLD

Wilhelm Windelband, before the turn of this century, saw two different formats for studying history — a particularizing mode emphasizing the uniqueness of events and a generalizing mode extracting larger similarities and arriving at abstracted patterns of relationships. Wilhelm Dilthey, using Windelband as a springboard, went on to develop the distinction between idiographic knowledge of substantive content about particular site-specific phenomena and nomothetic abstract generalizing ways of knowing.[33] The distinction between ways of knowing about the world is fundamental and has implications that must be addressed if we are to grasp the challenge presented by policy assessment.

Idiographic knowledge consists of documenting — in proper names — the unique and particular in a unit of study. It is to focus intently on the unique patterns of weeds and seeds in a specific garden. To provide detailed accounts of plant populations in particular

18

patches may be of interest to some who plan to feast on those specific plants, but it would not constitute the science of agronomy.

Nomothetic knowledge, on the other hand, consists of statements asserting general form of relationships among phenomena that do not require reference to specific objects, events, dates, or places. The nomothetic idea entered sociology through the work of Max Weber, who abstracted general relationships by means of "ideal types," and via Georg Simmel, who stressed generalized properties of "forms" of interaction.[34] From the time of Simmel, Weber, Durkheim, and Marx, sociology has operated on the premise that insight about "forms" of systemic relationships between people can explain something important about what people do.

Science gains nomothetic knowledge by studying cohering aspects of reality, by formulating and testing abstracted relationships among variables that are postulated to occur under conditions in which confounding conditions are removed.[35] In science, the search for nomothetic organizing principles has pride of place — it is essential to parsimonious explanation. Theoretical science abstracts general rules to construct logically connected sets of propositions about relationships among phenomena — generalized nomothetic theory. Nomothetic knowledge is illustrated by the manner in which geometry abstracts key forms — that is, the square, circle, cube, triangle, cone, sphere — from a complex and tangled world. Obviously, such forms cannot exist in the world except as embodied in such site-specific material as clay, wood, steel, paper, or plastic. Yet geometry gains its analytical capability by abstracting the nomothetic forms from their particular material contents and by studying their characteristics independently of site-specific considerations, just as physics proceeded with concepts of mass, energy, and motion abstracted from any particular bodies and appreciated as features of all bodies.

Would it not be sufficient to keep focus only on observable entities, to express oneself in terms of observable vocabulary alone, and to eschew use of nomothetic terminology? The notion may be tempting, but statements of observable phenomena at low levels of abstraction lack power to provide insight and can be grossly misleading. For example, the statement that wood floats on water while iron sinks is grossly inferior to the formulation that an object will float in a liquid if and when its body sinks into that liquid to such a depth that the displaced volume of fluid weighs exactly as much as the whole of the floating body. The first formulation, stated in terms of specific observables (wood, iron, water) is flawed in the sense that a suitably shaped piece of iron will be buoyant whereas a wooden boat with a hole in its hull will sink. When Archimedes formulated his nomothetic proposition employing abstract nonobservable concepts of displacement, volume, weight, and buoyancy, he increased our conceptual power to think about the phenomena of floating and sinking in liquids.

Yet no science of nomothetic form can comprehend the full richness and complexity of life in sociotechnological systems nested within larger ecological environments. Nomothetic knowledge must proceed on the basis of rendering propositions about facets of the whole but never comprehending the whole. Nomothetic knowledge is limited to its particular slices. Archimedes' principle has everything to do with why objects float, but it is far less than a theory of a ship.

A distinctive subject matter, and key objective, of sociology has been to abstract social forms from the theory-defying complexity of particular social episodes and to use them to analyze social order and change. Generating high-level abstract "laws" may, however, become a rather pointless enterprise. It is of little interest to construct highly generic propositions that never apply to any observable time or place, that represent features common to everything but shed insight on virtually nothing. We must, therefore, walk a path between a simple-minded positivistic "law-giving" Newtonian view, on the one hand, and conceptually blind site-specific fact grubbing, on the other.

There is clear danger in abstraction that is not carefully linked to historical situations in which people have lived,[36] but there is at least equal danger in pretending to reconstruct historical episodes without the use of at least some acknowledged abstract theory. It is simply not possible to build a history of events without employing theoretical premises and lenses. "Facts" and "evidence" of the historical record are never independent of an author's particular use of theoretical abstraction.

One must also distinguish between nomothetic understanding of selected aspects of complex wholes and the capacity to predict events. Abstract comprehension of flow volumes, rates, pressures, and materials involved in the plumbing of houses in general does not constitute a theory of houses, nor does it allow the plumber to predict a break in a specific pipe at an exact time in any particular home. Yet we rightly refuse to throw out such general abstract considerations just because we find ourselves wading in a basement full of water on a particular morning. Having a grasp of general nomothetically codified propositions does not permit one to make forecasts of specific events, but specific events occur within general enabling and constraining contexts, some of which are apprehended by nomothetic theory. Specific happenings require a multicausal account that recognizes the contingency of things and that will almost always find that the factors operating in a specific situation were beyond a given theory. As Karl Popper pointed out, practically no sequence of causally connected specific events proceeds according to any single theory or "law" of nature. If we imagine, as Popper asked us to do, that the wind shakes a tree and Newton's apple falls to the ground, nobody will deny that it is possible, in principle at least, to describe the event in terms of some combination of causal nomothetic formulations. But there is no single law, such as that of gravity, capable of describing the actual succession of causally connected events involved in the plunge of the fruit. In addition to gravity, the analyst would have to tie together laws explaining wind pressure on the tree, branches, and the apple, the jerking movements of the branch, the tension on the apple's stalk, and other related matters.[37] The idea that any specific sequence of real events can be comprehensively explained or predicted by any law, or parsimonious set of laws, is simply mistaken.

There is a sense, therefore, in which a "science of society" is an absurdly pretentious idea — that sense being that there is, or can be, a theory of complex social systems, such as churches, economies, corporations, nation-states, irrigation systems, neighborhoods, and regions, taken as wholes. The complexity of components, the degrees of freedom in behavior, their loosely coupled and contingent nature, all make for poor grist for scientific mills that are suited for controlled observation of selected aspects of reality, not reality per se.

There is another sense, however, in which a "science of society" is a most defensible notion quite within our grasp. This is the notion that nomothetic science requires only clear statements of specific variables and the relationships among them, pertaining to selected aspects of sociotechnical systems. We forgo a theory of complex wholes but rather develop a theory of slices of these wholes — for example, socialization, decision-making, power, conflict, or cooperation. To advance a view that theory is limited to selected aspects of things does not represent a lowering of expectations for social scientists as compared to their natural science colleagues. Why should a sociologist feel chagrined to admit that the behavior of a given organizational-ecological complex does not yield to science when chemists and physicists proceed without a theory of the Boeing 747, a Buick, or a Schwinn?

Airplanes, automobiles, and bicycles would not serve us today if their designers had awaited a comprehensive theory of their whole assemblies. The theory of electromagnetic wave transmission undergirding radio technology is altogether different from the theory undergirding the understanding of combustion in jet turbines, lift and drag on wings, the chemistry of plastics lining the cabin, the physics of inertial guidance. There is no theory of a complex assembly called an airplane — only theories of selected aspects. Technologically competent manufacturers assemble aircraft because they impose an overarching technological grasp of what they are doing on a rich variety of scientific theories.

No one judges the success of physics by its comprehensive theory of aircraft, and to attempt to do so would be to misunderstand fundamentally what physics is and can do. So it is with the social sciences. If theory can be advanced about selected aspects of social systems, without pretending to comprehend fully the whole of them, and if that theory represents some strategic aspect of society such that it merits the attention of citizens and social scientists in conducting policy assessment, so much the better for the social sciences. But social scientists, and their critics, should not judge their efforts by the impossible standard of full comprehension of complex sociotechnical wholes and prediction of specific outcomes of the dynamics of those wholes.

Policy assessment therefore must rely on the simple and parsimonious to guide us with regard to the complex and theory defying. Policy assessment does not employ its abstractions to try to explain society, nor does it pretend to predict particular future events within society; it simply attempts to assess the effects of a proposed policy on one or more abstract strategic parameters of society about which defensible meaning and rationale can be constructed.

In the light of the nomothetic-idiographic distinction, technology — a driving force behind the need for policy assessment and focus of policy assessment — must be distinguished from science, an assistant in policy assessment. Technological know-how has historically developed in a stream quite different from that of science.[38] During most of the relatively short history of the scientific enterprise, scientists have moved without close and systematic ties to those men and women of practical affairs who innovated in the technological realm. Organized scientific attempts to set forth variables abstracted from the rich flow of life and to test relationships among variables under controlled conditions in delineated domains of inquiry have constituted a far different enterprise than those of the technological tinkerer who developed "know-how" to make things work with or without a comprehension of the scientific "why." People developed complex forms of settled agriculture without the science of agronomy, they made wind and water turn working wheels long before the several relevant sciences were available, and they guided themselves with the compass before scientific study of magnetism was formalized. James Watt's steam engine was releasing human beings from the constraints of living animal and plant energy before scientific formulation could be provided for its thermodynamic behavior. Not until the twentieth century did the largely separate streams of technology and science begin to merge. Science as a body of method and a logic of inquiry, itself, then became a method of invention in some areas of the practical technological world.

Our problem is clear: We must extract nomothetic order from the flux of human existence, and we must apply nomothetic principles for policy assessment in real socioecological units, each with its unique properties — and must do so with sensitivity to site-specific considerations. People located in specific settings, possibly unskilled in the processed nomothetic knowledge of the disciplines but possessing local knowledge of the particular, must collaborate in bringing abstractions to earth in ways that accommodate local realities. Knowledge of the local and specific must inform applications of the universal, general, and nomothetic. Policy assessment for social development must combine the positivist emphasis upon knowing about nomothetic relationships "out there" with the postpositivist emphasis on knowing "with the other." People possessing idiographic knowledge must, in turn, effectively participate in the application and interpretation of nomothetic policy-assessment processes. The challenge of this aspect of policy assessment is to formulate defensible ways to fuse local idiographic understandings with application of generalizable nomothetic principles, with a minimum of distortion to each.

THE PROBLEM OF KNOWING WHAT OUGHT — LOGICS OF VALUATION IN A VALUE-RELATIVISTIC WORLD

Men and women will act collectively in ways that shape their society. Action requires choice. Choice is the expression of value. Values are tools for choosing.[39] How adequate are the valuational tools for assessing policy with respect to advancing a coherent conception of social development? Valuation is the analytical process of holding up to rational scrutiny the uses and limits of value logics employed in the making of value judgments.[40] A strategic challenge, therefore, is to construct, in a socially constructed relativistic world, logics of fact and value that can give coherent meaning to the idea of policy assessment for social development.

The social sciences are pervaded by concepts with implicit and explicit value judgments built into them: prejudice, racism, sexism, imperialism, equality, liberty, democracy, per capita income, economic efficiency, social mobility, powerlessness, alienation, freedom, justice, responsiveness, public involvement and participation, mental health, social welfare, the public interest, and quality of life — to name a few. For the most part, serious students of the logical problems involved in defining development and methods for policy assessment have found that the valuative meanings of such concepts are not analyzed in their own right within their respective literatures.[41] They each have been associated with one or another conception of social development, but they provide no coherent view of it.

A defensible concept of development must do its analytical work without falling into the traps of dogmatism or cultural ethnocentrism. Furthermore, reasoned approaches to the assessment of policy choices involve doing things on principle whether or not acting on principle is advantageous for any given subset of the community. For what good reasons should one be asked to sacrifice personal interests? But on what basis do we say which groups "ought" to accept which sacrifices to install benefits when everyone demands that others should shoulder the burdens? Without justifiable collectively apprehended logics of value by which agents of the public household can make defensible choices in shaping technological and natural resource options, we are without standards that represent more than the sum of marketplace exchanges, or we are forced to live with profiles of benefit and harm imposed by valuationally inept and arbitrary decision-makers who assert that, in a valuationally bankrupt world, their valuations are as good as those of anybody else.

David Hume stands as a central figure in the debate over value judgments and their analytical worth by virtue of his important exploration of the logical gap between "facts" and "values." The selection of valuative criteria to guide policy assessment, he noted, lies beyond the demonstration that something "is."[42] Facts about light waves provide no basis for selecting preferred color. To conclude that something "ought" to be on the grounds that it "is" is to commit what G. E. Moore later identified as the "naturalistic fallacy."[43] To say that something "is" is to assert an empirically verifiable property. Normative "ought" concepts, however, assert that something has value, yet such claims can be made only if one has a standard or rule defining what is preferable. No amount of manipulation can legitimately generate a normative "ought" deductively from a descriptive "is" statement. One cannot derive moral conclusions from amoral premises without somehow inserting a value standard. To attempt to do so is to commit the naturalistic fallacy. The valuational question now becomes: How defensible is the value logic inserted between statements of factual conditions and normative conclusions?

Social scientists have learned to be sensitive to the lessons of cultural and value relativism; they are cognizant of overwhelming sociological and anthropological evidence to the effect that human beings construct multiple social realities with their language systems and have evolved highly diverse cultural meanings.[44] Social scientists know well the arguments that each sociocultural meaning system must be judged on its own merits against standards of valuation held by its members. Any observer who valuates uncritically in terms of his or her externally imposed cultural standards, and who assumes the superiority of his or her cultural tradition, is guilty of ethnocentrism. Given these lessons, most scientists have held that the matter of value judgment and, therefore, social development is simply beyond their domain — proper to religion, philosophy, and public affairs. If science is value free and provides no ground for developmental values and public choice, so much the worse for developmental values and public choice. The definition of "progress" is both arbitrary and relative to meanings of local cultures. If value systems of social groups come into substantial conflict, "life is a game in which clubs are trump."[45]

Human cultures, taken as systems of social meaning and analytically distinguished from social structures, have evolved in different natural settings out of very different histories of interaction. Like poetry, their meaning systems do not translate easily from one to another. We have little choice but to interpret others by our own cultural lights, hardly ever able to see others fully as they see themselves.[46] A degree of culture-blindness is inevitable when we attempt to transcend our cultural boundaries; we are all, at least to some extent, necessarily cultural imperialists. Herein lies a problem. Who understands whom on whose terms? Or, more to the point, who has the power to impose their cultural meanings upon whom? Elites

25

sustain existing cultures by smashing some cultural values while promoting others, and it is through social power struggle that the meanings of one culture or subculture are projected upon another. Cultural meaning systems simply do not exist independent of power bases.

There can be no denying wide differences in value systems of culturally diverse peoples or for that matter of people within any given cultural system. There can also be no denying that policies for technology and natural resources must be assessed and guided by information about values. But which values should be employed, since values asserted by specific groups can be expected to serve the interests of those same groups? Any given culture is composed of a mix of groups, organizations, and values distributed across a stratification system. The dominant cultural values are produced and sustained by the more powerful actors. To simply accept existing values as defining the local cultural definition of development is tantamount to accepting the valuational commitments of the existing power structure. Is development, as a concept, to be no more or less than what dominant groups say it is? To adopt this position is to commit the naturalistic fallacy; it is to blatantly assert that what "is," as organized by the powers that be, "ought" to be. Is our only option to assess alternative policy choices in terms of the values of the rich and powerful who have disproportionate means to purchase the effort, impose the results, and then commit fallacious naturalistic reasoning in the bargain?

Policies, if implemented, will confer advantage and disadvantage disproportionately — some groups will secure advantages at cost to others. It can all be accomplished under the legitimating influence of "our culture." Does policy assessment blindly and passively accept the value prescriptions of the culturally legitimate, socially prestigious, economically dominant, and politically stronger actors? Or are there grounds upon which to make value judgments for policy assessment on a reasoned cross-culturally viable basis?

Policy assessment requires the moral and social sensitivity that rides with cultural relativism and the reasoned fortitude in value commitment that travels with our common interdependence. How can valuational fortitude be reconciled with the insights of cultural and value relativism? One begins by distinguishing between individual preferences and matters of public collective normative "ought." Individual preferences are subjective, are fundamentally arbitrary in asserting taste, and are generally not open to reasoned analysis. In matters of personal taste one simply asserts that one prefers chocolate to vanilla. No justification is required. However in developmental matters of the public household, one cannot defensibly assert that one simply "prefers" a high-rise dam or a wild and scenic river, an irrigation project or a wildlife refuge, resettlement of thousands of families to make way for a reservoir, or racism in the distribution of benefits.

Individual culturally conditioned preference and valuational logics for social development are neither the same nor are they interchangeable. Policymaking in the public household, affecting the structural shape of the community, must be open to community reason to which all, including elites, are accountable. There has grown up in philosophy and social science a position that relegates value judgments to the realm of personal idiosyncrasy. Values have been taken to be subjective, vague, unverifiable by the senses. But others have demonstrated that the "judgment" in value judgment does not have to refer to conjecture, opinion, subjective preference, or logically baseless supposition.[47] A line of inquiry has opened up that holds value logics up to reasoned inspection.

Just because Hume and Moore correctly pointed out the logical gap between what "is" and what "ought," it does not follow that facts are irrelevant to value judgment, that rational calculation has no part to play in valuation, or that any given existing cultural pattern is as defensible, in terms of a given reasoned value standard, as is any other cultural pattern. If one accepts that cultural meaning systems are socially constructed and multiple, it does not follow that they are equally to be admired from any reasoned valuative standpoint. Some may be viewed as "better" than others for reasons that can be brought into open discourse and be inspected.

There is no ultimate fact upon which the edifice of science rests. Facts are accepted insofar as they are rooted in sound analytical procedures for approaching the empirical world. If the procedures employed to arrive at statements of fact are found to be deficient, the facts are suspect. Statements of fact are no better or worse than the procedures employed to arrive at them. Poor procedures of empirical investigation yield poor "facts." This is also the case in the normative domain of valuation. There is no ultimate value in any analytically useful sense. But there are better and worse valuational procedures, and values rooted in more defensible logics are more to be trusted in policy choice than are those that fail to stand up to the best tests that reason can bring to bear. Some value logics are superior to others and so have a greater claim on the direction of technological potential in the public household.

We are challenged, therefore, to construct developmental valuational logics for policy assessment: sets of tools for reasoning about developmental "oughts" in given contexts of factual "is" conditions. The enterprise must consist of both defensible empirical and normative procedures. We want to be able to carry collaborative nomothetic logics of fact and value from culture to culture in the name of our common humanity and our interdependence without being ethnocentric and without losing touch with site-specific idiographic conditions.

CONCLUSION

Our challenge is to shape collective futures, via reasoned policy assessment in the public household about matters of advantage and disadvantage occasioned by technological policy, using nomothetic theory of strategic slices of reality in a culturally rich ideographic world and using reasoned normative capacity to select "better" from "worse" in a value-relativistic world.

Good theory in any domain helps us to see — to see beneath and beyond the immediacy of events into underlying relationships obscure to common sense. In the domain of development, some theory must assist us to see factual consequences associated with proposed policies, and associated theory must provide normative capacity to choose the most developmental, or the least inferior, policy. Yet as theory permits us to see and valuate some dimensions of life, it obscures others. Nomothetic theory of fact and value must be employed, and interpreted, within idiographically rich contexts.

Citizens, and their political representatives, must deny some technological possibilities and promote others for good reasons open to inspection in civil discourse. Around such discussion a sense of civitas can grow. Civility is founded upon the recognition of public values, above and beyond individual preferences, and upon appreciation that individuals do not experience life as detached atomistic beings. What individuals experience is fundamentally conditioned by the shape of the social structure within which they exercise their individual choices and by their position within those structures. Civil discourse must develop capacity to deal with the problems of public choice about shaping social structures in socially developmental perspective, to choose defensibly among policy options, each of which imposes a profile of harm and advantage. Civility becomes something more than knowing how to decant wine.

Implicit in the idea of policy assessment for social development is the idea that the structural shape of society affects individual life chances and that humans are collectively responsible for the shape of their own social structures. In the public realm, when engaging in policy assessment, conflicting parties will necessarily see and hear from different positions and will interpret discourse from the vantage of a variety of cultural meaning systems. Policy assessment in the public realm must accept the fact of multiple and conflicting realities, but it must also accept the fact of our interdependence. Respect for social and cultural diversity does not permit us to duck the twin questions: How do we live together, and how do we shape our collective future?

Sociology cannot carry the whole burden of development policy assessment, but it must contribute to it. Members of many other disciplines must construct their particular developmental logics of fact and value, and as will become obvious in following chapters, sociological logics must work collaboratively with them. It is the purpose of this book to present sociological logics of fact and value that can advance the discipline's capacity to carry a part of the analytical burden in the domain of technology and natural resources. It is also to contend that sociology must, in a reasoned manner, explicitly recommit itself to the larger social development project initiated by the founders of the discipline.

II

Social Policy Assessment:
The Historical Problem

Social science falls short of needs of policy guidance, not only because it is specialized, but also because it involves a deliberate effort to escape from valuation. — Duncan MacRae[1]

When the intellectual history of contemporary social science comes to be written, one of its major themes will be the relation of social science to value. It will be a story of mutual isolation affecting theory and practice alike, with losses to both the social sciences and the philosophy of value. — Abraham Edel[2]

Debate about the relation of fact to value and the manner in which values can, or should, be subject to logical justification has been prolonged, bitter, and polemical. The quarrel broke loose during the Enlightenment; invective and incivility have marked the controversies right down to contemporary confrontations within professional associations.[3] There are those who argue that values mixed with science lead inevitably to bad science. There are others who cannot see knowledge apart from action; they reply that value-free science lends itself to terrible abuse and in any case is an impossible enterprise.[4] It is the purpose of this chapter to sketch the main outlines of the value controversy and to show that failure to cope with the valuational problem for policy assessment has created three antagonistic types of social science in general and three types of sociology in particular — pure, applied, and value critical.

HISTORY OF THE VALUATIONAL DEBATE

The Eighteenth-Century Moral Problem

The idea of societal progress, a vision of humanity advancing from a remote and primitive past to a better future on the foundation of cumulative advancement of knowledge, was well known to the ancient Greeks and Romans. By the third century A.D., classical notions of progress had become tightly interwoven with Judeo-Christian visions of unfolding providential design.[5] By the Middle Ages, thinkers read nature primarily to define how various phenomena served heavenly purpose. The will of God revealed itself in historical outcomes. That which existed, therefore, ought to exist by virtue of supranatural design — the baldest form of the naturalistic fallacy.[6]

With the slow and intermittent collapse of the medieval world view, human suffering had to be explained as existing in the world apart from divine intention. Over centuries of struggle, God was gradually eliminated from science as an explanatory principle for natural processes and social affairs. By the time of the eighteenth-century Enlightenment, thinkers began to shift the burden of societal choice from reliance on God's will to belief in the power of human rational understanding. This shift occupied Enlightenment thought, and it occupies us today.

Enlightenment thinkers still tried to read nature but in an effort to discern what people should do. They sought to discover natural laws to which society should conform to promote social progress and welfare. The new worship of science was focused on finding policy guidance in nature. For some, rational-deductive mathematical-geometric methods were God's gift to humankind — the foundation for seeking out a new and rationally based morality to guide human development.[7] For others, experimental methods were the key to nature's secrets that, when unlocked, would reveal meaning and value. Naturalistically fallacious reasoning about social values survived, even flourished, in an increasingly secular world.

Giambattista Vico, David Hume, Jean Jacques Rousseau, and Immanuel Kant stand prominently among their eighteenth-century contemporaries because they rejected the valuational naturalism of their time. Vico attacked the misguided notion that a science of human nature could be constructed on the basis of the study of physical nature. Hume struck out at value naturalism with his distinction between logics of fact and logics of value, and Rousseau offered romantic-poetic images of what human society could and should be. Kant

31

sought to provide a rational, but nonnatural, foundation for the rules of morality. Neither Vico, Hume, Rousseau, nor Kant could accept the fallacy that what was, ought to be.

The first to get reason down to matters of earthly social policy was Vico.[8] His radical idea, the centerpiece of his *New Science* (1725), was that the social world was the work of human beings. If human institutions were self-styled, why should people stand still and passively accept existing sociocultural arrangements? Thinkers, said Vico, must pursue matters of social progress through rational inquiry into comparative history. Detailed, empirical examination of histories of human groups would yield principles of societal progress. This knowledge would be rooted in patient study of records of actual people, not in divine will or the deductive logic of Descartes.

David Hume, in offering his *A Treatise of Human Nature* (1739–1740), sought to complete the Socratic search for a new secular vision of social progress: His attempt was to introduce the experimental method for reasoning about valuation. He wished to do for social progress what Newton's *Prinicipia* (1687) had done for physics. His program was to show that deductive logic cannot add anything to the meaning of premises; it can make explicit only implications of premises, and therefore what "ought to be" can never be deduced from factual premises whose meaning is limited to what "is."[9] Ought statements, said Hume, could only be deduced from "ought" premises, and such "ought" premises would emerge from a human-centered valuationally pragmatic social science.

Jean Jacques Rousseau (1712–1788) proceeded to establish a conception of primitive man living in the state of nature — what Max Weber would later instruct us to call an "ideal type." It is clear that Rousseau did not believe the "primitive man" to be real, but he posed his construct as a way of formulating a critique of society by investigating properties of what our contemporaries would view as an autonomous person — responsible, strong, not a passive receptacle for tradition, a source of critical values. For Rousseau, science was charged primarily with the task of changing society so as to better promote morally superior behavior.[10] Instead of blindly following passion, human beings could exercise reasoned discretion over human affairs and create the kind of world they wanted. The younger contemporary of Rousseau, Immanuel Kant (1724–1804), also became lastingly prominent, because he saw so clearly what needed to be done: "Knowledge remains forever incomplete and haphazard in character unless various scientific disciplines are brought into some intelligible relation with each other and directed toward such ends as will serve to give them purpose for human well-being."[11]

In his *Critique of Practical Reason* (1788), Kant made a project of discovering a rational justification for social values. He searched for a rational test that would discriminate those moral maxims that are a genuine expression of moral law from those that cannot enjoy such standing. It was the task of practical reason to lay down moral principles that are universal, categorical, internally consistent, and applicable to human intentional action in all circumstances. Morality was rooted in respect for duty, which is to be discovered through the exercise of reason independently of sense experience or religious dogma. His famous formulation of the "categorical imperative" was "So act that you could will that the maxim of your action should be a universal law for all men." From this he drew conclusions condemning slavery and war and supporting the equal right of people to participate in self-government. By virtue of his thought, Kant ranks along with John Locke and Jean Rousseau as one of the founders of the moral theory of the democratic state.

A central drift of eighteenth-century thought was, therefore, that valuational reasoning could provide a basis for social policy assessment. Reason could critique real world events and policy options. Philosophers and embryonic social scientists hoped for a critical pragmatic social science that would show the way to social progress. The value problem was clear. Rational thinkers must construct value logics for the definition of societal progress that would, in turn, undergird examination of social policy. Social development was possible, and it was not a matter to be left to divine will or natural physical forces.

One major consequence of the subversive "idea of progress" was growing dissatisfaction with the French ancient regime. When reason was removed from its abstract perch and applied to immediate problems of society, abuses of the ancient regime drew heavy critical fire from Enlightenment rationalists. However, the immense cataclysm of the French Revolution had negative effects on social activism and reform not altogether unlike that of the Stalinist experience of this century. So great was the bloodshed, the dislocation, and misery that counterrevolutionary forces obtained a broad hearing for arguments that it is better to be passive in the face of injustice than to take direct and precipitous action. Science in the service of social reform seemed most suspicious to conservatives such as Edmund Burke and Thomas Carlyle.[12] So it was, then, that the eighteenth century ended in the aftermath of the French Revolution amidst shattered hopes for social progress on the continent. European observers came to appreciate that society was more complex than had been thought; realists came to know that government by social philosophers, the bourgeois, or the people would not automatically produce progress, and the postrevolutionary advent of Napoleon crushed any lingering hopes of social reform.

Across the channel, English elites worked to emasculate radical social theory and to dethrone the dangerous idea of social development. The counterattack was sustained in large part by a clergyman who believed passionately in original sin — Thomas Malthus. Adam Smith, a predecessor to Malthus, had laid the foundations for "classical" economic analysis. The "wealth of nations," according to Smith, was dependent upon two factors: availability of natural raw materials and labor. Since raw materials were "gifts of God," income was determined by the efficiency with which labor could be applied to them. Labor productivity would, in turn, be dependent upon rates of savings in society that allowed investment in new technologies to generate more productive "labor power." Savings not only lay at the basis of productivity per unit of labor but also determined what percentage of the population could be employed. If savings could be increased, new technologies could be introduced and employment expanded.[13]

Smith's work yielded optimistic conclusions for the ability of humankind to achieve social development through free market exchange, until Thomas Malthus's analysis of population and resources came along and was incorporated into David Ricardo's economics — making for the labeling of that discipline as the "dismal science." Malthus held that population would increase until leveled by natural checks of war, disease, and famine. Land and other raw materials existed only in fixed amounts. Population would increase as a consequence of better productivity; pressures would mount to bring lesser-quality land and other raw materials into production. Inferior resources would yield a diminishing return to each additional unit of labor and capital applied. Societal development, over the long run, would be impossible. New technology would only allow more people to suffer grim miseries of bare subsistence and less.

Malthus, therefore, took the idea of social progress outside the realm of human implementation. The most one could hope for in social reform was a temporary palliative. Any attempt to transform the class system and reduce inequality would be undone by the workings of the law of population.[14] Many students of society retreated to abstract metaphysical contemplation.

Nineteenth-Century Enthusiasm

The story of the belief in general social progress thins substantially in the early nineteenth century, given postrevolutionary reaction on the Continent and conservative forces in Britain. But momentum for the idea of societal development accelerated substantially during the second two-thirds of the century, culminating in the tomes of Karl Marx and Herbert Spencer. Three main streams of thought on the subject are usually traced by scholars:

1. The sequence of thinkers who constitute the German historical idealist school, blending a vision of Christian divine providence with an amalgam of naturalist and romantic thought. Here, one finds ideas moving from Gotthold Lessing, Johann Herder, and Immanuel Kant to Johann Fichte, Friedrich Schelling, and Georg Hegel. Ideas of progress in this stream centered on progress in revelation and expanding spiritual freedom.[15]

2. The new sociologists and political economists who undertook to discover scientific laws of social development. Major figures here include Claude Henri Saint-Simon, Auguste Comte, John Stuart Mill, and Karl Marx.[16]

3. Those evolutionists who accepted the positivism of Comte in sociology but who went on to anchor their ideas of social development in a larger scheme of biological and cosmic progress. Here we have the evolutionism of Jean Lamarck and Charles Darwin translated into the grand synthesis of Herbert Spencer.[17] Thinkers taking this approach to development sought to discover and clarify grand irrefutable laws by which the social order operated independently of individual and collective action.

The story of the German historical idealist school will remain untouched here because it attempted to root values in revelatory modes, but the valuational search conducted in the second and third streams of nineteenth-century thought will be briefly addressed.

Claude Henri Saint-Simon (1760–1825) clearly understood the need for a policy-relevant social science. Though a member of the French aristocracy, Saint-Simon became an early and highly prominent utopian socialist — a dreamer who believed that a rational reorganization of economic production would solve central social problems. The earliest forms of industrialization had brought into stark focus the problem of defining social development. What price industrialization? How can one sort the good from the bad? When is industrialization developmental and progressive? When is it not? These were his big questions.

Saint-Simon deliberately took a home near the French Academy of Science and repeatedly invited leading scientists of his day to dinner in order to raise developmental valuational questions with them. Unfortunately, he did not find it on balance to be a rewarding enterprise. He observed: "Those gentlemen eat a lot, but they don't talk much."[18] Wishing them to use science to directly address the crisis of postrevolutionary France, Saint-Simon was enraged by their lack of social responsibility. "He began to see in the leaders of contemporary science the 'indifferentists,' men blind to the catastrophe of the European continent and the chaos of society. . . ."[19]

Saint-Simon's influence and doctrine underwent, in Alvin Gouldner's words, a "binary fission" into two theoretical systems that persist in contemporary sociology.[20] On the one hand, Auguste Comte took up Saint-Simon's torch; it was then passed on to the academic sociology of Emile Durkheim, English anthropology, Talcott Parsons, and functionalism. The dominant theme in this strand, after Comte, came to be the value of social order and consensus. On the other hand, a stream of thought developed a lineage passing through Saint-Simon's other disciples — Barthelemy Enfantin and Saint-Armand Bazard — that when fused with German romanticism and Hegelianism led straight to Marxism. One of the several Marxist offshoots eventuated in the contemporary German school of critical sociology at Frankfurt.[21] In this stream of thought, the quest has been criticism of modern technology and society in the name of human potentiality denied just fulfillment by repressive social structures.

Auguste Comte (1798–1857), Saint-Simon's secretary and disciple, who put his master's insights into systematic form while elaborating upon them, saw that the Middle Ages possessed what policymakers and social analysts needed most and had since lost — a world view against which to judge right from wrong and by which to subordinate personal desire to social interest. The morals that Comte envisioned would be based not on theological fiat but on empirical science. Comte intended his positivist science to be a complete system of morality, not merely a technical method for analysis of facts. By Comte's own definition, positivism meant the subordination of politics to morals.[22] Science enters the picture to provide a basis for morality and public policy choice. Scientists were to determine the causes of human unhappiness and indicate the proper path for social action. Sociology would be the superordinate science serving societal development, and all other disciplines would take their places in a general science of social progress. Sociology would point out developmental directions by promoting broad social interest as opposed to private selfish interest.[23] Comte's naive attempts to replace the lost medieval morality with a new sociological "religion of humanity" was later disemboweled by philosophers and social scientists who laughed at the crude handling of the is-ought question, but Comte had brought into sharp nineteenth-century relief the valuational problem posed by eighteenth-century Enlightenment thinkers.

The second strain fissioning from Saint-Simon's thought came to fruition in the analysis of Karl Marx (1818–1883). Marx was a premier nineteenth-century theorist who brought Rousseau up to date by providing a postrevolutionary critique of human alienation, who added a class analysis to the economics of Smith and Ricardo, and who formulated a comprehensive theory of social revolution and development. Marx needs to be warmly remembered for his attempts to keep alive the ideal of the Enlightenment commitment to scientifically based social activism. He threw his whole being into a protest against the failure of analysts to probe social values and action in any adequate manner. He was strident, relentless, denigrating of his opponents, but he was also a late Enlightenment figure who held fast to a vision of human progress.[24] He ridiculed the visions of the utopian socialists; the crank cults of Saint-Simon, Charles Fourier, and Robert Owen; and Comte's religion of humanity. He cut mercilessly through the "laws" of the British economists, and he held that parliamentary democracy was little more than a spoils system incapable of solving problems of industrializing and urbanizing society. This humanist Marx held that mankind could, and should, remake itself through radical reconstruction of society. Later, after the turn of the twentieth century, Albion Small would reflect back and contend that Karl Marx would occupy a place in social science similar to that of Galileo in the physical sciences. Why? Because he pointed the way to placing the mode of production and the question of valuation under control of reason.[25] Human beings should choose and create the kind of world in which they would want to live. Unfortunately this central idea was obscured by Marx's choice to throw the burden of valuation for human progress onto the automatic law of history manifested through class struggle. Critical valuative thought in the Marxian tradition became sacrificed to deterministic ideology ". . . which drew a veil of mechanistic scientism so thickly that later Georges Sorel had to struggle hard to see that socialism was part of a great historical moral problem."[26] Marx obscured the fundamentally value-critical nature of what he was trying to do.[27]

Herbert Spencer (1820–1902) readily assimilated Darwinian evolutionary concepts and saw in evolutionism a universal law of becoming. The main fact of evolution was movement from simple to compound societies, from the compulsory cooperation of the military society to voluntary cooperation of the industrial society. Throughout, nature was endowed with a providential tendency to destroy the unfit to make room for the fittest.[28] Whereas earlier theory of societal development had earned the wrath of good conservatives appalled by the excesses of the French Revolution, conservatives found in Spencerian Darwinism a more compatible new view of progress that was not only scientifically locked into nature but that justified social inequality. In Darwin's version, the pressures of population on a limited environment contributed to assure the "survival of the fittest," according to the automatic principle of natural selection. Spencerian versions of this process looked on social inequality as a natural product of life's inevitable struggle. Society still moved, as in the time of Malthus and Ricardo, by natural law that worked itself out at its own sweet and slow pace. There was no room here for radical action — individually or collectively. Spencer's system became a science of fatalism — a curious value position in which its students read nature to find its laws, but did so to do nothing more but continue to read nature.[29] The value conception informing societal development was blatantly naturalistic — what is, had to be, and ought to be.

In sum, then, the nineteenth century, particularly during the last half, witnessed the strong emergence of a variety of evolutionary conceptions of progress — each with policy implications. Even most of those sociologists whose work did not center on social evolution did not typically reject the doctrine.[30] Spencer advocated his cosmic conception of evolutionism, followed by a host of social Darwinists who dropped the biological underpinnings of Spencer but who promoted the idea of the survival of the fittest individuals, groups, and norms — as did William Graham Sumner, who postulated the evolutionary emergence of the fittest folkways. Ferdinand Toennies described evolution from Gemeinschaft to Gesellschaft, Gabriel Tarde perceived an evolution toward unification of humanity through imitation, and Durkheim traced evolution from mechanical to organic forms of solidarity. The psychic evolutionism of Lester Ward and Franklin Giddings, the technological evolutionism of Edward Tylor and Lewis

H. Morgen, were all found in the company of Karl Marx's social evolution via the dialectics of the forces and relations of production.

The Enlightenment search for an action-oriented science, disciplined by a rationally based theory of valuation, had become converted into the Comtian evolutionary triumph of the positive method in all departments of human culture yielding a sociological religion for humanity, the Marxian evolutionism guided by deterministic laws of historical class struggle leading from the kingdom of necessity to the kingdom of socialist freedom, or Spencerian evolutionism ultimately ending in the establishment of the greatest possible perfection via laissez-faire society.[31] Evolutionists worshiped a fundamentally spiritual idea of mankind advancing toward ever higher levels of well-being. All were prophets of a distinctively modern secular religion, each responding to the collapse of the medieval world view. Although these evolutionists provided a theoretical bulwark for Western civilization — capitalist West bloc and socialist East bloc alike — one must conclude that none produced a basis for a defensible approach to policy assessment serving a viable concept of societal development. Evolutionary naturalistic ethics could not be responsive to the Enlightenment valuational question. If a medieval supranatural basis for valuation is removed, if humankind is responsible for shaping society, and if "what is" cannot define "what ought," by what logics of fact and value shall social policy be assessed and the social order steered?

Fading Hopes of the Early Twentieth Century

Twentieth-century observers have witnessed an irregular retreat from the nineteenth-century aspirations and enthusiasms. Students of twentieth-century social thought find that the major discernible theme in the history of Western intellectual attempts to come to grips with the valuational problem has been that of disintegration.[32] Many observers have seen modern society being fragmented and individual meaning systems thrown into disarray by industrialization and urbanization. The modern world has been preoccupied with the specific, specialized, and the narrow. Emile Durkheim picked up this theme from Comte and substantiated it in his study of primitive society with its striking unity — leading him to coin the term *anomie* to describe experience in specialized social networks of disconnected meaninglessness.[33] By the mid-twentieth century, valuation for development would be reduced to little more than examining means by which to promote aggregate economic growth based on individualistic logics blind to the structural shape of society.

39

Friedrich Nietzsche (1844–1900), a slightly older contemporary of Durkheim, deeply questioned the Enlightenment project to discover rational foundations for an objective science that could serve any meaningful and sustainable conception of social progress. In the *Gay Science,* Section 335 (1882), he jeered at Hume's notions and at the Kantian categorical imperative. In an important sense, Nietzsche set himself against not only the Enlightenment project but also against the reworking of that thought in the late-nineteenth-century Europe — the morals, racism, militarism, and rationalism. For him, history consisted of great cultures created by vigorous peoples prone to lapse into decadence. In periods of disorder great leaders appear — for example, Socrates, Jesus, Shakespeare, Spinoza, Goethe — who succeed in transcending the weakness, disorganization, and self-destructiveness around them and thereby embody the future. In such great people the "will to power" — meaning self-control, self-supremacy, power over self rather than over others — is strong. Nietzsche did not relish the approach of Western social madness, but he hoped that out of the rubble of decadent Europe would arise a new social order of *Ubermenschen* ("overmen") who had mastered themselves — an idea to be later badly distorted by twentieth-century Fascists. The rational moral agent of the eighteenth century, giving effective reasoned guidance to society, was held to be an illusion, a fiction. "Will" would have to replace reason. Individuals would have to make themselves into moral agents through a heroic act of "will" and create their values rather than pretend to find them in nature.

A certain portion of Nietzsche is found in modern sociological form in Erving Goffman's role players seeking effectiveness and success in ways not to be measured by objective standards of achievement. Success is what passes for success; it is what can be sold to an audience. Moral standards are primarily of use in sustaining social interaction. The influence of the Nietzschean diagnosis grew with spreading disenchantment with naive Enlightenment aspirations. The twentieth century would find it easy to accept the premise that moral tenets are to be viewed as a set of rationalizations that conceal the fundamental nonrational phenomena of the "will."[34] Nietzsche was to become the moral philosopher of the present age, with his analysis of the irrationalities of both political left and right and his conception of modern individuals working out their morality by themselves.

Meanwhile, things were occurring beyond the academy in the world of action that were to influence the social development project. At the time of Comte, the Social Science Association movement in the

United States had been actively interventionist, based on humanitarian idealism and efforts to experiment with communal colonies. This movement was succeeded by the more conservative American Social Science Association's searching for more "realistic" working principles of social reform; this eventually transmuted into social welfare work's disdain of impractical theory.[35] But when theory separated from practice, and practice rejected theory, there was little option but to accept existing social structures and ideologies as guides to policy action.

Yet laissez-faire social Darwinism, Durkheimian observations of community fragmentation and anomie, Nietzschean attacks on the rational basis for collective social morality, and the separation of theory and practice did not crush all efforts to address the valuational basis for social policy assessment. A strain of thought advocating a frankly experimental approach to values emerged at the theoretical hands of Lester F. Ward and at the practical hands of the progressive movement. Unconscious evolution, and laissez-faire social policy, were formidable adversaries for Lester F. Ward, but he struck at them with all of his considerable talent. Ward tried to build upon Enlightenment thought by pulling together the best ideas of his time on evolutionary progress, education, and human plasticity. He made a case that science needed to be focused on problems of social action. As a latter-day Comte, he offered his synthesis to breathe new life into a sociology that was becoming, in his words, "a polite amusement," a "dead science."[36] In addition to his advocacy of an Academy of Political Science in Washington, D.C., to influence legislators in shaping public policy, he spoke strongly against disciplinary quest for its own sake.[37] Ward saw science as part of the continuing problem of social reconstruction.

Thomas Henry Huxley echoed Ward in important respects as he also attempted to confront the issues of ethics and public policy that the social Darwinian and Marxian evolutionists had fudged. At the center of Huxley's thought was the clear distinction between the "cosmic process" and the "ethical process" — what Lester Ward would have labeled as the "genetic" and "telic." Although the ethical process was clearly an evolutionary product of cosmic evolution, in Huxley's view the ethical competence of human beings could transform the natural world, through conscious planning, into a "garden" constructed to serve human needs.[38] Cosmic struggle for Huxley meant ceaseless conflict over possession of means of existence, but ethical advancement meant increased self-restraint and mutual assistance.

When Albion Small launched the *American Journal of Sociology* in 1895, he acknowledged policy commitments similar to those of Lester Ward by expounding, in the lead article of the pioneer volume, "the relations of man to man are not what they should be . . . and something must be done directly, systematically, and on a large scale to right these wrongs."[39] The whole point of sociology for Small, at this time in his life, was to conduct scientific investigations of society and use the resulting knowledge to transform the social order.[40] Whereas Herbert Spencer and William Graham Sumner opposed social planning on the grounds that planning would fetter the natural operation of the cosmic evolutionary process, Small argued in his *General Sociology* (1905) that sociology must take as its central purpose to explain "not how the world came to be what it is, but how to make it what it should be."[41] Small was joined in his vision of a policy-relevant sociology not only by Lester Ward but also by E. A. Ross, Thorstein Veblen, William James, and Charles Horton Cooley. By the 1920s, the challenge of social Darwinism had been met in most sociology graduate programs, and most sociologists in the major centers of graduate education in the United States — Chicago, Wisconsin, Columbia, Stanford, Brown — were sympathetic to the aims of an applied policy-oriented sociology.[42]

Simultaneously, the progressive movement in the United States centered on the idea of rationally conducted policy assessment as a handmaiden to planned social change. The movement was rooted in social transformations wrought by the twin forces of industrialization and immigration.[43] U.S. society of the late nineteenth century had experienced widespread erosion of local autonomy in what had previously been a collection of isolated small communities — the heart of early nineteenth-century democracy.[44] By the 1880s, the autonomy of local community had been all but destroyed. A new class of rich industrialists was rising to dominate small-town elites. In addition, immigration from southern and eastern Europe swelled urban centers with people of cultural orientations vastly different from those of the Yankee Protestant middle class, representatives of which were threatened by loss of economic and political power to ward bosses and industrialists. They watched the ward bosses consolidate their control by catering to material needs of immigrants in exchange for votes, and they feared the life-and-death power that absentee industrial capitalists held over local communities.

Small towns could be made or broken by a single distant decision. Merchants, small manufacturers, professional men of law, medicine, and the clergy — leaders of the former era — distrusted decisions made by powerful capitalists based on the pure calculation of profit, and they hated the politics of policy conducted by the urban political entrepreneurs geared to the newly arrived immigrant. The alternative was clear. National, state, and local planning, all of it rational, would make for a government run by politicians responsive to the old-fashioned virtues and free from the motives of crass economic and political materialism. Aiding political leaders would be scientific experts with lifetime tenure as government bureaucrats, who could specialize in particular problems and, free of short-term political pressures, could find solutions for poverty, ignorance, disease, crime, and urban squalor.

Progressivists launched themselves eagerly into problems of resource conservation, regulation of big business, control over environmental pollution, tariff reform, electoral reform, urban planning, and civil service reform. It is no accident that modern applied sociology should be rooted in this era.[45] The ideas were popularized by Walter Lippmann and were codified and extended by Thorstein Veblen, John Dewey, William James, and Charles Beard. Yet the thrust of an applied sociology serving the government as a steward of social welfare raised the ugly question about values and valuation. How were decision-makers to know evil and separate it from the good? Whose values should prevail? Why? Sociology divided into at least two camps over the issue.

On the one hand, there were those who advocated the activist role for an applied sociology; they adhered to Lester Ward's conception that sociologists should speak out directly against established ways and the evils associated with them. On the other hand, there were "objectivists" who opposed the advocacy role for social scientists, who argued that they had no claim to special valuational authority and that they should adopt an advisory role in the supply of technical knowledge and policy recommendations. According to Mary Furner, the debate was won by the "objectivists," not on the merits of the case per se but in part as a result of the impact of several academic freedom cases that created a reaction against direct policy involvement.[46] It was important to avoid radicalism and excessive publicity and therefore to maintain a reputation for scientific objectivity. Most academic social scientists stopped asking value questions and turned their attention to empirical studies of "social problems" (itself a necessarily valuative concept), the accepted goal of which was to gain recognition as an expert with technical competence. It was not, however, simple fear brought about by political dangers of open policy advocacy that moved sociology to the empirical world of the "is" divorced from "ought" questions. Profound attacks were made during this time upon logical capacities to reason in the domain of "ought."

The Twentieth-Century Valuational Collapse

The philosopher G. E. Moore published with considerable impact his *Principia Ethica* (1903), the major message of which was that the term *good* could not be derived from a natural property. Building upon this insight of David Hume, he concluded that conceptions of the "good" are matters of intuition, not open to rigorous logical analysis. To assert that evolutionary processes would lead to betterment was to assert that what is, ought to be — the naturalistic fallacy. One of Moore's contributions was to shift attention of philosophers from the problem of policy impact in the world to the problem of language structure and meaning.[47] Those social scientists who had resisted social Darwinism sufficiently to continue their focus on planning were now placed under counterpressure to separate fact from value and to recognize the implications of emerging cultural relativist thought.

Until about 1900, anthropology had followed in the same positivist evolutionary tradition established by Comte and Spencer. The master idea was evolution, but in the early twentieth century dissenting views began to be heard. When the general public still thought of anthropology as the study of human evolutionary progress from savagery to civilization with special emphasis on the savagery, some professional anthropologists began to openly reject evolutionary conceptions. One of the first to break sharply from evolutionism was Franz Boas, who assailed the prevailing idea that modern Western culture presented an acceptable standard against which all other cultures should be measured.[48] One of the few generalizations that Boas would risk was that history, to him, revealed no pattern of necessary uniform evolution across various culture areas. Each cultural group had its own history and had to be judged on its own terms against its own constellation of values. Anthropological cultural relativism led, necessarily, to value relativism, and any general cross-cultural idea of social development became inconceivable.[49]

Although it would be years before his thought would be widely read in the social science community in the United States, Max Weber provided strong support for a valuationally neutral conception of social science by virtue of his analysis of the problem posed by professional value judgment. Weber highlighted the distinction between "is" and "ought" — a distinction that had been obfuscated by many of his contemporaries who argued either that (1) society was ruled by evolutionary principles, and what was "inevitably emergent" defined the normatively right; or that (2) science should be placed in the service of particular ideological views.

The question of the place of value judgment in social science had risen with increasing frequency and intensity in Germany just as in the English-speaking countries. When, in 1904, Edgar Jaffe, Werner Sombart, and Max Weber took over editorship of the *Archiv fur Sozialwissenschaft and Sozialpolitik,* they published in their first issue a statement of policy on the matter.[50] In essence, the article laid down the principles of scientific value relativism without actually using the word relativism. The purpose of the journal had been education in judgments on social problems and criticism of practical policy matters while at the same time attempting to proceed with methods of scientific research. Were these two purposes compatible? What were the meanings of the value judgments found in the journal's pages? What validity did such judgments have?

Weber replied to these questions by holding that there must be no confusion between two separate operations: (1) making judgments of fact to which science applies and (2) making judgments of value to which science does not apply. Scientists qua scientists had no basis in their craft to assert valuations.[51] There must be scholarly submission to the limits of the scientific method. The question as to whether something is to be valued can be assessed only in relation to the goal held by persons specifying what is or is not valuable. It is impossible to establish scientifically what goals or purposes are most or least valuable. Values are simply grasped by intuition and held by faith. Science can analyze consequences associated with their pursuit, but the superiority or inferiority of alternative values cannot be established by the scientific method. Because value judgments cannot be nonpartisan, Weber expressed the fear that the lecture platform would be used for personal prophecy, and he opposed professional promotions in the university being given to prophets rather than to scientists.[52]

In 1918, Weber delivered two lectures later published as "Politics as Vocation" and "Science as Vocation."[53] In the first, he pursued the responsibility of the political leader in relation to the bureaucrat and discussed the valuational problems of political choice. In the second, he discussed the limits of the scientist in the study of fact. Science, Weber contended, is a vocation organized into special disciplines in the service of clarification of fact. Science is not the gift of seers dispensing value judgments and revelation.

By virtue of his telling arguments about the limits of science, Max Weber belongs to that select group of thinkers who revealed the difficulties to be faced by any honest scholar, in the role of scientist, who would believe in the possibility of reasoned knowledge about valuation for social development and policy assessment. Social scientists were limited to proving means to externally given ends or to telling policymakers how to obtain their own goals. Weber's name came to be the trademark of "value-free science," but he did not cease to personally believe in the value of values, nor did he ever underestimate the importance of belief in values for human dignity. Values were objectively valuable even if their content was a matter of faith, not science. Furthermore, scientists could (1) analyze better and worse means to ends and by so doing indirectly criticize the ends themselves by making the acting person realize that every action and inaction imply certain values and rejection of others, (2) make the choosing person see the significance of what one is after — the ideas underlying the value-laden goal, and (3) judge value judgments critically according to their consistency and lay bare the axioms from which value criteria are derived.[54] Although the making of the decision itself is not a task that science could undertake, Weber concluded: "We are far removed, then, from the view that demand for the exclusion of value judgments in empirical analysis implies that discussions of evaluations are sterile or meaningless."[55]

The proper conclusion to be drawn from Weber's analysis is not that reasoned valuation is impossible but only that logics of valuation must be clearly distinguished from logics of factual inquiry and that science of fact qua science cannot speak to issues of valuation. There is, however, no reason to believe that Max Weber would be distressed by the thought of logics of value working in collaboration with logics of factual inquiry to assess proposed policy options affecting the structure of society.

Whatever the state of the troubled relationship between fact and value, by the 1920s sociology had undergone a startling change from the naive value commitments of the nineteenth-century evolutionists and social reformers. Evolutionism was receding, Lester Ward was soon to be largely forgotten, and the debates over the place of value in science laid the foundations for social science's stressing discovery of "facts" at the expense of valuative context and meaning. Valuative contributions were quite correctly seen to be no longer a part of science per se, and their status in reasoned discourse was open to question.

What was soon to be clear, however, was that sociology did not want to be hampered by value commitments of either the superordinate social science of Lester Ward or the immediate action imperatives of social reconstruction. The idea of social development would have to fight a desperate battle to remain alive in the interstices of a heterogeneous discipline. Stuart Rice, writing in the early 1930s, asked: "What is sociology?"[56] He answered that sociology was a plural set of subject matters in uneasy relation to each other but that whatever sociology was, there was one thing it was not and should not be, namely "ethical valuations."[57] Sociology, in the period between World Wars I and II, came into the hands of those who would champion "scientific objectivism" — for example, Stuart Rice, George A. Lundberg, F. Stuart Chapin, and William Fielding Ogburn.[58] For Ogburn, Chapin, and their allies, a scientific sociology was "nominalist, statistical and advisory," concerned with means, not ends. It had a vision of society allowing structure to recede into the background and emphasizing perceptions of aggregates of individuals.[59] For Chapin, social class could be reduced to a point system for recording items of home furnishing. Some protest was heard from time to time from the likes of people such as Luther Bernard, who reminded contemporaries that sociology should retain a value-critical stance,[60] but for the most part sociology settled into a secularized version of nineteenth-century American Protestantism with its celebration of "hard fact," the "rigors of research," and its implicit faith in serving undefined notions of "efficiency" and "growth." There was more than a little transmuted missionary zeal in all of this, but open discussion of valuation became taboo. Vigorous consideration of valuation would threaten the pose of disinterested sociological teaching and research.

Sociology had divided the issue of valuation into three sometimes bitterly opposing schools. Antagonistic positions taken on the matter have yielded bitter conflict dividing "value-free" sociologists, the applied value-committed sociologists, and radical value-critical theorists. Struggles over the issue of valuation have fundamentally conditioned sociological discourse on policy assessment, and it is to these positions that the discussion now turns.

THE TWENTIETH-CENTURY VALUATIONAL ANTAGONISM

Valuation and the Pure Science Orientation

Professionals taking the pure science position, the dominant one in sociology in the United States from the 1920s through the 1980s, argue that Weber's central message is clear and compelling: There is no intersubjectively transmittable proof of the validity of value judgments. Sociology is a pure science different from the natural sciences only in degree; its purpose is to discover and refine general principles of human behavior. Sociologists must avoid having their values bias their research and teaching. Galileo's espousal of heliocentric theory and Darwin's connection of humankind to the evolutionary process did violence to religious views at a cost to scientific progress; the natural sciences, therefore, quite rightly found a path to scientific advancement by freeing themselves from commonsense categories and especially from the value-laden ideologies shared within power structures. The separation of fact and value has opened the way to discovery of the complex web of relationships that makes up modern science — something that could only occur when scientists were freed from the necessity of seeking factual relationships supporting valuative systems of ideologists in power. Social scientists, too, must be freed from the burden of value-laden concepts so as to see the world more clearly as it "is," and they must remain neutral concerning the issue of which values "ought" to guide policy assessment.

This conception of social science has rested centrally on the logical positivist argument that value statements are meaningless — nothing more than the expression of personal emotion. Knowledge of what "is" does not include normative policy directions and therefore does not lend itself to valuative interpretations.[61] Value neutrality is, therefore, the central norm of scientific endeavor; scientists are to be disinterested in motivation and are thereby freed to choose problems on deductive theoretical grounds rather than according to practical pressure or personal bias.

Value-free scientists come in at least two varieties. One is the complete value skeptic who contends that all value statements are equally nondemonstrable. The other is the much less extreme relativist who argues that various value stances are valid relative to individuals within their respective cultural systems and that such values therefore are possible candidates to guide development planning in those sociocultural contexts.[62] Still, the values adopted by agents in a given culture cannot be scientifically or logically appraised. Yet both total skeptics and moderate relativists agree that social scientists as such must confine themselves to the study of facts or facts about values.[63] Through role differentiation, and a commitment to the value-free posture, the sociologist can be value free in the role as scientist while still holding values as a citizen. The positivist is no less the whole person by abstaining from mingling value judgments in scientific work than is the physician who tries to keep ideological values out of mind while performing surgery. Science and citizenship are two different things. Taking positions on social and political issues would compromise sociologists in their basic investigative tasks, but as citizens they can express their value judgments without dragging sociology into the political arena.[64]

The pure scientist contends that science best serves humankind by fostering the best science — that is, a value-neutral science. It is perfectly reasonable to expect science to aid the condition of human beings, but it must do so indirectly. The most effective road to the application of scientific knowledge is to study social uniformities for their own sake — as an investment that will ultimately yield important returns for human welfare.[65] The application, eventually, will be carried on by the marketplace, the political system, and the applied branches of the university — engineering, social work, public health, city planning, and public administration.

Most professionals who take this position recognize the right of the applied scientist to work in practical domains, provided that s/he never fails in her or his duty to reveal underlying value judgments and admit their nonscientific basis, and insofar as the applied scientist never abuses authority in the classroom as a teacher indoctrinating students in value biases under the cloak of academic freedom. Yet the pure scientist claims that applied colleagues opt for a second-best choice of scientific behavior on the grounds that

1. when governments provide funds for applied policy research, it diverts attention from the higher priority of seeking new knowledge;

2. when social scientists accept government funds they are placed in the position of giving advice prematurely on the basis of inadequate knowledge, and such brashness brings the discipline into disrepute;

3. by accepting research problems set forth by government or other nonacademic agendas, social scientists distort the development of their disciplines while issues of greater theoretical salience become neglected;

4. social scientists who not only address research problems set by governments but who address them in terms of the value orien-

tations of incumbent office holders abdicate their role as scientists and become mere technicians serving powers that be;

5. employing scientific knowledge and skill in service to any setting government — whatever the guiding ideology — makes social scientists handmaidens of the state rather than unattached critics of any and all social arrangements.[66]

This value-free conception of sociology came to have substantial influence by the 1920s, and the separation of value-free science from an applied value-laden social science became highly crystallized by the 1950s. By 1929, W. F. Ogburn, in his presidential address to the American Sociological Society, proclaimed: "Sociology as a science is not interested in making the world a better place to live . . . Science is interested directly in one thing only, to wit, discovery of new knowledge. . ."[67]

Later, George A. Lundberg, a resolute champion of rigorous technique, held that sociology had arrived at the full stature of science and no longer needed to concern itself with values or history. Said he: "The history of social thought will be relegated to approximately the position that the history of chemistry occupies. . ."[68] Robert Bierstedt, writing in the late 1940s, pronounced clearly the dominant consensual position on the matter: "It [sociology] is a science or it is nothing. And in order to be a science it must diligently avoid all pronouncements of an ethical character. As a science it cannot answer questions of value. It can have no traffic with normative statements because there is no logic of the normative."[69]

By the 1950s, this position represented the dominant orthodoxy. Professionalized describers of fact and searchers for factual relationships plied away at giving them value-free order. The rare appearance of a frankly valuative article in a major journal was almost always credited to the privilege of a presidential address. Only a minority of thinkers disturbed, in a marginal way, the calm. It is to them — in both the applied and radical postures — that we now turn.

Valuation and the Applied Science Orientation

The social-problem-solving, policy-assessing, applied science position was hit hard by G. E. Moore's and Max Weber's reassertion of David Hume's fact-value distinction and by the ensuing cultural relativism that questioned possibilities for a defensible intersubjective and cross-culturally viable notion of progress to which science could be applied. To this challenge, applied sociologists in general, and Robert S. Lynd in particular, replied that the positivist faith in the ultimate benefit of value-free science is predicated on a master system of evolutionary progress. If there is no evolutionary scheme leading to inevitable progress, there is no reason to assume that science will serve beneficial ends in the long run. A valuationally neutral science can be employed for harmful as well as for beneficial ends; it is totally unwarranted to assume knowledge will lead to social improvement.[70]

The applied scientist views the Weberian position as not preventing the assertion of values as long as they are recognized as such. Furthermore, although it is true that there are no proofs of value, there are clearly superior and inferior values. In the view of applied scientists, the value-free approach implicitly accepts the value of existing arrangements, but not all existing social arrangements are equally desirable, and "pure science" fails to recognize that it implicitly relies upon a nonexistent automatic evolutionary process to ensure that advances in knowledge will be constructively applied.

A sharp test of the "pure science" position came with the onslaught of fascism in the 1930s. To be systematically irrational, to "think with the blood" as a principle elevated to a maxim of social organization and public policy, was not just one cultural value among many about which nothing could be said by scientists. It was decidedly inferior and must be opposed, especially by scientists whose very enterprise depends on values of reason, open sharing of evidence, and toleration of dissent. Many philosophers and scientists called a halt to unthinking application of cultural relativist doctrine when confronted by a mobilizing European fascism led by Adolf Hitler. Julian Huxley summed up matters for many when he proclaimed: "We live under the grim material necessity of defeating the Nazi system, ethics and all, but no less under the spiritual and intellectual necessity not merely of feeling and believing but of *knowing* that Nazi ethics are not just different from ours, but wrong and false; or at least less right and less true" (emphasis in original).[71] Robert Redfield was later to add that it is easy to be benevolently value free and impartial about value systems so long as the values are of "unimportant peoples remote from our concerns," but such neutrality is harder to maintain when issues are closer to home.[72]

Talcott Parsons saw that the problem required attention, and he viewed his theoretical effort as providing something of a valuational framework. By the 1930s, when Western liberalism was under sharp attack from the anti-intellectualism of the Fascists and the collectivism of the left, Parsons launched a project to save liberalism. He began in 1937 by publishing *The Structure of Social Action*. Noting that the liberal theory of laissez-faire capitalism was focused almost exclusively upon individually rational social "atoms" pursuing self-interests and judging that theory to be blind to effects of social structure, Parsons pointed out that liberalism worked without anything approaching an adequate conception of the collective good. Parsons then went about the sociological business of placing decision-making agents in the context of a social system constructed out of emergent social norms. Liberal individualism in the classical economic tradition suggested social atomism; it was, therefore, an important part of the Parsonian effort to demonstrate that liberal individualism could only emerge in a certain variety of culture and social structure and that this social order deserved systematic elucidation. There were, asserted Parsons, supra-individual standards against which analysts must judge social life.[73] Parsons advanced a collectively moral vision of a humanistic, stable, democratic society organized around a common value system. Parson's theoretical effort was, in no small measure, an attempt to identify the social conditions within which both collective reason, and respect for individuality, could be achieved. It was within this framework during the 1940s, 1950s, and 1960s that many applied sociologists worked out their value commitments.

Although most applied sociologists conceded that social values cannot be ultimately established as valid, they held that value judgments are unavoidable in definitions of social problems generally, in the specification of particular research problems, in the selection of variables, and in the choices made in interpreting the significance of factual conclusions. Value judgments are, therefore, at the heart of the social science enterprise. The only real choice, they contend, is between expression of one's values as honestly as possible or persistence in a sham ritual of moral neutrality that leaves valuation at the total mercy of irrationality.[74]

Some applied professionals have followed the footsteps of those who have urged an experimentalist approach to values. John Dewey emphasized this option. Let us experiment with values, said Dewey, so that we may have ever more dependable ones, just as physical science seeks ever more dependable facts through systematic experimentation.[75] Values are something to be achieved, to be systematically examined in light of their consequences for human beings — not something to be passed down and received in an uncritical fashion.

Dewey found that the lessons of antiauthoritarian experimental science extended to systematic investigation of values to determine which worked best — best being defined as that which instrumentally furthered the survival and development of the species.[76] There may not be scientifically verifiable ultimate value criteria, but logical and scientific observation of empirical consequences of value choices in action would hone our value sensibilities. Since value judgments cannot be avoided in problem selection and interpretation of research results, our only alternative is to extend our capacity to pursue humane values. Robert Lynd took a sympathetic stance when he held that the basic data for the social sciences are the values that human beings seek to satisfy. If culture pattern x exists, but is not working given the best values that can be agreed upon, social scientists must assist in the examination of alternative cultural patterns. Said Lynd, "Research without an actively selective point of view becomes the ditty bag of an idiot, filled with bits and pebbles, straws, feathers, and other random hoardings."[77]

Contemporary applied scientists seek to define practical problems in sociological terms and to examine implications of alternative policy proposals as hypothesized solutions. To this end the Society for the Study of Social Problems was organized, in 1952, to promote research on the problems of U.S. society so as to provide knowledge for sound social action. Social problems texts have routinely confronted, and fudged, the fact-value problem entailed in the definition of a social problem. For example, Morris Janowitz has distinguished two basic models for the conduct of applied social-problem-oriented science: the "social-engineering" and the "enlightenment" approaches.[78] The analyst employing the engineering model attempts to communicate technical knowledge to decision centers of the client organization, who then consume the knowledge subject to the controls placed on the organization by the political system and marketplace. Critics of the engineering model of applied science are quick to point out that this approach does not sufficiently serve the consumer, the citizen-voter, or even political elites responsible for policy.[79] This is to say that it serves the implicit value judgments of elites and their organizations. Employing the Enlightenment model, social analysts recognize that they are part of the broader social process by seeking to educate the responsible decision-makers and relevant publics as broadly and deeply as possible with respect to the problem under consideration. Yet this begs the question: What values will guide Enlightenment efforts?

Whether proceeding according to either or both of these models of applied science, researchers in the applied tradition focus their inquiry on dependent variables with distinctly normative content — for example, some aspect of quality of life such as educational opportunity or delivery of health care — and independent variables are then ferreted out that are expected to influence realization of the dependent value-laden variable in question. The larger the number of independent variables open to manipulation by decision-makers, the better.[80]

Harold Lasswell, while at the University of Chicago (1924–1938), connected his dependent variables to the values of income, safety, and respect. Later, while at Yale University (1945–1975), Lasswell developed a matrix of eight values to guide applied science. Lasswell teamed with Daniel Lerner in the publication of the post–World War II landmark statement, *The Policy Sciences* (1951).[81] When Lasswell proposed the applied policy science approach he was thinking of a comprehensive conception of societal development.[82] Lasswell distinguished between a less-desirable applied social science that would serve as a handmaiden of setting governments and a more-justifiable policy science that would advance theories of public choice to advance more developmental social policies. He envisioned a policy science revolving around a general theory of social choice attached to development values. The promise of this effort was widely discussed, but it was the 1970s that were to become the decade of policy analysis. Yet even then, valuational issues would remain neglected.

Meanwhile, in the early 1950s, the Columbia School of applied research emerged by building on the work of Paul Lazarsfeld and associates at the Bureau of Applied Social Research, which was for more than a decade the mecca of policy analysis in U.S. social science.[83] The core of this effort was to take existing policy issues and subject them to systematic empirical observation; this was facilitated by advances in electronic data processing that made it possible to go beyond the Lazarsfeld two-by-two contingency table that limited empirical analysis to examination of one hypothesis at a time. By the 1960s, applied scientists had at their disposal the increased multivariate power of the correlation matrix, multiple regression, and factor analysis. Then path analysis was popularized, which allowed researchers to examine whole sets of hypotheses together in mutual interaction.

Unfortunately, methodological advance did not bring contentment to the world of applied sociology. Whereas Rexford Tugwell had gone confidently to Franklin Roosevelt's Washington to "speak truth to power," the contemporary mood in applied social science has been bleak. Weaknesses of applied social science in general, and of applied sociology in particular, have been widely acknowledged. One example is represented by the report of the Special Commission of the Social Sciences of the National Science Board, *Knowledge into Action: Improving the Nation's Use of the Social Sciences* (1969). The Commission clearly attempted to substantiate the importance of the social sciences for analysis of social problems, but at least in the eyes of some sympathizers, the arguments were not at all convincing.[84] More recent assessments of the contributions of applied sociology are, at best, subdued. Gone are the strident tones that once promised progress via applied policy research.[85] A recent review raised the issue of valuation, among others, and concluded: "In summary, we feel that rural sociology has generally failed to achieve its dual aspirations of becoming a science and applying scientific knowledge usefully in solving rural social problems."[86]

In contemplating this pessimistic assessment, Professor Patrick C. Jobes clearly saw the importance of the unresolved value problem as he commented:

> What, then, can rural sociologists do as applied scientists? First, they can continue to muddle through, plying their analytical skills with as much skill and integrity as they can muster. Then, they can don the moral robes of their personal persuasion. Some will adopt the perspective of society's elite, others will take that of the disenfranchised . . . of course neither has the essential knowledge that the good they seek to implement will serve well more than some people for a limited span of time.[87]

That contemporary applied social science is viewed as problematic in its attempts to improve policy and is, therefore, on the defensive attributed by various critics to a range of factors. Some inadequacies are attributed to the fact that applied social science is inherently conservative, not capable of serving the needs of consumers, patients, voters, and that it is almost exclusively in the service of producers and bureaucratic agencies.[88] Some inadequacies are perceived to be rooted in the failure of social scientists, especially sociologists, to develop an accurate view of the policy process, a deficiency that yields studies with conclusions that cannot be implemented.[89] Also, it is pointed out that single disciplinary research necessarily misses the multifaceted realities of actual policy problems — there is no clear and simple truth that completely falls within the boundaries of any single discipline.[90]

Furthermore, it is frequently the case that favorite variables of the applied sociologist — childhood socialization, class and status, father's occupation, position in the family, consumer or voter attitudes — are those over which a policymaker has no control via policy manipulation.[91] The failure to seek out variables that can be manipulated — actionable variables in applied contexts — is a frequent target of criticism.[92] Furthermore, under the most favorable of circumstances, the policymaker operates with many sources of information beyond the content of the best and most comprehensive study. Professional applied social research, however well crafted around manipulable variables, is only one small source of relevant information for the decision-maker. Too often, it is asserted, applied research fails to supplement the other sources in a useful manner.[93]

Astute observers of the scene have asserted that it is unlikely that disciplinary applied social research, especially that of sociology, will be routinely relevant for policy purposes.[94] Insofar as this proves to be the case, one of the primary justifications for public financial support for academic social science is thereby seriously undermined. Yet for all of the problems, many sociologists refuse to abandon the applied policy enterprise. Many agree with Edgar F. Borgatta and Karen S. Cook that ". . . if sociology is to have a future, it has to be able to do work — useful work."[95] They hold on to the hope that useful work will yet be done. A viable policy-assessing sociology must be constructed that is equipped to work both in the domain of empirical fact and in that of reasoned collective values. Applied sociology must directly, and openly, confront its valuational problems before its full potential can be fulfilled.

Valuation and the Critical Theory Orientation

The message of the critical theorist is that positivist science in general, and positivist social science in particular, constitute a conservative ideology that accepts the world as it "is" and overlooks what "could be" and "should be." In Western societies, therefore, positivism is the ideology of bureaucratic capitalism and state socialism. Positivist "value-free" scientists are viewed as being conservative because they have sustained the power of the capitalist ruling class in the West and that of the apparatchiks in totalitarian socialist nations.[96] Whereas the old Marxist left feared capitalist exploitation and wars of imperialism, the new radicals — also taking cues from Marxist theoretical foundations — reject socialist totalitarianism while also fearing the "gentle apocalypse" that comes with capitalist elite manipulation of the masses in affluent consumer societies. The movement bemoans the failure of ideology and the triumph of the instrumentally rational, socially value-blind, corporate organization. It regretfully finds the world in the pocket of giant U.S. and European corporations and their Eastern European and Soviet bureaucratic counterparts — a fact that makes a mockery of both parliamentary democracy and the dignity of the worker.

Professional sociologists in the West wait for the call of the marketplace or state capitalist bureaucracy to offer research opportunities; likewise, in the U.S.S.R. and Eastern Europe, the sociologist waits eagerly for signals from the party and bureaucracy. Both serve the smooth functioning of the existing order, and neither promotes human liberation from oppression — the central value of the critical theorist. Authentic liberation is taken to mean a condition in which individuals have the chance to participate equally and continuously in the policy formulation and implementation processes of organizations affecting them and thereby to maximize their potentialities.[97]

The path of what has been too loosely deemed social development, say the critical theorists, has led less from savagery to humanity and more from the spear to the nuclear missile. So-called progress provided by positivist science has made possible the worldwide construction of oppressive social structures that have undercut the capacity of citizens to move toward eighteenth-century Enlightenment ideals of emancipation, equality, and civic participation. The concern of these thinkers with the larger structural and cultural shape of society forced into the open the valuation problem.

On the U.S. side of the Atlantic, value-critical sociologists were few and isolated well into the 1960s. C. Wright Mills, his voice raised against the isolation of science and value and for a value-aware sociology, was ignored in his department and ostracized by his profession. Mills bemoaned the degeneration of political discourse into vapid sloganeering, and he criticized social scientists for trading away critique of mindless social policies associated with the high consumption society in favor of enhancing their professional status.[98] The proper role of sociology, according to Mills, was to make reason relevant to democratic public discourse that would involve challenging prevailing definitions of reality propounded by elites.

With the possible exception of Mills's *The Power Elite* (1956), most radical sociology in the United States was little more than polemic — a fact that began to change markedly in the 1970s.[99] By the mid-1960s, however, the oppositional stance of many U.S. sociologists became pronounced as the goals of the government were highlighted with respect to problems of racism, poverty, urban deterioration, and the military involvement in Vietnam. Pursuit of value-free positivist science was increasingly called into question — especially after the killing of students at Kent State University, the radicalism of Malcolm X, the assassination of Martin Luther King, the intensification of the air war in Indochina, and the continuing failure to stem the deterioration of the quality of urban life in the United States.

A radicalized stratum of social scientists mobilized across disciplinary boundaries.[100] New-left activists challenged not only national political leaders but also professors in the seminar room. Academic departments seethed with conflict over the fundamental character of their respective disciplines; campuses and streets were witness to guerrilla theater, workshops on counter culture, and overt attempts to convert social scientists to social causes.

Within this politically sharpened context, Alvin Gouldner published his widely read *The Coming Crisis of Western Sociology* (1970).[101] Gouldner argued that since society would not accept the values of the founding fathers of the discipline, sociologists came to accept society's values, such as they were. Every social theory, argued Gouldner, is predicated on "domain assumptions" representing not the results of controlled professional and objective inquiry but the influence of prevailing ideology and the investigator's social position. The task is not to rid the discipline of such assumptions — an impossible notion. Rather, it is to accept their inescapable presence and to choose domain assumptions proper to a world waiting to be born rather than those tied to a collapsing system. The dominant paradigm of value-free sociology, functionalism, could be neither value free nor value critical.[102] It could not be value free because functionalism celebrates the value of existing orders, and it could not be value critical, said Gouldner, because it can do nothing but accept the kind of social order in which it finds itself. Functionalist theory provides a sociological posture for affluent middle-class sociologists who no longer relate to historical patterns of conflict, dominance, and subordination and who fail to envision a future radically different from the present.[103]

Gouldner made a case that theories are accepted or rejected because of the appeal, or lack thereof, of the background domain assumptions embedded in them. At some point, old assumptions come to operate in new conditions within which they are vulnerable to attack by a new generation whose dissent from the old premises precipitates a crisis — the condition of contemporary sociology. Sociologists must deliver their domain assumptions — and the values built into them — up from the dim realm of subsidiary awareness into the light of explicit analysis where they can be brought to the bar of reason and evidence — a task best accomplished via the procedures of Gouldner's proposed "reflexive sociology."[104] Reflexive sociology accepts the dangers of value commitment. It prefers the risk of "ending in distortion" to that of "beginning in distortion." Gouldner's critical sociologist prefers "soul searching" to the "soul selling" of the applied technician or the "pure" researcher.[105]

On the European side of the Atlantic, recent years have seen much attention focused on the work of social philosophers and sociologists associated with the Frankfurt Institute for Social Research — the Frankfurt School.[106] The Institute was founded in 1923 in Weimar, Germany. Many of its illustrious members migrated from the homeland when Hitler came to power and found their way to the United States. After the conclusion of World War II, most returned to Germany.[107] For the Frankfurt group — men such as Max Horkheimer, Theodore Adorno, and Herbert Marcuse, the definitive experience was the coercive manipulation of German fascism and the artificial need creation of late capitalism. Both ideological systems, in their view, used political propaganda and sophisticated marketing psychology to break down barriers between private and public spheres of life to engender artificial needs in support of the power structure. They disapproved of the Stalinist and post-Stalinist system in the U.S.S.R. because of its failure to be emancipating, but as Marxists they have made their primary target the oppressions of state capitalism. Their Marxism has been partly an attack on the pretensions of capitalist societies to provide for all citizens the rights set out in that eighteenth-century Enlightenment document — the Declaration of Independence — and partly a vision of society in which liberty, equality, and fraternity will be realized without state coercion.

In the 1960s, Herbert Marcuse became the most widely proclaimed figure in this stream because he detailed ways in which contemporary technology eroded social bases for fundamental opposition by abolishing the working class as a force for radical social transformation.[108] Marcuse argued, furthermore, that the immense productivity of science and technology had already minimized time spent in production of necessities. There is, he contended, no longer any necessity for civilization to be repressive in order to provide the daily bread — at least if there is proper guidance from a liberated critical social science.

Critical theory was extended substantially in the 1970s by Jürgen

Habermas, whose work has ranged over the methodology of the social sciences; the relationship between science, politics, and public opinion; and the poverty of public discourse in advanced industrialized countries.[109] Habermas demonstrated, to his satisfaction at least, the failure of positivist science. Such science is rooted in the natural world wherein manipulation of objects is the goal; positivist social science carries this into the domain of manipulation of people and public discourse. Positivist social theory becomes a "hypostatization of the actual" — it confines inquiry to "what is the case" and rules out "what could be."[110] Advocates of positivism are mistaken, says Habermas, in supposing that natural science is value free; on the contrary it is value committed to mastery of the environment. What people have learned about nature is used to dominate both nature and other human beings.

Positivist natural science is thereby stood on its head. Far from natural science providing the model for social theory, it cannot properly be understood except in terms of prior social theory that specifies natural science's role in the social division of labor.[111] A purely descriptive social science cannot comprehend the meaning of social structure — it cannot recognize facts for what they are because social theory must place "facts" in proper social perspective for us to recognize them. There must be a collectively shared value stance from which facts can be judged as to their significance and meaning.

In *Legitimation Crisis* (1975), Habermas developed an old sociological theme: the disintegration of the community under the onslaught of modern science and technology. As late capitalism advances, the traditional store of collective values associated with the church, family, and nation is dried up. But it is collective values that shape personal identities and discipline demands that citizens make upon each other in political struggle. Self-interested and socially atomistic economic growth notions dominate whatever is left of public discourse in technologically advanced societies, but such ideas are no longer sufficient to sustain the legitimacy of the social structure. There is a legitimation deficit.

As legitimation of social structures weakens, because of inadequate processes of collective valuation, the state is expected to carry ever greater burdens of social integration. A welter of conflicting demands advanced by narrowly interested parties presses upon a public household without the socially legitimate analytical tools with which to conduct defensible dialogue about the social well-being of the community. Spent public value traditions leave both individuals and organizations of the state exhausted and without the direction that can only come through practical reason about common values.

What should be the value commitments of a value-critical social science? Marcuse offered the values of freedom, beauty, peace, justice, satisfaction of human needs, and abolition of misery and cruelty.[112] Habermas has advanced the basic value expressed in German as *Mundigkeit* — roughly translated as "individual autonomy," with strong connotations of freedom and equality.[113] In addition to reflecting a basic human need, Habermas argues that individual autonomy is justified as a basic human value because the very structure of human language expresses unequivocally the moral intention of universal and unrestricted consensus — a consensus possible only in a fully emancipated society free from repression and domination.[114]

How are such values to be realized? Habermas contends that advanced scientific-technical societies can be rational only if development and application of science and technology are subject to public control through civil discourse. Exercise of such control is possible only if the autonomy and responsibility of workers is so secure that the framework of public discussion is free from domination. Then dialogue can be established about the ends of life.[115] Habermas holds that the domain of modern public life has been constricted to intermittent public spectacles and periodic acclamation of one or another representative of the power structure. General unrestricted discussion of "practical" questions — genuine policy options — has disintegrated under the onslaught of elitist positivist scientific and technical rationality. The answer to this problem lies in the creation of an ideal situation for public discussion within which communicative distortions are eliminated — an ideal speech situation based on an analysis of the forms of distorted communication. Actual speech situations can then be compared to the ideal and judged accordingly.

The structure of communication is said by Habermas to be free of constraint only when all participants have an effectively equal chance to take part in dialogue; therefore, conditions of the ideal speech situation imply an ideal form of social life in which autonomy and responsibility are possible. Here, the split between the "is" and the "ought" is bridged. The nature of language — the communicative "is" — specifies a normative "ought" for egalitarian social structure that will enable public policy discussion. Whereas Marx derived his "ought" from an analysis of the work process in forces and relations of production, Habermas derives "ought" from his theory of "communicative competence."[116]

Moral claims, for Habermas, are not simply to be derived from human wants; such wants are entitled to regulation by others provided the regulations can be justified in intersubjectively rational discourse occurring according to rules serving the requirements of the ideal speech situation. Claims to truth or rightness, if challenged, can be investigated through argumentation leading to a rationally constructed consensus that is to emerge out of the equality of the "dialogue roles."[117] Mutual recognition of incompatible needs places tension on discourse; the tensions are to be resolved though adherence to accepted normative rules for conduct of policy discourse. All of this is to advance human life chances and promote global consensus.[118]

One must appreciate the critical theorist's concern that sociology can be, and is, used as a weapon in social struggle. Furthermore, one must be struck by the tenacity and stridency with which critical theorists believe in the idea of societal development — a much beleaguered notion in the latter part of the twentieth century. While in deep agreement with Marx's assertion that no partial aspect of social life can be comprehended unless it is related to the historical whole — to social structures as a unified entity — the critical theorists no longer believe, as did Marx, that progress will come from revolutionary action of the proletariat. They no longer believe that social development is guaranteed by a logic of history. Whereas Marx posited that contradictions of capitalist production were self-undermining and would lead to inevitable revolutionary crisis, the Frankfurt analysts see that advanced technologies of production have had an opposite effect — the stabilization of the status quo wherein real interests of the disadvantaged are bought off by the power of capitalism to "deliver the goods" and by manipulation of perceived needs that "the goods" can satiate. Critical theorists have moved the classic Marxian analysis of the crisis of society away from economic production into the cultural domain — especially into the sphere of mass communications.

Karl Marx sacrificed his valuational reason to precharted historical determinism; for Marx, proletarian victory through class struggle was a prerequisite for value discourse, and appeals to common values would camouflage oppressive interests. The Frankfurt theorists, on the other hand, have introduced a bit of welcome ethical ferment in the is-ought debate. Even so, they retain the classical Marxian notion that the pretense of common value bonds in a world of inequality, and exploitation of the poor by the rich, heaps insult on the injury of the disadvantaged. Nevertheless, they collectively lament the eclipse of practical reason in matters of public policy assessment.

One is still left without a clear set of logically based value standards by which incompatible interests can be sorted out in the public household — even by liberated communicatively competent equals. In a world characterized by powerful technological capacity for the most unexploited people to interfere with each other, how are liberated people supposed to choose among policy directions, each of which represents a different profile of advantage and disadvantage? Critical theorists have articulated, in modern form, the normative Enlightenment question: How can reason be employed to steer society in developmental directions? Yet they have sidestepped the problem of formulating logics of value other than those holding forth the expectation that people liberated from oppression will somehow do so.

CONCLUSION

The valuational question and its linkage to the world of factual inquiry have been central to the history of social thought, especially since eighteenth-century Enlightenment thinkers advanced the modern view that shapes of societies, and public values with which to guide them, are not dictated by supranatural forces beyond human control. Social structures, now recognized to be human constructions, require steering. Steering of human communities, in turn, requires value criteria for collective choice. Such criteria should be products of collective reason, not the outcome of personal whim, taste, or preference of the stronger party who, in the absence of viable public organization, would impose its arbitrary will upon the weaker.

During the first round of this great valuational debate, thinkers postulated that they should read nature for clues to finding ways to advance human progress. This was called to a logical halt by David Hume, who pointed out the distinction between fact and value and persuasively contended that moral conclusions cannot be drawn from "amoral" facts without the insertion of a value premise that must, in turn, be based on reasoning independent of the factual situation.

Over the course of the nineteenth century, Hume's distinction between facts and values was once again obfuscated by many — especially by evolutionists who saw ethical prescriptions in their various evolutionary dynamics. This "round two" of the "is-ought" debate ended when G. E. Moore picked up on David Hume's arguments and reiterated the fact-value distinction in his warning against commission of the naturalistic fallacy. In addition, Max Weber and influential anthropologists put forth strong arguments for cultural relativism in the domain of valuation, which brought into serious question the notion that cross-culturally defensible values could be formulated to meaningfully define "societal development."

No sooner had cultural relativist doctrine become widely accepted, round three, than the rise to power of Adolf Hitler brought into serious question the notion that cultural values could not be criticized on rational grounds; some — most notably Robert Lynd, Talcott Parsons, Harold Lasswell, and theorists in critical tradition — openly advocated an involved social science serving preferred collective values. Scientists with a wide variety of value allegiances had little trouble mobilizing themselves in the grand effort to defeat Fascist madmen, but the post–World War II years have witnessed the crystallization of bitter splits between three rival social science camps — the fourth and continuing round of debate. Conflict about valuation has conditioned the professional lives of social scientists and is to be found today in most academic departments of any size. Breakdowns in normative logics constrain ambitions of value-critical and applied workers just as they provide grounds for the refusal of the pure scientist to openly participate in valuation.

The valuational discussion has proceeded for well over two hundred years and neither the pure, the applied, nor the critical social scientist has succeeded in arriving at valuative logics for assessing social policy in the name of societal development. Just what are the available value criteria? The discussion turns in the next chapter to an analysis of their problems.

III

Valuation for Policy Assessment: Problems in Economics and Sociology

It is necessary to study sociology in order to learn why the advice of economists is so consistently ignored. — Vilfredo Pareto

It is necessary to study economics to learn why the advice of sociologists should be consistently ignored. — Anonymous

POLICY ASSESSMENT: ECONOMICS AND THE NORMATIVE FAILURE OF MARKETS

To an economist, every asset that lies within the scope of marketplace exchange is measured by a single yardstick calibrated in the local currency — rupees, pounds sterling, marks, yen, won, or dollars. Examined in the light of how much currency it can command in marketplace exchange, a book is twelve loaves of bread or a pair of sneakers. People advance their welfare by exchanging those resources providing utility in return for those promising more. For over two hundred years, economists have been going to the blackboard to establish that, under conditions of a fully free market, welfare of the exchanging parties — and by extension that of society — is advanced by such transactions.

The fundamental economic logic of valuation centers on obtaining the greatest possible efficiency of resource use in the service of consumer demand. Free markets serve efficiency in two fundamental senses:

1. static or allocative efficiency, meaning the value of obtaining the greatest possible quantity of preference satisfaction from a given bundle of goods and services; and

2. dynamic efficiency, meaning the value of promoting new technologies that make resources available at lower cost, improving product quality, and creating new products for enhancing preference satisfaction.

Free markets do well in securing the two efficiency values, and in a world of scarcity, one does well to obtain as much of both as possible. However, markets must function within a social nexus, and market-generated efficiencies cannot by themselves prescribe the shape of "developed" social structures within which markets function any more than the chemistry of the blood corpuscle can by itself adequately define the structural shape of the human body. Pursuit of aggregate economic growth in the name of social progress has been a central feature of twentieth-century public policy, especially after agents of the public household digested John Maynard Keynes's analysis of the interaction between aggregate demand and employment,[1] but economic growth cannot be synonymous with a defensible conception of societal development.[2]

It may be true that the welfare of any given set of exchanging parties is improved by free-market exchange, but it is not necessarily the case that what is good for a given set of exchange partners is good for members of society taken as a whole. However, given our need for a guiding valuational light, and given the bankruptcy of developmental valuation in the noneconomic social sciences, decision-makers have frequently acted as though efficient growth of aggregate product can substitute for a vision of social development.

Basic to the economic valuational problem is the assumption that social decisions are made in terms of a price system reflecting true costs. But if prices fail to reflect all of the benefits received by some and all disadvantages imposed on others, the policy that maximizes dollar returns will not necessarily be the one that best advances societal development, assuming defensible value standards are available with which to judge such matters. Given that prices may not adequately reflect true costs and benefits, the preferences to which the market responds are not necessarily those to which it should respond.[3] A society that turned itself into a giant vending machine efficiently delivering anything and everything in return for the proper number of coins would not necessarily be a desirable social order, as many economists have been quick to recognize.[4]

Just because a prevailing social structure induces situations within which people become sufficiently desperate that they are willing to sell themselves into the status of indentured servants does not mean that such conditions can be justified and that public policy should promote such sales. Or, to take another example, if pursuit of aggregate growth measured in quarterly reports directed capital from productive investment to speculation on hostile corporate takeovers in the American "casino society" of the 1980s, the results may have had little to do with societal development. Blind pursuit of economic growth per se, within unexamined social structures, has no necessary connection to social development, even though static and dynamic economic efficiency is a necessary, but insufficient, condition of it.

Problems of marketplace exchange can be best understood by examining specific market breakdowns — concentrations of power that erode consumer sovereignty, technological externality, the failure of private marketplace calculations to lead to an adequate provision of public goods, the tyranny of small decisions, and the problem of resource distribution.

Concentration of Power and Erosion of Consumer Sovereignty

For orthodox economics, the sovereignty of the consumer is the fundamental article of faith and axiom of theory. Within this system the twin value premises are that individuals know best what is good for themselves and that conceptions of social well-being must be based on the respective positions — good and bad — of individuals in society. Then it follows that persons exchanging in a free market, under conditions of pure competition in which prices reflect true costs, will pursue the exchange of goods and services by trading away those resources that have less value to them in order to obtain those promising greater utility on the margin. Since the days of Adam Smith, economists have been busy proving that under these conditions free and pure competition working through the price system will produce a movement toward the Pareto optimum condition wherein it is not possible to make someone better off without making someone else worse off.[5] Because somebody is made better off, without making anybody worse off, up to the Pareto equilibrium point, society is thought to be made better by voluntary exchange in free markets.

The power of economic sellers is, therefore, theoretically sanctioned by denying its existence. Sellers are viewed as being totally constrained by buyers in a purely competitive marketplace. Markets are free and competitive when (1) there are sufficiently numerous buyers and sellers such that each constitutes so small a proportion of the total market that any one's output or purchase has no effect on price; (2) there is freedom of entry and exit such that new firms can enter markets on terms as good as those available to firms already there; (3) buyers do not care from which seller they buy because the products offered are homogeneous — those offered by one seller are indistinguishable from those offered by another; and (4) each firm and each customer is fully informed about products and prices.[6] Given these conditions, the competitive seller has no influence over price — the consumer is sovereign.

If actions of the seller are totally constrained by buyers, either as consuming households or as factor owners, then consumers and not the sellers are accountable for the sellers' activities and for the direction of marketplace exchange. In this view firms, corporations, and conglomerates simply follow the dictates of freely choosing consumers who, it is assumed, bring to bear on their choices "good" socially responsible values. Corporations are, then, nothing more than legally chartered servants of social development, individual welfare, and the public interest as controlled by consumer preferences. If something is wrong with the developmental direction of society, look not to corporations or other producers but to faulty consumer decision-making.

In most marketplaces, however, the assumptions of free markets and pure competition are grossly violated. The power of sellers is concentrated in the hands of a few large corporate enterprises that exert influence over the behavior of consumers and over public policy formulation, assessment, and administration much more than orthodox economic theory allows. The problem of market power has long been a focus for economists, especially the institutionalists such as Thorstein Veblen, Wesley C. Mitchell, John R. Commons, Gunnar Myrdal, Robert Heilbroner, C. E. Ayres, Robert Lekachman, J. Ron Stanfield, and John Kenneth Galbraith.[7] One of their major contentions has been that large corporations produce oligopolistic market structures in which market power and financial strategies determine production and consumption outcomes, not the supply and demand curves of neoclassical economic theory.

John Kenneth Galbraith developed this point in his *The New Industrial State*.[8] According to Galbraith, the economy consists of the corporate planned sector and the small business competitive sector. Public policy has become captured by a technologically based military-industrial elite, rooted in the large-scale corporate sector, that is referred to in the aggregate as the "techno-structure." The techno-structure consists of the full organization of specialists required for complex technological decision-making and planning, extending from senior management to the foreman on the factory floor. Since major industrial production involves long-run planning and massive resource commitment, the decision-making agents of the techno-structure cannot leave corporate fortune to chance — public response to output must be anticipated and controlled within tolerable ranges in the name of corporate stability. Corporations control their environments in several ways: Carefully negotiated contracts stabilize relationships with suppliers, customers, and labor unions. As in all negotiation, advantage goes to the strongest, but there is substantial common interest in mutual survival, and negotiations often approximate alliance bargaining more than adversary bargaining. Through close collaboration with each other and government to secure arrangements for necessary resources, to obtain restrictions on production and market entry, to maintain growing aggregate demand for products, and to mount aggressive media campaigns to influence consumer preference, the techno-structure works to attain the greatest possible growth measured in sales. Since that which is produced must be consumed or production will halt, high levels of aggregate demand for products are maintained in collusion with government through excessive military expenditures that are easier to justify to the public than alternative civilian spending more essential to the public interest. The whole business is obscured by notions of consumer sovereignty.

In a similar vein, Charles E. Lindblom, after a thoroughgoing study of politics and markets, concluded that:

> It is possible that the rise of the corporation has . . . more than offset the decline of class as an instrument of indoctrination. That it creates a new core of wealth and power for a newly constructed upper class, as well as an overpowering loud voice, is also reasonably clear. The executive of the large corporation is, on many counts, the contemporary counterpart to the landed gentry of an earlier era, his voice amplified by the technology of mass communication. A single corporate voice on television . . . can reach more minds in one evening than were reached from all the platforms of all the world's meetings in the course of several centuries preceding broadcasting. More than class, the major specific institutional barrier to fuller democracy may therefore be the autonomy of the private corporation. . . . Enormously large, rich in resources, the big corporations . . . command more resources than do most government units. They can also, over a broad range, insist that government meet their demands, even if those demands run counter to those of citizens. . . . It has been a curious feature of democratic thought that it has not faced up to the

private corporation as a peculiar organization in an ostensible democracy. . . . The large private corporation fits oddly into democratic theory and vision. Indeed, it does not fit.[9]

There is nothing so threatening to orthodox economics as this conception that corporate elites are anything less than passive servants of consumer sovereignty in the marketplace.[10] If freely competitive consumption does not control production, what is left of the normative welfare content of economic thought? If consumers are necessarily advancing neither individual welfare nor social development by exercise of their preferences in the marketplace, by what standard are alternative production and consumption patterns to be judged?

Technological Externality

A second major source of market failure is that of technological externality. It has always been true that any one individual's welfare is at least partly a function of other people's choices. Activities in one part of the social system, or in one location, generate effects — positive and negative — that impact members of other groups who did not participate in the initial decision to undertake the precipitating action. Such spillover effects are technological externalities.[11]

Two major kinds of externalities must be distinguished: pecuniary and technological. Pecuniary externalities are the result of self-interested decisions of sellers and buyers in the marketplace to buy or sell goods or services that increase or decrease demand, thereby affecting prices to others in the market system. Pecuniary externalities are central to a market economy as changing demands cause the rise and fall of prices that, in turn, serve to allocate scarce resources to those who are willing to pay. Therefore, pecuniary externalities pose no problem of market failure.

Technological externalities, on the other hand, do pose a problem: They represent unpriced costs and benefits uncounted in marketplace exchange. Urban congestion, environmental pollution, aircraft noise, and littered mountain trails all represent the unkind rub of activities on each other where there is no intermediation of a market to enable negatively affected parties to confront their tormentors through the price system. The "no deposit — no return" message on a beer bottle blatantly proclaims that the cost of disposing of the container will not be paid for by either the brewery or consumer but will simply be imposed on others who must pass by. In producing steel, industrialists also produce smoke, which imposes damage on the surrounding community in the form of grime, lack of sunlight, and respiratory disease. These unpriced externalized costs are paid by someone other than the manufacturer or consumers.

In complex technological societies, whether capitalist or socialist, much decision-making is placed in a competitive framework made up of individuals, firms, bureaucracies, communities, provinces, and nations. Within the framework decision-makers seek immediate and local advantage by disregarding wider external effects and thus can be said to exercise rational behavior — maximize returns, minimize costs. Costs to the organization can be minimized by imposing some of them on neighbors who are impacted across geographical or organizational boundaries or by placing them on future generations.

Socialist managers are not immune from this logic of suboptimizing for organizational self-interest. Adoption of socialist ideology, served by totalitarian control over economy and society in the Soviet Union, Eastern European nations, and the People's Republic of China, has provided no prophylactic against the ravages of environmental degradation. In agriculture and industry alike, socialist management in these nations has produced massive pollution of land, air, and water and wanton destruction of important raw materials. Some knowledgeable analysts have seen the situation as so serious that modernization goals have been significantly undermined.[12] Now that "openness" has accompanied the demise of totalitarian socialism in Eastern Europe and the U.S.S.R., environmental horror stories have become the stuff of the popular press.

Returning now to the North American scene, residues produced by oil shale mining in Colorado contain salts that, if leached by rainwater, can significantly raise salinity levels of the Colorado River. Increased water salinity occasioned by future oil shale exploitation in western Colorado would represent a significant negative externality imposed on the farmers of Arizona, Mexico, and California for many years. Petroleum producers could raise the price of their oil shale products sufficiently to pay for controls on leaching and thereby "internalize" the costs, which would then be passed on to consumers — the ultimate beneficiaries. But price competition within the industry creates an incentive to externalize as much of the costs as possible. The producers would find it "irrational" to pay costs of maintaining higher levels of water quality for the benefit of others; furthermore, any cost internalized by one competitor but not by another would reduce the competitive position of the former. Yet the Colorado River is already

71

highly saline, and the Mexican government has had occasion to complain about the substandard quality of Colorado River water that has driven many Mexican farmers, and much Mexican land, out of agricultural production.[13]

The time dimension of externality may be as important as the spatial. Oil shale residues must be dammed to prevent their leaching. After companies have extracted the commercially profitable supplies and departed the area, who will then maintain the containment structures? Will their deterioration create severe leaching problems in the future, or will somebody pick up the costs of continued maintenance? Who? Will it be those producers and consumers who benefited from the production? Given the basic value premise that decision-makers should be rewarded for the benefits they confer on others and that they should pay costs that they impose on others, one would seek to find mechanisms by which such decision-makers — producers and consumers — would internalize the costs that would otherwise be externalized to nonbeneficiaries. Unfortunately a competitive world — whether the market competition of the capitalist or the bureaucratic competition of the socialist — creates incentives to externalize as many costs as possible across space and time.

If market prices do not reflect real costs of production and consumption — if they create incentives to take mortgages out against the environment and other people in the form of fouled air, dirty water, contaminated soil, congested traffic, and spoiled works of art and architecture — self-seeking behavior through free marketplaces will not lead to any viable conception of social development.

Public Goods

Related to the problem of externality is another form of market failure. Welfare economists have been insistent that the market performs unsatisfactorily in the case of public goods.[14] A good is said to be "private" if its benefits can be captured by the investor-owner and denied to those members of the community who do not invest in it. A "public" or "collective" good is one that has a significant benefit that cannot be denied to those who do not help bear the costs — "free riders." Pure public goods are characterized by two attributes: (1) nonrivalness of consumption, meaning that the quantity of a good available to others is not diminished by any one person's consumption of the good; and (2) nonexclusiveness of consumption, meaning that if a good can be consumed by one person it can be consumed by others in the community at no significant marginal cost.

Many important goods possess these attributes. Flood control projects indiscriminately benefit all those subject to the rampaging river. A pollution control program for air or water will generate benefits that cannot be denied to noninvestors. One person's breathing of the cleaner air does not deprive others from likewise doing so, and cleanup programs once in place can be made available to the next inhabitant of the improved community at little or no marginal cost. So it is also with a meteorological forecast, street lighting, and national defense.[15] It is not possible for consumers to go into the marketplace and purchase their own share of flood control, traffic regulation, irrigation water control, or clean air. Public goods must be products of collective decisions by which organizational effort pools resources for the purchase and maintenance of the good and then preserves the good from the depredations of potential free riders.

Herein lies the difficulty. In collective-good situations, the logic of the individually rational decision-maker is irreconcilable with the logic of the community.[16] This conflict of logics is illustrated by an example of two rational farmers who each ponder the possibilities of building an improved watercourse for channeling irrigation water to their adjacent fields. The total improvements will cost, shall we say, sixty dollars. However, the benefits to farmer A equal only forty dollars, whereas to farmer B the benefits amount to fifty dollars. From the standpoint of their collective benefit as a whole, the improvements should be made: The benefits accruing to both farmers equal ninety dollars and substantially exceed the sixty-dollar total cost. But if each farmer looks at only his or her private costs and benefits, neither will build the improved structure. Each farmer individually does better not contributing while hoping that the other, in an economically irrational altruistic spirit, will build the improved watercourse and thereby allow the noncontributing free rider to enjoy benefits of increased water supply and control. Because the economic rationality of each constrains altruism, neither invests and the improvements are not made. Both suffer. They are both perfectly rational in an individual sense, and they are simultaneously perfectly irrational in a collective social sense.

In markets in which decision-makers have no incentives to take into account the consequences of their action on others, an economic equilibrium may exist, but it will not be the most efficient, nor will it be the most developmental, given the incentive for each individual to be a free rider at the expense of others.[17] Laissez-faire economic philosophy assumed that what was good for individuals as they rationally sought economic advantage in markets would aggregate to that which was good for all society. This simply does not hold in matters of public goods.

Tyranny of Small Decisions and Freezing of Decision-Makers

Alfred Kahn has shown how, through the tyranny of small incremental decisions no one of which is notable, a cumulative effect is generated that produces a defective allocation of resources.[18] Big changes frequently are the result of an accumulation of small decisions, and individual consumers who are affected by the outcome never get an opportunity to vote with their dollars in the marketplace on the larger changes as such. If they were given such an opportunity, consumers might not approve of what their cumulative small decisions wrought, and this constitutes a fourth source of failure in marketplace capacity to facilitate social development.

If one hundred consumers choose option x and this brings about a market decision of X (where X = 100x), it is not necessarily true that the same consumers would have opted for X if that large decision had been presented for their explicit consideration.[19] For example, a passenger railroad service for a set of communities can disappear when no particular decision-maker prefers it to do so. The lack of competitiveness of the railroad with the automobile and the interstate highway system in good weather has frequently killed off the only all-weather transportation option. Slowly working cumulative effects of individual transportation decisions lead to the much bemoaned death of passenger railway service. Yet no particular decision-maker may have wanted that death, and many might have been willing to pay a premium to retain the service had they been presented with an opportunity.

Associated with the tyranny of small cumulative decisions is the phenomenon that decision-makers become "frozen" into patterns of investment through cumulative sinking of funds into options that, when found to be unsatisfactory, are difficult and expensive to modify or reverse.[20] When technologies burst on the scene, they are designed to solve the problems of specific groups, firms, or public bureaucracies located in particular socioeconomic sectors of activity. A technology has somebody's values built into it. Technologies are not adopted by societies as a whole with overall social development in mind.

Promoters of the technology, seeing an opportunity to solve a problem to their advantage, are often ignorant of the risks involved in potential negative externalities. They may be blinded by enthusiasm or loath to point out foreseen difficulties for fear that opponent groups will seize on perceived negative consequences to block project advancement. Given that decision-makers have considerable incentive to externalize costs across space and time whenever possible and to "free ride" on benefits provided by others as much as possible, promoters plant and harvest their technologies without adequate attention to the larger range of secondary and tertiary social, economic, and ecological impacts — beneficial or harmful.

By the time undesirable consequences are discovered by affected social groups and by the time concerned publics can be mobilized for action, the sunk costs in the particular technological pattern are so great that the initial planning, innovating, and promoting decision-makers are "frozen" into postures that even they might not have preferred.[21]

Because of the great sunk costs in automobile production, interstate highway linkages, and dispersed suburban land use patterns for housing, schooling, work, and play all geared to the automobile, it becomes extremely costly to reorient a community to mass transit usage when gasoline prices rise from one to three constant dollars per gallon. Decision-makers in the United States have substantially "frozen" their transportation options in many towns and cities in a manner that no particular decision-maker would have opted for given the altered economic, ecological, and social conditions of the 1990s. That which the marketplace signaled as being developmental under one set of circumstances based on low-cost petroleum will become nondevelopmental under an altered set of conditions. The freezing of decision patterns by irreversible commitments, built up through a long series of decentralized cumulative decisions, prevents the marketplace from rapidly responding to new realities.

Distribution

A central tenet of marketplace theory is that free people, making uncoerced and mutually beneficial exchanges, will advance their welfare and therefore that of society. Unfortunately, the capacity to drive an advantageous bargain depends in large measure on what one possesses and can offer potential exchange partners. One with little to offer tends to be ignored or exploited. The marketplace adjusts to the demands of those with assets. Those who control key assets can coerce those who do not. A person with a surplus of bread to offer can extract concessions from another who faces starvation and who cannot raise the going price.

One hidden assumption of market exchange theory is that existing distributions of assets are the product of past meritorious performance: Each individual possesses the assets that she or he deserves based on the quantity and quality of past services rendered. Therefore, if one is at a disadvantage in today's exchange, it is purely because of past deficiency. If one's reading of history is that those who currently possess the greatest asset shares obtained them only through productive effort and free exchange untinged by any coercion or by taking advantage of any other market imperfection and only by dint of their own meritorious service to the community, then one might be willing to make the case that they "deserve" their advantage. Such inequalities as are found would be justified by differences in merit. On the other hand, if one's reading of human events is that some people obtain disproportionate shares of assets through coercion, luck, access to privileged information, capacity to dominate unfree oligopolistic or monopolistic markets, or judicious selection of wealthy parents, then marketplace bargaining reflects, not earned rewards, but capricious happenstance.

Policymakers who accept marketplace exchange as the arbitrator of technology policy must assume that existing distributions of assets are just — that they have emerged out of an unflawed historical exchange process.[22] If, for any reason, there is doubt that past exchanges were the product of anything less than free uncoerced willingness to enter into bargains for mutual advantage in perfect markets, then there is doubt that current asset distributions are "deserved," and there is serious question that market outcomes have anything to do with promotion of social development. Markets reflect values — those that bubble up in the hardscrabble struggle for market advantage by the more powerful in confrontation with the weaker. But those values are not necessarily ones that "ought" to be served. Particular technological applications that succeed in marketplaces are not necessarily those that "ought" to be so favorably assessed.

The requirements of perfect competition may never be fulfilled, and when even one requirement is unsatisfied, the valuational justification of market outcomes falls apart.[23] Competition is either perfect or it is not; if it is not, market outcomes lack valuational legitimacy. There is only one way out in a world wherein markets rarely fulfill the conditions for free-market functioning. It must be squarely admitted that markets cannot be abstracted from their social structural context; it must furthermore be admitted that the economic growth generated by the play of markets should not be confused with social development. Imperfect markets must be guided by imperfect governments responsive to citizens who have contemplated the uses and limits of alternative imperfect value logics and who insist that technological and natural resources policies be assessed by value standards that amount to something more than contribution to aggregate economic growth.

POLICY ASSESSMENT AND THE NORMATIVE FAILURE
OF SOCIALISM

Marxian thought has had a powerful grip on many twentieth-century intellectuals. For one thing, it represented one of the most comprehensive efforts to critique the deficiencies of political economies where markets have allocated resources to values in ways blind to the structural shape of society. For another, Marxism placed an emphasis on eighteenth-century Enlightenment egalitarian values by positioning proletarian workers in a morally positive role vis-à-vis inegalitarian capitalist political economy. Marxism has been both a secular religion and a form of social science. As a means of secularizing the religious impulse, Marxism offers an explanation of human history, a messianic vision of the future, an eschatological conflict between "good" and "evil," and hope for rejuvenation of society. However, Marxism has also represented a real social science in that it contains penetrating sociological theories of social stratification, knowledge, social change, alienation, class formation and inequality, and technology's role in society.

All of this has been packaged as a "science" of social development that has always worn its normative commitments on its sleeve. Generally celebrating the most egalitarian strands of the Judeo-Christian tradition, attacking liberal individualism, rejecting anything more than minimal use of markets for social coordination, and calling for more community, Marxism has promised salvation through revolution against capitalist political economy. But determination to make revolution does not, in itself, make for defensible public value logics, and socialist approaches to social development and the "good society" have long been seen as being deeply flawed, even by those who are sympathetic to socialist ideals.[24] The valuational and policy assessment crisis is to be found at the heart of socialist theory in general, and of Marxist theory in particular.

It is too easy to hold that the problems of choice in the public household are simply a consequence of capitalism and can be remedied by socialism.[25] Calls for the social ownership of the means of production do not address problems of technological externality, market dominance, tyranny of small decisions, the freezing of decision-makers, and distributional problems. Such calls have provided no clear and logically defensible policy-assessment criteria for allocating scarce goods and services among competing social demands. The valuational deficiency of socialist theory has revealed itself to practical people as well as to theoreticians — all of whom have seen the terrible results of sacrificing economic static and dynamic efficiency in the name of highly suspect and poorly formulated communitarian value logics. In the face of this widespread socialist failure, the distrust of markets in central Europe, the Soviet Union, and China has dramatically lessened in recent years. However, as Socialist leaders see new virtue in markets that promise to restore some static and dynamic efficiency in resource use, they come full circle to face the enduring question: What higher-order values can guide markets in the name of some justifiable vision of developmental change?

Classical Marxist theory worked on the premise that bourgeois capitalism would "solve" the problems of production and would leave a legacy of productive capacity after proletarian revolution to supply such great abundance that scarcity would be eliminated. In such a society "needs" could be served for Mutt without depriving Jeff ("Mutt" and "Jeff" are used here and elsewhere in the book to acknowledge that people differ from one another in many ways.) Marx truly believed that after the revolution and abolition of classes there would be no need for a policy-assessing, or conflict-resolving, agency. What mattered was which class held power. As long as proletarians were in control, armed with the truths of "scientific Marxism," it was by definition the case that rationality would solve problems and carry society forward to its greatest developmental potentials. How to assess merits of proposed policies was a detail to be somehow worked out by others in future circumstances.

The very distinction between "is" and "ought" simply disappeared in the Marxian use of Hegelian dialectics. Emancipators simply must struggle for a higher form of society, and in doing so, they will pass through transforming circumstances. They have as individual agents no ideals to realize; they simply must act out their historic mission to set free elements of the new society trapped in the old collapsing order. This commitment to working with "objective forces" of historical materialism is what distinguished Marxism from utopian socialisms and what Marx regarded to be their contemptible moralisms. Marxist analysis rested upon the forces behind the ascendancy of the proletariat and not upon sufficient analysis of the fact-value problem. Marx saw discussions of such matters, within his epoch, to be futile.

Socialist theory to this day has not adequately confronted the task of distributing scarcity among alternative equities and conflicting rights. A socialism that assumed that competition, envy, and social evil resulted from scarcity and capitalist maldistribution of resources and that abundant production would make conflict and evil unnecessary has little to say about logics of policy assessment.

Marx flatly rejected the most coherent theory of social coordination that could harmonize conflicting interests — classical market theory. Yet nowhere did Marx offer an alternative theory of social coordination or social choice of anything approaching comparable explanatory power.[26] Marx's laws, insofar as they are laws at all, are laws of capitalism and its dynamics. Marx did not work out any value blueprint for a policy-assessing socialism or communism. For Marx, a Joseph Stalin was unthinkable, and a humane communism was inevitable. One was simply to stand with the working class while the laws of capitalism worked themselves out. The task of constructing a socialist society would belong to those who lived in it and who would operate it as a true egalitarian and majoritarian democracy.[27]

Marx was, in a sense, a libertarian democrat who saw his values thwarted by the workings of capitalist political economy. The Marxist view, and that of leftists in general, has been that socialist countries are far more democratic than capitalist ones. In capitalist political economies, although people appear to choose their leaders and govern the public household, in fact leaderships represent interests of monopoly capitalists. Formal freedom may exist, but this cannot be translated into real freedom. Everyone may be free to own newspapers, but the fact is that newspapers are controlled by a tiny elite. Votes cast in an election simply reflect interests of capitalist bosses who set electoral agendas. For Marx, the basic civil, political, and legal rights that individuals enjoy in the parliamentary democracies associated with capitalist economies are valuable only as ways of coping with those sorts of conflicts of interest that are themselves produced by capitalism. Only after this system is destroyed by working-class capture of state power can authentic democracy exist. But that democracy would have little need for conceptions of individual rights, interests, and collective conflict-resolution mechanisms because the communist nonmarket system would somehow be so efficient and productive that scarcity would be eliminated and clashes of interest would disappear. Marx did not admit that individuals would have preferences or needs divergent from the requirements of their neighbors or the development of the community at large. Proper socialization, elimination of false consciousness, and adoption of the most efficient scientific means for achieving given ends were seen somehow to eliminate any requirement for working out valuational principles.

Some thinkers on the left have recognized the problems presented by this stance and have begun to investigate those aspects of social life that advance possibilities of rational citizen public discourse about policy-assessment matters. They have examined the social forces promoting and retarding this possibility.[28] They see Marxism less as a "science" of society and more as a moral engagement with social structures and problems of valuation appropriate to advancing the development of a free community of citizens. Valuational questions, therefore, continue to ferment in at least some niches of leftist theory.

Nevertheless, for the greater part, the need for coherent principles to guide social choice by agents of the public household has been simply glossed over and hidden by myths surrounding ideas of social harmony and reduction of inequality. What logics are to be employed by liberated people to work out their policy-assessment values? If one envisions a society that attempts to maximize every individual's ability to do x, where x is anything a person genuinely wants to do as determined without pressures from alienating or oppressing forces, one sees little more than a utopia or the perpetual war of all against all associated with Hobbes's state of nature.

It behooves one to be careful about inferring failure of socialist theory from the experience of any given set of socialist experiments. Alasdair MacIntyre, before *perestroika*, cautioned that "the barbarous despotism of the collective tsardom which reigns in Moscow can be taken as irrelevant to the question of the moral substance of Marxism as the life of the Borgia Pope was to that of the moral substance of Christianity."[29] But political and intellectual elites of socialism have not sufficiently addressed problems of valuation for policy assessment. There simply is, within the corpus of socialist theory, no antidote for problems posed by lack of static and dynamic efficiency produced by markets and by the presence of technological externalities, the tyranny of small decisions, the bedeviling problems of maldistribution, and the failure to define appropriate mixes of public and private goods. The theoretical deficiencies have led straight to societies that can produce missiles but few potatoes; giant factories produce pollution but to little end since there is all too little demand for the shoddy products.

Marshall Goldman and Malcolm Pryde have cogently argued, for example, that subordination of the economy to the government and party in the Soviet Union, rather than solving the problems of the public household, has developed an institutional preference for economic growth and industrial production that mitigates against a state's enterprise's being rewarded for sound environmental practices. Important natural resources such as commonly held air and water are regarded as free and thereby abused; bureaucratic rivalries undercut rational planning — all of which result in unnecessary pollution and wastage.[30] If socialist managers are told to minimize costs in the name of furthering economic growth, and if pollution is not adequately charged as a cost, socialist smoke will degrade air quality as readily as capitalist smoke. If fees or regulation can make socialist managers respect the environment, the same types of rules can be imposed by liberal governments on private enterprise — unless, of course, one finds that governments are so dominated by private interests that they are powerless to do so. Yet if capitalist states are pushed and pulled by the competing alliances of producers and consumers, this is no less true in state socialist societies.

Socialism, as implemented in various nations, has produced alternative forms of industrial societies. But nowhere has scarcity been eliminated, and nowhere is there to be found a nonmarket system of democratic decision-making, theoretically or practically viable, that can usefully guide policy assessment in the public household. The failure of socialism to adequately confront the problems of policy assessment has led to recent experimentation with "market socialism" — no small concession given that it signals an abandonment of the classical Marxist position that markets are irrational in resource allocation and require replacement by rational planning and given that market socialism accepts competition among firms as the engine of production and distribution.[31] Given that markets are to perform policy-assessment functions in market socialist societies, in lieu of failed attempts at central planning, socialist experience comes full circle to face the central valuational question raised at the outset: How can agents of the public household assess policy and defensibly constrain markets in the name of developmental change?

Marxism has become the unofficial creed of radical intellectuals

81

around the world who employ it to critique deficiencies of modern market-oriented societies. They have rejected a world created by modern technology insufficiently constrained by any value higher than that of economic efficiency in the service of aggregate economic growth, especially a world in which grossly distorted markets dominated by powerful elites establish most values. Interest in socialism is motivated not by any success with its policy-assessment methods but more by an abiding fear that something is deeply wrong with the direction of technology policy in affluent market-oriented industrial and postindustrial societies. The issue is not whether the Western societies have, or have not, won the ideological cold war. Rather, it is how to defensibly construct viable developmental logics of fact and value for guiding the assessment of public policy.

POLICY ASSESSMENT AND THE NORMATIVE FAILURE OF SOCIOLOGICAL DEVELOPMENT THEORY

Does the sociology of development literature hold forth viable policy-assessment value criteria? This is not an unreasonable question given that sociology, as a discipline, germinated in the hope that fundamental principles of societal development could be discovered and employed to promote human welfare.[32] Sociology was born out of this act of secular faith, and after generations of muddled experience with the idea, social development still provides the fundamental rationale for the effort of sociology. In the contemporary words of Immanuel Wallerstein, "It is, in the end, only some variant of the idea of progress that justifies the enormous social energy required by social science."[33]

Developmental change for sociologists has always had some connection to expansion of choice opportunities for members of society. Study has always focused on some combination of two things: (1) the facts of choice opportunity expansion and distribution in social structure, and (2) the values served or destroyed by changes in the structure of choice opportunities. The several literatures of development are too rich and varied to be adequately reviewed in this small section. Discussion here will focus on two major traditions within the sociology of development literature — social development as modernization and as an escape from dependency status.

For some sociologists, working in the traditions established by Herbert Spencer, Emile Durkheim, Ferdinand Toennies, and Karl

Marx, development has been viewed in evolutionary and "modernizing" terms. Societies "developed," "evolved," or "modernized" from simple social structures of highly constrained choice to complex ones yielding greater generalized adaptive capacity for social organization and wide arrays of personal choice.[34] Whereas the early evolutionists held out a belief that humankind was inevitably moving toward conditions somehow better satisfying vague notions of social progress, that nineteenth-century optimism was dropped in mid-twentieth-century neoevolutionary theory. It then came to pass that the whole valuational issue of the meaning of progress was swept under the theoretical carpet by adopting the supposedly more value neutral language of modernization.[35]

Much post–World War II "development as modernization" theory consisted of little more than plundered versions of the dichotomies advanced by earlier sociologists who organized their work around constructs such as preindustrial-industrial, gemeinschaft-gesellschaft, status-contract, folk-urban, and mechanical-organic solidarity. Modernization theory was essentially cultural theory. To be "modernized" was to take on cultural attributes of the more advanced nations — their forms of rationality, empiricism, efficiency, and industrial organization. Modernization theory took, as its ideal, the industrial liberal United States and Western Europe, and it suggested that "underdeveloped" nonmodern societies would emulate technological-cultural practices of the more modernized.

Modernization theory was a post–World War II substitute for the earlier civilizing mission that had justified colonial practice. There was an explicit view that all people and societies would "develop" or "modernize" along the lines pioneered by the West, but on an accelerated calendar. Much of this was found to be bad history, a crude cover for ethnocentrism and cultural imperialism, and wrongheaded in its view of tradition.[36]

Development studies came to mean examination of the "facts" of industrialization, urbanization, bureaucratization, and social mobilization, generally in a normative framework wherein aggregate economic growth and increased per capita income were the driving values. This is a literature too vast to be reviewed here,[37] but one assertion can be safely made: An explicit critical consideration of valuational logics has not been a priority in it. Valuations, insofar as they are found, are suspect in that they consist of no more than assertion of the premise that technological advancement is good, that traditional society was too restrictive, that modernity brought about conditions of a "better" life. Valuational logic to support any of this was virtually nonexistent, and what did exist consisted of a view that more choice, as defined by the modernizers, was better. The idea of social development, in such literatures, was reduced to little more than uncritical promotion of the values of economic growth and mass consumption laced with notions of political adaptation, human rights, and pluralist democracy.

Three who kept the normative aspects of social development explicitly in the forefront of the modernization paradigm were Gunnar Myrdal, Peter L. Berger, and Denis Goulet.[38] Myrdal set forth values defining what he meant by the concept of development in the opening portions of his *Asian Drama* (1968). For him the "ideals" included rationality and planning in the service of increased per capita productivity, social and economic equality, and improved institutions and attitudes that would support efficiency, diligence, orderliness, punctuality, frugality, honesty, preparedness for change, alertness to opportunities, energetic enterprise, integrity and self-reliance, cooperativeness, and willingness to take the long view. In addition, development was defined by national independence and political democracy, especially at the grass roots. Myrdal acknowledged that this list, while "usually mutually supporting," was "somewhat indeterminate and vague."[39]

Peter Berger pulled sociologists into normative discussion of the development idea in his *Pyramids of Sacrifice: Political Ethics and Social Change* (1976). During the course of debunking the capitalist myth of economic growth and the socialist myth of revolution — each of which permit sociologists to skirt the real issues of valuation — Berger forced his readers to confront the fact that development policies impose a mix of gains and losses. Unfortunately, he argued, too many analysts have not adequately examined the losses imposed on affected publics by development policies because they have been caught up in one or another of the modern development myths. Berger successfully argued that social scientists must put the value question in the forefront of their work.

Another who saw much value-blind modernization as destructive to authentic social development was Denis Goulet. In *The Cruel Choice* (1973), he pointed out that much modernization undercut his proposed values — esteem, freedom, and a sufficient supply of properly distributed life-sustaining goods for all citizens. Goulet issued a clarion call for philosophers to engage issues of policy choice, and he succeeded in drawing the attention of many social scientists to the fact that their modernization commitments involved difficult value choices in need of explicit normative analysis.[40]

Other values with which to define development in the modernization mode have been forwarded. Kyong-Dong Kim has seen development as consisting of "happiness" or "life chances" for all members of society, which in turn requires social and economic justice, economic prosperity, political freedom, health, and education. Attainment of these goals calls for a flexible social structure so that all members of society can perceive, demand, and attain their fair share of resources.[41] Dudley Seers argued that development means increased food production, increased employment opportunities for income and self-respect, and equality of income distribution.[42]

The relative honesty with which Myrdal, Berger, Goulet, Kim, and Seers approached the normative dimension of modernization is laudable, but none provided a specific valuational logic by which to sort among options that promise to impose alternative mixes of advantage and disadvantage. They provided us no answer to the question: Why should the combination of pain and gain associated with policy X be preferred to the mix entrained by policy Y?

During the course of the late 1960s and 1970s, a sociological concern crystallized that focused on international stratification as an obstacle to effective social development — whatever that beleaguered concept meant. Underdevelopment — the lack of "good things," or at least the inequitable distribution of them — came to be viewed as a consequence of the "dependence" of subordinate political economies to dominant ones, a situation that leads to gross inequality, internal colonialism, and underdevelopment for occupants of lower social strata, especially in the dependent economies.

Dependency theorists, building upon the insights of John Atkinson Hobson and Nikolai Lenin, have viewed underdevelopment as being created by the very processes that generated development for the rich in the advanced industrial nations composing the core of the global economy.[43] Development values, largely the same conceptually unprocessed lists advanced by the modernization theorists, are viewed as being undercut by unequal exchange emergent between the dominant and subordinate.[44] Exploitive exchanges prevent technology from being appropriately employed to serve genuine developmental values. The problem, of course, is that this literature leaves the definition of authentic social development in the same sad state — an amorphous list of "good things." There is still no policy-assessment valuational muscle.

The sociological struggle with the problem of valuation was the focus of Chapter 2. It is sufficient to mention here that, whether working within the modernization or dependency traditions, sociologists have viewed social development as involving a wide range of "good things" — liberty, dignity, equality, equity, freedom from hunger and disease, fulfillment of basic needs or felt needs, increased real income, political freedom, quality of life, social cohesion, participation in public decisions. But simple lists of "good things" are not particularly helpful in policy assessment. One "good thing" may be incompatible with another. Conceptions of equity oppose equality; cost effectiveness may well be inconsistent with the demands of social justice; individual liberty stands against collective responsibility. Moreover, any given "good thing" is open to divergent interpretation. Freedom for the wolf threatens freedom for the sheep. A value logic that simply advocates more "good things" is a logic itself without values and is suited only for a utopia beyond the need for policy assessment. What all this reveals is that, for the most part, the idea of development operates without any clear and logically justifiable value bearings.

In the conflict of visions between modernization theory as "development" and dependency theory as "development," we see development as both humanizing and dehumanizing, constructive and destructive, good (choice creating) and demonic (choice destroying). The "development" concept, unsupported by any intersubjectively coherent logic of valuation, has become different things to different people. The sociology of development has operated without any meaningful logic of value that can give coherent meaning to an essentially normative concept.

Loaded up with various and vague meanings, the idea of development had became so confused by the mid-1960s that Herbert Blumer felt called upon to remind sociologists that they did not know what they were talking about when using the concept.[45] Two decades later, another analysis by Fred Riggs reconfirmed Blumer's earlier assessment that the idea of development was badly muddled.[46] Riggs noted that development can refer to either (1) a process by which a social system is transformed from state x to state y; or (2) a condition x or y in which conditions are viewed as "rising" or "descending." Obviously, to "rise" is to "develop" and to "descend" is to retrogress. Now, a system may rise or descend on many variables simultaneously, but none are served by a defensible value logic for sorting out the mixes that represent "better." Given the failure to define developmental values in any coherent manner, Riggs noted that social scientists cannot agree when they look at a given case as to whether it represents development or not.[47] What a liberal social scientist accepts as developmental may well be rejected by a Marxist. As one analyst reviewed by Riggs lamented, "until more is accomplished, . . . development will be meaningless. . . ."[48]

Reacting in frustration against the failure of sociology and political science to generate policy-relevant normative choice criteria with which to address the development problems of decision-makers, Warren F. Ilchman and Norman T. Uphoff concluded that development theory had been largely irrelevant to the problem of policy choice.[49] They proposed an approach that employs the concepts of economics, political science, and sociology combined into a new political economy that assesses the costs and benefits of alternatives from the perspective of regime builders who hope to create the conditions of long-term development.[50] Ilchman and Uphoff succeed admirably in generating a range of insights about productive investment of economic, political, and social resources to shore up shaky regimes, and there can be little doubt that regime stability is a prerequisite for development. Their analysis yields insights about what policy strategy is likely to "pay off" for those who have or want power, but such considerations cannot define social development for guiding policy assessment. To serve the interests of existing regimes is one form of useful policy analysis, but it is not necessarily what serves social development and cannot produce a normative basis for policy assessment.

Recently, Amitai Etzioni has also noted the absence of a viable value logic with which to restore the idea of development to coherence, and he has powerfully argued for a cross-disciplinary association of sociology and economics to address the problem of valuation for development policy. Building upon his much-read *The Active Society* (1968), he makes a case for the necessity of building a viable normative developmental vision in his *The Moral Dimension: Toward A New Economics* (1988).[51] Although he does not construct a value logic with which to assess policy, he does succeed in pointing out that the shape of social networks is more influential in framing choices of individuals than the individuals themselves, that individual decisions of the firm or person — the kind economists study — largely reflect their position within society, and that collectively produced social structures must be shaped according to some set of openly announced, investigated, and justified values.[52] Etzioni expresses his value preferences as those of economic efficiency, dispersion of power, separation

87

of economic and political power, and limitations on the political power of economic competitors.[53] Etzioni may not have put together a logic of value for policy assessment, but he has clearly placed policy assessment within the larger developmental project. He has, furthermore, made a powerful case that sociologists and economists must turn their attention to social structural logics of value that can give meaning to a revived idea of social development. Etzioni argues forcefully that sociologists and economists must address themselves to the task of building normative theory that can guide policy assessment in the public household.

CONCLUSION

In this chapter I have contended that although economic markets are powerful coordinators of complex demands, they suffer from breakdowns that prevent one from concluding that technological and natural resource use patterns that emerge out of marketplaces are necessarily the patterns that serve any normatively defensible conception of social development. Furthermore, Marxian socialists — while highlighting deficiencies of markets and offering scathing criticism of what they see to be the inferior capitalist economic base for democracy — have themselves failed to advance viable policy-assessment logics for the conduct of policy assessment. Socialist elites are as blind to the resolution of normative policy-assessment issues as are elites of capital.

Not that the alternatives before us are either unfettered marketplaces or socialist bureaucracies. The real issues have to do with how to provide valuational direction to markets by agents of the public household, whether those agents stand in the shadow of free enterprise or socialist theorists. Public authority must contribute to improved functioning of markets; and markets, in turn, are important to the improved functioning of public agencies.

Development sociology has evolved in multiple directions over the last century, but nowhere does the analyst find a defensible valuational logic that posits clear, and defensible, value criteria against which proposed policies can be usefully assessed. Lists of "good things" abound in the literature, and although it may seem self-evident that people everywhere prefer food to starvation, health to sickness, variety to monotony, freedom to servitude, and life to death, there is nothing in such statements that can carry the policy-assessment burden. Unfortunately, values are in conflict and most contending interests are on the side of the angels. But the "good thing" for one can be expected to interfere with achievement of a "good thing" for another.

A policy-assessment logic serving a conception of social development must provide specific ways to trade off one "good thing" against another. It must be able to select from among conflicting conceptions of "progress" in a way that avoids ethnocentrism. Such normative capacity is not to be found in the sociology of development literature. Why has valuation for policy assessment been so neglected? There are profound reasons, which are to be examined in the next chapter.

IV

Valuation for Policy Assessment: Problems With Contemporary Value Criteria

Familiarity with alternative value systems, critical examination of the doubtful claims for so-called "scientific" or "self-evident" values, a skeptical look at prevailing value axioms dominating much Western based policy science — these are steps on the arduous road to taking up value exploration as an essential and neglected dimension of the policy sciences. — Yehezkel Dror[1]

What value logic justifies the imposition of costs of an action on some people and parts of the environment and not on others? Costs are inevitably present; sufferers are always chosen. Any method of policy assessment for public choice must entail justification of a distribution of suffering. It is the purpose of this chapter to continue the examination of major market and nonmarket value logics that have been advanced for justifying profiles of advantage and disadvantage. Discussion of logical problems in valuation, in the first section of this chapter, will reveal why the valuative component of the social development concept has fallen into disrepute. When the idea of social development failed to attain sufficient valuative meaning, many particular policy-assessment activities were cast adrift without connection to each other or to an encompassing analytical framework. The discussion in the following section will trace major fragments of the valuational heritage that have survived into the late twentieth-century.

PROBLEMS WITH CONTEMPORARY VALUE LOGICS

Seeking a Value Logic in Utilitarianism:
The Failure of Welfare Economics

Welfare economics is that part of the larger discipline that attempts to explain how to arrive at socially "better" solutions to resource allocation problems of the national or local economy.[2] Welfare economics attempts to identify "better" alternatives by eliminating inferior ones that are less "efficient" in the service of individual "preferences."[3] Individual preferences are to count as constituting end values. More of any one output, or less input per unit of output, is desirable in serving preferences if the supply and distribution of other commodities and services are held constant.[4]

Preference satisfaction constitutes the "good"; what the hedonists want by way of utility is what they ought to want. Policy rationality, therefore, consists of economic efficiency in the pursuit of a given set of utilities.[5] Yet welfare economics has been an uneasy science, in no small measure because of trouble with its valuational logics for drawing "ought" conclusions in given factually described situations. The trouble can be traced through three phases of thought — the old welfare economics centering on Jeremy Bentham's notions of cardinal utility, the new welfare economics of Pareto optimality, and cost-benefit value logics.

Jeremy Bentham hated the inconsistencies of English common law, which he considered to be archaic, irrational, and ruinously expensive. Furthermore, Bentham was first and last a reformer who clearly advocated studying what is — the facts — in order to promote what "ought."[6] He saw the "ought" to be defined by the ethical commandment of utility maximization, that is, one should always act to increase the greatest happiness for the greatest number. Happiness was the greatest amount of pleasure with the least possible pain. What is pleasure? What is pain? Each is whatever a person considers it to be.[7] Utility meant welfare, happiness, want satisfaction. Utilitarianism has always been a comparatively clear theory of social betterment easily grasped by practical men and women. In essence, the commandment to the decision-maker is: When assessing the value of proposed policy alternatives, turn your attention to the actual states of mind of persons who are, or will be, affected. Those states of mind are all one needs to consider in one's assessment. There are no duties to abstractions such as states, constitutions, or religions but only to actual human beings who feel pain and pleasure.[8] The whole machinery of the natural and social order is useful or harmful in proportion to its promotion of pleasurable states of feeling. Policy, and science for policy, should serve individual hedonism in which the satisfaction of each person's desires, and the composite of individual satisfactions, is to be aggregated into the social good.

Attacks on the primary tenets of Bentham's utilitarianism have been favorite sport for philosophers and social scientists; the full range and subtlety of the criticism cannot be encompassed here, but key themes can be summarized. First and foremost, the utility principle is spongy. Happiness of numbers of people cannot be defensibly aggregated so as to compare the effect of alternative policies. We simply do not know that policy X will produce more or less net utility than will policy Y. In addition, it has long been admitted that wealth and utility are not necessarily associated. Money is not equivalent to happiness. People define many nonmonetary values as critical to their well-being and to a good society. For example, are animals to count? Is contentment for a breeding population of 270 grizzly bears equal to that of sixteen cattle ranchers and two philosophers? How is one to know? If one narrows consideration only to people, utilitarianism can be criticized as being arrogant in the face of nature. Destruction of the grizzlies, a plant species, or of a scenic vista is to be avoided only if it should entail a net loss of pleasure among the aggregate of human beings — as if that net loss could be calculated. Is the natural order to be viewed only in terms of the comfort and pleasure of human hedonists with no restriction except the pleasure of present and future human beings?

Yet utilitarianism has also been criticized because it belittles humanity. By making morality a kind of psychic engineering, men and women might be trained to accept chemically induced pleasures that reduce them to pleasure-obsessed beings manipulated by technicians for whom private and public morality is just another manageable problem. It belittles human beings in another sense. Individuals can be sacrificed on the altar of greater preference satisfactions of others who attack their lives and dignity. Killing off grandfather might well make for greater aggregate utility — if that concept had any operational meaning — given the utility levels conferred by the inheritances upon the children. Should such a fact justify grandfather's murder? Is a rapist to be allowed to defend himself by arguing that his satisfactions exceeded the pain of the raped? Furthermore, utilitarianism, by focusing on the aggregate of preference satisfaction, seriously fudges distributional questions. If one were to be able to defensibly measure utility across populations, various policies might equally increase the aggregate of social utility but do so by imposing very different distributional patterns on the social order. Should one manage the public household so as to maximize average or total happiness? If the poorest of a society were killed off, the average utility of the remainder would increase, but total aggregate utility might well diminish. Utilitarian thought provides no defensible answers to such problems.

Finally, utilitarianism represents a naturalistic ethic. In spite of Hume's distinction between "is" and "ought," Bentham and later utilitarians engaged in naturalistically fallacious reasoning when they argued that what the preference maximizer does want is what s/he ought to want. Utilitarianism takes people as it finds them, aggregates their pains and pleasures through logically unspecified spongy devices, and then fallaciously concludes that what serves the existing preferences "ought" to serve. All of this illicit business goes on without examining the social structure within which people come to define and evaluate their preferences.

The utilitarianism of Bentham lay at the heart of the "old welfare economics" until it was struck its death blow in the 1930s. Until then, analysts had assumed utility to be represented by a cardinal number, comparable among consumers, that measured both satisfaction derived from consumption of goods and consumers' relative preference for such goods. If one holds that interpersonal comparisons of utility have meaning, then presumably one can order social outcomes according to the sum of utilities of individuals under each outcome — the solution of Bentham that was accepted by Edgeworth and Marshall.[8] In 1938, Lionel Robbins successfully attacked the notion that interpersonal comparisons of utility were possible when he noted: "Every mind is inscrutable to every other mind and no common denominator of feeling is possible."[9] There was, for Robbins, no scientific status for interpersonal utility comparisons:

> In Western democracies we assume for certain purposes that men in similar circumstances are capable of equal satisfactions. . . . But, although it may be convenient to assume this, there is no way of proving the assumption rests on ascertainable fact. . . . If the representative of some other civilization were to assure us that we were wrong, that members of his caste (or his race) were capable of experiencing ten times as much satisfaction from a given income as members of an inferior caste (or an inferior race) we could not refute him.[10]

After Robbins's well-taken argument, analysts could no longer defensibly hope to add up utilities into measures of alternative social states. Furthermore, Robbins pointedly noted that distinction must be made between scientifically ascertainable matters and those derived by convention. Economists could not make policy recommendations without going beyond their status as economists and passing into the separate realms of ethics and local cultural meaning systems.[11] If interpersonal comparisons of utilities have no meaning, then there is no meaning to comparisons of policy options based on a summation of individual utilities under each alternative. There was then no defensible method in the old welfare economics for passing from individual tastes to ideas about what policies better serve social development.

The old welfare economics was characterized by a naive naturalism and bogus hedonistic psychology. When notions of interpersonal comparisons of utility fell by the wayside, the criterion of Pareto optimality became the centerpiece of the "new welfare economics."[12] The Pareto optimal state of affairs is taken to be a condition in which no individual could be made "better off" in terms of his or her preferences without another being made worse off. Or, if some individuals prefer x to y, then so does society if other individuals are no worse off under condition x given their particular tastes.

Pareto optimality as a social value logic is easily assailable, however, on several grounds. First, it almost never applies to real-world situations — it says nothing about those choices as a consequence of which one individual gains and another loses in some respect. In response to this severe limitation, some British economists asked whether they could justify the repeal of the Corn Laws (tariffs on grain), even though landlords were clearly worse off as a result. Kaldor and, following him, Hicks argued that there was a sense in which an analyst could hold that one state is better than another without assuming the interpersonal comparison of utilities and while fudging Pareto optimality.[13] Nicholas Kaldor and John R. Hicks endorsed the hypothetical compensation of the losers. A policy would be desirable if the gainers could hypothetically compensate losers and thereby attain a Pareto-type improvement even if compensation for losers was not actually instituted.[14] In effect, the argument is that state x is better than state y from the viewpoint of society if winners could hypothetically compensate losers and still retain a surplus of advantage. A deep objection to the Kaldor-Hicks compensation principle is that there is no necessary provision of compensation.

Table 4.1. Pareto Optimality and Problems of Plausibility

		A	B	C
Policy Alternatives	One	100	10	10
	Two	101	10	10
	Three	99	100	100

Also, in a world of more than one commodity, there is no unequivocal meaning to comparing total production in any two or more social states.[15] In a one-commodity world, the idea is to maximize total output of that one commodity, but in a multiple-commodity world, the standard of value changes meaning and must fall to pieces over the fact that, given no interpersonal comparisons of utility, the measurement must shift meaning from commodity to commodity, from individual to individual, and income level to income level. Furthermore, in order to accept an outcome as Pareto optimal, with or without employing the Kaldor-Hicks condition, one must accept the initial distribution of resources among members of the society. The defensibility of existing distributions is a matter to be settled separately. It is very possible, therefore, that within a prevailing exploitive maldistribution a Pareto optimal solution may be found that is blindly accepting of that great distributional injustice.

In addition, the Pareto criterion suffers a major defect because it generates results that simply are not plausible. The problem can be viewed by inspecting Table 4.1, wherein parties A, B, and C obtain various distributions of valued items under policy alternatives one, two, and three.

It is plausible that alternative three would be considered superior to alternative one on the grounds that alternative three offers a greater total of utility and equality — namely 99, 100, and 100. However, the Pareto value criterion will not permit a shift from condition one to condition three because agent A would lose one unit of advantage in the transition. It is simply not plausible that condition three is not at least as good as condition one even though party A would lose that single unit. Furthermore, a shift from option one to option two would be sanctioned by the Pareto criterion even though the gap between the rich and the poor would be widened — giving pause to those concerned with great inequality of resource distribution. The Pareto principle emasculates even moderate redistributional action. If one analyzed income redistribution between the rich agent A under option two and poor agents B and C, the Pareto optimality criterion would make all income transfer entirely a matter of A's volition.

The modern welfare economics of cost-benefit analysis simply runs roughshod over the problems of cardinal utility measurement, interpersonal comparisons of utility, and Pareto optimality while also running counter to widespread concerns with distributional justice.[16] Basic data for cost-benefit analyses are still the preferences of individuals; as with the old welfare economics, such preferences are not directly revealed to the analyst, so market prices are used in their place. Therefore, if one wishes to compare the effects of two policies, one proceeds to estimate the amount of goods each policy would produce. One would calculate the decision-maker's preferences for the policies in terms of the prices and quantities of goods received under each. Costs associated with each policy are subtracted from the projected returns — appropriately discounted for the time that they must be waited for — and benefits relative to costs are netted out. Policy assessment is then a matter of identifying and choosing the option that promises the greatest quantity of net benefits.

The use of common monetary yardsticks leads to the addition and subtraction of monetary benefits and costs across commodities and individuals; it is assumed that the benefit value of a given monetary unit is equal among all affected parties.[17] The analysis further assumes that when costs and benefits are decomposed into their component parts (for example, transport costs, crop prices, air pollution costs, and so on), the corresponding values may be represented by market prices for all goods and services that constitute the components. There is a problem when market prices do not reflect true costs and benefits because of externalities, public-goods distortions, market power of oligopolies, the distortions accompanying the irreversible tyranny of small decisions, and problems of resource distribution.

There is also a problem in the assumption that benefits and costs are the same for all people — rich and poor who receive the same goods or who pay the same taxes. Different people with different incomes, located at varying distances from desirable and undesirable activities, generating their unique social meaning systems, are variously benefited by the same amount of additional dollars. An additional thousand dollars simply does not mean as much to the millionaire bachelor as it does to the struggling sharecropper with six children and a bare subsistence income. In addition, to assess the value of later versus present consumption, a common discount rate is generally applied to all parties. That discount rate may not fairly represent the costs of postponing consumption for parties in different resource and cultural situations, but what grounds are there to employ different discount rates in a world wherein interpersonal utility comparisons are not defensible? Valuations built into discount rates become subjective and arbitrary. Finally, cost-benefit analyses accept the Kaldor-Hicks compensation principle that winners should be able to compensate losers, but without any requirement that they do so.

In sum, cost-benefit welfare economics is carried out without overcoming the logical problems raised by the old Benthamite utilitarianism or those associated with the new welfare economics of the Pareto value logic. Cardinal utility measurement and interpersonal comparison of utilities have simply been performed — no questions asked. The notion of the greatest utility for the greatest number of people represents a value logic for leaping from the "is" to the "ought," but it fails on several grounds. It is simultaneously arrogant in the face of nature, while belittling human beings by making them subject to base hedonism; it derives "oughts" from "is" conditions in illicit naturalistic fashion; and it wrongly assumes that utilities can be interpersonally compared and aggregated into a conception of social progress. The new welfare economics has centered on the Pareto optimality criterion, which is so restricted in application that it cannot address most policy problems. Even where it can be applied, it can lead to less than plausible conclusions, and it emasculates any possibility for redistributional action irrespective of circumstance except as voluntarily endorsed by those who would lose.

Most fundamentally, welfare economics leaves out considerations of social structure — it never reaches up to the level of social and political organization and attendant resource distributions. Maximizing welfare in these terms merely describes what can be done given the possibilities of existing social arrangements, and the value logic assumes the justifiability of existing asset distributions. Proposed options are, indeed, assessed, but this logic of policy assessment for the public household is constructed on shaky analytical foundations.

Valuational failures, however, are not confined to welfare economics. There are also valuational breakdowns in nonmarket logics — majority-rule notions and principles of distributive justice. To these, the discussion now turns.

97

Seeking a Value Logic in Majority Rule

A supreme danger in any democracy, James Madison argued, is the possibility that a "passionate majority" might sacrifice rights of other citizens and the public good. Majorities can act out of ignorance, miscalculation, emotion, racism, and greed and can commit actions counter to any idea of societal development.[18] Even if the U.S. government's transfer of more than one hundred thousand Japanese-Americans to inland camps from their West Coast homes in 1942 was popular with the majority of U.S. voters and that majority had expressed itself through a procedurally fair plebiscite on the issue, popularity could not have justified the act. Majority will as expressed through voting has no necessary connection to "better" or "more developmental" social policy. To assess policy according to what majorities prefer might be politically savvy, or even constitutionally necessary, but such assessments cannot identify which policy one "ought" to choose.

Powerful arguments exist for participatory democratic forms of government, and this is not to argue against constitutional democracies and responsive governments. Furthermore, democratic forms of government assume a valuationally competent citizenry in possession of viable logics of fact and value for policy assessment. Democratic government in which majority interests rule within constitutional parameters may be a necessary condition for viable policy assessment, but democratic elections operating on a majority-rule basis are not a sufficient condition. Majorities of citizens, unhinged from any viable value logic serving a coherent conception of social development, may well (1) construct inferior options from which to choose as voters, and (2) endorse collectively destructive policy options.

The disjunction between majority preferences and social welfare has been most systematically investigated by Kenneth Arrow, who formulated his insights in terms of his famous "Impossibility Theorem."[19] Arrow demonstrated that where there are at least two choosing parties, and three or more alternatives from which to choose, it is impossible to aggregate majority votes into a stable and meaningful conception of collective welfare. For example, assume that a decision-maker is faced with choosing among three alternative ways of using technologies and natural resources and that it is estimated that each alternative will distribute some valued outcome differentially among affected parties A, B, and C, as displayed in Table 4.2.

In the situation depicted in Table 4.2, the choice of any one policy will result in one party receiving the most payoff (3), one receiving the

Table 4.2. Payoffs to Affected Parties Under Each Proposed Alternative

		A	B	C
Policy Alternatives	One	3	1	2
	Two	2	3	1
	Three	1	2	3

First Agenda: {two/three} — two — {two/one} — one.
Second Agenda: {one/three} — three — {three/two} — two.

second most (2), and one receiving the least (1). If no side payments are allowed (in which case the affected parties could agree on an alternative and then compensate the losers), there is nothing in the structure of the situation that makes the mix advantage of one alternative more preferable to any other. Furthermore, if parties A, B, and C are allowed to choose alternatives by a majority vote, the selection of the preferred alternative is a function of the sequence in which pairs of alternatives are compared.

For example, if alternatives two and three are compared first (see first agenda), alternative two will be selected by the majority because party A will vote for two (2 is greater than 1), party B will vote for two also (3 is greater than 2), and party C will cast the only vote in a losing cause for alternative three. Alternative two, when compared to alternative one, loses to the first option. Alternative one wins majority approval as the most desirable option, reflecting the greatest good for the choosing parties under conditions of perfect information and complete rationality.

Now, if the second agenda for comparing options is employed, and the first comparison is that of alternatives one and three, then three will defeat one, and the runoff between alternatives three and two will yield two as the winner. A different definition of what is collectively "best" emerges simply as a function of a change in the order of comparison. There are grounds for despair in this, if one seeks to advance social development by learning what people prefer and then by investing in those policies that serve majority preference. There is no such thing as the "greatest good for the greatest number" because the majority will not select the same "greatest good" as the agenda of comparison changes. Majorities select different definitions of collective good under conditions of perfect rationality, perfect equality, and perfect information simply as a function of a different ordering of comparisons.

Serving majority preferences may well have its political advantages in a constitutional system capable of protecting minority rights, and there is virtue in responsive public authority, but there is no necessary connection to any stable, meaningful, logically defensible notion of societal development. If Jeremy Bentham's "greatest good for the greatest number" value criterion were to have survived the assaults of Lionel Robbins on interpersonal comparisons of utility, Bentham's logic would be smashed by Kenneth Arrow's demonstration that it is impossible to aggregate individual preferences into meaningful definitions of the collective good.

Seeking a Value Logic in Equality

Equality has been proposed as a value criterion defining social "betterment" almost since the beginning of organized thought about social welfare. More equality in society is taken to be better; policies should be assessed according to their estimated impact on reducing inequalities.[20] Critics of utilitarian welfare economics — especially critics of the Kaldor-Hicks approach — hold that there can be no meaning of output independent of its distribution. To enlarge total output in the aggregate, without paying attention to whether resources are distributed to millionaires or to the impoverished, undercuts the very meaning of increased production. An additional thousand dollars for the poor individual struggling on the brink of starvation contributes much more to the aggregate welfare than would the same money added to the consumption of the millionaire. This is a utilitarian, and not inconsiderable, argument for more equality. The diminishing marginal utility of money and goods as income rises means that a dollar transferred from a rich person to someone without enough to eat represents a gain to the latter greater than the loss to the former. This transfer would be justified in these terms for the next dollar and so on for numerous dollars as the gap of inequality is reduced.

A major drawback to the utilitarianism of the old, new, and cost-benefit welfare economics, say the critics, is that it is insensitive to grossly unequal income or wealth distributions and that the Kaldor-Hicks logic, which focuses on the capacity of gainers to compensate losers without requiring such compensation, is an ethical travesty. Welfare economics uncritically accepts the marginal utilities associated with the existing distribution of resources in its calculus of most favorable cost-benefit ratios and Pareto outcomes.

It is hard to argue with the contention that a dollar flowing from the rich to the poor increases the welfare of the poor more than it reduces the welfare of the rich, but the matter becomes complex. At what point should the dollar flow from the rich to poor halt? Is perfect equality of wealth or income a value worth seeking? If so, why? If not, what amount and kind of inequality is justifiable? Would the terrors of the Chinese cultural revolution be justified if they could be established to have increased equality in distribution of wealth in the People's Republic of China?

By itself, the logic of equality tells us no more than this: Where there is much of some resource, it should be subtracted and given to the less advantaged; where there is insufficiency, something should be added. The value judgment is that superfluity and insufficiency are destructive of human well-being. But when is much, too much? When is little, too little? What is the relationship between means of enhancing equality and the goal of equality? When is inequality deserved and justifiable? We must possess a notion as to what superfluity and insufficiency are to mean and a notion of what conditions call for transfers and of what means are to be employed to effect transfers. Are we simply to feed the hungry from the granaries of the prosperous? Must we not inquire as to whether hungry people are so because they chose to be irresponsible with their resources or gluttonous in their consumption while the prosperous are so because of their superior diligence? Such considerations bring into focus the question of equity — fairness. Contemporary welfare economists regularly discuss this topic, but they refer to it as a moral or political problem beyond economics because they do not possess a theory of distribution that copes with the multiple problems associated with equality and its various definitions.[21]

Problems associated with the use of equality criteria for a policy-assessing value criterion are too numerous to be fully treated here. A more thorough, but still partial, discussion will be presented in Chapter 7.

The equality of the lottery can easily lead to dismal consequences. This kind of simple-minded egalitarianism that allocates, by chance of random draw, advantage or advantage equally to all in the group may send the skilled musician to war while the crack-shot war hawk sulks at home. Lotteries are blind to relevant differences and therefore impose outcomes that gratuitously destroy individual and collective welfare.

Inequality may be justified on grounds of relevant differences,

Table 4.3. Equality and Welfare of Affected Parties

		A	B	C
Policy Alternative	One	90	90	89
	Two	90	90	5
	Three	5	5	5

including differences in merit. If Mutt produces much and is rewarded accordingly, he will acquire greater resources relative to Jeff, whose intemperate eating and drinking substantially compromise his productivity. Should distribution be equal as between Mutt and Jeff? Is it equitable to deprive Mutt of admittedly nonbasic needs in order to enhance Jeff's terrible position? Most scholars examining the equality criterion conclude that there is no ethical or welfare reason for an equal distribution of resources per se.[22]

Furthermore, use of the equality criterion can lead to absurd results that would impose unnecessary hardship and gratuitously destroy human welfare, as shown in Table 4.3, which displays three alternative proposed policy situations affecting parties A, B, and C. The welfare situation under each option for each party is displayed by numerical values in each cell. The higher the cell value, the greater the advantage. If one were to employ the equality value to assess the desirability of the optional policies, situation three is clearly to be preferred to the policy that produces alternative two or that which results in option one. There would, however, have to be gratuitous destruction of much human well-being to actually choose policy alternative three over option one. In order to reduce absolute inequality by one unit (that is, to shift from option one to three), we would have to be willing to destroy 254 units of benefit. The idea of equality has no respect for resource levels and can lead to tragic destruction. Who would prefer the equality of the graveyard to the inequality of the vineyard?

Is there an approach to the problem of distribution that is superior to that of simple-minded equality? The discussion turns now to a notion of justice as fairness — the maximin value logic.

Seeking a Value Logic in Rawls's Concept of Maximin Justice

The maximin criterion — that is, maximize the minimum share of benefits or maximize the benefits to the least advantaged — has been at the center of the valuational debate since John Rawls brought it

Table 4.4. **Plausibility of the Maximin Value Logic**

		A	B	C
Policy Alternatives	One	100	100	100
	Two	120	120	20
	Three	20	25	21

Table 4.5. **Plausibility of Maximin Justice Under Altered Payoff Matrix**

		A	B	C
Policy Alternatives	One	100	100	99
	Two	100	100	10
	Three	11	11	11

forward in his *A Theory of Justice* (1971).[23] The maximin criterion has been widely hailed because it represents a sophisticated attempt to synthesize the utilitarian focus on aggregate utility with a concern for reducing inequality. In essence, the maximin criterion holds that if given two states of affairs (x and y), x is at least as good for society as is y if the individual in the worst position in x is no worse off than the worst-off person under y. If the worst-off actor in x is better off than the worst-off person in y, x is socially preferable to y.

A stronger variant of the maximin logic holds that if x is indifferent to y in the comparison of the worst cases, then one should proceed to compare the next worst-off cases under x and y. Situation x will be preferable to y if the second worst-off person is better off under x than the second worst-off individual under y. If this comparison results in a tie, go to the next pair of cases and so on up the line until the tie is broken.

It is obvious by now that the maximin criterion requires interpersonal comparisons of utility, but it does not require addition of utilities across society. It requires only that the utilities of the worst off in each situation be compared. The maximin criterion gets into serious trouble, however, for reasons other than requiring interpersonal comparisons of utility — even in this reduced form.

The maximin criterion falls down on the consideration of plausibility.[24] To illustrate the problem, Tables 4.4 and 4.5 array payoffs to individuals A, B, and C under three policy-induced alternative situations. Examination of Table 4.4 reveals that, employing the maximin logic, alternative one is preferable to three — something that is perfectly reasonable. One finds that alternative two is indifferent to alternative three because party A under three ties with party C under two. When the tie is broken between the two worst-off cases by comparing the next worst off pair, policy-induced situation two wins. This is also a plausible outcome. So far so good.

However, if one modifies the payoffs in Table 4.4 in the manner arrayed in Table 4.5, one sees a problem with maximin logic. Under this modified situation, alternative three is now preferable to situation two. Yet it is simply implausible that policy alternative three should be preferred to the second option given that, in order to gain one unit of advantage for party C under option two, parties A and B would have to sacrifice 178 units in shifting to policy three. We therefore obtain a problematic result and come to seriously question Rawlsian maximin justice.

The Failure of Contemporary Value Logics

The value logics reviewed are seriously problematic. The naive enthusiasm of eighteenth-century thinkers, so certain that reason could adequately assess social policy to steer society in the direction of social development, has withered under the glare of twentieth-century analysis. Given problems with existing value logics, the idea of social development has fallen into a muddle of incoherent meanings.

Men and women of goodwill and of analytical competence, equally committed to societal development, may well disagree over preferability of policy proposals. They can do so because they differ over which criteria are most appropriate and over the relative weighing of the criteria when employed in combination. Furthermore, none of the value logics earns high marks for logical coherence or capacity to produce plausible outcomes. Careful review of the value premises leads to pessimistic conclusions about their utility in guiding collective decision-making.[25]

Technologically advanced societies have evolved great capacity for action, but they have failed to arrive at defensible value criteria for assessing technological options much more advanced than those available to John Locke, Jean Jacques Rousseau, or Thomas Jefferson. Serious consequences attend our collective valuational failure: Decision-makers and their clients employ value logics in uncritical fashion without acknowledging their defects; valuational procedures undergirding policy choices are often not explicitly recognized and opened to reasoned critique, and allocations of advantage and disadvantage simply evolve out of the struggle in the marketplace and political arena. The public choices made rely heavily on an uncritical legitimacy ascribed to existing rules of the game and on coercive forces that can be brought to bear upon those who protest. Opponents and proponents of any specific action typically do no more than claim that policy X is or is not desirable. Claims that "gains" outweigh "losses" are amusing at best, given their highly problematic logical basis. Sufferers are not chosen for defensible reasons.

Furthermore, failures in valuation have led to confusion and fragmentation in contemporary sociology and in social science generally. Given conceptual disarray, a range of responses to unresolved valuational issues has split off bits and pieces of the larger value question; analysts specialize in fragments without placing their effort in larger valuational context. Major fragments of the mangled social development enterprise are found in the contemporary study of social problems, the economic growth debate, technology and social impact assessment, discussions of social indicators and "quality of life," concern with public involvement in public bureaucratic decision-making, and search for "appropriate technology." A brief review of these fragmented components of the long-standing policy-assessment problem now becomes the focus of the second portion of this chapter.

FRAGMENTATION OF THE SOCIAL DEVELOPMENT ENTERPRISE

Caught between the insights of cultural relativism, the dangers of ethnocentrism, and the failures of extant value logics for coping with policy assessment, social development has become a loose label for a great accumulation of problems for which the private marketplace or bureaucratic intervention did not, or could not, provide satisfactory solutions. The idea of development has become an object of scorn for pure researchers, a political appendage of liberal parliamentarianism in the West, party dogmatism of the totalitarian socialists, and an elite aspiration for society-building in the Third World.

However, there is much more at stake than loss of clarity and meaning of a social science concept. A sociology that cannot bring matters of fact and value together in a logically coherent manner has unclear relevance for social policy choice. Disciplines that cannot coherently speak to matters of alternative collective shapes of society, and to policy options that induce such structural shapes, must inevitably suffer from slackened patronage, narrowed readership, and lessened appeal. This, of course, is exactly what has transpired. Yet the valuational struggle has not ended; it still surfaces in specialized problem areas, however incoherently.

The Social Problems Movement

The largest, and most visible, sociological remnant of the failed hopes of eighteenth- and nineteenth-century visions of social reconstruction is that associated with those who have retained a focus on "social problems." It is a rare department of social science or sociology, however small and underfunded, that does not offer a social problems course. Social problems have historically consisted of "problematic" situations insufficiently addressed by marketplaces. The essence of the approach has been to hold up observed conditions against eighteenth-century Enlightenment ideals of equality, justice, and material advancement — whatever they may be taken to mean — and then to proceed to investigate discrepancies between what "is" and what "ought." Generally, there is a clear desire to "improve" matters.

Antecedents of the social problems orientation in sociology go back to nineteenth-century England and the United States in the work of the clergy, philanthropists, and humanitarians who were laboring in variety of reform movements having to do with prisons, settlement work, child rescue, the temperance movement, public health and sanitation, literacy, housing, and unemployment. In 1865, the American Social Science Association was established via the merger of several local and regional meliorative organizations.[26] The Association became active in promotion of social science courses in U.S. colleges and universities and in touting the potential usefulness of systematic study of social problems. The activities of the Association peaked in the decade following 1885.

Around the turn of the century, the social problems approach began to lose out to the need to validate sociology as a science. By the middle decades of the twentieth century, mainstream sociology was preoccupied with matters of research methods and general theory unhinged to social policy. As the older nineteenth-century sociological thrust faded, the gulf between value-neutral social theory and the study of social problems grew wide, leaving intellectually stranded those who still clung to the notion of linking scientific knowledge directly to the solution of crucial social problems.[27] The discontent of problems-oriented people culminated in the establishment, in 1952, of the Society for the Study of Social Problems that, although affiliated with the American Sociological Association, advanced its own identity and nurtured its own journal. The Society was established by, and continues to serve, sociologists with multiple commitments to research, policy assessment, and action.[28] Perusal of the pages of *Social Problems* leaves little doubt that the Society views sociology as a strategic contributor to the investigation of, and as a source of potential solutions for, social problems in areas such as poverty, racism, sexism, environmental quality, crime, delivery of essential services, distributions of work and leisure, employment conditions, disarmament, and war.

The problem with all this, of course, is that a social problems focus must rest uneasily with a value-neutral sociology and that analysts who are unhinged by cultural relativism from any viable conception of valuation cannot make logically explicit defensible value commitments with which even a small proportion of the involved professionals can agree. Social problems as taught in contemporary programs remains a remnant of an earlier day when developmental values could be advanced with less embarrassment. Social problems teaching, regretfully, has become a prudent carping from the safety of the lecture room.

"Problems" emerge from popular opinion, moral indignation, environmental threats, and specialized technocrats speaking in esoteric languages. They are, by definition, situations that at least some observers view as wrong, troublesome, and in need of remedy. It is obvious that the very definition of a social problem entails the assertion of value judgments. Social problems texts routinely acknowledge the problem of valuation by including obligatory disclaimers about the valuative nature of definitions of problematic situations.[29] The valuative mess is obscured, but not lessened, by the attempts to gloss it over under labels such as *social disorganization* (Charles H. Cooley, W. I. Thomas, Florian Znaniecki), *dysfunction* (Robert K. Merton, Robin Williams), or *deviance* (Howard Becker, Edwin Lemert, Erving Goffman).

To identify a "problem" one must specify a value standard against which some observed situation falls short. But what value standards are to be employed? Standards vary from group to group, time to time, place to place, and power structure to power structure. Lying at the heart of the matter is the fact that "solutions" for some are "problems" for others. Gigantic trusts were not seen as a social problem by J. P. Morgan; however, members of the progressive movement and President Theodore Roosevelt were quite prepared to define them as such.

Slavery in the antebellum South was not a social problem for many whites, but slave revolts were. Furthermore, definitions of social problems do not cut evenly across populations. There will always be dissent over the definition of "problems" as some groups muster the clout to insert their definitions into the public arena and others lose out.

In the tangle of competing groups and organizations, the social problems approach has avoided coming to grips with the question of valuation.[30] The formulation of problems, the selection of data, and the forging of arguments all follow current fashion, but logics of valuation are typically obscured. Usually there is an expressed desire to avoid uncritical acceptance of problem definitions as they are constructed by power elites. Deplorable conditions are to be examined even if not sanctioned by the local power structure, but what standards define deplorable? Sociologists with a social-problems focus frequently see themselves functioning as attorneys for the defense of the powerless and disorganized. They may seek to pass responsibility from those less able to bear it to those more able to affect policy, but they do not offer carefully reasoned logics of valuation.

The Growth Debate

Sustained growth in gross national product and average real income per capita has become the modern secular religion — the source of individual motivation, the basis for political stability and legitimacy, a most basic value premise for policy assessment in both capitalist and socialist societies. That which promotes continuous growth in investment and production has been assessed as "better." The comfortable belief that societal progress could be equated with continuous economic growth, which was assumed to assure to all a high quality of life, came apart in the late 1960s. By 1972, the Club of Rome warned all who would listen that growth, especially exponential growth, had significant and unsettling attributes.[31]

Exponential growth occurs when a quantity increases by a constant percentage of the whole over a constant time period, resulting in a doubling of quantities in fixed time intervals. Doubling of a quantity — whether of population, energy production, income, fertilizer applied per unit of crop, or pollution — at regular intervals means that the last term in a series of doubled values will always exceed the cumulative total of all preceding terms. In a doubling series 1, 2, 4, 8, 16, the value of sixteen will exceed the sum of the preceding numbers. Exponential growth is, therefore, treacherous because a quantity can proceed through a series of doublings without seeming to reach significant size, but values can become overwhelming in one or two additional time periods. The quantity will be one-half of any limit on growth only one time period before the limit is reached or breached. Crises emerge precipitously with only a short period for adjustment.

Exponential growth curves rise forever only in the abstract world of mathematics; in the real finite world, limits exist for energy extraction, atmospheric capacity to bear pollution, supplies of minerals to support industrial production, and plant, animal, and human populations. The Club of Rome report concluded that continued exponential growth would bring the world to collapse and catastrophe within a century. Soon after those dismal forecasts were being debated, the Arab attack on Israel on October 6, 1973, launched the "energy crisis" into popular consciousness, marked the effective entry of Arab states into a powerful position in world politics, and destroyed the post-World War II illusion that petroleum supplies could be regarded as a simple function of the demand of technologically advanced nations. Men and women from all walks of life in North America and Europe began to picture deserted motorways and the specter of petroleum-induced standstill in the machinery of economic growth.

Soon a spate of literature emerged around the theme of the no-growth society, and the debate between growth and no-growth advocates blossomed as a central issue in the 1970s.[32] The Science Policy Research Unit of Sussex University, England, reviewed the Club of Rome report, worked with its assumptions and data, and arrived at much more optimistic conclusions about prospects for continued economic growth.[33] The central argument of the Sussex group was that the Club of Rome estimates did not give adequate weight to negative feedback from human social structure, politics, and changed preferences under increasing scarcity, environmental pollution, and price shifts — all of which could be expected to flatten out growth curves. The Sussex group contended that "overshoot" and "collapse" are not inevitable modes of behavior and that more flexible responses are probable. There was no disagreement, however, over the impossibility of long-term exponential growth in strategic domains — energy consumption, pollution, population, and important minerals.

The debate between the growth pushers and gloom merchants became sterile because the real issues have to do with the composition and distribution of the products of growth. "Better" composition and distribution are qualities to be determined by resolving the valuational problem to which neither the proponents nor the detractors of growth have adequately attended. Some types and patterns of growth are more compatible with reasonable levels of environmental quality and resource use than are others. Growth in sailboating has different consequences than does growth in powerboating. Growth in the use of small cars, bicycle transport, mass transit, and high-density housing has far different ramifications than does continued growth in the use of large automobiles and low-density suburban land use patterns. The question is not: Is economic growth in the aggregate good or bad? The question is more properly: What kinds of economic growth fulfill defensible value criteria serving a viable conception of social development?

The growth debate reflects our systematic incapacity to address matters of valuation; the debate has collided with those intractable issues of valuation that have preoccupied us since the eighteenth century.

The Social Indicator, Social Impact Assessment, and Quality of Life Movements

Apparent deficiencies of the market system for controlling technology and allocating natural resources have stimulated creation of yet another fragment of the contemporary social development enterprise — the social indicator and quality of life movement that is closely associated with the debate over the meaning of economic growth. The term *quality of life* has no single agreed-upon meaning except that it represents an attempt to measure aspects of the human and environmental condition ignored by narrow economic growth definitions of societal progress.

What is clear is that social indicators embody values; they have built into them some conception of the common good, a normative vision of some aspect of social development. Any indicator statistic, if it changes in a direction defined as "better," is seen to indicate a condition in which society is thought to have somehow improved.[34] Writers on social indicators have been ambivalent about the value questions that necessarily arise in the construction, use, and interpretation of social indicators, and many have downplayed the value question by emphasizing that the indicators project was centered on a more value-neutral scientific social change research.[35]

Duncan MacRae, however, has clearly seen the valuational problem posed by social indicator construction, and in 1985 and 1986 he issued clarion calls to social scientists involved in the activity. He challenged social scientists to quit sweeping the value question under the conceptual rug, to restore to the full light of day the value meanings of social indicators, and to see that the only viable reason for undertaking to build social indicators is that they have potential to be useful for public discourse and collective decisions.[36] MacRae wants to organize sets of social indicators into "democratic information systems" and advocates that such systems be employed to contribute to reasoned analysis of public issues and policies.

The social indicator movement is so diverse, so snarled in theoretical and methodological difficulties, that a thorough review of the state of the art is well beyond the scope of this effort. For present purposes the major branches of this diverse domain of activity can be categorized under a few major headings.

First, there is the important set of efforts to monitor social change. One of the earliest efforts to compile a system of social indicators for this purpose was the report of the President's Research Committee on Social Trends, *Recent Social Trends in the United States* (1933).[37] More recent efforts include the work of Sheldon and Moore (1968), Smith (1973), Hauser (1975), and Campbell, Converse, and Rodgers (1976).[38] This stream of thought emphasizes attempts to identify and measure major structural and attitudinal changes in society and to project trends where possible. A major issue centers around the relationship, if any, between subjective attitudes and objective criteria of well-being. Analysts must either assume that certain items expressed by objective indicators are in fact desired by people, turn their objective indices into measures of perceived satisfaction, or mix both approaches. Is welfare a state of mind? Is it represented by objective conditions irrespective of attitudes? If people without indoor plumbing, and possessing little income, report high levels of personal happiness, is that a problem?

A second thrust in social indicator activity has been that of forecasting the future.[39] A central objective is to anticipate alternative socioecological states and thereby to identify potential crises sufficiently in advance such that they might be judiciously acted upon. The question as to which value criteria should guide action in response to projected problems is largely ignored or resolved by fiat.

The third major approach is that of revealing the social impact of government policies. For example, one might focus on energy development in the western United States, where attempts have been made to measure social consequences on impacted communities experiencing economic "boom" conditions, or on those effects associated with major public works projects such as high rise dams or regional development schemes. The objective is to serve policy by providing it with a wider range of information and insight than can be gleaned from economic growth analysis. In the United States, the National Environmental Policy Act (1969) provided major impetus to this use of social indicators. This legislation not only established environmental quality as a leading national priority for the public household, it established procedures for incorporating environmental and social concerns into agency decision-making, and it created the Council on Environmental Quality in the Executive Office of the President to oversee all federal government environmental efforts.[40] In addition to physical dimensions of the environment, social indicator studies and impact analyses are to be responsible to archaeological, historic, and social dimensions of human well-being. Subsequently, the U.S. Water Resources Council issued *Principles and Standards for Planning Water and Related Land Resources* (1973), which explicitly called for establishment of a "social well-being" account to supplement economic and environmental quality accounts.[41] Many measurements of a social nature have been proposed for such accounts — population size and composition, labor force composition, dwelling conditions, family cohesion, bank receipts, attachment to place, intergroup conflict, and community cohesion to name a few.[42]

A fourth stream of social indicators effort is that of attempting a theory-based systematic mapping of social dynamics. The effort is less focused on immediate practical decisions and more intended to build better social theory. Social indicators work, in this stream, is viewed as a tool of basic research.[43]

The problem posed, except possibly in the case of the theory-construction approach, is the valuational one. For a social indicator to be relevant to policy assessment, it must consist of two components: (1) a numerator value stating the existing state of affairs as measured in a given unit of analysis, and (2) a denominator stating the desirable state of affairs in that unit. The result is:

$$\frac{\text{Existing Level of Phenomena in Unit X}}{\text{Desirable Level of Phenomena in Unit X}}$$

If one cannot specify a value judgment for the denominator in a defensible fashion, there is no reason from a policy-assessment standpoint for employing the indicator in the first instance. For example, if one wishes to compare several proposed policy alternatives in terms of their impact on employment or social cohesion, it is necessary to first define increased employment up to some level as desirable, or increased cohesion of some type up to some point as being in the social interest. Then estimated effects of each proposed policy alternative can be compared against the value criterion in the denominator of the indicator variable. If such value criteria cannot be formulated, or if their desirability cannot be agreed upon, there is no policy-assessment reason for making measurements on the indicators.

In many instances, it can be expected that value criteria can be formulated in the denominators of impact variables — less crime will be largely accepted as desirable as compared to increased crime rates, lower divorce rates will be viewed as better than higher ones, housing with bathrooms will be taken as superior to structures without indoor plumbing. The real valuational problem comes in making trade-offs among conflicting criteria. How much increase in banking receipts is worth how much decline in community cohesion? How much aggregate increase in per capita income, and in housing starts, is worth what amount of decrease in reported loss of control over local events by community old-timers? How much decline in air quality is compensated for by the new availability of x jobs and y new shopping centers? How are we to know which mix of benefits and losses on a set of indicators represents betterment when every technological option imposes noncommensurable costs differentially over the affected population?

What is "quality of life" in all of this? As a social science concept, it has been little more than a conceptual cover-up for the fact that analysts do not know how to make such trade-offs among conflicting values. It has been a term used to avoid even more blatantly valuative words such as *the good life, progress,* or *social development.*[44] It gives dim luster to lists of "good things." Given the lack of agreement as to what should go into the denominators of many social indicators, and given the more basic problem of developing logical criteria with which to make trade-offs among competing criteria, one witnesses the desultory collection of social indicators data with the implicit hope that out of all this will evolve some notion of progress and a strategy for fostering it.[45]

Technology Assessment

In the private sector, technology assessment occurs when entrepreneurs contemplate investment. A new technology goes into use when it reaches a point at which a firm can offer it on the market and make more money than if the technology were to be withheld. There have been, however, negative external side effects, anticipated or un-anticipated, which have brought agencies of the public household into the technology assessment arena. In the 1830s, when a series of boiler explosions on steamboats brought pressures for assessment action, the U.S. Congress authorized the Treasury Department to grant research funds to the Franklin Institute in Philadelphia for experiments that would yield a body of data essential to the improvement of steam boiler design.[46]

The ultimate technology assessment organization is the legislative assembly, which can prohibit hazardous applications and prescribe regulatory controls. Typically, a legislative assembly assigns operational responsibilities to administrative bodies, but legislatures and their bureaucratic appendages tend to react to technological problems only after those problems have reached significant levels of intensity — and then only after protracted struggle with vested interests.

Marketplaces do not necessarily offer realistic appraisal of technological hazards because of problems of externality, concentration of power, public goods and the logic of the "free rider," and the tyranny of small decisions. Furthermore, legislative assemblies encounter constituency resistance to prompt and balanced assessment. Prompted by these realities, a technology assessment movement emerged in the late 1960s with the objective of redressing matters. In October 1972, the U.S. Congress established an Office of Technology Assessment (OTA), and similar agencies have been established in other countries.[47] The objective has been to develop methodologies for revealing positive and negative externalities in advance of widespread diffusion. Technology assessments attempt to provide balanced appraisals of the positive and negative consequences in their physical, biological, economic, political, and social dimensions as soon as possible so as to supplement the signals emerging from the marketplace, the courts, and the legislature.[48]

Assessment of technological impacts in social life, and upon the wider physical environment, forces the analyst to confront problems of valuation. What technology, under what circumstances, is to be preferred? So far the answer has been to put the value question in the hands of the politician or agency bureaucrat in the hope that the political process will yield a conception of public welfare that, in time, will guide decision-makers to the best possible choices. But the political process can only yield a justifiable conception of social progress if citizens and their representatives possess some shared logics of social fact and value.

Politicians, in turn, fully comprehend that balanced assessment may well limit their freedom of action to serve parochial interests back home. Politicians survive according to their ability to serve conflicting constituencies in terms of current problems and understandings of their well-organized supporters. Reasoned policy assessment may suggest that today's decision should be made in the light of criteria that violate current common sense and that might undercut immediate interest of certain clients in order to serve constituencies that are relatively powerless or even unborn. Politicians know their constituencies and take pains to become fully sensitive to technology's implications for their political future. But what is politically expedient does not necessarily easily associate with what is socially developmental. Politicians, to promote developmental values, must find support of constituencies who can powerfully insert reasoned value logics into public discourse.

Appropriate Technology

Enthusiastic response to *Small Is Beautiful* (1973), by E. F. Schumacher, made for another fragment of development discourse.[49] Since its publication, observers have witnessed the emergence of many social scientists who advocate "intermediate technology," "gentle technology," "soft technology," or "appropriate technology."[50] The essence of the argument, under any of the labels, is that capital-intensive technology based on exploitation of nonrenewable raw materials, developed in the industrial West under conditions of relative labor scarcity and hydrocarbon energy abundance, is highly inappropriate for poor nations that possess abundant labor but for which capital and fossil fuel supplies are severely constrained.

Advanced capital-intensive technologies of the Western world may be highly productive in terms of labor hours applied but at the cost of obtaining little product per unit of capital investment and per gallon of fossil fuel. For example, farmers in the United States may be highly productive in turning out great quantities of food per hour worked, but productivity per unit of labor has meant that great quantities of capital and hydrocarbon energy are inserted into the production process. High labor productivity has meant low capital and energy productivity. It takes roughly the equivalent of sixty-four gallons of diesel fuel to grow an acre of corn in the United States.[51] Such agriculture simply should not, and cannot, be replicated in many nations. It is inappropriate to blindly export such capital-intensive, raw material–depleting, laborsaving technologies.

115

Soon the appropriate technology argument was extended to advanced industrial countries themselves. Principal advocates of appropriate technology in this quarter have been Amory Lovins and Barry Commoner.[52] Industrial societies will make a major mistake, it is contended, if they continue to plunge into highly irreversible commitments to capital-intensive, nonrenewable energy technologies — coal, oil, gas, and nuclear. These technologies represent to Lovins a "hard path" to energy sufficiency. Advanced societies should be employing remaining stocks of nonrenewable energy to build a future society that can sustain itself when strategic minerals and fossil fuels can no longer be economically extracted in sufficient quantities. The more appropriate "soft path" to future energy sufficiency emphasizes renewable energy sources and relatively small scale decentralized technologies designed to extract energy from locally available gradients.

Appropriate technology advocates are commendably clear about their value criteria — there is no pretense of value neutrality here. They advocate technical options that are thermodynamically efficient, that produce waste products that can be absorbed by naturally existing ecological cycles (the source of gentleness or softness), and that are relatively reversible in impact such that they can be adapted to local ecological settings without causing long-term disruption. There can be no denying the persuasiveness of such values as criteria for policy assessment. Chapters 5 and 8 will be responsive to such insights, but appropriate technologists do not adequately cope with the development question. There is nothing in present conceptions of appropriate technology per se that prohibits injustice, poverty, and other threats to societal development. Is a long-term sustainable society a sufficient definition of the "better" or "more developed" social order? Will "soft" technology always be used for socially developmental ends? Such value criteria as the advocates of appropriate technology propose may be necessary to a conception of social development, but they are insufficient.

Public Involvement

Throughout the early years of the United States as a republic, a battle over issues relating to citizen involvement in governmental decision-making raged between Alexander Hamilton and Thomas Jefferson.[53] Hamilton argued that there are two categories of people. First, there are the few well born and privileged with capacity to make intelligent policy; in the second category are the mass of common people. The masses were viewed by Hamilton as being fickle, turbulent, and untrustworthy, seldom capable of judging public policy matters in rational and deliberate fashion. Give, therefore, the reins of government to elites who could check the unsteadiness of the masses. Jefferson readily agreed with Hamilton that the world consists of two kinds of people, but he differently defined the categories. The members of one group, said Jefferson, fear and distrust the people and wish to draw all possible power away from them into the hands of elites. On the other hand, a second category of people identifies with the commoners and has confidence in them. Maximum possible involvement of the average citizen, said Jefferson, was to be encouraged in affairs of the state.

For years, public involvement meant the exercise of influence on legislative assemblies. However, as policy matters became more complex and as government intervened in new domains of life as a result of needs raised by technological collisions in the private sector, legislatures were forced to delegate increasing amounts of discretionary authority to the chief executive and, thereby, to administrative agencies. In addition to lacking sufficient staff and technical skill to monitor policy decisions down to the field level on a sustained basis, politicians in the legislative bodies frequently have not been able to agree on specific policy statements in enabling legislation — a fact that has shifted the burden of making concrete policy decisions and specific interpretations to administrative agencies acting as agents of the legislature.[54]

Given that it is virtually impossible for any legislature, regardless of how great its cohesion, to set forth terms of public policy in sufficiently specific ways to eliminate significant administrative discretion in policy interpretation and execution, public involvement has come to mean efforts by public administrative agencies to reach out and systematically incorporate views of affected publics in the bureaucratic decision-making process.[55]

In a bureaucratic world of monopolized supply and inarticulate demand, some public agency administrators have been seeking, not just to inform affected publics of their intentions, but to involve them in a two-way communications process. It has been suggested that, as a basic ethical norm, those who are the objects of policy should have the opportunity to participate in the specific decisions and in the definitions of the situation on which decisions are based.[56] Discretion is left to agencies in the federal government of the United States as to how much public involvement to promote, and those agencies have considerable latitude to determine at which stages of the decision process to promote public involvement. So far preparation of environmental impact statements for proposed actions has engendered substantial efforts to galvanize public involvement by agencies such as the Forest Service, the Army Corps of Engineers, the Department of Defense, and the Bureau of Land Management.[57]

There can be no questioning the value of administrators casting their information nets more broadly in local communities to more effectively take into consideration preferences and needs of local constituencies affected by agency action. However, there can also be no question that public-involvement programs cannot resolve fundamental issues of valuation. After publics have been effectively involved, after the array of preferences and needs has been documented, assuming such information is well integrated into the organizational decision process, the question still remains: What is to be preferred and why? Is information about local desires to be evaluated according to cost-benefit ratios, Pareto optimality, majority votes, conceptions of equality, or maximinization? Effective public involvement can be expected to increase the sensitivity of agency decision-makers to the range of advantage and disadvantage perceived by involved publics, but involvement mechanisms alone cannot be expected to provide defensible value criteria for leaping from factual situations to defensible policy choice.

CONCLUSION

To defensibly choose the most developmental policy from among alternatives, one must formulate and employ a procedural logic of fact and value. That logic must address the problems of guiding technological applications in the public household identified in Chapter 1, traced historically in Chapter 2, and brought into contemporary focus by Chapters 3 and 4. What troubled the Enlightenment thinker, and what troubles us today, is that there is no shared logic of valuation to be had to give meaning to the idea of social development and to make policy assessment more fully open to reason.

Is there nothing more to say than that policy assessment is a game in which "clubs are trump"? Is policy simply to be preferred because the rich and powerful say it is to be so and because they successfully wrap their confused and inconsistent policy rationales in norms of salient constituencies? Is the social scientist to set aside policy assessment on the grounds that nothing logically defensible can be done with it, or to engage it with logically vulnerable conceptual fragments arising out of utilitarianism, Pareto optimality, cost-benefit logics, aspects of equality, and maximin justice or the lists of "good things" associated with the study of social problems, the growth debate, "quality of life," technology assessment, appropriate technology, and public involvement in bureaucratic decision-making?

The valuative logic of utilitarian welfare economics in its old, new, and cost-benefit forms has been the most systematic and popular among those offered by the social sciences, but it is highly problematic. Yet nonmarket value criteria for guiding policy assessment are also seriously flawed. The consequence for policy assessment is that both scholars and decision-makers make do with an amalgam of technical practices and politics, limping along as valuational mystics.

Within academia, pure researchers cling to the faith that disinterested science will somehow automatically benefit humankind over the long run. Judged by the needs of times, their faith is arrogant; judged by the evidence of history, it is naive. Applied scientists realize that their work is always applied to problems of choice, but they blindly trust that the mix of value criteria employed by their clients is fundamentally humane, and they hold faith in the benign disposition of the state. Critical theorists cry for an applied policy-assessing social science that will restore meaningful forms of public discourse about the direction of society. Yet critical theory also flounders on issues of valuation; along with other versions of social science it too lacks capacity to pick sufferers, and beneficiaries, for good reasons.

Social science struggles on; since mid-century its growth has been largely quantitative — more money, more departments, more faculty, students, journals, books, conferences, and specializations. The qualitative advances in theory and method that have been witnessed have not secured a place for logically defensible policy assessment. Failure to cope with the Enlightenment valuational problem has led to the fragmentation associated with the social problems squabbles, economic growth debates, the social indicator movements, the social impact assessment and quality of life efforts, technology assessment, the appropriate technology thrust, and concern with effective public involvement. All have of necessity broached value issues while avoiding direct confrontation with explicitly value-laden terms like *social development.* Sociology now bears witness to the desultory collection of data and fudging of the valuational issues that have hounded us for over two hundred years.

Nothing exists resembling a defensible policy-assessment framework for uniting, without confusing, a science of empirical fact with a logic of value. Such a framework could integrate the fragmented endeavors of policy-oriented social science and by so doing respond to the challenge thrown up by the Enlightenment thinkers who so firmly held that reason provided better foundations for policy assessment than brute force, the blind exercise of social power, or interpretations of supernatural authority. The failure of the social philosopher, and of the social scientist, to provide a minimally satisfactory resolution of the valuational problem is the fundamental reason for a social science simultaneously uncomfortable with pretensions to value neutrality and value commitment.

V

Response to the Policy-Assessment Challenge: Assessing Social Development Policy With Logics of Fact and Value

A social science that sees its value bearings, and a value theory that sees its scientific linkage, need no longer be a dream . . . it can instead become a powerful instrument in human growth. — Abraham Edel[1]

The issue of value freedom vs. value ladeness should finally be laid to rest by sociologists, and be replaced by an integrating principle linking facts and values in a policy context. — Irving Louis Horowitz[2]

INTRODUCTION

The sociological enterprise has banked heavily upon the promise of policy assessment rooted in some encompassing vision of social development. The promissory note remains largely uncashable, but most members of the discipline readily admit that most of our dependent variables are of empirical interest primarily because of their valuative implications. It is the purpose of this chapter to advance an argument consisting of specific sociological logics of fact and value that will operate together to guide technology and natural resources policy in the direction of a coherent working idea of social development. However, prior to specifying the policy-assessment logics, three questions must be addressed: (1) in what sense can we say the value judgments are justified, (2) what criteria are to be employed in critiquing alternative value judgments and their rationales, and (3) to what domain — individual or structural — does the logic of fact and value apply?

Justifying Value Logics

Justifications for value logics fall into one of two broad categories — hard or soft. Those who demand "hard justification" demand ultimate proof of value assertions. In a sense they are modern descendants of Archimedes who seek the ultimate value fulcrum on which they can rest the logical lever that will move earthly policy.[3] Hard justificationists require identification of first principles that, by definition, cannot be deduced from any higher principle or procedure. One must, then, deductively establish some self-evident truth for all times and peoples and then demonstrate that one's value judgments are true to the deduced implications of such first principles.

Soft justificationists, on the other hand, deny the possibility of finding ultimate skyhooks upon which to hitch value criteria for policy assessment, or at least they deny that acceptable ones have, as yet, been found.[4] The assertion that the validity of value criteria is not ultimately demonstrable does not necessarily lead to the conclusion that one cannot employ reason to formulate and critique them for policy-assessment purposes any more than admission that there is no ultimate fact destroys the enterprise of empirical science. One might imagine revisions in our factual and valuational knowledge to be analogous to repairing a ship at sea. One fixes parts without tearing down the whole structure and sinking it. Just as there is no single rivet, plate, or brace upon which the integrity of the whole ship rests, so there is no single ultimate bedrock fact upon which the entire enterprise of science is founded. The adequacy of a particular fact must be judged according to the logical adequacy of the procedures out of which the fact has been generated.

There is, likewise, no ultimate value criterion upon which the entire domain of policy assessment rests. Value criteria for the public household are to be judged as superior or inferior according to the defensibility of the logical procedures upon which such criteria are based.[5] Some value criteria can be judged superior to others and, therefore, claim priority in guiding technological potentials in the public household because they are rooted in logically superior procedures that better withstand searching criticism just as do the procedurally more trusted conceptions of fact. It is a fundamental task for analysts of social development and policy assessment to continuously repair and improve the valuational navigational apparatus, just as they must never cease to advance improved scientific hypotheses about the factual matters. Human dignity and social development are served by reasoned but fallible human investigation into both fact and value, not by slavish obedience to permanent stipulations deduced from someone's attempt to formulate ultimate facts and first principles. Soft justificationists worry that hard justification will all too easily slip into uncritical dogmatism and freeze into moral paralysis.[6] The argument that follows will rest upon soft justifications.

Meta-Criteria — How to Judge a Value Logic

Valuation, the process of formulating and critiquing value criteria, must be approached at two levels: (1) the meta-normative level where one poses and examines criteria for evaluating substantive developmental value criteria, and (2) the level of specific value criteria that meet, at least to some degree, the meta-level tests. Appendix I discusses the question of meta-level normative analysis in greater depth, but now the meta-level question can be posed: How should value logics be judged?[7] They should be judged according to their capacity to fulfill at least six tests:

1. Value criteria and the logics that tie them together must be clear. Clarity refers to the capacity of a verbal or written expression to indicate precisely its meaning and to note those observations to which it would and would not apply independently of the speaker, listener, or subsequent qualification. The opposite of clarity is dependence on context.

2. Value criteria must be hierarchically ranked. Multiple criteria must be ordered in priority so that conflicts among them can be resolved in the same direction by analysts working independently, who will know how each criterion is to be ranked relative to all other criteria.

3. Value criteria must be operationally measurable. One must be able to tell when each criterion has been fulfilled. Measures of fulfillment must be capable of independent replication. Value criteria must be logically justified in terms of some empirically knowable, methodologically replicable conception of human welfare rooted in the experience of actual human beings, not God's will, historical necessity, or perception of ancestral wish.

4. Value criteria must deal with the problem of forced choice. Not to decide is, in fact, a policy choice in favor of the status quo situation and its attendant pattern of benefit and misery. To choose to do nothing, therefore, is to choose the existing policy situation, and that choice has immediate consequences in the form of benefit and harm just as do other options. To hold that one will do nothing unless an alternative to the status quo reaches some given standard of goodness not also applied to the status quo situation is to give privileged position to the existing state of affairs. The status quo policy should not have a privileged position in the valuative system for any a priori and unexamined reason.

5. The valuative system must acknowledge the omnipresence of risk and uncertainty. One cannot say with certainty that a given policy option will actually fulfill the value standards when implemented. Very seldom in complex dynamic social and ecological situations can consequences of policy choice be established in advance with certainty. Formulation of value criteria must assume the presence of risk and uncertainty in policy implementation.

6. Value criteria must acknowledge the relevance of time. One must think of policy outcomes as temporal sequences of events; analysts performing a policy assessment must be able to see trade-offs between short- and long-run effects. Policies have both proximate and distant consequences, and a valuative system that focuses on only one or the other would be seriously deficient. In a risky and uncertain world, the policy-assessment logics must be capable of iteration. One might make a five-, seven-, or ten-year estimate, but it will be necessary to frequently remake corrected estimates.

The more a value logic fulfills these six meta-criteria, the more value judgments ensuing from it will earn trust, leading to the conclusion that all valuations are not equal. The norms of science are invoked to ensure that rational dialogue controls and critiques valuation. (See Appendix I.) The norms of scientific dialogue are not universal in the sense that everyone does employ them, but they are universal in the sense that any individual representing any given culture can employ them.

How should one judge a value judgment? One does so, not on the basis of subjective preference, but on the basis of systematic application of the six meta-criteria applied through mutual dialogue governed by norms that have emerged to sustain scientific communication. Therefore, one judges a value judgment in a manner analogous to the manner in which one judges a fact. There are sciences of empirical fact and there are logics of value. The two must never be confused as being the same — strictly scientific investigation of the "is" can never logically yield a policy "ought" — but both activities are open to reason. Inquiry in both domains, and the harnessing of logics of fact and value to the social development project, are essential to defensible policy assessment. Men and women, as inquirers, are toolmakers for constructing logics of both "is" and "ought" in specific problem areas. The search for improved factual and valuational logics is a search for empirical relationships and value criteria that are ever more discriminating and justifiable.

Clarifying the Level of Analysis

One must begin by distinguishing between individual preferences that typically may be subjective and not open to reasoned analysis and value judgments relevant to community concerns that are open to rational discussion and investigation. Assertions about private preference, assuming they are independent (that is, Mutt's choice of vanilla does not interfere with Jeff's selection of chocolate), require no public justification. However, natural resources and technology policy intended to advance social development of a collectivity has to do, not with personal taste, but with consequences of action upon members of the community taken as a structural whole. One cannot defensibly assert that one simply "prefers" war, racism, genocide, or denial of occupational opportunity to a minority group. Individual preference and social development values are not interchangeable concepts.

At the individual welfare level, it is impossible to determine whether there is necessarily more aggregate individual welfare to be obtained from a given amount of timber cut for housing construction or a given amount of timbered acreage to be placed under the protection of wilderness designation. This is the lesson of Arrow's Impossibility Theorem, the failed calculus of utilitarianism, and the neglected messages of externality and public-goods problems.[8] One cannot aggregate incommensurable personal preferences into any defensible social development notion. On the other hand, the problem of constructing a value logic does not grind to a halt at the structural level — the level of collective choice patterns.

To think structurally is to think in terms of relationships among components — to perceive stable relationships among such real social units as persons, informal groups, formal organizations, and nation-states. To think structurally about choice is to inquire into the structural array of choices available to real social units in a collectivity.

Conceptions of social values have always presupposed interaction between people and their organizations in patterned social networks. There is little interest in developing collective social values and policy-assessment logics for solitary individuals on desert islands. The major error of subjective value theorists, who deny that values can be open to reasoned analysis, comes about because they fail to adequately apprehend that "good" behavior necessarily involves patterned relationships among subjects and between subjects and their environment. The relation of subject to subject and subject to environment is not a subjective phenomenon about which no logic of value can be constructed.[9] The argument so far, then, is that one must distinguish between individual preference and personal welfare, on the one hand, and social structural contexts of choice within which private parties choose, on the other hand.

Role expectations and sets of role expectations, organizations and sets of organizations, combined into patterned networks compose the structural subject matter of sociology. The discipline was never intended to be aggregated psychology but has always asked how individual behavior is constrained and guided by patterns of prevailing social relations. Social structures have always been viewed as consisting of emergent and stable patterns of social life not reducible to properties of individuals — for example, polarized conflict patterns, divisions of labor, social distances between status positions among classes and castes, group cohesion and fragmentation, equality and inequality of power, prestige, income, and wealth.

At the micro level, social structure is composed of the stable exchange of resources within small networks of individuals. At the meso level, social structure consists of patterned exchange of resources within and among organizations, and at the macro level it is the repeated exchange of resources among sets of organizations composing regions and provinces within nations and among nations themselves.

What is exchanged? Exchange centers on money (or material rewards), information, and power taken as capacity to threaten sanctions so as to elicit compliance. Some theorists see structures produced as a consequence of individually rational self-seeking behavior as people seek exchanges where the most profitable payoffs are to be found. Others emphasize the importance of collective political power struggles as some groups and organizations impose their choices on subordinates. Still others have focused most centrally upon maintenance of traditional cultural meaning systems as the key force in structuration. These are not mutually exclusive theoretical approaches, and much ink has been spilled in advancing them over the years.[10] It is not the purpose of this effort, however, to examine the several traditions of social structural thought; it is only essential to note that sociological valuation for policy assessment must somehow focus upon properties of social structure as distinct from properties of individual people.

Social structures are regularly repeated choice patterns; they are established "contexts of choice" made available by human beings employing technologies in given sectors of human activity (for example, agriculture, industry, recreation and leisure, education, health) upon defined spatial units (for example, villages, neighborhoods, cities, forests, river basins). A context of choice refers to the array of choice opportunities available at a given time and place to at least some members of the several social strata.[11] What is handed down from parent to child, from teacher to student, is not just a legacy of material goods and personal knowledge but structured social forms themselves. In becoming a person today in the occupied territories of the West Bank of the Jordan River, whether Jew or Arab, one is handed a structural legacy, a pattern or form of social interaction within which individuals will come to know themselves and society. Sociology, especially a policy-assessing sociology, is potentially liberating because it promises to examine, assess, and enable consideration of alternative proposed policies as they affect, and are affected by, encompassing social structures without falling into methodological individualism or sociocultural determinism.

Social development is a property of social structures and of the underlying technologies and natural resource uses that enable the preferred forms of structuration. There is no implication that individual actors can or should exercise all possible opportunities in the name of individual private welfare. No particular individual or organization can or should pursue all structurally available choice opportunities any more than an individual should eat everything on a luncheon smorgasbord. Context of choice is a structural concept and does not speak to issues of individual preference or welfare.

A LOGIC OF FACT AND VALUE FOR POLICY ASSESSMENT

In sum, then, it has been concluded that the policy-assessment logics to be presented here will not rest on "hard justifications" of fixed conceptions of ultimate value, that they will be set forth with a desire to fulfill six meta-value criteria to the greatest possible extent, and that they will be suited to application to units of social structure nested on geographic units of land and water. The discussion now turns to an overview of the policy-assessment logic of fact and value. Detailed consideration of its elements will be provided in the three following chapters.

Structural Description of Choice Context:
Identifying What Exists

In a given unit and sector of analysis, there will be a set of existing choice opportunities. The character of the choice context will vary from unit to unit, time to time, and sector to sector. Contexts of choice are to be mapped for given social-geographical units such as cities, neighborhoods, counties, forests, river basins, districts, provinces. Furthermore, the focus is on specific impacted technological sectors of activity within such units — for example, agriculture, recreation, mineral extraction and processing, transportation. The specific boundaries to be employed are left to the discretion of the analysts and the citizens with whom they work. There are no universal rules for defining such boundaries in any ultimate fashion except that they must reflect as accurately as possible choice opportunities presently afforded that will be importantly affected by the proposed policy options to be assessed. The adequacy of any chosen set of boundaries is, itself, the subject of discussion and review.

Valuational Analysis of Choice Context:
Identifying What Ought

Original specification of proposed policy options to be brought to assessment is an activity exogenous to assessment per se. However, the assessment of proposed options can be expected to result in reformulation of policy proposals. Given an original set of proposed policies for a unit and sector of analysis, the assessment process generates revised policy options.

Policy options might revolve around extension of wilderness recreation versus increasing intensive timber management practices designed to enhance commercial logging. Or they might center around provision of increased highway linkages for intracity commuting versus establishment of specific traffic lanes for buses on arterial highways during rush hours. Policy proposals for a Third World village community might well reflect optional regimes for delivery and control of irrigation water and alternative cropping patterns.

The normative question is: Which proposed policy option, each with its mix of advantage and disadvantage, will alter existing structural contexts of choice so as to better fulfill the value logic and thereby be recognized as more socially developmental? An overview of the value logic designed to address this question is provided by Figure 5.1. The reasoning is straightforward. On the left side is a qualifying item followed by five value criteria, each of which reflects a strategic value-laden empirically measurable variable. As the meaning of each value criterion is fulfilled by the proposed policy option, it is advanced to the next criterion. If, however, a policy proposal fails a test, the analyst proceeds to the right side of the figure and returns the proposal for reformulation or rejection. Means to modify a failed proposal may become apparent; if so, one again advances the revised policy option through the assessment hierarchy.

It should be clear that this analysis cannot reveal precisely which proposed policy alternative or combination of alternatives will maximize social development, but it can identify those proposals that importantly violate the logic of value. Policy options are to be ranked from most to least desirable, and the least inferior can be identified, though there can be no guarantee that a superior proposal could not be devised and brought to assessment. Searching for superior policy options must never cease.

The value logic summarized by Figure 5.1 possesses a lexicographic construction in important ways. Strictly speaking, a lexicographic ordering requires that the first criterion be fulfilled, or be declared nonoperative, before the second is employed. This logic is then applied as one proceeds down the list.[12] Without fulfilling the higher, the lower lose their interest and value. Failure to fulfill lexically prior principles cannot be compensated by overfulfillment of subordinate criteria. First, there is no yardstick that allows some number of units on one criterion to be defensibly translated into units on another. Secondly, deficiencies with respect to one criterion are not to be compensated by superiority in another; trade-offs are not operative. Just as cardiovascular superiority does not make up for failing kidneys, so added strengths in one facet of the policy-assessment hierarchy cannot cancel weakness in another. Each higher item in the series possesses its status because its fulfillment is an essential precondition to the enjoyment of following values. In this sense, the value logic is truly lexicographic. However, three qualifications are in order:

1. The highest-ranked value criterion, while deserving of its position, is not sufficient to define developmental policy. This stipulation

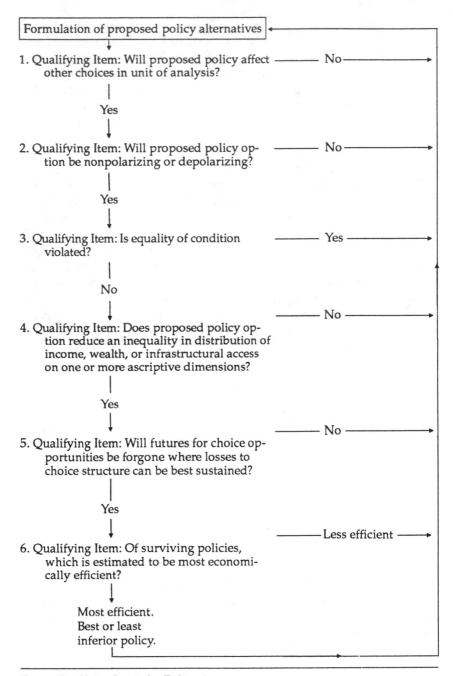

Figure 5.1. Value Logic for Policy Assessment

holds for each subsequent criterion. This is to say that the developmental value analysis will not be terminated as soon as a tie is broken between proposals X and Y by virtue of the fact that X passes a higher-order criterion while Y fails. Alternatively, a "best" or "least inferior" proposal for social development must minimally fulfill all tests. One is not at liberty, therefore, to declare proposal X to be a developmental policy by virtue of the fact that it passes the first test in an instance in which no other proposal does so. At that point one can only conclude that no policy fulfilling the requirements of social development has been formulated, although policy X has a better start than the alternatives.

2. The first three criteria in Figure 5.1 each advance minimum conditions to be fulfilled. Failure of policy proposals to attain minimum values results in return for reconstruction or rejection. However, the fourth normative test — futures for choice opportunities forgone — generates a ranking from among the survivors of the prior value analyses. Policy proposals that are tied or are trivially separated by their respective futures forgone scores are then ranked according to the criterion of economic efficiency. The "best" or "least inferior" proposal for expanding the context of choice is that survivor of higher-order value tests that is estimated to be the most economically efficient.

3. If two or more proposed policy options survive all tests in at least minimal fashion, the assessment loops back through the value framework for more careful scrutiny until either the deadlock is broken or the analyst concludes that the surviving policies are each roughly equivalent in developmental potential, even though they will, in all probability, impose different profiles of hardship.

In sum, by way of an overview of the assessment logic portrayed in Figure 5.1, a specific proposed policy is most socially developmental that

- is most depolarizing of social conflict;
- does not compromise equality of condition;
- narrows an inequality in income, wealth, or access to infrastructure on any one of the ascriptive dimensions — age, ethnicity, and gender;
- imposes a profile of forgone choice opportunities that can be most afforded;
- efficiently accelerates per capita real income.

This policy-assessment logic values the economically efficient production of income and wealth and finds merit in coordinating complexities of that production via marketplace exchange. However, increased economic growth via the most efficient possible marketplace production and consumption is to occur within a structural context in which authorities of the public household ensure that higher developmental values are fulfilled.

The method of economic choice, which has come to dominate so much of modern policy assessment, has traditionally run counter to any system of lexicographic priority. In economic theory budgets are allocated among choices at the margin; objects of expenditure are equally important because one spends on bread, heating oil, and medicine in such a way as to maximize personal utility. This undisciplined economic logic — while serving structurally blind aggregate growth — must be subordinate to higher values. Value principles establishing the shape of larger society set parameters within which market efficiency works to satisfy demands. To put the matter plainly, developmental change does have to do with becoming richer in an economic sense, but a society must become more wealthy while serving higher-order values that shape the manner in which income and wealth is employed. The discussion turns now to a consideration of each element of the general policy assessment logic as shown in Figure 5.1.

Determination of the Need for Assessment

Do policy alternatives under consideration have implications for affecting structures of choice opportunities in a nontrivial manner? Earlier this chapter addressed the distinction between private preference, individual welfare, and public choice. One is reminded that those private behaviors that are not socially significant because they do not generate negative consequences for others in the social web do not require public justification. Policy assessment is brought into play when problems arise associated with technological externalities, purchase and maintenance of public goods, the tyranny of small decisions, concentrations of market power, and structural distributions of assets. Policy proposals that do not involve such matters are essentially private proposals and are not to be a focus of public household assessment.

The Value Logic and Conflict Polarization

A specter is haunting this planet — less that of gaunt revolutionary workers heroically mobilized against capitalists on polarized horizontal class cleavages as envisioned by Marx and Engels and more that of people caught in destructive conflict organized around a variety of ethnic, linguistic, religious, territorial, economic, and ideological divisions.

Moses of the biblical account, caught up in the pattern of conflict polarization between Hebrews and their Egyptian hosts, one day slew an Egyptian who was beating a Jewish worker (Exod. 2:11–12). For Moses, the significance of his murderous aggression was to strike a blow against the degradation imposed by Egyptians who viewed Hebrew people, across polarized relationships, as lesser beings. The point is that good people will commit the most destructive of actions when in high threat situations occasioned by conflict polarization.

In our own century, World War I, fought with exceptional brutality, ignited around polarized cleavages in Serbia and Austria-Hungary that to the rest of the horrified world appeared to be almost laughably trivial. Yet millions of intelligent men and women walked open eyed into that hell, an experience repeated by those caught up in the global polarizations of World War II and the more recent intranational polarizations of the Korean Peninsula, Vietnam, Afghanistan, El Salvador, Northern Ireland, the Indian subcontinent, South Africa, Sudan, Ethiopia, Sri Lanka, and the Middle East. Seeing the U.S.S.R. turning toward its own long internally suppressed ethnic cleavages, and anticipating the loss of virtually automatic support of the Soviet Union for militant Arab states against Israel and the United States, Saddam Hussein grabbed for oil and regional leadership by invading Kuwait on August 2, 1990. By so doing, he galvanized long-standing cleavages polarized around matters of ethnicity, religion, and control of wealth. The United Nations' coalition waged a short war against Saddam Hussein's Iraq to keep Kuwaiti oil from his grasp, but at a cost of untold thousands of lost lives and vast environmental destruction to land, sea, and sky. Prior to that episode Iraqi and Iranian soldiers, some hardly reaching puberty, had laid down their lives by the hundreds of thousands over historical polarizations barely comprehensible to onlookers. Sikhs of northwest India, having been attacked in their temple, have launched deadly revenge upon Hindus; in Sri Lanka, Tamil and Sinhalese terrorists have gunned and bombed innocents in response to what they each see as the degradation and violence imposed upon them by the other. In the Sudan and Ethiopia thousands have starved to death in refugee camps because available foods could not be delivered across polarized conflict fronts.

Polarization exists in the United States just as in other countries. During the summer of 1963, serious violence broke out across polarized ethnic, territorial, and economic cleavages in several U.S. cities — especially Birmingham, Savannah, Chicago, and Philadelphia. White racists shot and bombed black people, and blacks retaliated by looting and burning white-owned businesses in black neighborhoods. During subsequent summers violence continued until, during the summer of 1967, almost 150 U.S. cities were ripped by violence and thousands of people dehumanized and brutalized. The conditions of divided urban America have not been removed, and leadership groups of many communities continue to be paralyzed by the polarization.

In sparsely populated areas of the western United States, far from the deterioration of U.S. cities, ranchers have polarized between those who saw personal welfare in the sale of their mineral rights to mining companies and their neighbors who possessed no rights but who would be left to deal with the negative externalities of mining. Elsewhere, citizens of rural communities have polarized over the impacts of ski development — some profiting handsomely, others left to be driven off their land by inflated prices, higher taxes, and lack of marketable resources in the new order. In polarization situations — whether urban/rural, white/black, black/black or white/white, legitimacy broke, civil discourse terminated, and developmental values were pitched aside.

The list of matters about which human beings have polarized is discouragingly extensive. But destructive polarized conflict is not inevitable. Lines of division between people may run on nonpolarized crosscutting patterns, making negotiation possible, civic life healthy, and economic life productive.

Conflict cleavages may be viewed as running along a continuum from polarized to crosscutting (see Fig. 5.2). Highly polarized conflict cleavage patterns exist when the same opponent groups confront each other over differences on all value fronts. Adversaries on one issue are opponents on all. There is no common ground to facilitate compromise, no incentive to negotiate. Crosscutting conflict exists when groups, although opposed across some cleavages, are allied on others — a condition that makes for nonpolarization. Highly polarized conflict threatens choice context because opposing groups on issue after issue threaten each other and mutually feel that they have little option but to undercut each other's choices. Social development at the structural level is served when crosscutting cleavages can be established across which opposing groups can negotiate their noncommensurable and conflicting preferences or private conceptions of welfare. Non-

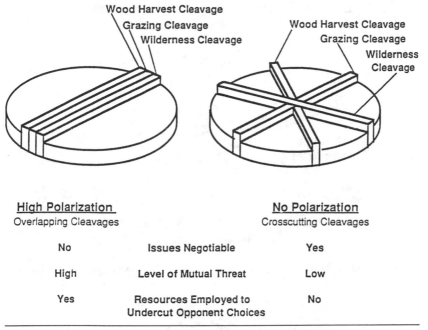

High Polarization		No Polarization
Overlapping Cleavages		Crosscutting Cleavages
No	Issues Negotiable	Yes
High	Level of Mutual Threat	Low
Yes	Resources Employed to Undercut Opponent Choices	No

Figure 5.2 Meaning of Conflict Polarization

polarizing conflict patterns stand at the root of civic society by allowing civic exchange, compromise, trade-offs among opponents, and the exercise of instrumental (means-regarding) and practical (ends-regarding) rationality for developmental purposes.

The policy-assessment task is to estimate which proposed policy alternatives from among the set of options would, if implemented, generate the most nonpolarizing pattern of conflict cleavages. The more a given proposed option is estimated to increase conflict polarization, the more destructive it will be to the capacity to afford a developing context of choice — a point that Chapter 6 will discuss in detail. Three analytical operations must be completed in order to estimate social conflict patterns associated with proposed policy options:

1. Existing conflict cleavage patterns must be mapped in the relevant policy planning unit. The task is to determine who is in conflict with whom over what salient cleavages. A sociological logic of fact must be constructed to ferret out existing cleavage lines. Such cleavage divisions will be referred to as "base cleavages" (see lower portion of Fig. 5.3).

Determine Which Groups Support or Oppose
Policy Alternative X

Policy Alternative X Cleavage

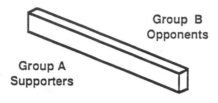

Group B
Opponents

Group A
Supporters

Superimpose Policy X Cleavage
on Base Cleavages

Transmountain Highway Cleavage

Electricity Generating
Plant Cleavage

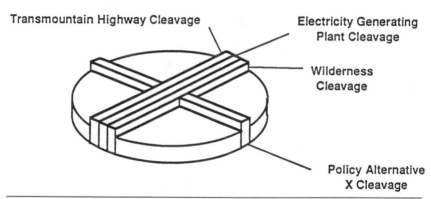

Wilderness
Cleavage

Policy Alternative
X Cleavage

Figure 5.3. Measuring Conflict Polarization

2. Each proposed policy alternative must be inspected for the pattern of support and opposition that it can be expected to arouse. Data will reveal which people engaged in specific activities will support, oppose, or be neutral about the proposed policy. This is also a challenge for an empirical sociological logic of fact (see upper portion of Figure 5.3).

3. A sociological logic of value must then join with the logic of fact to rank proposed policy options according to the estimated amount that each will reduce or increase conflict polarization. In essence, the analytical procedures superimpose conflict cleavages associated with each proposed policy on the base conflict cleavage structure to reveal

the extent to which policy-induced cleavages are, or are not, polarizing. The logic of value selects those policies that most decrease conflict polarization. Those proposed policies that pass this value test are then advanced to the next criterion.

It becomes, therefore, a legitimate criticism of a proposed policy to determine that its induced conflict pattern, when examined in the light of existing base cleavages, would increase conflict polarization and thereby reduce the capacity of impacted parties to keep issues negotiable. When polarization increases mutual threat levels, antagonists have little choice but to employ their resources to reduce each other's choices and those of innocent bystanders. No matter how economically efficient, no matter how technically feasible, no matter the redistributive consequences, a policy that fails the conflict polarization test will be sent back for reformulation or rejection.

Nonpolarized conflict is an essential precondition of the enjoyment of the lower value criteria — it lays the foundation for civil dialogue and the use of reason in policy assessment. Expanded ranges of choice, accelerated rates of choice, and increased standards of choice that are highly polarizing are not socially developmental. The theory, rationale, and methodological procedures of conflict polarization analysis is the topic of Chapter 6.

The Value Logic and Distribution

One cannot simply ask: Will policy X be "better" or "worse"; the distributional question must be asked: "better" or "worse" for whom? Abandonment of the ancient idea that some people by nature are privileged and that others by nature are destined to be subordinate with lesser capacity for enjoyment of choices represented a great step forward. It has become a hallmark of the modern age. Modern societies took much of their distinctive shape when it became accepted that every law-abiding citizen has equal right to unfold personal potential and that it is for agents of the public household to create the preconditions for exercise of this right. Yet a specter haunts this planet — the specter of billions of people in nations, rich and poor, deprived of meaningful civil rights and of the minimum material resources essential to lives of dignity and civic participation.

Equality has many meanings, and an unpacking of this troublesome concept must await Chapter 7. A good utilitarian would argue that income should be distributed to maximize satisfaction of all, but as was noted in Chapter 4, it is impossible to make meaningful interpersonal comparisons of utility. It is, therefore, impossible to know whether the satisfaction given up by Mutt's sacrifice of four concerts is really greater than, or less than, the utility gained by Jeff's use of his new bicycle.

Furthermore, people are equal or unequal along different dimensions simultaneously, and different dimensions of equality can be expected to be incompatible. A policy that provides greater access of females to jobs might undercut access to jobs for male members of a minority ethnic group. There is simply no way of adding and subtracting the interpersonal gains and losses as between age categories, ethnic groups, and income, wealth, and educational levels to net out gains or losses associated with alternative policy directions.

Out of the confusion in the literature, however, there has emerged a basic set of distinctions essential to clear thinking. First, equality of condition can be specified to mean equality of public liberties, equality before the law, equality of movement in public places, one person–one vote, equality of civil rights of citizenship. Second, equality can refer to equality of opportunity — equality of access to the means of developing personal potential. Such means may well include equal opportunity to compete for employment and openings in educational programs, marketplaces, and political arenas. Third, equality of outcome must be distinguished. Equality of outcome ignores relevant differences among parties and focuses on the question: Are outcomes of an activity the same for all parties? Is there equality in distribution of prizes?

If one employs a race track analogy, the three kinds of equality would highlight fundamentally different aspects of the distributional problem. Equality of the first variety — condition — would guarantee all law-abiding citizens an equal right to identify themselves as runners and appear at the track, not to be abridged by considerations of ethnicity, gender, religion, or other matters not relevant to racing. Equality of opportunity would focus on the question of whether all citizens have an equal opportunity to condition themselves for the race within individual constraints — short legs, excess weight, a taste for chocolate bars — and to start from the same point as all other runners. Equality of outcome would focus the question on the allocation of prizes: Did all runners cross the finish line at the same instant and collect the same prize?

Given the essential distinctions between equality of condition, opportunity, and outcome and considering that inequalities of the latter two varieties can simultaneously occur on multiple dimensions, it becomes possible to formulate a set of distributional value criteria. Inequalities of policy outcomes will be acceptable insofar as they meet two criteria.

1. They do not abridge equality of condition. No proposed policy shall violate the fundamental equality of condition of citizens. If a proposed policy should be found to abridge equality of condition, it fails assessment and is returned for reformulation.

2. They reduce inequalities of opportunity by employing inequalities in outcomes to reduce gaps in income, wealth, or access to infrastructure along one or another of three ascriptive dimensions over which individuals can exercise no personal control — ethnicity, age, and gender. Does the proposed policy reduce an inequality of opportunity by reducing a gap in the distribution of any one or more of the three types of resources on any one or more of the three ascriptive dimensions? If the proposed policy cannot be expected to reduce a gap, the proposal shall fail the distributional test and be returned for reformulation.

It is a legitimate criticism of a proposed policy to show that it would widen the gap in equality of opportunity or compromise equality of condition. To enlarge the range of choice, to accelerate rates of choice, or to raise standards of choice by violating these distributional values is to earn a negative assessment. Structural choice contexts must be sustained and expanded by policies that ensure that people possess absolute equality of condition and by increased equalities of opportunities via unequal policy outcomes. Income, wealth, and access to infrastructure are the foci of the distributional analysis because each represents a generalized medium that provides individuals a capacity to prescribe for themselves personal life plans and definitions of individual welfare. The distributional analysis will be presented in Chapter 7.

The Value Logic and Choices Forgone

A specter haunts this planet — the specter of industrial toxic waste discharges, soil erosion, declining air and water quality, ozone depletion, acid rain, atmospheric warming, and carelessly lost diversity in ecological communities of which human societies are but a part. A ravaged environment, unable to sustain human structures of choice such as they are and might be, represents a monumental threat to any viable conception of social development. Given the limits of a dominating economic calculation, many policies are adopted without sufficient attention to important kinds of losses to choice not reflected in economic income accounts.

The concept of cost has always centered on sacrifice — the cost of X equals the value of the combined sacrifices necessary to obtain X. Cost can only be reduced to money forgone if all dimensions of cost have been captured in marketplace exchange. The problem is, of course, that significant costs — sacrifices — are frequently not validly reflected in money accounts; they have not been, and often should not be, entered into market exchange; they have thereby not secured a market value based upon willingness to pay. To exploit an energy gradient available in falling water by building a high dam is to forgo a whole range of activities incompatible with the hydroelectric facilities — for example, fly-fishing, white water rafting, or wilderness experience. To construct the Aswan High Dam, decision-makers had to forgo the freshening and nourishing effects of the annual floodwaters on the agricultural lands of the lower Nile, and they had to accept submergence of ancient monuments in Lake Nasser. To build an industrial plant in a neighborhood may well demolish essential local services and the long-standing social cohesion of the place. To maintain minimum stream flow may well eliminate irrigation water for hard-pressed farmers. Such costs are experienced by people and ecological communities as negative externalities, tyrannies of small decisions, the absence of needed public goods. Since all costs are opportunity costs, and since opportunity costs are inevitable and many significant sacrifices cannot be adequately measured in monetized economic accounts, the question becomes: How can important nonmarket costs associated with alternative proposed policies be assessed? As formulated here, the answer is to advance an analysis of choice opportunities forgone in the social and ecological structure — futures forgone.

A forgone future for a choice opportunity means that implementation of a particular policy will cancel a future for that incompatible activity. The concept of futures forgone consists of three measurable dimensions.

1. *Scope of loss.* A scope value expresses the proportion of any given human activity or ecological community anticipated to be lost in the unit of analysis if the designated policy alternative is implemented (see Fig. 5.4). If a proposed policy permitting construction of a ski area were estimated to reduce winter habitat for an elk herd by half, the

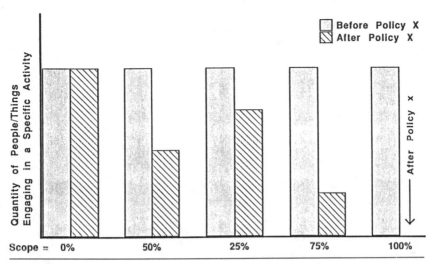

Figure 5.4. Impact of Management Policy Alternative on Scope

scope of loss value for elk would equal 50 percent. If a proposed policy for energy extraction in a given planning area would reduce the availability of high-quality roadless recreation by 16 percent, the scope of loss would be that same value.

2. *Intensity of loss.* Intensity measures the extent to which resources lost in a particular location can be made available in the surrounding primary and secondary planning areas. Intensity values for each choice suffering a given scope of loss increase as an inverse exponential function of the remaining possibilities for sustaining that choice (see Fig. 5.5). If a ski area were to reduce a particular winter elk habitat by a given proportion (scope), and if there are many alternative winter habitats in the relevant planning area, the intensity of loss would be low. If, on the other hand, a policy were to permit human fuelwood gathering to ravage a piece of tiger habitat for which there were few alternative habitats of equal or superior quality, the intensity of loss would be high. Intensity scores do not measure a human psychological attribute — intensity of feeling; they measure the extent to which alternative choice opportunities exist in the relevant surrounding socio-techno-ecological choice structures given a specified scope of loss within a given local environmental and historical situation.

3. *Duration of loss.* What will be the length of time, in years, before the choice structure in the unit of analysis can again sustain each anticipated loss at least to the present standard of quality if the proposed policy alternative inflicting the loss should be terminated, and if

141

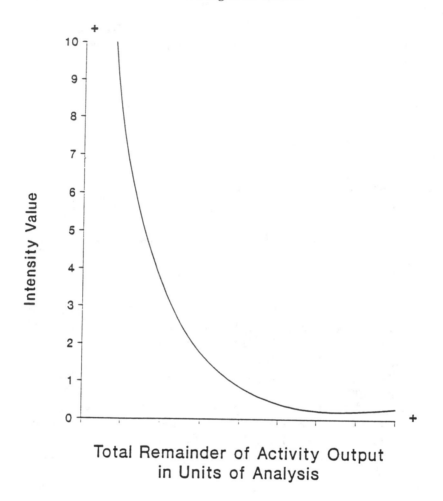

Total Remainder of Activity Output in Units of Analysis

Values increase exponentially as total remainder of activity in the secondary unit of analysis diminishes.

Figure 5.5. Intensity of Loss Curve

the decision-makers should wish to restore the sacrificed choice (see Fig. 5.6)? This question is answered given existing budgetary levels and technological know-how. If a proposed ski area were to reduce a particular winter elk habitat by a certain proportion (scope) and intensity, the duration question asks: How many years would be required to restore that habitat to present condition if decision-makers were to

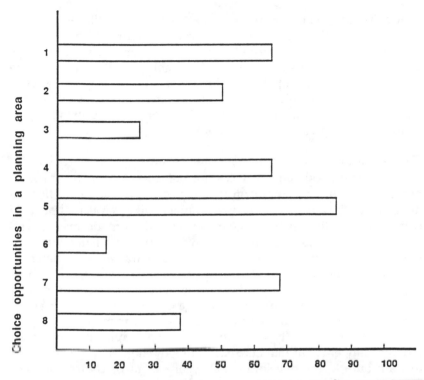

Years required before activity can be restored to present condition given existing technology and budgets.

Figure 5.6. Duration of Loss Associated With Policy X

decide that they wished to restore it given present budgetary resources and technological know-how?

A proposed policy alternative that forgoes futures for choice opportunities with greater scope and greater intensity and for longer duration is one that undercuts the context of choice more than another policy that is estimated to inflict lower futures-forgone values. Intensity is employed in the futures-forgone calculations as the most important weight on scope. Duration, although important, is given less weight than intensity because it is easier to forgo a future for X a long time on that unit if a future for X is abunduntly sustained in other accessible units.

Futures-forgone values reveal which policy proposal will produce a pattern of loss that can be most afforded in the existing context of choice. Those policies are inferior that impose a profile of losses to choice context that are of high intensity and for which a lengthy duration is required to restore lost choices to their present condition. Losses of choice opportunities are inevitable, but it is a legitimate criticism of a proposed policy to show that it would impose losses to choice context where they can be least afforded — that is, where the losses earn highest intensity and duration scores. The futures-forgone analysis will be presented in Chapter 8.

The Value Logic and Acceleration of Income Flows

Economic goods and services are not allocated on the basis of needs, wants, or wishes but on the basis of possession of "effective demand" or "real income." Income embraces all receipts that provide command over the use of scarce resources and, in modernized societies, is most commonly represented by currency and bank assets. In the absence of voluntary or involuntary income transfers, the determinant of "effective demand" that an actor can make on a socioeconomic system is the capacity to produce some good or service sufficiently valued by others, such that an exchange can be made that attracts a flow of resources per unit of time — an income stream.

To accelerate the flow of annual real per capita income in an economically efficient manner that fulfills the higher value criteria is to contribute to the developmental enlargement of choice contexts. People who attract more real income can exercise more choice than people with less. Economically efficient acceleration of real per capita income is, therefore, an important policy-assessment value criterion. Within constraints imposed by higher-order values, scarce resources should be placed in their most productive uses so as to expand the structural context of choice from which people may choose for themselves. The fact that we have no ultimately defensible way to choose from among different domains of endeavor — for example, health, education, irrigation, transport, courts of law, recreation, prison construction, the arts — is the most compelling single argument for policies promoting growth of the overall resource pie. Increased real income sustains the pursuit of noncommensurable choices.

What does efficiency mean in an economic sense? Static efficiency focuses upon allocation within a given resource pie. To say that a piece of furniture costs $435 is to say that $435 worth of other products had to be sacrificed to produce and merchandise it. Prices that accurately reflect the real trade-offs among combinations of factors in production are efficiency prices. Given fulfillment of the assumptions of a properly functioning free marketplace, the proper efficiency price will clear the market — it will neither be so low as to create demand in excess of supply nor so high as to inspire production for which there is no buyer. Uncoerced willingness among buyers and sellers to exchange in a market, moving resources from less to more productive employment, will generate an efficiency price.

Dynamic efficiency, however, focuses upon qualitative improvement of technology that creates new resources and products. Much of the significance of dynamic market efficiency has to do with the fact that it has promoted much technological innovation in the quest for market advantage. We are fundamentally separated from the world of Thomas Jefferson, not just because we more efficiently allocate the bundle of goods and services known to the late eighteenth century but because dynamic efficiencies have provided us with a great range of products undreamed of by Jefferson.

It is a legitimate criticism of proposed policy X, after it has succeeded in fulfilling higher value criteria, to demonstrate that it will sacrifice economic efficiency, in either a static or dynamic sense. Economic efficiency in the service of accelerated private per capita real income is a necessary condition of developmental policy and a tie breaker between policy options that have passed higher-order tests. Efficiency in accelerating private income flows is best regarded as an instrumental value — a tool for assisting people in their quest for private problem solving, but one that must be constrained by higher-order developmental vision.[13]

Increasing per capita income may be a necessary condition for development, but it is not sufficient. It is quite possible that money will be invested by individually rational people in marketplaces in ways that are destructive to developmental expansion of contexts of choice. For example, citizens opted in the marketplace to switch to private automobiles in such numbers as to leave mass transit in a state of high deterioration or even extinction in many U.S. metropolitan areas by the early 1950s. The switch to private automobile transportation exacted a toll largely ignored by private income accounts. Transportation options diminished within and among cities as passenger train service declined in both quantity and quality, as trolleys were banished from the streets, taxis forsaken, buses abandoned, and walkways destroyed under the onslaught of the automobile. The compactness and efficiency of the urban core was destroyed in city after city, to be replaced by the shopping center and the low-density suburb. Friends no longer met on streets, urban air thickened with smog, and highway construction to serve jammed-up cars tore up neighborhoods and their attendant contexts of choice in housing, health care, worship, shopping, education, and recreation. As traffic shifted from high-capacity transit to low-capacity autos, increasing numbers of cars each carried a decreasing number of people. Segments of society without access to autos — children, the old, the sick, the disabled, the poor — became deprived of formerly available transport options. The economically viable "solution" for many healthy middle-class individuals was not efficient from the community standpoint. Private individuals choosing the automobile did not have to count costs imposed on the wider community by a money accounting system that disastrously equated aggregate private welfare with social development.

Quantitative economic growth cannot fully define societal development any more than the rate of blood circulation can define the organism. However, economic growth harnessed to normative social structural principles, as specified in the assessment value logic, is important to a viable conception of social development. Such valuationally informed growth can efficiently expand choice structures in socially developmental directions within which individuals and organizations can prescribe, and pursue, their unique and noncommensurable private welfare and preference mixes.

Placing economic efficiency last in the valuational scheme does not suggest that economic efficiency considerations should be less than foremost when considering means of fulfilling higher-order value criteria. Each of the higher values should be pursued by as economically efficient means as is possible.

RATIONALE

In the history of an individual, the pattern of choices made centrally reflect a person's character. So it is also the case that values guiding construction of choice contexts for the community at large define the character of society. This chapter has asserted a socially developmental logic of fact and value with which to assess public policies in the domain of technology and natural resources. Policies are assessed according to their capacity to fulfill five value criteria that, taken together, reveal those proposed options developmentally "best" or "least inferior." The logics, working in concert, represent a set of "good reasons" for imposing particular profiles of advantage and disadvantage on members of the community.

All of this must be inspected in light of the meta-ethical criteria advanced in the first section, and it must be associated with a conception of the relationship of the individual citizen to the public household. The discussion turns to these two tasks.

The Value Logic and Meta-Ethical Criteria

1. The value logic is clear. It consists of much more than vacuous slogans that could be reshaped as required to support preordained needs of whoever occupies a seat of power in a local culture area. Structural properties, given nomothetic form, can be employed across cultural meaning systems and retain their integrity — their clarity. Each criterion directs the analyst to the range of observations to which it will and will not apply. Each criterion retains its nomothetic meaning as it is employed in, and across, cultural and political contexts. The criteria are not context dependent. "Good reasons" found in the "form" of social relationships are employed to allocate advantage and disadvantage among people expressing conflicting definitions of problems and solutions in a rich variety of cultural idioms. Each local cultural meaning system will uniquely establish specific settings for particular policy choices. But the policy-assessment logic provides a basis for legitimate criticism of policy proposals without respect to their cultural source or content. The value logic avoids tying desirable public ends to any particular culturally substantive pattern.

2. The value logic responds to the problem of hierarchy in ranking. Criteria for policy assessment are linked together in a meaningful manner. Each criterion is placed in its position for a defensible reason that can be inspected for adequacy. It must be acknowledged, however, that the ranking serves to guide the sequence of assessment discourse; a policy cannot be judged developmental unless it has at least minimally fulfilled all criteria. Trade-offs among criteria are not operative. An excess of virtue on one will not compensate for a deficiency on another.

3. The value logic consists of criteria that are each operationally measurable. Empirical research can establish the extent to which proposed policies for guidance of technological application have fulfilled, or are estimated to fulfill, each criterion. The logic is accountable to empirical outcomes knowable by real people, not unverifiable expectations of the spirits — past, present, or future. The context of choice

concept, and the value criteria, are obviously abstractions, but the analysis of choices created and crushed by policy options is something to which human beings relate in an immediate and empirically knowable sense.

4. The value logic can deal with the problem of forced choice. To continue with the status quo is a policy with a pattern of attendant benefit and misery. Existing policies are not to have a privileged position but are to be held up for inspection along with other alternatives. Existing policies will or will not be polarizing; will or will not compromise equality of condition or reduce inequalities of income, wealth, or access to education; will or will not forgo futures for choice opportunities with high intensity and extended duration; and will or will not promise economic efficiency in accelerating income flows. All of this is to be compared to the estimated effects of alternatives to the status quo policy.

5. The value logic acknowledges the omnipresence of risk and uncertainty. There is no supposition that risk and uncertainty are obliterated, that strict application of the criteria will eliminate chance of policy error. Error in empirical research employed to establish relative fulfillment of the value criteria by proposed options, confoundedness in the implementation of policies chosen, and failure to calculate real costs due to incompleteness of logic and theory force the analyst to acknowledge that risk and uncertainty always accompany any analysis of fact and value. The analyst copes by making the best estimates today with available information and then continuously reanalyzes options informed by new data as policy implementation proceeds.

6. The value logic acknowledges the relevance of time. The analyst assessing proposed policy options can see trade-offs between short- and long-term effects of conflict polarization, equality, lost futures, and prospects for increased income. The analysis of fact and value proposed here is expected to be iterated and reiterated. There is nothing in the assessment logic that focuses attention on short- or longer-term effects to the exclusion of the other.

The Value Logic and the Citizen

Nobody can compel me to be happy in his own way. — Immanuel Kant[14]

"Freedom" is too often used rhetorically to mean "we do as we please." The value logic advanced here, however, sees freedom located in the selectively necessary infringement of individual pursuit of private advantage when that private action would bring harm to the community. When agents of the public household learned to infringe upon the individual's capacity to mug travelers and rob banks, people in society became more free, not less so.

A major ground for distinguishing between public development logics and private morality is the greater requirement of explicitness of reasoning in public affairs. Private action, not affecting others, can be left to private reasoning. One can do what one likes behind the wall of privacy subject only to the justification of one's private morality. But when one's action adversely affects others, the public agent must choose among alternative courses of policy action for "good reasons" for which explicit accounting is due. The "good reasons" advanced in this chapter are those that are to guide the alterations of choice contexts from which individual citizens can choose for themselves. The "good reasons" allocate benefit and harm to individuals according to a coherent conception of commonly apprehended interest in social development. Those who view the development project may do so from a variety of personal and cultural perspectives. Muslims, Jews, Christians, Hindus, and Buddhists can commonly concern themselves with keeping salient conflict cleavages depolarized; keeping intact equality of condition; supporting reductions of inequalities in income, wealth, and infrastructure; forgoing futures for choice opportunities where they can be most afforded; and within the constraints imposed by the above, efficiently employing resources to accelerate income flows via marketplace exchange.

The attempt to aggregate individual pleasures and pains into some definition of social welfare or progress must end in failure — a central point of Chapters 3 and 4. Not all pleasures for individuals are socially good; not all individual pains are necessarily socially bad. Just as one cannot expect to make good frankfurters with bad meat, one cannot expect to construct adequate value logics for guiding technological potentials in society out of the grist of individual preferences or welfare definitions. To shift analysis away from the probing of individual preferences and meaning systems is not to deny dignity and worth of the individual citizen. To the contrary, to fulfill the five value criteria in the service of developmental expansion of choice contexts allows each citizen to act in accordance with personal values and to actualize individual potential without social policy analysts meddling where they do not belong — namely, in private lives.

One value that scientists, philosophers, and artists hold most dearly is freedom of inquiry and creation of meaning — the ability to choose problems for oneself and to raise possible solutions independently of superior prescribing authority. This kind of freedom should be as open as much as possible to all unless scientists, philosophers, and artists possess some peculiar attribute that fits them exclusively for such freedom. It is not the business of the policymaker or the social scientist to prescribe to people how they should privately live. It is the essence of liberty and human dignity that individuals should remain free to prescribe for themselves. Yet people in the possession of powerful technologies cannot be free to bring ruin to their neighbors and to coming generations. Therefore, individual pursuit of personal welfare must be bounded by requirements of the public household. Imposition of limits on private action is legitimate insofar as those limits can be justified in terms of creating more developed choice contexts.

This developmental logic of fact and value for policy assessment finds nourishment in the thinking of several philosophers of human freedom. Two, in particular, deserve explicit acknowledgment — Karl Popper and Isaiah Berlin. Karl Popper's message has been clear: Ultimately we cannot know.[15] We can only make tentative best guesses. Ultimate truth always escapes us. None of the theses of science can finally be proven right. It is, therefore, important to continue to see if accepted theories are wrong and to inquire as how to make them better fit the best data and experience we can bring to them. In order to continually question, people must maintain the conditions of rational discourse in which it is possible to disagree. The importance of disagreement is not limited to the sciences of fact but also extends into the realm of values. Careful critical discourse and civil disagreement is fundamental to the proper guidance of technology. The fundamental uncertainty of the human condition, the acknowledgment that we do not, and cannot, ultimately know what is best for us, makes it important to continually explore alternative possibilities. The need for an "open society" arises out of this bedrock uncertainty, and that society requires that dogmatization of error be prevented. Whosoever adopts this position has committed himself or herself to continual controlled testing of factual statements and experimentation with values — activities predicated upon the existence of "open" societies where incompatible views can be forthrightly expressed, where all are free to propose solutions or to criticize proposals of others, where it is safe to be unpopular, and where policymakers are responsive to fact and logic. It is in this Popperian spirit that the policy-assessment value logic is forwarded.

Isaiah Berlin also provides an undergirding rationale.[16] Says Berlin, there is no one overriding goal for people in society. We live for a variety of conflicting purposes, yet we must structure a society such that individuals are protected in their choices. If all could agree on the highest good, there would be no conflict over whether we should be free to pursue our private ends; our ends would be the same and only the incompetent or mentally deranged would pursue perverse ends. The very plurality and perpetual antagonism of individual ends, however, prevents them from enjoying consensus and even from being ranked in any meaningful order. There can be no one best set of private goals, but since freedom for the wolves can mean death to the sheep, society must require that we privately live in such a way as not to deny to others the possibility of making their own choices about life.

Berlin argues for a conception of "negative" liberty as a base value.[17] Human dignity is seen to be rooted in the absence of others' prescribing or choosing one's goals for oneself. People must have a secure base in negative liberty that guarantees that their actions are truly their own. Liberty for the sake of being or doing something prescribed by others is not liberty. Without negative liberty — the freedom to choose one's own private ends — other values are rendered meaningless. To speak of freeing people to pursue our ends is a mockery of freedom. Human beings can only be freed to pursue their own ends. In Berlin's words: "I wish to determine myself, and not be directed by others, no matter how wise or benevolent; my conduct derives an irreplaceable value from the sole reason that it is my own, and not imposed upon me."[18]

To deny human beings the choice of their own life plans is a violation of their personhood. For Berlin there is no ultimately knowable system to the cosmos, no predetermined plan for human development that justifies one person's determination of a life plan for another. Only each individual's creative capacity can provide meaning for that being. Individual meanings should not be programmed by the powerful as a matter of public policy. Roots of oppression are to be found in those theories that would rank private ends, determine the superior, and then assert the obligation to show the unenlightened the way to "progress" against the latter's own will — behavior that reduces people to objects to be manipulated in the light of higher truths comprehended by the more enlightened or powerful. To manipulate people, to propel them toward goals that social engineers see, but which the impacted people may not view, is to treat them as lessers without wills of their own. This is the essence of human degradation, and the crafts of this manipulation have become highly refined in our time.

Berlin emphasizes freedom from external constraint, a negative conception that views freedom as a function of the degree to which actors carve out areas within which they can do as they please without interference. Others have emphasized a positive conception of freedom; they see freedom as the capacity to do what one chooses. Here freedom denotes that human beings are free, not from something negative (for example, coercion) but for something positive (for example, autonomy, creativity, self-development). Joel Feinberg, after examining the debates between proponents of the two seemingly opposed views of freedom, concluded that there can be no special positive freedom "to" that is not also a freedom "from."[19] Positive and negative freedom are two sides of the same coin. The value logic employed here accepts this integration of the two views. To reduce polarization, for example, is to simultaneously remove the constraint upon behavior produced by high levels of mutual threat and to create the capacity to invest resources in nondestructive activities. The value logic advanced here does not associate only with advocates of one view of freedom or another.

CONCLUSION

Radical thinking is not necessarily the advocacy of extreme action; it is that which goes to the root of the problem. The root of the policy-assessment problem, of course, is that current value criteria employed to guide technologies by agents of the public household are grossly insufficient. Furthermore, many late-twentieth-century social scientists have so removed themselves from the valuational problem that the task of policy assessment is only dimly seen. There is a glaring discrepancy between the urgent need for value logics to harness and steer technological prowess and the contemporary inability to provide, or even discuss, defensible logics of good reasons for public policy choice in the service of a coherent conception of social development.

The essence of the argument is that it is possible to create a cross-cultural policy-assessment language for sociology. The neglected message of externality, public goods, the tyranny of small decisions, concentrated market power, and problems of distribution is the primacy of social structures — patterned relationships within which individuals must make their private lives. I seek a set of concepts that focus analysis on patterned social relationships emergent out of interaction among individuals, organizations, and their environments. How is valuation for policy assessment possible? To this philosophical (Kantian) question, I have constructed a structural sociological (Simmelian) answer. Each of the three chapters that follow takes up a specific sociological component of the value logic to provide it policy-assessment status by attending to particulars of theory and method.

VI

Policy Assessment for Development: A Science of Fact and a Logic of Value in the Domain of Social Conflict

> A wasp settled on the head of a snake and stung it repeatedly. The reptile, in great anger and unable to retaliate at its tormentor, placed its head under the wheel of a wagon. The two died together. — Fable by Aesop

Social conflict exists when actors engage in incompatible activities and thereby consciously interfere with each other.[1] Lewis Coser, following the intellectual lead of Georg Simmel, demonstrated that conflict is an inevitable component of social structure, that the very form of society is defined by the nature of conflict sanctioned.[2] Antagonism creates structure; it provides people with roles, organizations, identities, and purposes. Specific issues may be settled so as not to reappear, but complete elimination of conflict is not seen as being possible or even necessarily desirable.[3] The question is not how to eliminate conflict; rather, it is how to distinguish between its productive and destructive forms. The policy-assessment problem then becomes one of determining how to promote the former and retard the latter in the name of developmentally expanding contexts of choice.

Multitudes of disputes have been recorded in which participants opposed one another so intensely that physical violence and risk of death became preferable to compromise or acceptance of defeat. The pages of economic history are littered with industrial conflicts in which workers accepted job loss and owners chose bankruptcy rather than meet each other's demands. Political and religious conflicts are all too easily recalled in which one or more opponents have risked extinction for themselves and their progeny. Conflicts in the small community are known wherein one faction has been prepared to forgo its own welfare to ensure damage to rivals. The specter of violent warlike aggression in the larger community has cast its shadow across the social landscape from earliest recorded time.

Conflict, however, has also been closely associated with progress, innovation, and advancement of human welfare. It has been viewed as central to formation of group identity, sustained social cohesion, rapid innovation, and expansion of opportunity. Any number of thinkers have placed positive value on certain varieties of conflict because they strengthen the social web and are viewed as intrinsic to advancement of social justice.[4] Therefore, a three-part question emerges:

1. What kind of conflict is destructive of social development, and what kind is associated with progress?

2. How can one measure the extent to which a given conflict pattern is likely to be constructive or destructive?

3. How can one assess the conflict implications of any given proposed policy to ascertain whether it will tend to generate a conflict condition of greater or lesser destructiveness and thereby gain or lose merit?

It is the purpose of this chapter to address these questions and to illustrate the use of conflict analysis in the assessment of proposed technology and natural resources policy. Concepts and procedures will be illustrated with examples from the United States and Pakistan.

CONFLICT THEORY

Overview

Technological and natural resource policies, programs, and projects are inevitably involved in, and generate, social conflict.[5] Gains and losses are differentially conferred as some groups find their interests advanced while others are penalized. Some values are promoted; others are undercut by virtue of the fact that they are harder to fulfill under the altered circumstances. Conflict between the advantaged and disadvantaged, therefore, becomes a strategic component of policy assessment.

Many students of the subject have employed the concept of conflict cleavage — that is, a patterned division between actors over value differences creating a front of mutual opposition.[6] Because conflict

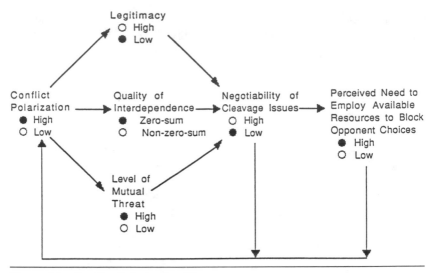

Figure 6.1. Conflict Polarization Theory

cleavages cannot be eliminated from social life, the significant question has to do with their arrangement or structure. There are two ideal-type cleavage patterns, each with distinctly different implications for negotiability of conflict and social development. These two cleavage types and their hypothesized relationships with legitimacy, qualities of mutual interdependence, levels of mutual threat, negotiability of issues, and choice are specified in Figure 6.1.

The polarized cleavage pattern exists when the same opponent groups are repeatedly cleaved apart over all significant lines of division.[7] Adversaries in one conflict are opponents in all. There are no crosscutting attachments, no common grounds upon which to build compromise, no incentive to negotiate. A winner with respect to one cleavage will gain advantage to be employed on all. Legitimacy declines; opponents view their mutual interdependence as being zero-sum in nature — that is, any gain made by one adversary is seen as a loss to the other. Negotiability of the issues is reduced, and mutual threat levels increase. Each opponent group develops internal cohesion based on the need for unity against clearly delineated out-group threats, and each side must employ whatever resources are available to prevent opponents from advancing their incompatible values. Polarized cleavages threaten developmental expansion of choice contexts, and they create conditions hostile to reasoned discussion of either facts or values. When conflicting social groups become highly polarized they feel compelled to block opponents at whatever cost to themselves and to reason in valuation.

Crosscutting cleavage patterns, on the other hand, exist when opponent groups are in opposition over a limited proportion of cleavages but are allied in common cause in other significant conflicts. Actors cleaved apart over one issue find shared attachment in other conflicts. Here lie roots of social cohesion based in mutual legitimacy, positive-sum perceptions of interdependence, negotiability of issues, and low levels of mutual threat among groups who are sometimes opposed and sometimes allied. Total threat of one opponent by another is precluded. Multiple involvements in crosscutting cleavages prevent polarization on any one axis and keep opponents open to ideas, values, and needs of each other. Crosscutting conflict patterns are preferred to polarizing ones in the name of enlarging choice contexts according to the logic of value because opponent groups are not compelled to employ resources to deliberately harm each other and the structure of choice; furthermore, crosscutting conflicts provide a basis for dialogue and openness to reason in matters of both fact and value.

The general hypothesis that polarized conflict cleavages are associated with nonnegotiable, intense, and choice-destroying conflict is one that has been endorsed by many analysts. Review of the relevant literature is a challenge because the notion has been taken up by so many. There can be no pretense of completeness in the literature review that follows, but strategic themes will be organized around the variables displayed in Figure 6.1.

Conflict Polarization

Karl Marx was a theorist of polarization on heroic scale. He argued that "laws" of capitalist political economy ensured that all social groups and strata would be absorbed eventually into two hostile and highly polarized classes — the bourgeois owners of the means of production opposed to proletarian workers, sellers of labor power.[8] Traditional conflicts associated with precapitalist society, organized around matters of religious belief, language and cultural orientation, ethnicity, and nationalist commitments, would be subordinated to an overwhelming horizontal class cleavage. As horizontal class polarization was predicted to become complete in capitalist industrial societies, the increasingly homogeneous proletariat would become class conscious, disciplined, and focused on its class enemy. It would, in time, overthrow the progressively weakened bourgeois as a succession of economic crises depleted the ruling class. Marxian economic "laws" may have been miscast, and polarization along class lines may not inevitably occur in the sense Marx claimed, but even the greatest critics of Marx accept the essential meaning and violent consequences of polarization outlined by Marx.

Ralf Dahrendorf reformulated Marxist conceptions; with Marx, he posited that class conflict of nineteenth-century capitalist societies was due to the overlapping of political and industrial conflict. Opponents in the industrial sector, capital versus labor, met again in the political arena as bourgeois and proletariat.[9] Against Marx, Dahrendorf argued that industrial and political conflicts have been depolarized in modern capitalist societies. Crosscutting cleavages have emerged in place of the former polarized patterns, making for reasonably stable industrial democracies. This analysis may have differed from Marx's in its conclusions about the fate of industrial peoples, but it accepted the connection between polarization, nonnegotiability, and violence.

In his significant work on theory of social structure, Peter M. Blau echoed Marx and Dahrendorf:

> When parameters are highly correlated — for example, when ethnic differences neatly coincide with differences in religion, occupation, and politics — they do not further intergroup relations, as cross-cutting parameters do, but on the contrary inhibit them. . . . The lower the correlations of parameters, the more extensive are the intergroup relations that strengthen macrosocial integration.[10]

Rudolph Rummel built an elaborate social psychological conflict perspective in an ambitious multivolume work that centered on the general hypothesis linking polarization to destructive forms of conflict. He noted that if interests of opponents begin to coalesce into a polarizing pattern, "forming a conflict front that traverses society and divides groups into opposing clusters of homogenous interests, conflict will be intense, violent and possibly revolutionary. . . . This notion is central to my perspective. . . . "[11]

Another line of thinking about conflict polarization can be identified among those who have examined traditional conflict in preindustrial societies based on primordial loyalties of blood ties, race, language, region, religion, and custom. Clifford Geertz, in particular, has shown how such conflicts tend to be overlapping and undercut efforts toward national integration.[12] Max Gluckman found it strategic to employ the study of primordial conflict cleavages as a chief means to comprehend aspects of social life. Using Evans-Prichard's data, Gluckman examined how polarization led to destructive conflict and how crosscutting allegiances were associated with social cohesion among Nuer tribesmen.[13] Other analyses of instability in new nations have emphasized how forces of modernization have frequently superimposed new social and economic divisions on old ascriptively based lines of cleavage.[14] The basic idea has been that high levels of political instability and violence are precipitated by overlapping of primordial antagonisms with new divisions related to industrialization and urbanization. A profound cause of destructive conflict is viewed as being the shared perception of one communal group that the transfers of welfare involved in rapid technological change add to the economic, religious, linguistic, and ethnic subjugation by another primordially defined group. Such overlapping cleavages have been lamented as constituting obstacles to societal development. It is postulated that the world will witness more destructive conflict along ethnic, religious, and racial lines so long as these coincide with socioeconomic divisions.[15] The conflict polarization argument, therefore, has been employed in a rich array of non-Western cultural settings.

In the North American context, James S. Coleman described numerous instances of community polarization in the early 1950s. He noted how polarization led to emergence of extremist leaders who pushed aside older moderate leadership elements who had failed in their efforts to conduct the conflict in a contained and reserved manner.[16] As polarization increased, disputed issues tended to move from the specific and negotiable to the general and nonnegotiable; genteel disagreement gave way to bitter antagonism. Coleman formulated his "Gresham's Law" of conflict — namely, that the harmful and dangerous elements tend to drive out those that would keep the conflict within bounds.[17] In William Gamson's terminology, conflict shifts from "conventional" to "rancorous" as polarization proceeds.[18] Conflict is rancorous when opponents do not simply regard each other as mistaken or as pursuing different but legitimate ends, but feel compelled to engage in "dirty" tactics and therefore violate norms generally accepted for the proper and nonviolent waging of conflict.

Louis Kriesburg, summarizing the insights of many scholars, has described how conflict polarization feeds on itself. As polarization increases, moderates withdraw because they are unwilling to engage in more intensive and destructive action. This leaves a partial vacuum to be filled by those pushing for escalation.[19] Each extreme and uncivil act erodes crosscutting attachments. Such attachments are defined as less relevant and are subordinated to overlapping cleavages or are redefined so as to add to polarization. Extremists are less and less constrained; they become more free to indulge in increasingly intensive, threatening, and coercive behavior. Neutrals are reduced in number as they come under intensive pressure to choose sides. As the coal miners in Harlan County, Kentucky, sang in the 1930s, "You either are a union man or a thug for J. H. Blair. Which side are you on, man, which side are you on?"[20]

Moderates, who attempt to see at least some virtue in the positions of opponent camps, are distrusted by extremists on all sides. Moderates are frequently subject to violence or threat of violence by the fervently committed, who have a stake in eliminating any definition of middle ground providing a basis for compromise that would threaten the appeal of extremist positions. As the decencies are coarsened, and scruples murdered, moderates who fail to withdraw from polarized conflict arenas are frequently driven from them by intense partisans.

In a classic series of studies, Muzafer Sherif examined social consequences of conflict polarization.[21] Sherif described a field experiment that graphically revealed how polarization led to destructive behavior between opponent groups of boys in a summer camp setting. The boys were not initially divided by cultural, class, or observable physical differences, but during the course of the experiment polarized divisions sharpened, intergroup communication distorted and withered, and violence flared. Sherif made a point of concluding that destructive intergroup conflict is not the result of neurotic or other psychological tendencies of individual personalities but is the consequence of polarization in the social web.[22] Normal, healthy, and socially well-adjusted boys engaged in destructive conflict behavior when the conducive social condition (polarization) was obtained.

Morton Deutsch picked up this theme and built a case that conflict under conditions of polarization becomes characterized by impoverished communication among adversaries who have great incentive to withhold information from each other in conditions of high threat. Furthermore, opponents become highly sensitive to mutual differences. Gestures of good faith, offered across polarized cleavages, become interpreted as objects of distrust.[23] Both Sherif and Deutsch have shown how the growth of solidarity within a given conflict group comes at the expense of intensified hostility toward the outgroup. Pressure for uniformity of in-group opinion increases, and individual challenges to group orthodoxy become viewed as signs of weakness or heresy. Such individualistic interpretations of situations tend to be resisted and subordinated by leaders who insist that all energy must be focused on the external threat. Conflict groups, mobilized against enemies across polarized cleavages, are not fertile ground for individual freedom of thought and action.

If numerous analyses of conflict behavior have associated conflict polarization with impoverished and distorted communication, absence of mutual grounds for compromise, high levels of threat, and destructive violence, what do analysts have to say about the opposite types of cleavage pattern — the nonpolarized or crosscutting? The hypothesis that crosscutting cleavages contribute to the regulation of social conflict for constructive purposes has also been widely accepted among sociologists, anthropologists, political scientists, and students of international affairs. It has been attested to by such widely respected scholars as Arthur F. Bentley, David B. Truman, William Kornhauser, S. M. Lipset, Stein Rokkan, Raymond Mack, Richard C. Snyder, Ernest B. Haas, and Claude Ake.[24] An anthropologist who put the crosscutting cleavage hypothesis at the center of his work was Thomas Sterns Elliot, who in 1949 put the case succinctly:

> I now suggest that both class and region, by dividing the inhabitants of a country into two different kinds of groups, lead to a conflict favorable to creativeness and progress . . . and . . . these are only two of an indefinite number of conflicts and jealousies which should be profitable to society. Indeed, the more the better: so that everyone should be an ally of everyone else in some respects, and an opponent in several others, and no one conflict, envy, or fear will predominate.[25]

A decade later, Max Gluckman employed the same conception in his analysis of Evans-Prichard's work on the Nuers: "If there are sufficient conflicts of loyalties at work, settlement will be achieved and social order maintained."[26] This contention has been advanced by others.[27] Ethnic groups, tribes, and classes have been stitched together by factional cleavages running vertically along lines of patron-client relationships that unify people of different social standing in the search for ways to advance specific material interests.[28] Given that traditional vertical ethnic and factional cleavages crosscut horizontal lines of class cleavage, they have been viewed as a source of interclass solidarity.

Among sociologists, there has been much debate as to whether conflict is or is not functional for society. Georg Simmel, disagreeing with those who saw conflict as necessarily harmful, emphasized the "socializing" and "civilizing" functions of conflict.[29] Simmel contended that conflict, sufficiently controlled by crosscutting attachments so as not to call into question the foundations of the social order, would help sustain and invigorate society. The crisscrossing of cleavages, he thought, served to sew the social system together by preventing disintegration along any one primary line of cleavage. E. A. Ross later articulated this theme:

> A society . . . which is ridden by a dozen oppositions along lines running in every direction may actually be in less danger of being torn by violence or falling to pieces than one split just along one line. For each new cleavage contributes to narrow the cross clefts, so that one might say that *society is sewn together by its inner conflicts*. (emphasis in original)[30]

Literature developing this hypothesis was assembled and examined by Lewis Coser, who built a substantial case that conflict, if organized along nonpolarizing lines, could have positive functions.[31] Beneficial conflicts (that is, crosscutting) integrate society, allow adversaries to negotiate their disputes, develop rules and organizations that represent resources for control of still newly emerging conflicts, promote moderation among opponents, allow for dissent within conflict groups, and make for social cohesion based on mutual respect. Crosscutting conflict patterns facilitate constantly renewed willingness to seek grounds for compromise and create conditions for acceptance of new ideas, values, and innovations from out-group representatives. Coser's analysis has received much support.[32]

Polarization and Legitimacy

Legitimacy is critical because actors exercising leadership do not have carte blanche to compel obedience of followers to orders. Willingness to accept leadership authority depends upon the degree of legitimacy recognized to exist by followers. Legitimacy, in turn, is dependent upon the degree of perceived congruence between norms and values of leaderships and followers. Leaders of conflict groups, to develop and sustain legitimacy, must play upon, and resonate with, norms and values important to local audience culture. Leadership messages in violation of audience norms tend to be treated as "noise" and bring the actor's legitimacy into question.[33] When cleavages arise in a sharply polarized pattern, leaders who enjoy legitimacy by virtue of close identification with the norms, values, and definitions of the situation held by one faction will necessarily cut themselves off from identification with opponent groups. By playing to the strongly held views of one conflict group, they lose legitimacy in the view of antagonists. Mutually reinforcing cleavages, therefore, undercut the capacity of conflict group leaders to effectively formulate compromises legitimate to antagonists. Norms and values are not sufficiently shared, and grounds for compromise are thereby eroded.

Polarization and Perceptions of Interdependence

Between the extremes of desire for annihilation of the opponent and perfect consensus are various degrees of zero-sum or non-zero-sum interdependence.[34] Zero-sum interdependence between conflicting parties is characterized by a perception that a gain for one side necessarily means an equal loss for the other, as in a game of checkers. On a checkerboard one may advance one's position only at the expense of one's opponent. There are no common causes in which both sides can simultaneously benefit. Such interdependence becomes mutually detrimental and is associated with polarization and non-negotiability of issues.[35] Zero-sum interdependence violates the basic principle of mutual benefit upon which peaceful and constructive social relations are founded. The interests of conflicting parties are diametrically opposed: What one wins the other loses; there can be no exchange of concessions.

Non-zero-sum situations, however, are those to which resources are added as the conflict proceeds — as in a horse race with spectators contributing to the purse. Although a given opponent may gain more than others, all are capable of advancing their values to some extent. The horse, jockey, and owner who finish second may well be better off for having run the race. They may have gained in knowledge and experience, and their share of the purse may have made the effort more than worthwhile. In such situations, the sum of payoffs does not add to zero — hence non-zero-sum conflict. Interests partially converge and partially diverge.

Polarization and Negotiability

Bargaining and negotiation, which must constitute the core of social life, are the constant search for mutually beneficial arrangements. Polarized conflict structures forestall this search.[36] The continuous bargaining of social life is inherently a positive-sum exercise since, by definition, parties mutually prefer the newly agreed outcome to the status quo. This requires at least modest levels of legitimacy to be extended to opponent messages, needs, wants, and beneficial non-zero-sum relationships. The extent to which a concession or conciliatory act is exploited or reciprocated depends upon the situation in which the concession is made. In polarized contexts, where legitimacy is low or nonexistent and where perceptions of interdependence are zero sum, actors estimate that it "pays to be tough" and tend to feel that they must exploit any opening to their exclusive advantage. Concessions are to be exploited, and leaders who attempt to make concessions in polarized situations are viewed by their adversaries as false, tricky, crafty, and to be distrusted. Such leaders are also viewed with suspicion by their own followers and are typically placed under great pressure not to risk in-group advantage. Each side, therefore, finds the course of choice-destroying conflict to be necessary, even if regrettable.

Polarization and Choice

To insert new conflict associated with support for, and opposition to, a proposed technological policy for resource use, on a crosscutting vector in the affected social web, is to contribute to conditions that make expansion of choice contexts possible in a manner that will fulfill other developmental value criteria. But, to insert new conflict on a vector that polarizes existing conflicts is to threaten the structural context of choice from which individuals, groups, and organizations can prescribe for themselves their particular and noncommensurable definitions of welfare. As polarization increases, negotiability of conflict declines, mutual threat levels rise, and the propensity increases of each antagonist to employ resources to block or undercut choices of the opponents. Those technological policies for the public household that would promise to increase range, rate, or standards of choices, but would do so at the expense of significantly polarizing a social unit, must be assessed as inferior to those that would depolarize or sustain a condition of nonpolarization.

Rules of the social game for conducting and resolving conflict are necessary to the continuation of social life and choice — they protect the survival of parties in conflict, contain injury, introduce a degree of predictability, and protect noninvolved parties. Unfortunately for social tranquility, rules for restraining conflict are always in a precarious state. An acceptable rule at one point may prejudice outcomes at another juncture. Procedural rules are multiple, open to constant reinterpretation and redefinition through constant reaffirmation in negotiation. Crosscutting conflict structures, associated with legitimacy and non-zero-sum interdependence, exhibit socially binding supports for sustenance of conflict management structures as well as valuationally defensible expansion of choice contexts.

Many investigators of social life have recognized the close connection between conflict and choice. A tradition of social analysis has emerged that considers traditional ascriptive cleavage affiliations, imposed by accident of birth, to be inherently constraining to individual choice. As societies modernize, both person and organization are seen to be released from primary group bonds and permitted to operate in a variety of secondary networks based on preference. Opportunities for multigroup affiliation have been viewed as central to choice.[37] In situations of high polarization, loyalty to the in-group and exemplary opposition to the adversary are at a premium — all at the considerable expense of individual predilection. Demands for unflinching opposition become exacting, and at the structural level, people engage in collective actions designed to cut each other down to erode the context from which all may choose. Simmel pointed out how even our language reveals the meaning of conflict. In polarized situations, opponents must each "pull themselves together."[38] All energies must be concentrated on the adversary. In peaceful situations, however, one may "let oneself go," meaning that one can allow interests to develop independently in various directions. The consequence is clear. Conflict has implications for choice at two levels: (1) the personal level at which individual welfare is prescribed; and (2) the structural or contextual level.

At the personal level, dynamics of polarization force subordination of individual personal needs and preferences to the demands of highly threatened conflict groups. At the structural level, opponents maneuvering to deny choice corrode the capacity of people in the web to offer choices to each other in the private household, marketplaces, or the public household. We are graphically reminded of this awful reality by daily media reports of the effects of destructive conflict. The United States and the Soviet Union have exhausted national treasuries in the half-century pursuit of a global arms race in the face of deteriorating public services, eroding natural environments, and extensive domestic and global poverty. In the Middle East, Israelis and Arabs have forgone civilian consumption to maintain high readiness of destructive capacity, and the United States–led United Nations coalition became locked in combat that devastated Saddam Hussein's Iraq. In Lebanon people have been forced to violently struggle for control of a water tap, and innocents have been subjected to wholesale slaughter.

In Afghanistan, armies have destroyed grain crops amidst grievous hunger, and in Northern Ireland much wealth of the nation has been bound up by zealots bent on a campaign of terror against the authority of the English Crown rooted in cleavages that go back several hundred years. Ethiopian and Sudanese civil wars, involving the respective central governments and a half-dozen guerrilla movements, destroy what precious agricultural infrastructure exists, while millions starve and famine relief convoys are bombed. In U.S. cities opponents have eroded school systems for all students in bitter struggles over matters of interracial busing.

Implications

All of the above is intended to give policy-assessment status to a strategic sociological variable — conflict polarization — abstracted from the social whole. It is beyond the scope of this effort to further empirically establish all of the posited relationships specified in the model however much such empirical work is needed. Insofar as the theoretical propositions have credibility, measurement and tracking of conflict cleavage polarization is of central strategic importance for the sociology of social policy assessment. If the theory should lose credibility — if polarization should be found not to have the posited relationships with humans' capacity to negotiate differences and with their propensity to employ available resources in ways destructive to choice contexts and to reasoned discourse about fact and value — then interest in measurement of conflict polarization will accordingly diminish. The discussion proceeds on the premise that there is good reason for isolating the conflict polarization variable, that it is as strategic as is claimed.

Before proceeding to the details of computing polarization scores and the use of such scores to rank proposed policy options, several important implications of the polarization argument require explicit discussion. First, despite the lengthy litany of political science, sociological, and anthropological investigations that have employed the hypothesis that conflict polarization is associated with nonnegotiability of issues, high levels of mutual threat, and propensity to cash in available resources to cut down opponents with greater or lesser violence, many researchers have pointed out that the actual systematic empirical support for the hypothesis is skimpy.[39] It is posited that the lack of more conclusive empirical support for the hypothesis is, at least in part, due to the lack of adequate measures of conflict polarization and to the failure to control for potentially confounding variables such as distribution of power, mutual spatial and social access of antagonists, and the relative salience of cleavages. I hope that the analysis advanced here will contribute to improved comprehension of the polarization phenomenon and energize research into its implications for issue negotiability, mutual threat, and propensity to engage in destructive forms of behavior.

Second, one must clearly distinguish conflict cleavage patterns from power distribution. The power of A to compel B is intimately associated with decisions to be aggressive or passive, violent or nonviolent.[40] The procedures that follow in the next section clearly measure one property of a social unit and one property only — the degree of conflict polarization. No measurement of social power distribution is advanced here. Conflict polarization and the associated loss of negotiability are therefore preconditions for violence and destruction of choice context. Polarization constitutes a necessary but insufficient condition to explain outbreaks of violence, the course of violence, or the outcomes of violence. Many variables that enter into the explanation of the decision to commit violence are beyond the domain of conflict polarization per se — for example, power distribution, organization of antagonists, relative isolation of opponents, distribution of technologies of violence, and state repression. Intensely violent conflict has been avoided in highly polarized social units by use of coercive power of a third party or by one dominating antagonist. Resorting to overt violence is a tactic that depends heavily on the respective power and position of the contestants. Therefore, the conflict analysis here makes no pretense of offering a theory of war or revolution. Whether polarization leads to war among sovereign nations, coups d'etat among competing governing groups, revolutions between elites and counterelites, or insurgencies between challengers and state core coalitions is a matter affected by many variables not addressed here. The argument is only that nonpolarizing conflict patterns are to be valued because crosscutting cleavages create the essential conditions of civil life — dialogue, dissent, compromise — and make possible developmentally expanding contexts of choice. Those who wish to inquire into the factors affecting the dynamics and outcomes of conflict in polarized settings must seek elsewhere for such analysis.[41]

A third implication requires explicit statement. There is no expectation that policymakers can easily manipulate cleavages that have been deeply rooted in history. One can, however, monitor existing cleavages and evaluate proposed policies so as to increase the probability that such policies, if implemented, would advance crosscutting patterns. Long-standing polarized conflict cleavages are unlikely to be easily redefined and redirected, but cleavages inherent in policy proposals can be manipulated as policies are formulated, assessed, and reformulated. Technology and natural resource conflicts tend to involve weighty matters and may constitute substantial crosscut cleavage material. At the very least one can hope to prevent further polarization while chipping away at polarized cleavages.

Fourth, an important distinction should be made between "peace" and a given amount of conflict polarization. Peace can be found under conditions of either polarization or nonpolarization. Peace, the absence of overt violence, can coexist with heavy polarization and gross violation of the developmental value logic. One might witness peace in a situation characterized by deeply polarized cleavages, but in which one antagonist controls overwhelming means of coercion and domination, leaving the subordinate parties no alternative but acquiescence. Certain social structures of peace in that state may be polarized and promote the harshest variety of injustice and the most limited choice context for the exploited. Systems polarized as between slaveowners and slaves have known peace. In the aftermath of the French Revolution, Napoleon endeavored to extend French reforms throughout the Continent — to do for Europe what had been done for France. Tired of the Corsican's mania for rearranging things, a coalition of reactionary elites imposed the peace of Prince von Metternich, which again made Europe safe for aristocracy. One does not necessarily have to view Napoleon as a force for European development to note that peace is a tricky notion that associates as easily with the venal and oppressive as with humane developmental values. The value logic advanced here holds that a peace based upon a condition of crosscutting cleavages wherein cohesion is founded upon negotiation and voluntary and mutually acceptable trade-offs is vastly superior to a peace rooted in the capacity of the powerful to oppress the weak across polarizing cleavages wherein cohesion is based upon control of force by the dominant.

Fifth, the question might be posed as to whether the conflict value is inherently conservative. Is there a tendency to serve the status quo in a formulation of value that favors nonpolarized conflict? It is true that regulation of highly charged polarized conflict, especially when it erupts in violence, is one of the necessary conditions of civil life. Elimination of destructive conflict has long been a cherished ideal associated with visions of the good society. Most citizens and theorists have indicated a preference for negotiation and compromise over destruction, to talk and accommodate rather than to coerce and kill. However, does the position taken here necessarily imply that one should prefer peace at any price, that one should negotiate any issue under any circumstance and thereby forgo possible benefits of revolutionary change? The issue is more complex than it may first appear.[42] Several points are in order:

1. Valuing the reduction of conflict polarization does not imply a value of maintaining the status quo. Status quo policies may, in fact, be as destructively polarizing as any proposed alternative. The status quo does not enjoy a special privileged position in policy assessment. Furthermore, crosscutting cleavages are associated with an increased capacity to undertake and absorb change. Multiple involvements in crosscutting cleavages keep social groups open to innovation and to the ideas of others. Low threat levels mean resources are released for instrumental technological change to solve problems and to serve expansion of choice — not to be confined to countering opponent threats from across highly polarized cleavages.

2. By definition, the tools of oppression, coercion, and destructive violence are more available to elites than to the dispossessed. Disproportionate access to the means of violence and oppression is another privilege of high rank. Wishing to reduce polarized conflict and its associated nonnegotiability of issues, high mutual threat levels, and propensities to employ available resources destructively cannot be viewed as prima facie evidence of serving elite or status quo interests.[43]

3. It is easy to imagine polarized and exploitive social arrangements so brutalizing, so destructive of choice context, so denigrating of human dignity, that one simply must accept that use of overt violence to overthrow existing "peaceful" arrangements is preferable to systematic exertion of nonovert structural violence during periods of peace. Thoughtful people love peace, but not peace at any price. When forms of "peace" emerge around such coercive polarizations in ways that undercut any reasonable hope of securing developmental expansions of choice context, no alternative may present itself other than conduct of a winning fight against those who would systematically and gratuitously destroy structures of choice. There is nothing in this analysis to suggest that one must patiently negotiate with an Adolf Hitler while Jews are marched to ovens. Strategies of peaceful negotiation and nonviolent pressure to advance interests in the context of crosscutting cleavages are methods preferable to those of violence — if a nonpolarized setting exists to open up such creative possibilities for peacefully enlarging choice contexts according to a defensible logic of

developmental value. But when one is confronted by powerful elements who are consciously bent on the systematic destruction of human dignity and choice, it is idiocy to fold one's arms and declare that there is nothing to be done in the name of pacifism. If those with defensible conceptions of developmental value for managing the public household stand idealistically aside from violence under all conditions, thugs will rise to the top and rationality in the normative domain will fall to the bottom to be discussed only in whispers. What is needed is not a general commitment to pacifism but a discriminating capacity to sort justified violence from unjustified violence. The refusal to take part in all war under any conditions is an unworldly view that accepts the status quo no matter how antidevelopmental, unjust, or degrading of human dignity.

4. One cannot determine the morality of war or other forms of violence by investigating who threw the first rock or shot the first bullet. It may all too often be the unsophisticated who fail to appreciate the maneuvers of opponents who await with bigger stones and more guns. Agents of oppression, claiming allegiance to peace, can skillfully mobilize community opinion against the dupe in ways that strengthen injustice and undercut developmental values.[44] The morality of violence must be determined by a logic of value rooted in human reason — a logic that simultaneously refrains from cultural ethnocentrism, prescription of individual welfare, and a thoughtless cultural relativism that suggests that the values of the thug cannot be differentiated from the best of developmental values constructed through open, careful, and reasonable dialogue.

5. Just wars, by definition, must be fought not only with an eye to certain rules for soldiers, but for just causes.[45] Just wars must be fought in the service of some defensible developmental value logic. Given the failure to define social development in any defensible manner, there has been a distinct lack of value logics to give credibility to conceptions of just war. Madmen may not be inclined to listen to reasoned analysis, but such analysis is essential to citizens contemplating the morality of war as an option for agents managing the affairs of the public household. Just wars may be required to resist those who are determined to employ technology and resources to provide narrow advantage by violating developmental logics of value, whose vision is to construct only ever more efficient mechanisms of oppression to destroy choice contexts, who refuse to be constrained by reasonable public normative dialogue. In crosscutting situations, agents

of antidevelopment may be effectively resisted by nonviolent means, but in highly polarized situations, violence in the name of social development may be the only reasonable recourse. This position is not different than that of the signers of that eighteenth-century Enlightenment document, the American Declaration of Independence, who held forth a conception of unalienable rights that said "to secure these rights, governments are instituted among men, deriving their just powers from the consent of the governed; that whenever any form of government becomes destructive of these ends, it is the right of the people to alter or abolish it . . . " and "when a long train of abuses and usurpations . . . evinces a design to reduce them under absolute despotism, it is their right, it is their duty, to throw off such government and to provide new guards for their future security."

Those who would employ technology to enslave must be opposed in the last resort; there is nothing in the factual or normative theory of conflict polarization that would stand in the way. Decision-makers operating on behalf of the public household are not given carte blanche to go to war or to commit acts of civil disobedience, by judging matters according to personal preferences. To act responsibly, citizens and decision-makers must look to fundamental criteria expressed in some reasoned developmental logic of value applicable to the affairs of the larger political community. If one comes to a conclusion that war or civil disobedience is justified and acts accordingly, one acts conscientiously in principled fashion. Although one must admit the possibility of error in application of developmental logics of value to particular situations, the decision-maker has not simply acted out of whim, preference, or self-interest. Reasonable debate about the nature of possible error, and about appropriate alternatives to violence, must force to the forefront valuative principles.

Finally, whereas the polarization concept cannot carry the burden of explanation for the complex and subtle dynamics of violent conflict, it does speak to the problem of nonnegotiability of issues in human networks — no small matter in a nuclear world that has known an abundance of senseless violence. Citizens face twin dilemmas: 1. Just wars fought for coherent community values may be necessary as an alternative to the destructiveness and inhumanity of grossly unjust forms of social "peace," but we have collectively wired the planet for our destruction by building doomsday machines; use of nuclear weapons on any significant scale would be more choice destroying than almost any evil they could attack.[46] Nuclear war, in all probability, would mark the death of highly developed human choice contexts for any foreseeable future.

2. If governments should ever succeed in getting the nuclear genie back into the bottle, the danger of catastrophic collapse of human society and the ecosystem in the aftermath of an accident or moment of madness will be reduced, but then one has made conventional war somewhat more safe as a human institution. As weapons become less globally destructive, they become more usable. By simply getting rid of nuclear weapons, one increases the chances that Europe, Asia, the Middle East, Africa, and the Americas will become theaters of war. The weapons of large-scale conventional war, including the biological and chemical, give little comfort to the analyst in a postnuclear world. It is not obvious that such a world would be immune from high risk of massive destruction. Elimination of threatening weaponry must go hand in hand with reduction in social conflict polarizations within and among nation-states.

Mutual deterrence leaves us hopelessly teetering on the brink of holocaust; it suspends disputes but does not make for their resolution; it consumes massive resources that could otherwise be developmentally invested. At best, deterrence means stalemate, a freezing of the global situation into spheres of influence, and makes developmental change within and among nations dangerous because of its implications for shifts in sensitive alliance systems. Developmental rearrangements for the Poles, peoples of the Middle East, or Central America may not be good for global stability in a highly polarized hair-trigger world. World government offers little by way of hope. For one thing, the chance is negligible that dominant sovereign nations would share in world government except in ways that would advance their interests at the expense of lesser powers. For another thing, it would be dangerous to create a central global government capable of imposing resolution of conflicts upon affected peoples without first creating value criteria, rooted in common valuational reasoning, for management of the global public household. That community of value must come into existence along with the authority to ensure the safety of nations. Local polarized and nonnegotiable conflicts offer opportunity for escalation and intervention in a world that can afford neither nuclear nor large-scale conventional war.

These realities give weight to the absolute priority of reducing conflict polarization while simultaneously advancing other developmental values. Human beings, caught in highly polarized cleavages and struggling for their particular conceptions of victory at specific times and places, can end developed human existence for all times and places. The eternal question of how to respond to the reality of conflicting human purposes has been placed in the hands of mortals who must accept responsibility for the structural shape of their societies. There can only be one general response: Keep cleavage polarization down, legitimacy up, interdependence of a non-zero-sum nature up, threat levels down, and conflicts negotiable. All of this, then, is to sustain cultural diversity and human creativity and productivity as constrained by lower-ranked value criteria.

CONFLICT ANALYSIS FOR POLICY ASSESSMENT — ESSENTIAL STEPS

How can one conduct a policy assessment to determine the degree of polarization associated with any proposed policy alternative in a social unit? Four essential tasks are involved:

1. Determine the existing conflict cleavage pattern in the unit of analysis. This involves the mapping of significant cleavages dividing opponent groups (refer again to the lower portion of Figure 5.3).

2. Gather data that reveal which actors take positions for, against, or neutral to each proposed policy (refer to the upper portion of Figure 5.3).

3. Employ analytical procedures to determine whether the cleavage associated with each proposed policy as determined in step 2 will increase or decrease polarization, given the existing pattern of conflict delineated in step 1.

These first three steps represent a sociological science investigating factual conditions. The fourth task is to rank proposed policies in the order of their contribution to decreasing polarization — a step that involves a sociological logic of value.

The discussion turns to procedures for performing each of the above four analytical steps. The reader who does not wish to follow the data may skip ahead to the case studies. It is only necessary to know that the Conflict Polarizations Coefficient (C_{ij}) varies from 0 (no polarization) to 1 (complete polarization).

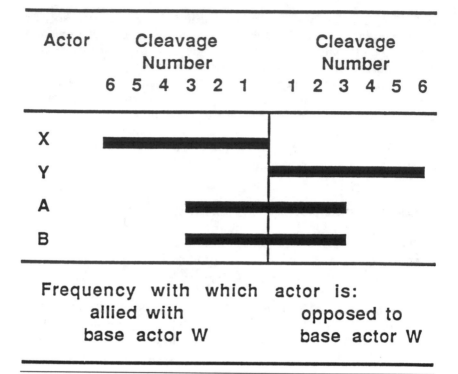

Actor	Cleavage Number						Cleavage Number					
	6	5	4	3	2	1	1	2	3	4	5	6
X												
Y												
A												
B												

Frequency with which actor is:
allied with   **opposed to**
base actor W   **base actor W**

Figure 6.2. Polarization Measurement Given Six Cleavages

Determining the Degree of Polarization
in the Base Conflict Situation — Mapping What Is

Several analysts have addressed the problem of polarization measurement.[47] What follows is a procedure that, although it draws insights from several approaches, has been developed for practical policy assessment at the structural level — a task not specifically addressed by others.[48] Pie figures with cleavages represented by bars, as in Figure 5.3, communicate an intuitive feeling for the meaning of polarization but are not helpful for computational purposes. Figure 6.2 presents a computationally more useful way of looking at the measurement problem. Imagine a social unit in which there are six conflict cleavages. Each actor's position must be compared to that of each other actor on each cleavage in order to comprehend the extent of polarization. The most straightforward way to make this comparison is to select one actor as a base for comparison and then to locate each

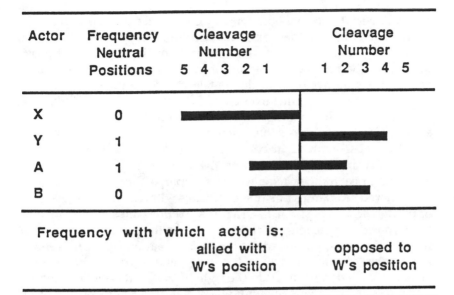

Actor	Frequency Neutral Positions	Cleavage Number 5 4 3 2 1	Cleavage Number 1 2 3 4 5
X	0		
Y	1		
A	1		
B	0		

Frequency with which actor is:
allied with W's position   opposed to W's position

Figure 6.3. Polarization Measurement Given Odd Number of Cleavages and Neutral Positions

other actor on Figure 6.2 in terms of who allies with, is neutral to, or is in opposition to this base actor (W). In a perfectly polarizing situation, actors in opposition on any one cleavage will be in opposition on all. Examination of Figure 6.2 reveals this to be the case as between actors X and Y. X is six times in support of W's position, Y is six times opposed to W. On the other hand, given six cleavages, a perfect cross-cutting situation would entail actors who are three times allied to be also opponents three times. Figure 6.2 displays this condition for actors A and B.

One now notes the possibility of actors being neutral with regard to cleavages and also notes that conflict cleavages do not necessarily come packaged in even numbers. Such possibilities are easily represented in Figure 6.3. Actor X (Fig. 6.3) takes no neutral positions and is totally committed to W's positions on all five cleavage fronts, but actor Y is neutral on one cleavage while being in opposition to W in four instances. The number of times a given actor chooses to be neutral in a given social unit is recorded in the left (neutral) column of Figure 6.3. Cleavages in any number, odd or even, can in principle be represented. Odd numbers are noteworthy only in one respect. Given an odd number, it is impossible for any given actor to take exactly the same number of positions for or against W unless one — such as A in Figure 6.3 — assumes one or more neutral positions, making it possible to split the remaining even number of cleavage positions equally across the center bar. If actors do not take an even number of positions because they are in conflict over an odd number of cleavages (the case of B in Fig. 6.3), the analysis simply accepts this fact. There will necessarily be imbalance across the center bar.

The steps involved in computing a polarization score are now straightforward. First, one selects the base actor W against which positions of each other actor will be compared.[49] Each other actor is then viewed as taking a position of alliance with, neutrality toward, or opposition to W's position. Each actor's positions are recorded relative to W's position by extension of the bars out to the positive (support) or negative (opposition) side of the figure. Each bar on Figure 6.3 reports the number of times a given actor supports or opposes the position taken by W. A bar extended to the right of the center line in actor X's row indicates the frequency with which X is opposed to W. The number in the neutral column reports the frequency with which X assumed neutral positions. The actual pattern of support and opposition for base actor W is now compared to the ideally expected pattern that would occur if all cleavages were perfectly crosscutting.

If conflict were perfectly nonpolarized, one would expect that each actor would be half the time for W and half the time against — that is, all bars would evenly balance on the center line of Figure 6.3. Given an even number of six cleavages on which an actor is estimated to take a nonneutral position, the expected pattern for perfectly crosscutting cleavages would be three times for W and three times opposed. Given an uneven number of cleavages, such as five, the ideally expected pattern would be 2.5 for and 2.5 against W. Odd-numbered cleavage situations, therefore, guarantee at least one unit of deviation from purely crosscutting patterns on the part of any given actor unless a neutral position is taken such that actors are involved only in an even number of cleavages. In instances where neutral positions are taken, the ideally expected pattern of support and opposition to W is based only on nonneutral involvements. If actor Y (see Fig. 6.4) takes one neutral position, leaving four positive or negative positions vis-à-vis W, the ideally expected pattern would be two in support of W and two in opposition.

The question now becomes: How much deviation occurs between

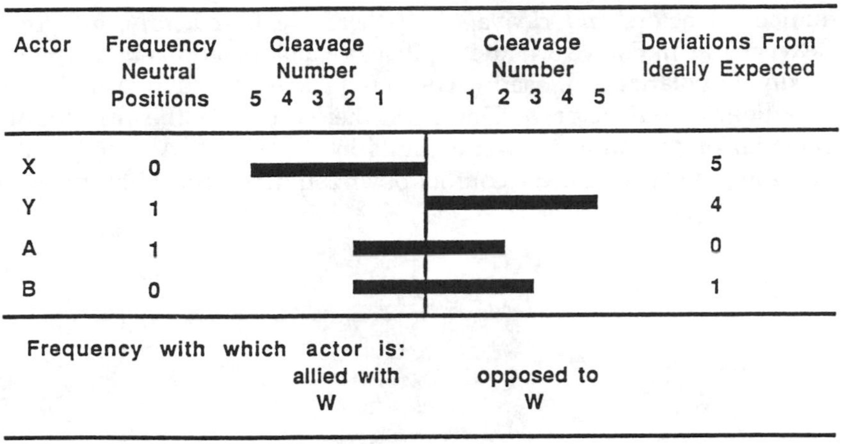

Actor	Frequency Neutral Positions	Cleavage Number 5 4 3 2 1	Cleavage Number 1 2 3 4 5	Deviations From Ideally Expected
X	0			5
Y	1			4
A	1			0
B	0			1

Frequency with which actor is:
allied with   opposed to
W   W

$$C_{ij} = \frac{\sum D_a}{\sum D_p} = \frac{10}{20} = .50$$

Figure 6.4. Logic Underlying Polarization Coefficient (C_{ij})

the observed conflict pattern and the ideally expected? Figure 6.4 reproduces the situation presented in Figure 6.3, but it also includes a deviation column. Deviation scores are easily computed by determining the difference between the number of times an actor assumes a position of support for W and the ideally expected value, plus the difference in the number of times an actor opposes W and the ideally expected value. For example, in Figure 6.4 actor X is five times for W, or 2.5 times more than ideally expected, while at the same time never allied with W or 2.5 times less than ideally expected. These two departures from the ideal are summed to five and entered into the deviation column for actor X. Actor Y presents us with the interesting case of being neutral on one cleavage and opposed to W on four. Since Y is involved in four cleavages, one would expect that ideally Y would be twice for and twice opposed to W. In fact we observe that Y deviates from the ideal pattern by being two units more in opposition to W and two units less in support. These two deviations above and below the ideal sum to four units of deviation and are likewise recorded in Y's deviation cell.

The sum of deviations can now be compared to the sum of potential deviations that could have occurred in a given table with a given number of actors and cleavages. If there are four actors and five cleavages, as in Figure 6.4, and if all actors took positions that would maximize polarization, then each would have earned five units of deviation, as did actor X. One sees, therefore, that the maximum potential of deviation is twenty units in Figure 6.4. A social unit, therefore, can be assigned a conflict polarization score as follows:

$$C_{ij} = \frac{\sum D_a}{\sum D_p}$$

where:

C_{ij} = conflict polarization score for social unit i at time j;

$\sum D_a$ = sum of actual deviations from the ideally expected;

$\sum D_p$ = sum of potential deviations that could occur if no neutral positions were taken by any actor.

Substituting values from Figure 6.5 into the formula, we obtain the following result:

$$C_{ij} = \frac{10}{20} = .50$$

This simple conflict polarization coefficient provides one with a value, varying from 0 to 1, that can be employed in comparing the relative polarization of actors in conflict in different social systems and within the same system at different points in time.

The use of bars to denote positions in Figure 6.4 illustrates the meaning of conflict polarization and of the logic employed to measure it, but such graphic display becomes clumsy when tabulating large amounts of conflict data. Fortunately, it is but a small step to eliminate bars and replace them with a table in which numbers are employed in their stead (see Fig. 6.5).

The analysis of conflict polarization, so far, is promising, but there is a serious omission. Not all cleavages are equal in importance — salience — for parties to conflict.[50] One must distinguish between

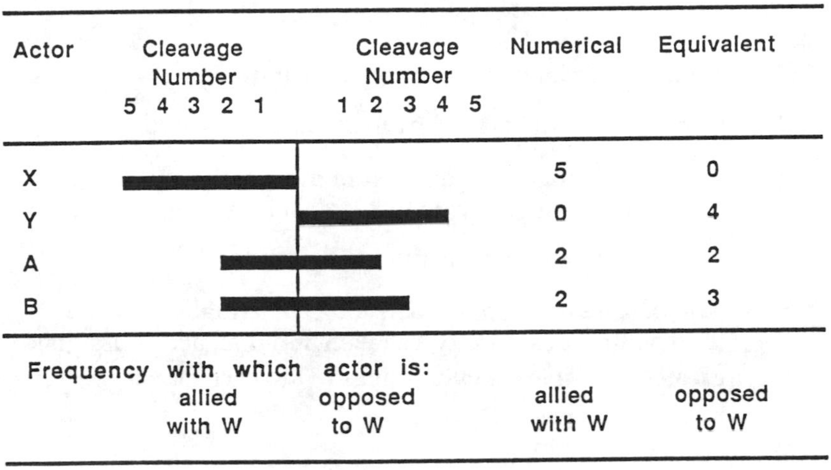

Actor	Cleavage Number					Cleavage Number					Numerical	Equivalent
	5	4	3	2	1	1	2	3	4	5		
X											5	0
Y											0	4
A											2	2
B											2	3

Frequency with which actor is:

| | allied with W | opposed to W | allied with W | opposed to W |

Figure 6.5. Identity of Graphic and Numerical Presentation of Conflict Polarization Data

compelling and trivial cleavages. Fights over weighty issues of identity, fundamental rights or principles, and highly valued material rewards must be distinguished from those that are defined by conflicting parties to be of relatively little real consequence. Conflict cleavages can be weighted according to their degree of salience — operationalized as the cost of defeat — for each actor. This is exactly what can be accomplished by multiplying deviation scores for actors by salience values (see Table 6.1). Salience scores will be assigned to conflict cleavage positions based on each particular antagonist's perceived cost of defeat on each cleavage, ranging from none (0), low (1), or moderate (2) to high (3). Salience scores, like values representing positions of actors on cleavages, are generated by the modified Delphi process described in Appendix II.

The addition of salience scores to the analysis, as displayed on Table 6.1, requires an adjustment in computation of the conflict polarization value. The revised formula is written as follows:

$$C_{ij} = \frac{\sum D_a \left(\sum S_a \right)}{\sum D_p \left(\sum S_p \right)}$$

where:

C_{ij} = conflict polarization score for unit i at time j;

$\sum D_a$ = sum of actual deviations from the ideally expected;

$\sum D_p$ = sum of potential deviations from the ideally expected if no neutral positions were to be taken by any actors;

$\sum S_a$ = sum of salience scores actually observed;

$\sum S_p$ = sum of salience scores which could potentially occur if no neutral positions were taken and if all actors assigned greatest possible salience values (3) to each cleavage.

Assessing Proposed Policies in the Base
Conflict Situation — Determining What Ought

The analysis can now proceed to the next step — assessing and ranking proposed policy options. One now asks: Given that actors are estimated to constitute a given base conflict pattern or structure, will a policy proposal increase or decrease polarization? More polarization will be revealed by increasing deviation units from the pure crosscutting distribution weighted by salience scores and a C_{ij} score moving in the direction of unity (1.0). Less polarization will be revealed by a C_{ij} score moving in the direction of zero. Each policy-induced cleavage will generate a new division among affected parties, but will it fall on a more crosscutting or overlapping pattern? If actor X were to once again side with W over the proposed policy, then X would be six times for W and still never be allied with opponents of W — a fact that would increase polarization. A unit of deviation would then be added in X's cell 1 in the column in Table 6.1 headed "Deviation Associated With Policy 1." Likewise, if actor Y were to react to the policy proposal (P_1) so as to again be opposed to W's position, there would be a unit increase in polarization (shown in the same column in Table 6.1). Deviations induced by Policy 1 are algebraically summed and then multiplied by the sum of associated salience scores. Policy 1 adds somewhat to polarization (C_{ij} = .26 as shown at the bottom of Table 6.1).[51]

On the other hand, Policy 2 (P_2) is depolarizing in impact, as shown in Table 6.1. Policy 2 has the opposite effect of the first policy

Table 6.1. Illustration of Polarization Measure Including Cleavage Salience Values and Assessment of Policy Proposals P₁ and P₂

Actor	Frequency of Neutral Positions	Frequency Actor Allies With W	Frequency Actor Opposed to W	Deviation From Ideally Expected (D_a)	Salience Score Sum (S_a)	Deviation Potential (D_p)	Salience Potential (S_p)	Deviation Associated With Policy 1 (D_aP_1)	Salience Associated With Policy 1 (S_aP_1)	Deviation Associated With Policy 2 (D_aP_2)	Salience Associated With Policy 2 (S_aP_2)
X	0	5	0	5	15	5	3	+1	3	-1	3
Y	1	0	4	4	12	5	3	+1	3	-1	3
A	3	3	2	1	3	5	15	0	0	0	0
B	3	3	3	0	0	5	15	0	0	0	0
				$\Sigma D_a = 10$	$\Sigma S_a = 30$	$\Sigma D_p = 20$	$\Sigma S_p = 60$	$\Sigma = +2$	$\Sigma = 6$	$\Sigma = -2$	$\Sigma = 6$

Base Cleavage Computation

$$C_{ij} = \frac{\sum D_a \left\{ \sum S_a \right\}}{\sum D_p \left\{ \sum S_p \right\}}$$

$$C = \frac{10 (30)}{20 (60)} = .25$$

Base Cleavage Combined With Policy 1 Cleavage

$$C_{P_1} = \frac{\left[\sum D_a \left\{ \sum S_a \right\} \right] + \left[\sum D_a P_1 \left\{ \sum S_a P_1 \right\} \right]}{\sum D_p \left\{ \sum S_p \right\}}$$

$$C_{P_1} = \frac{[10 (30)] + [2 (6)]}{20 (60)} = .26$$

Base Cleavage Combined With Policy 2 Cleavage

$$C_{P_2} = \frac{\left[\sum D_a \left\{ \sum S_a \right\} \right] + \left[\sum D_a P_2 \left\{ \sum S_a P_2 \right\} \right]}{\sum D_p \left\{ \sum S_p \right\}}$$

$$C_{P_2} = \frac{[10 (30)] + [2 (6)]}{20 (60)} = .24$$

181

because actor X, for the first time, takes a position of opposition to W over it. The effect of Policy 2 is to stitch together old enemies who are now allied. These reductions in polarization are reflected in the deviation column for Policy 2 by negative units (-1) for actors X and Y in the column in Table 6.1 headed "Deviation Associated With Policy 2." Deviations from the ideally expected have been reduced by a unit each, yielding a sum of minus 2 (-2) recorded at the bottom of the Policy 2 column. Inspection of Table 6.1 reveals that Policy 2 is to be preferred to Policy 1 because it slightly reduces polarization. Proposed policies, therefore, can be ranked from most to least desirable in terms of their estimated polarization impacts. Given the policy assessment logic advanced in Chapter 5, any policy that increases conflict polarization is to be sent back for reformulation. Only those policies that do not increase polarization scores are to be advanced for further assessment on the remaining value criteria. Obviously, the greater the decrease in polarization, the more desirable the policy — especially in highly polarized units.

CONFLICT ANALYSIS IN THE UNITED STATES — THE CASE OF "BIG VISTA DIVIDE"

Background

The 126,530 acres of this U.S. Forest Service planning unit[52] straddle the Continental Divide in north-central Colorado. Elevations range from 8,300 to 13,000 feet above sea level. With snowcapped peaks of the Rocky Mountains dominating the middle of the unit, the western reaches are distinctively rural, sparsely populated, and isolated from sizable population centers. Several large metropolitan areas, in rapidly urbanizing counties, are situated less than one hour's drive from the unit's eastern boundary. The high quality and variety of the outdoor recreation opportunities make them a valued attribute of this unit, which is characterized by outstanding scenery, local social color in the form of small rustic communities, 131 miles of perennial high-quality fishing streams, and 572 surface acres of lakes and reservoirs. Fish habitat is in good condition in most places, and there is good summer range for deer and elk. However, poor winter range severely constrains the size of the big game population, which has been slowly declining in the face of competitive human uses of the land and water.

The terrain is employed for limited livestock grazing, but forage production capability is sharply constrained by the generally high and rugged landscape. About 65 percent of the unit is forested; ponderosa pine and Douglas-fir trees inhabit lower elevations, but they are succeeded by lodgepole pine and Engelmann spruce as elevations rise to the timberline. Timber productivity, although commercially significant, is limited by steep slopes, variable soils, and difficulty of access. The unit serves as an important water collector because of its location along the Continental Divide — a major barrier to Pacific weather fronts that drop the bulk of moisture on the west slope. Eleven water storage facilities deliver water to metropolitan and agricultural users — mostly on the eastern plains. Virtually all of the water flowing from either side of the unit is impounded and diverted for human uses.

Sharp conflict emerged over Forest Service management policies for Big Vista Divide. Some groups pushed hard for designation of a major portion of the unit as wilderness area; others hoped for increased economic development. Groups from the rural western slope tended to opt for polices that would enhance local growth of population, employment opportunities, and diversion of water to support their growth ambitions. Leading spokespeople for eastern slope communities, already experiencing rapid urbanization and industrialization, strongly endorsed measures to slow or stop economic growth and to preserve the unit's distinctive amenity values in the name of counterbalancing their own sense of immediate environmental loss. Groups located on the western slope, in particular, saw their progress in construction of a transmountain highway through the unit — a highway that would also provide a utility corridor to the west side. Road proposals constituted an anathema to many urbanites on the eastern side, who also resisted development of a ski area promoted by interests who clearly won the sympathy of western slope residents. Decision-makers in the public household, once again, were confronting that basic fact of life: Bitterly contesting groups carried different and mutually incompatible prescriptions for promoting social development.

The Policy Options

A conflict analysis was conducted as one of several means of assessing impacts of four proposed policies. Each policy option was developed in detail; specific activities provided by each alternative were defined and located on high resolution maps of the planning unit. The four alternatives are briefly synopsised in the following paragraphs:

In alternative A, protection and enhancement of wilderness, aesthetic, air, and water quality values would be the primary emphasis. Other resource uses and activities would be subordinated to the goal of environmental protection and wilderness use. The maximum amount of wilderness within the definition of the Wilderness Act would be provided. This option would exclude the possibility of a transmountain highway and associated utility corridor.

Alternative B called for long-term continuation of present uses and activities. Primary emphasis would be placed on maintaining endangered and threatened fish and wildlife habitat coupled with maintenance of historical and cultural sites. Dispersed recreational activities in a natural environment would be emphasized along with protection and use of unique natural areas. No wilderness would be made available, although opportunities for primitive, nonmotorized recreation would be provided. The transmountain highway and utility corridor would be possible.

Alternative C would promote recreation diversity. Primary emphasis would be to provide maximum diversity of moderate- to low-intensity recreation opportunities no more than a tank of gasoline from "metroplex." Amenities and intangible values would be protected and enhanced in support of recreation diversity — for example, developed campgrounds limited to the proposed highway corridor and a mix of low-intensity recreation sites in areas removed from the corridor. There would be no provision for ski areas. The amount of wilderness provided would be less than that under alternative A but more than that provided by alternative D.

Alternative D focused on promotion of tangible forest product production. Major emphasis would be placed on stimulating local and regional economic growth through development of high-intensity recreation sites (for example, ski areas and developed summer campground facilities), production of commercial timber, and utilization of forage, wildlife, and water. Policy emphasis would provide for maximizing economic values at minimum possible amenity costs. A lesser amount of wilderness would be available than provided by either alternatives A or C, but it would provide a minimum wilderness designation in comparison to alternative B, which would provide no designated wilderness. A transmountain highway would be possible.

Source of Data

A modified Delphi procedure (see Appendix II) was employed to generate data for the conflict analysis.[53] Panels of locally knowledgeable citizens representing a cross section of activities afforded by the planning unit were assembled. During each round of the conflict assessment, each citizen judge made a series of estimates about the positions on cleavages — for, against, neutral — of the several conflict groups. After each round of judgment, each citizen was allowed to inspect the judgments and rationale of others on the panel in a manner that protected the anonymity of each. During the course of each round, citizen judges consulted detailed policy proposals, data, and maps showing distributions of activities under each proposed policy alternative. The process was cumulative; each round built on the information generated in earlier ones.

This modified Delphi procedure, therefore, consisted of a series of sequential interrogations based on review of judgments of others at each step. It provided means to keep communication of informed judgments free from the biases of personality factors, social status, and power. The focus throughout was not on what participants preferred but on which conflict groups would take which positions on specified cleavages. The data defined a factual conflict condition obtaining on the planning unit. There was no attempt to arrive at any value judgment by aggregating panelist preferences.

Panel Operations

Panel members were asked to independently identify significant conflict cleavages dividing conflict groups over policy for the Big Vista Divide unit. Working with this list for two rounds of review, panels arrived at a list of six base conflict cleavages:

1. A cleavage over promotion of population growth and economic development in the unit. Some groups, especially those identified with Western Slope communities, advocated such growth while other groups strongly opposed it.

2. A cleavage over construction of a transmountain highway through the unit. The available east-west, north-south highway system connecting west slope communities with urban areas and markets of the east severely curtailed movement of people and goods to and from west slope communities even in summer.

In winter there was no available direct all-weather transportation facility. People on the west side had to travel a considerable distance north or south to reach transmountain highways. Opponents saw that such a highway and utility corridor would compromise amenity values and substantially reduce the area that could be placed under wilderness designation.

3. A cleavage over allocation of agricultural water to municipal and industrial uses. All water presently generated in the unit had been committed. Additional industrial and municipal uses could only be accommodated by water transfers from agriculture, and strong opposition to such transfers had crystallized.

4. A cleavage over development of utility services along the proposed transmountain highway corridor. Electric power lines could bring cheaper energy from the east but at cost to scenic values.

5. A cleavage over proposed construction of a ski area designed to accommodate a moderate volume of skiers.

6. A cleavage over more restrictive county zoning to more effectively control patterns and composition of growth within and adjacent to the planning unit.

After establishing the list of base conflict cleavages judged to be central to the planning unit, the panel of judges proceeded to the second step. Again employing a sequence of anonymous Delphi interrogations, reviews, and iterative adjustments, panelists arrived at:

1. Estimates of the positions (for, against, neutral) that each of sixteen conflict groups took on each of the six base cleavages (see Table 6.2).[54]

2. Estimates of base cleavage salience importance to each conflict group (see Table 6.2).

3. Estimates of positions and salience of each proposed policy option for each conflict group (see Table 6.3).

Results

To render the descriptive data of Tables 6.2 and 6.3 into a form suitable for polarization analysis, Table 6.4 was constructed. Interpretation of Table 6.4 proceeds in several steps. First, a base group category

Table 6.2. Estimated Positions of Conflict Groups on Six Base Cleavages With Salience Scores

Organizational Categories	Issue 1 Population Growth and Economic Development	Issue 2 Construction of Transmountain Highway	Issue 3 Allocation of Water to Municipal Use	Issue 4 Development of Utility Services and Roads	Issue 5 Ski Area	Issue 6 More Restrictive County Zoning
Sawmills/planing mills	+3	+3	+1	+3	-1	-3
Logging contractors	+3	+3	+1	+2	-1	-3
Cattle, sheep, grazing	+2	+2	-2	-2	-1.5	-2
Other livestock	+1	0	-1	0	0	-2
Minerals/mining	+3	+2.5	+1	+3	-1	-1
Watershed/water users	+2	+2	+3	+2	+3	+3
Eating/drinking	+3	+2	+3	+2	+3	0
Personal services	+3	+2	+2	+2	+3	0
Wilderness recreation	-3	-3	-3	-3	-3	+3
Wildlife recreation	-3	-2	-2	-3	-3	+3
Dispersed recreation	-2	-2	-2	-2	-0.5	+2.5
Developed recreation	+2	+2	+2	+2	+3	+3
Auto/gas	+3	+3	+2	+3	+3	0
Transportation/warehousing	+2.5	+3	0	+3	+2	-1
Food processing	0	0	+1	+0.5	+1	-1
Other retail	+3	+2	+3	+2	+3	-0.5

Position: + = For, - = Against, 0 = Neutral
Salience (Importance): 3 = High importance, 2 = Moderate importance, 1 = Low importance, 0 = No importance

187

Table 6.3. Estimated Positions of Conflict Groups With Salience Scores on Four Proposed Management Policies

Organizational Categories	Alternative A Continue Present Management	Alternative B Maximum Wilderness	Alternative C Recreation Diversity	Alternative D Economic Development
Sawmills/planing mills	+2	-3	-2	+3
Logging contractors	+2	-3	-2	+3
Cattle, sheep, grazing	+2	-2	-1	+3
Other livestock	+2	0	+2	+1
Minerals/mining	+3	-3	-2	+3
Watershed/water users	+3	-2	-1	+2
Eating/drinking	+1	+1	+2	+2
Personal services	+1	+1	+2	+2
Wilderness recreation	-2	+3	-2	-3
Wildlife recreation	+2	+3	+1	-2
Dispersed recreation	+2	+2	+3	-2
Developed recreation	+2	-2	+3	+2
Auto/gas	+1	-1	+3	+2
Transportation/warehousing	+1	-1	+1	+3
Food processing	+1	0	+1	+2
Other retail	+1	+2	+2	+3

Position: + = For, - = Against, 0 = Neutral
Salience (Importance): 3 = High importance, 2 = Moderate importance, 1 = Low importance, 0 = No importance

Table 6.4. Conflict Patterns Over Six Base Cleavages

| Social Organizational Unit | Observed Social Organizational Category Position Relative to Base Group on Six Base Cleavages Sawmills/Planing Mills | | | | Ideally Expected Social Organizational Category Position | | Observed Deviation From Ideally Expected | | B5 | Maximum Possible Salience | Maximum Possible Deviation |
	A1 For	A2 Against	A3 Neutral	A4 Salience Σ	B1 For	B2 Against	B3 Above	B4 Below	Total (B3 + B4)	B6	B7
Logging contractors	6	0	0	13	3	3	3	3	6	18	6
Minerals/mining	6	0	0	11.5	3	3	3	3	6	18	6
Watershed/water users	5	1	0	13	3	3	2	2	4	18	6
Transportation/warehousing	5	0	1	11	2.5	2.5	2.5	2.5	5	18	6
Auto/gas	5	1	0	15	3	3	2	2	4	18	6
Other retail	5	1	0	13.5	3	3	2	2	4	18	6
Eating/drinking	4	1	1	13	2.5	2.5	1.5	1.5	3	18	6
Personal services	4	1	1	12	2.5	2.5	1.5	1.5	3	18	6
Developed recreation	4	1	1	11	2.5	2.5	1.5	1.5	3	18	6
Cattle, sheep, grazing	4	2	0	11.5	3	3	1	1	2	18	6
Other livestock	2	1	3	4	1.5	1.5	0.5	0.5	1	18	6
Food processing	3	1	2	3.5	2	2	1	1	2	18	6
Wildlife recreation	1	5	0	16	3	3	2	2	4	18	6
Dispersed recreation	1	5	0	11	3	3	2	2	4	18	6
Wilderness recreation	1	5	0	18	3	3	2	2	4	18	6
				$\Sigma = 177$					$\Sigma = 55$	$\Sigma = 270$	$\Sigma = 90$

$C_{ij} = .400$

Table 6.4 (continued)

| Social Organizational Unit | Management Policy A Environmental Quality Position of Social Organization Relative to Base Group — Sawmills/Planing Mills | | | | | Management Policy B Continue Existing Position of Social Organization Relative to Base Group — Sawmills/Planing Mills | | | | |
	C₁ For	C₂ Against	C₃ Neutral	C₄ +/- Units of Deviation	C₅ Salience Position	D₁ For	D₂ Against	D₃ Neutral	D₄ +/- Units of Deviation	D₅ Salience Position
Logging contractors	X			+1	3	X			+1	2
Minerals/mining	X			+1	3	X			+1	1
Watershed/water users	X			+1	3	X			+1	2
Transportation/warehousing	X			+1	1	X			+1	1
Auto/gas	X			+1	1	X			+1	1
Other retail		X		−1	2	X			+1	1
Eating/drinking		X		−1	1	X			+1	1
Personal services		X		−1	1	X			+1	1
Developed recreation	X			+1	2	X			+1	2
Cattle, sheep, grazing	X			+1	2	X			+1	2
Other livestock		X		0	0	X			+1	2
Food processing		X		0	0	X			+1	1
Wildlife recreation	X			+1	3	X			+1	2
Dispersed recreation	X			+1	2		X		−1	2
Wilderness recreation	X			+1	3		X		−1	2
				Σ = +7	Σ = 27				Σ = +11	Σ = 23

CP_A = .408   CP_B = .411

Table 6.4 (continued)

Social Organizational Unit	Management Policy C Environmental Quality Position of Social Organization Relative to Base Group — Sawmills/Planing Mills					Management Policy D Continue Existing Policy Position of Social Organization Relative to Base Group — Sawmills/Planing Mills				
	E_1 For	E_2 Against	E_3 Neutral	E_4 +/- Units of Deviation	E_5 Salience Position	F_1 For	F_2 Against	F_3 Neutral	F_4 +/- Units of Deviation	F_5 Salience Position
Logging contractors	X			+1	2	X			+1	3
Minerals/mining	X			+1	2	X			+1	3
Watershed/water users	X			+1	1	X			+1	2
Transportation/warehousing		X		-1	1	X			+1	3
Auto/gas		X		-1	3	X			+1	2
Other retail		X		-1	3	X			+1	3
Eating/drinking		X		-1	2	X			+1	2
Personal services		X		-1	2	X			+1	2
Developed recreation		X		-1	3	X			+1	2
Cattle, sheep, grazing	X			+1	1	X			+1	3
Other livestock		X		-1	2	X			+1	1
Food processing		X		-1	1	X			+1	2
Wildlife recreation		X		+1	1		X		+1	2
Dispersed recreation	X			+1	3		X		+1	2
Wilderness recreation	X			-1	2		X		+1	3
				$\Sigma = -2$	$\Sigma = 29$				$\Sigma = +15$	$\Sigma = 35$
	$CP_C = .398$					$CP_D = .422$				

191

was selected; it is listed above columns A1, A2, A3, and A4. For this exercise, the category "sawmills/planing mills" was employed as the base category against which positions of other conflict groups were measured. Each other set of actors was seen to take a position of support for, neutrality toward, or opposition to the position of the sawmill group on each cleavage.

Second, the frequency is recorded with which each conflict group is estimated by panelists to either ally with, be opposed to, or be neutral to the position taken by the base group. These values are found in columns A1, A2, and A3 of Table 6.4. Values of 6 entered under the heading "For Sawmills" (Column A1) and 0 under the heading "Against Sawmills" (Column A2) indicate that the group was estimated by the panelists to support the sawmills/planing mills position six of six times.

Third, an "expected" pattern of support and opposition was constructed — the pattern expected to occur if there were to be a perfect pattern of crosscutting conflicts on cleavages where nonneutral positions were taken. These values are found in columns B1 and B2 of Table 6.4.

Fourth, the "observed" pattern of support and opposition was then compared to the "ideally expected" (perfectly nonpolarizing) pattern (see columns B3, B4). The question can now be asked: How much deviation occurs between the observed patterns of conflict and those ideally expected? Deviation scores are computed simply by determining the difference between the number of times a given group category was "for" sawmills and the expected number, by doing the same in regard to the "against" column, and summing the two values (see column B5). In those instances where conflict groups are found to be neutral on one or more cleavages, the ideally expected conflict pattern is based on the number of nonneutral positions taken.

Fifth, the units of deviation in column B5 are then summed. In Table 6.4, this sum equals 55.

Sixth, a conflict polarization score was computed for the assessment unit prior to consideration of the impact of any proposed public policies. Recall that the conflict polarization coefficient is defined as:

$$C_{ij} = \frac{\sum D_a \left(\sum S_a \right)}{\sum D_p \left(\sum S_p \right)}$$

where:

C_{ij} = conflict polarization in Big Vista Divide in the spring of 1976.

$\sum D_a$ = sum of actual deviations from the ideally expected on the base cleavages (column B).

$\sum D_p$ = sum of potential deviations that could occur if no neutral positions were to be taken (column B).

$\sum S_a$ = sum of salience scores actually estimated (observed) on base cleavages (column A).

$\sum S_p$ = sum of potential salience scores that could occur if no neutral positions were taken (column B).

Substituting the values displayed in Table 6.4 into the formula, one obtains:

$$C_{ij} = \frac{55\,(177)}{90\,(270)} = .40$$

The coefficient of cleavage polarization summarizes what a careful inspection of Table 6.4 reveals — the Big Vista Divide unit was the object of a substantial degree of conflict polarization over the six base cleavages. Actors who ally on one cleavage tend to be allies on others, and cleavage saliences tend to run high. Forest Service custodians of this small piece of the public household were besieged with conflicting definitions of progress. Providing a coefficient of polarization and a table of data may focus anxiety of decision-makers and conflicting publics; furthermore, it may provide some insight into their difficulties; but it can hardly instruct them as to what should be done by way of policy choice. A science of fact has been exercised, but no logic of value has yet been applied. One must proceed to the policy assessment and ranking as initiated in the next step.

A question now frames the seventh step: Given the conflict patterns estimated to prevail among base cleavages, will any given proposed policy introduce more or less crosscutting conflict? Each proposed policy alternative can now be compared to the existing conflict pattern presented in the A columns of Table 6.4. The positions estimated to be taken by each group category on each of the proposed policies are displayed in Table 6.4 under the columns labeled C, D, E, and F. A value of plus 1 (+1) appears if the position on a policy taken by the group would increase the deviation from the purely crosscutting pattern. A positive 1 (+1) indicates that old allies or old enemies on the base cleavages are once again allies or enemies on the proposed policy cleavage. A value of minus 1 (-1) appears if the position taken would decrease the deviation from the ideally expected pattern — that is, old enemies on base cleavages are estimated to be allied on the proposed policy cleavage. A zero appears if a group is estimated to assume a neutral stance on the policy proposal.

Eighth, a conflict polarization coefficient, reflecting the increase or decrease in polarization occasioned by the estimated impact of each proposed policy, can now be computed.

$$C_{px} = \frac{\left(\sum D_a \sum S_a\right) + \left(\sum D_{ax} \sum S_{ax}\right)}{\sum D_p \sum S_p}$$

where:

C_{px} = conflict polarization coefficient in Big Vista Divide unit in 1976 given implementation of policy x.

$\sum D_a$ = sum or actual deviation from the ideally expected on the base cleavages.

$\sum S_a$ = sum of actual salience score from basic cleavages.

$\sum D_p$ = sum of potential deviations from the ideally expected on the base cleavages.

$\sum D_{ax}$ = sum of actual deviations (plus or minus) contributed by policy x.

$\sum S_{ax}$ = sum of actual salience scores contributed by policy x.

Substituting values from Table 6.4 into the formula for proposed policy A, one finds that:

$$C_{px} = \frac{55\ (77) + 7\ (27)}{90\ (270)} = .408$$

Policy A, therefore, is found to increase polarization by a small amount. Table 6.4 displays polarization scores as computed for each of the other three policy options. Three of the four policy proposals

Table 6.5. **Ranking of Proposed Policy Options for Big Vista Divide**

Rank Order	Proposed Policy Alternative	Coefficient of Polarization Associated With Policy
1	Alternative C Recreational Diversity	.398
2	Alternative A Environmental Quality	.408
3	Alternative B Continue Present Mgt.	.411
4	Alternative D Economic Development	.422
Base Polarization of Big Vista Divide		.400

are seen to increase polarization and thereby fail the test. However, alternative C slightly reduces polarization. The economic development policy option is established to be, by good margin, the most polarizing and therefore last ranked. The results of this policy assessment are lifted from Table 6.4 and are arranged for easier viewing in Table 6.5.

There is no way, at this time, to estimate how much of an increase in conflict polarization can be tolerated before it exceeds critical unknown thresholds and generates significant problems of social cohesion and negotiability of differences among affected groups. The current inadequacy of conflict theory prevents one from determining the amount of increased conflict polarization that one can add to various base amounts before endangering the social fabric. Given the limited knowledge available, the recommendation is to avoid increasing levels of conflict polarization. This can be accomplished by selecting a proposed policy that reduces polarization or by revamping attributes of currently polarizing policy proposals so that their polarizing potentials are removed. Furthermore, it must be stressed that in this study alternative C, recreation diversity, was not the best of all possible alternatives — only the least inferior of those that were formulated and brought to assessment.

CONFLICT ANALYSIS IN PAKISTAN — THE CASE OF JALARABAD

Background

The agricultural sector of Pakistan[55] possesses extraordinary potential for the production of food and fiber. Deep alluvial soils, favorable climate for year-round cropping, a large rural labor force, and the world's largest single irrigation system operating under one management (it incorporates 32 million acres of the Indus and tributary river valleys) could combine to become one of the planet's great agricultural regions.[56]

The Indus River, nearly 1,800 miles in length, drains a basin of approximately 387,000 square miles — an area roughly equivalent to the combined areas of Texas, Colorado, and Connecticut. Major tributaries are the Jhelum, Chenab, Ravi, Beas, and Sutlej, which gave the Punjab province its name — land of five (*punj*) waters (*ab*). The Indus, along with the tributaries, forms the natural center of Pakistan's irrigation system around which human engineering has stitched a complex of reservoirs, river barrages, huge link canals for connecting river beds, major and minor distributaries, and local watercourses. Overall, the flow of water originates in high Himalayan watersheds and proceeds to one of the major rivers, from which it is diverted into major and then to minor canals and run through a fixed outlet (*mogha*) into a community watercourse (*sarkari khal*) to individual farmer ditches and finally to fields where bunded units are flooded on a regular rotation.

It is not the purpose of this discussion to examine the rich history and operation of this irrigation system — something found elsewhere.[57] Neither is it the objective to provide an ethnographic description of village life.[58] It is important, however, to sketch fundamental features of village social organization within which farmers strive to live and work. The central building block of village social organization is the brotherhood network (*biradari*). Biradaries are combined into caste networks. A faction of such a network (a *patti*) — is linked to higher governmental authority through a headman (*numbardar*). Villages are divided into agricultural and artisan castes.[59] Traditionally, people of artisan (*moeen*) castes have performed nonagricultural services for each other and for members of agricultural castes for a share of the crop. Artisans typically do not have access to cultivatable land.

Birardari groups, based on male lineage, form the core of village social organization. Obligations within this network typically carry more weight on individuals than obligations to any other social network. Headed by the eldest competent male, answerable to other village authorities for the conduct of brotherhood associates, the biradari is a social unit that can be expected to take common positions on issues and candidates for political office. It is a social security unit that takes care of its own in the event of financial reverses, ill health, and death. It is, furthermore, a social unit for managing the factors of agricultural production — land, water, animals, tools, seeds, fertilizers, and credit.

The village, here fictitiously referred to as Jalarabad, was established in the nineteenth century by migrants into the area who sought opportunities provided by the then newly constructed irrigation system. By the 1970s, the village consisted of approximately eight hundred people, the landowning farmers of whom were organized into two major agricultural caste groups — Jat and Arain — which in turn were divided into a total of ten biradaries. Jalarabad is deeply divided between the sizable Jam Jat biradari on one hand and, on the other, the remaining biradaries in coalition — led by Rid Jats, Pahore Jats, and Arains who stand united in opposition to Jam Jats.

Current conflict cleavages have their roots in a bitter land dispute between Jam Jat people, who were the original nineteenth-century settlers, and the other biradaries, members of which settled in the village soon after the partition of the Indian subcontinent in 1947. The problem centered on division of land vacated by fleeing Hindu farmers. "Locals," the Jam Jat farmers, struggled with incoming refugee groups dispossessed by the upheavals of partition and seeking to reestablish their lives. The land dispute quickly escalated to violence and lives were lost in the early fighting. Within a few years the land and refugee/local cleavages were overlapped by another cleavage created when refugee farmers adopted a government-sponsored cooperative society program strongly opposed by Jam Jats, who without a single exception in over three decades refused to participate in the cooperative society's farming effort. Furthermore, because the cooperative society played a major role in financing the local elementary school, Jam Jats refused to contribute to it or allow their children to attend — placing another cleavage on top of the refugee/local, land, and cooperative society divisions.

Life in Jalarabad is characterized by constant verbal abuse and mutual exclusion from hooka smoking groups and ceremonies of marriage and circumcision. Sporadic outbursts of fighting occur, which have led to physical injury and, on some occasions, death. Constant intrigue occupies everyone's attention as opponents maneuver to embarrass each other, to steal each other's irrigation water, to take advantage of opportunities to press charges of water theft, and to arrange to have opponents jailed on such various allegations as linkage with district police authority will permit.

Analysis and Discussion

A conflict analysis of Jalarabad is presented in Table 6.6. The four base cleavages dividing the village are:

1. refugees (assorted biradaries) versus locals (Jam Jats),
2. land division among refugees and locals,
3. cooperative farming society dominated by refugees and rejected by locals, and
4. local elementary school dominated by refugees and opposed by locals.

Employing the data displayed on Table 6.6, and substituting those values into the conflict polarization formula, one finds:

$$C_{ij} = \frac{\sum D_a \left(\sum S_a \right)}{\sum D_p \left(\sum S_p \right)}$$

$$C_{ij} = \frac{33\,(99)}{36\,(108)} = .840$$

A glance at Table 6.6 reveals that Jalarabad is highly polarized. There is an absence of crosscutting attachments and very few neutral positions taken by the several biradari groups. Allies on the issue of land are the same as those who are allied over cleavages having to do with refugee rights and status, cooperative activities and goals, and elementary school affairs.

No carefully formulated set of policy alternatives was formally assessed with respect to Jalarabad. However, a group of irrigation technicians, operating under the auspices of the central government and an international agricultural assistance program, determined to improve the local irrigation system in this highly polarized community. Noting that approximately half of the irrigation water was lost in conveyance from the minor canal outlet (*mogha*) to farmer field ditches by its passage through the poorly maintained community watercourse,

Table 6.6. Cleavage Patterns in Jalabad Over Four Base Cleavages

Social Organizational Unit (each represents a biradari unit)	Observed Social Organizational Unit's Position Relative to Base Unit on Four Cleavages Base Unit = Arain				Ideally Expected Social Units Position		Observed Deviation From Ideally Expected			S_p Maximum Possible Salience	D_p Maximum Possible Deviation
	A_1 For	A_2 Against	A_3 Neutral	A_4 Actual Salience (S_a)	B_1 For	B_2 Against	B_3 Above	B_4 Below	B_5 $(B_3 + B_4)$	B_6	B_7
Rajput	4	0	0	12	2	2	2	2	4	12	4
Owd	4	0	0	12	2	2	2	2	4	12	4
Awan	2	0	2	6	1	1	1	1	2	12	4
Khosal	4	0	0	12	2	2	2	2	4	12	4
Syed	3	0	1	9	1.5	1.5	1.5	1.5	3	12	4
Pahore Jat	4	0	0	12	2	2	2	2	4	12	4
Mahey Jat	4	0	0	12	2	2	2	2	4	12	4
Rid Jat	4	0	0	12	2	2	2	2	4	12	4
Jam Jat	0	4	0	12	2	2	2	2	4	12	4
				$\Sigma = 99$					$\Sigma = 33$	$\Sigma = 108$	$\Sigma = 36$

$$C_{ij} = .840$$

the technical field team decided to assist in the reconstruction of that facility as a demonstration effort.[60] An improved community conveyance channel would reduce waterlogging and salinity for the farmers located toward the head reaches and would produce additional water supplies toward tail sections, thereby allowing greater cropped acreages for all. The objectives were clear and everyone involved would be better off — or so it seemed. Local labor and materials would be mobilized to do the reconstruction with assistance of the technical team.

Unfortunately, the field party — in its enthusiasm for a project so apparently advantageous and in its ignorance of the social situation — dealt exclusively with leaders of the majority anti–Jam Jat refugee coalition, who had no particular desire to elevate their opponents by pointing out their importance to the overall scheme of things. Because the technicians did not realize they were overlooking the effects of their effort on the significant Jam Jat faction, the improved watercourse plan that took shape had two unfortunate attributes. First, being designed in consultation with refugee coalition leaders, it tended to take up the sixteen-foot right-of-way in a manner disproportionately to the disadvantage of Jam Jats. Second, being disproportionately located to take Jam Jat land out of production to the advantage of their opponents, the watercourse reconstruction effort could be effectively held hostage by Jam Jats. They waited to sabotage the project until after their longtime antagonists had planned, invested money in the purchase of materials, and labored in digging approximately the first third of the improved channel through their own land.

Although failure to consult with Jam Jat leadership was a most innocent oversight on the part of the expatriate technical field party, the direct consequences were disastrous. As soon as the digging reached parcels of Jam Jat land, work abruptly halted. Those of the anti–Jam Jat refugee coalition pressured the technicians to push the construction work over Jam Jat resistance. In effect, refugee leaders counted upon the field party to politically humiliate their long-established Jam Jat opponents.

Field party technicians, after overcoming the initial shock of learning that not all village members of the irrigation community were enthusiastic supporters of their "development" efforts, engaged in futile negotiations. They soon determined that the situation was hopeless. Changes demanded by Jam Jats were unacceptable to the refugee groups. The field party withdrew, leaving the polarized community with a new cleavage over which to fight, new wounds to discuss, new stories of perfidy to tell, new grist for indoctrination of the young on both sides. The technicians, for their part, could only draw misplaced conclusions about irrationality of villagers. Villagers, on either side of the local conflicts, could only bemoan the untrustworthy nature of outsiders representing remote governments.

Given the state of social conflict polarization in this unit, one can only sadly note that the burden of irrationality and irresponsibility may lay heavily on those agents of the public household who, however unwittingly, further polarized villagers. How a highly polarized social unit such as Jalarabad can be successfully crosscut and opened to constructive social development is a serious and unanswered question. Three points can, however, be made. First, the amount of conflict polarization that can be successfully crosscut by a policy-induced cleavage must be the subject of further research. Second, natural resource policy conflicts tend to produce inherently weighty, or salient, cleavages with much crosscut potential because they are so centrally connected to income, social identity, and capacity to sustain important cultural symbols. This becomes a source of hope. Third, change agents, even if in no position to depolarize conflicts, should avoid operating so as to increase polarization — especially in situations already highly polarized.[61]

CONCLUSION

Technological policies are inevitably involved in, and generate, social conflict cleavages because such policies differentially confer advantage and disadvantage. That which one actor will enthusiastically endorse, members of other groups will just as heartily reject. When social life becomes polarized, not only do values come into intense and nonnegotiable conflict, but the very concept of fact falls apart. Each opponent group refuses to acknowledge the "facts" advanced by the other; each faction advances its version of fact in antagonism to the other. Neither sciences of fact nor logics of value prosper in such situations.

The nomothetic form of conflict, its degree of polarization, is of greater interest to policy assessment than the specific idiographically apprehended cultural substance of conflict. This logic accepts the wide variety of local site-specific cleavages and operates cross culturally. Furthermore, conflict structure is connected to choice in that conflict in polarized form is inherently destructive of choice and reasoned discourse, whereas crosscutting forms of conflict sustain choice structures and opportunity to negotiate. The value criterion for assessing proposed policies for management of the public household is that conflict polarization should be reduced. Those proposed policies that are estimated to create new conflicts on crosscutting vectors are assessed as superior to those that insert overlapping cleavages into the social web.

The problem, then, becomes one of measuring whether a proposed policy for the public household will increase polarization. A solution has been presented that operates in four stages: (1) existing cleavages in a unit of analysis are identified, and a conflict polarization coefficient is computed for the base situation; (2) patterns of support, neutrality, and opposition are determined with respect to each proposed policy option; (3) each policy-induced conflict pattern is superimposed on the pattern of preexisting base cleavages operative in the social unit to determine the extent to which each policy can be expected to increase or decrease conflict polarization; and (4) proposed policies are ranked from most to least polarizing.

Each of these steps involves a sociological science of fact. Working on this factual base, a sociological logic of value locates those policies that reduce polarization by any amount and passes them on for assessment on lower criteria. Proposals that would increase polarization are rejected and returned for reformulation. Careful examination of patterns of support and opposition associated with failed policies may result in reformulations that produce reduced polarization and thereby earn the chance for such policies to advance downward in the policy assessment logic.

Computational procedures have been illustrated by examination of situations obtaining in a Forest Service planning unit in northern Colorado and in a South Asian village irrigation command area. The procedures are appropriate for use in planning units at different levels of analysis — villages, districts, neighborhoods, cities, counties, states, and nations.

The analysis constitutes a critical component of policy assessment. There are other important dimensions in analysis of proposals for affecting choice ranges, rates, and standards, but social conflict assessment is placed first in the value logic. It is strategic because it is central to the sustenance and expansion of choice context in the service of reason about fact and value. To erode ground for negotiation among continually conflicting and cooperating parties by increasing polarization, thereby raising threat levels and encouraging opponent employment of resources to mutually block and destroy choices, is to fundamentally threaten choice context and collective reason itself. By itself, this value criterion cannot be sufficient to define "best" or "least inferior" policy, but it represents a necessary condition to be fulfilled. No matter how economically profitable or ecologically viable an option, no matter how properly redistributive, no matter what the merits of the profile of futures forgone, if a proposed policy option can be shown to significantly increase polarization, the public household decision-maker who pushes forward with implementation of that alternative undercuts developmental potential of the policy.

Social Policy Assessment: A Science of Fact and a Logic of Value in the Domain of Choice Distribution

Equality is an absolutely necessary condition of freedom. — Mikhail A. Bakunin[1]

I love liberty, and I hate equality. — John Randolph[2]

Neither equality, freedom, nor democracy can long survive without the other two, for they together form an integral trilogy of social justice. — Francis M. Wilhoit[3]

The foundation of modern egalitarian thought has been constructed on three bedrock premises: (1) normal human beings are roughly equal in their capacities to experience pleasure and pain, (2) people are similar in their capacity to exercise rational control over their personal lives — to create individual life plans within moral constraints imposed by community requirements, and (3) people possess equal right to participate in public policy discourse regarding the shape of society within which they live. Grossly unequal resource distributions have been seen as threatening these assumptions and any conception of a more developed society.

It is the essence of modernity that all human beings are viewed as being members of the same species and that each individual's potential can only be realized if s/he possesses means of access to choice. People are different, and in order to be different in their own right they must have equality of condition and access to education, wealth, and income. The very purpose of equality is inequality in the sense of being able to pursue different individual lives. We typically judge whether individuals or groups are free by estimating the diversity and attractiveness of their alternatives. Slaves are not free because their alternatives are stifled. Poor people are less free than the rich because of their relatively diminished ranges of options, the slower rate at which their options can be exercised, and the inferior quality of those options.

Public policies, in the name of social development, must therefore somehow promote equality of condition and at least some amount of greater equality of resource distribution than imperfect markets are likely to generate. At least two general arguments constitute the heart of the rationale.

First, gross inequality threatens democratic forms of civic life. It has been observed since the days of Aristotle that great inequality of income, wealth, and education undermines the stability, and the very meaning, of democracy. When such inequalities are great, the rich and poor live in parallel social universes between which little is shared in common. Such systems tend toward either oligarchy in behalf of the rich against the poor or tyranny in the name of the poor against the rich. Aristotle, Marx, and Rawls — reflecting rather different social standpoints and perspectives — each has noted that great inequality of resource distributions undermines any authentic meaning of political democracy. No social scientist or philosopher has been able to specify precisely where the limit to inequality in resource distribution is or should be, but it is argued that great inequality, if permitted too long in a manner that deprives very many, threatens the survival of political democracy and the open society. A liberal conception of democratic institutions, where issues of social development are to be addressed by citizens considering alternative conceptions of "good reasons," is fundamentally threatened by a social structure within which the many are poor, great wealth is concentrated in the hands of the few, and the middle class is small and weak. Freedom of speech — freedom to meaningfully participate in sustained public discourse — depends upon having material resources at one's disposal. Scarcity of speech opportunity rides with great inequality.

Second, gross inequality in resource distributions undermines the operation of markets as coordinators of supply and demand and as partners of liberal-democratic governments in preserving open societies. This line of reasoning has been addressed in the discussion in Chapter 3 of distributional problems as a source of market breakdowns. It suffices here to note that, at a given level of production and per capita income, the more unequal the distribution of income, the more aggregate demand (and therefore the shape of production) will be influenced by the consumption preferences of the rich to the disadvantage of the poor. If a rich person transmits $100,000 worth of market vote signals to producers each month, whereas a poor person has only $250 to spend during that same period of time, producers will quite rationally respond to the much greater economic effective demand of the rich. Since the rich have a markedly greater propensity to consume luxury goods and services than do the poor who seek essentials of subsistence, producers following market signals turn toward the demand of the well heeled and away from the needs of the worn heeled. This provides an example of a situation where the traditional theory of consumer sovereignty represents not the sovereignty of all citizens expressing their diverse preferences in the marketplace but the pull of the few against the many. One can argue that the rich are obtaining their "just deserts" only if they have acquired their great wealth and incomes from a historically unflawed process of marketplace exchange, a process wherein no part of their current economic advantage can be attributed to any market breakdown, as described in Chapter 3. There simply have been, and are, no such pristine historical economic exchange processes.

For both reasons, then, great inequality in resource distribution threatens a viable conception of social development rooted in a liberal conception of the open society in which people contend with each other and with public policy by reasoned dialogue rather than by coercion. One cannot, therefore, simply advocate more choice, more production, more income, more wealth, more consumption. One must ask: More for whom? Much of the meaning of an additional unit of production depends upon who has the opportunity to benefit from it.

Technological and natural resource policy would be paralyzed by a requirement that precluded redistribution of choice opportunities. A policy will have the following implications for distribution of choices:

1. It will affect the location of jobs and services, thereby affecting accessibility of choice opportunities that can be obtained only at the price of overcoming distance and time. For example, every dollar, peso, or rupee spent on a private physician in the city is diverted from expenditure on safe community drinking water in the village.

2. It will affect values of property rights by making some property close to undesirable things — pollution, noise, ugliness — while making other property proximate to such desirable attributes as parks, open spaces, police protection, or transportation terminals.

3. It will enhance or undercut productive power of individuals and organizations by creating new work opportunities and obsolescing old ones. Policies promoting the production of small scale diesel- or solar-powered pumps for irrigation by small farmers will produce a very different pattern of employment opportunities than those that emphasize centralized large-scale production of electricity.

Shifts in resources and choices from group to group, time to time, and place to place will be inevitable. Redistribution in a no-growth context necessarily raises the issues of winners and losers in sharpest relief. However, even in situations where slow redistributions are undertaken during rapid increases of resource supplies, winners and losers there must be. Losers will emerge in the sense that someone's share will be below what it would have been if redistributive policies were not in effect. If not in absolute terms, redistributions will still occur in a relative manner. Losers are an essential part of any redistribution no matter how it is accomplished. The problem of distribution of choices, therefore, must be seen as strategic to any system of technology and natural resources policy assessment. Defensible policy assessment for the public household must address that roguish problem that has been hotly debated over the ages: Which policy should gain merit by virtue of being associated with a defensible redistribution of advantage? It is the purpose of this chapter to review the essentials of distributional theory and to formulate and justify a distributional logic of fact and value for policy assessment in the name of social development.

PROBLEMS IN FORMULATING A DISTRIBUTIONAL SCIENCE OF FACT

Alexis de Tocqueville warned us that "An abstract term is like a box with a false bottom; you may put into it what ideas you please and take them out again without being noticed."[4] What has been true of abstract terms in general is more than evident in discussions of equality. The literature is filled with discussions of the difficulties presented by that concept.[5] What do we mean when we say that we wish to reduce or eliminate inequality? An examination of the conceptual issues is essential as we prepare ourselves to construct a logic of distributional fact and value.

The concept of equity often enters distributional discussions early on. As distinguished from equality, equity connotes an ethically just distribution, and justice may or may not entail equal distributions.[6] Going back as far as Aristotle, equity has been associated with "fairness," similar treatment for similar cases, different treatment of different cases, the allocation of "just deserts." Equity is, therefore, not to be confused with equality.

Concepts of equity may make sense at the small-group level where individual accomplishment and failure can conceivably be known, but such conceptions make little sense in macro policy-assessment situations. There can be no definition of *just desert* applicable to broad policy assessment in sizable social units.[7] Even in micro situations we frequently do not know, and cannot calculate, the exact extent to which an individual is deserving of reward for service rendered over the course of a given year. Let anyone who doubts the veracity of this statement contemplate the explosiveness of debate among any dozen university faculty as they attempt to determine just desert in allocation of whatever modest salary increase has been made available by the dean for teaching, research, and professional service. There is no reasonable way to know, when engaging in macro policy assessment, whether successes of particular individuals, groups, or organizations are products of joint effort, individual diligence, or lucky windfall. There are deep uncertainties in any conception of just desert that will not go away, especially at the macro level where social policies are assessed. Therefore, what follows will focus on valuation regarding the pursuit of greater or lesser equality. No more will be said in this chapter about equity.

Equality, strictly speaking, posits what appears to be a simple empirical notion.[8] Given a specified quantity of a resource, it is to be distributed among the relevant population in equal shares. This seemingly innocuous statement, however, turns out to be most problematic. Although some inequalities, such as those having to do with income or wealth, can be measured in straightforward ways, other things are not so easily measured — for example, satisfaction with work or leisure activities. Furthermore, some resources are inherently divisible and complete equality of distribution is theoretically feasible, as in the case of income, whereas other resources are not divisible in the same sense, such as infant death.[9] For example, if the infant mortality rate is 10 percent, it is not possible to have the same percentage occur in each family. Each family unit must experience a whole death in infancy or none. Such inequalities can only be meaningful to collectivities in terms of deaths per thousand, a concept of equality quite different than what one usually associates with a divisible good such as income.

Equality of a resource distribution is often measured by use of a Lorenz curve and a Gini coefficient (see Fig. 7.1).[10] Given a situation of perfect equality, the least advantaged 20 percent of the population, as represented on Figure 7.1, would receive exactly 20 percent of the resource, the least advantaged 40 percent would obtain 40 percent, and so on. This logic leads to the construction of a straight line at a forty-five-degree angle — a line representing perfectly equal distribution.

However, an actual observed distribution may be far from equal, as seen in the Lorenz curve. As the curve drops away from the line of perfect equality, greater inequality of resource distribution is represented. A Lorenz curve has the property, therefore, of measuring the cumulative distribution of a quantity against a theoretical norm defining perfect equality. A Gini coefficient has been devised that consists of the ratio of the area between the Lorenz curve and the line of perfect equality and the total area in the triangle — the maximum possible area of inequality (see Fig. 7.1). As the Gini value approaches unity, the degree of inequality increases to its maximum.

So far, so good, but problems arise. Two distributions (X and Y) may yield the same Gini coefficient by having the same area under their respective Lorenz curves but place the burdens of inequality differently (see Fig. 7.2). When Lorenz curves intersect, conceptual problems emerge. Has inequality increased or decreased as between distributions X and Y? The two distributions are equally unequal, but each produces a different pattern of advantage and disadvantage. Distribution Y is more to the advantage of the least well off as compared to X. Methodological tools do exist that permit us to explore the implications of distributions when Lorenz curves and Gini coefficients are indeterminate.[11] Furthermore, methodological alternatives to the Lorenz curve and Gini coefficient are available.[12] It would not be fruitful to examine the methodological options here; that is a task better done by others.

For present purposes it is sufficient to note that once again we confront the reality that "truth" in both the world of fact and value is procedural; our methodological procedures shape our conception of "fact" about distributions, just as they shape our logic of value about distributions. There is no ultimate procedure that will define the ultimate distributional fact or value. We have learned a great deal about how to measure equality and inequality, and further inquiry can be

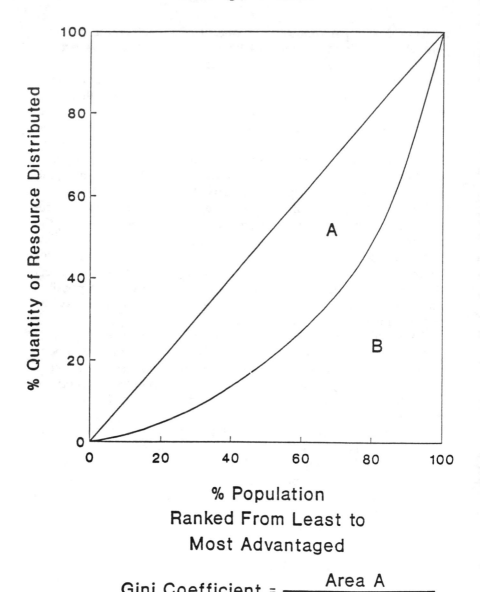

Figure 7.1. Lorenz Curve

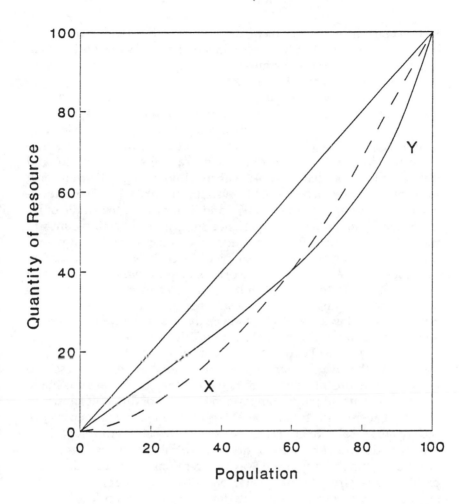

Area Under Curve X Equals Area Under Curve Y

Figure 7.2. Two Intersecting Lorenz Curves

expected to make better tools available. As our tools improve, so will our understandings of distributional problems. Each of our methodological options for defining distributional "facts" is characterized by a mix of advantages and disadvantages.

Additional problems of inequality measurement and interpretation turn on still other serious matters. Foremost among these is the fact that people experience inequality in society (1) not in terms of any one good or service but in terms of many simultaneously; (2) not at one point in time but over an entire life cycle; and (3) not only as isolated individuals but also as members of social groups.

First, inequality can occur in terms of a wide variety of goods — for example, income (a concept of flow), wealth (a concept of stock), prestige, suffrage, social influence, employment, job satisfaction, health care, housing, clean air or water, education, and police and fire protection. All of these, and other, items can be simultaneously and differently experienced. When we abstract nomothetic distributional principles from the rich flux of life, we capture only a few distributional facets regarding certain resources and thereby miss the whole of it.

Second, human beings experience society, not in a single instant that a Lorenz curve reflects on a decision-maker's graph, but over a lifetime. A retirement policy that yields great advantage for senior professors who are allowed to work extra years will deprive some newly minted doctorates of faculty positions and may slow rates of advancement for others. Or, to take another example, who is better off: a sixty-year-old with \$200,000 in wealth or a seventy-five-year-old who has accumulated \$125,000? Although the younger of this pair has more assets, s/he will expect to live more years and therefore need to portion out the wealth over a longer time frame. A person's resource position, therefore, must be examined according to where one is in the life cycle, not just in crude comparison to others of different ages.

Third, there is the fundamental fact that human beings experience society not as isolated atoms but as members of social groups. Socially constructed conflict cleavages, dividing social groups one from another, determine in important ways perceptions of the distributional problem. The struggle for greater equality is a struggle of groups, organizations, factions, and classes defined by a variety of vertical and horizontal social cleavages. If one confronts a situation in which cross-cutting conflict cleavages C_1, C_2, and C_3 (for example, anglo-Hispanic, anglo-black, and Hispanic-black) divide groups as in Figure 7.3, different consequences flow from selection of different cleavages as the primary one around which to reduce an inequality. If C_1 is selected as primary, and efforts are made to reduce inequalities with regard to this division, one may exacerbate inequalities with respect to C_2 and C_3. Improving conditions for Hispanics relative to anglos may well come at disadvantage to black people.

Should the social group, or the individual, constitute the relevant unit for distributional analysis? O'Neill has pointed out the difficulty

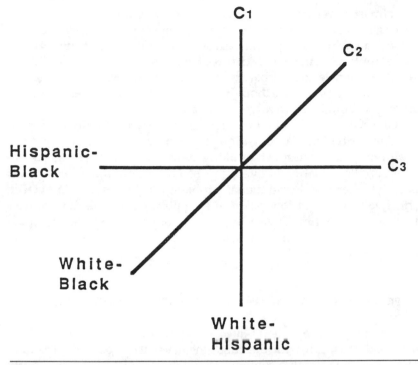

Figure 7.3. Illustration of Equality-Equity Problem Under Conditions of Multiple Cleavage

that this distinction poses in the liberal democratic tradition, which tends to ignore group claims in the name of an individualism that views groups as transitory expressions of individual interest with little standing before the law.[13] Can only individuals experience inequality? Or should one focus on problems of inequality as viewed from the standpoint of groups taken as a whole — the fundamental issue in the famous case of *Bakke v. The Regents of the University of California?*[14] When Bakke applied to medical school, he presumably thought in terms of equality, meaning that applicants would be judged according to individual merit without reference to ethnicity. But the admissions office had another conception of equality in mind — one having to do with rates of admission of ethnic group representatives.

If all members of a social group or statistical category have identical individual characteristics, equal treatment for the group or category would be equal for each individual member. This circumstance will almost never be encountered. When individuals are judged according to data representing their group, unequal treatment is dealt to individuals whose individual attributes are not those of their group. For example, if teenage male drivers tend to have more auto accidents than their female counterparts, all teenage males will pay higher insurance premiums even though some will negotiate these years of driving without being involved in an accident.

Given that one can be expected to confront inequality as experienced by individuals, among groups qua groups, between individuals of all groups thrown together along different discriminating dimensions simultaneously, and over time, serious question has been raised as to whether the distributional problem can be resolvable even in principle.[15] As a decision-maker in the public household manipulates an inequality on dimension X in the name of promoting greater equality, the likelihood is that inequality on dimension Y will expand in some questionable fashion.

PROBLEMS IN FORMULATING A DISTRIBUTIONAL LOGIC OF VALUE

Delegates to the United States' Constitutional Convention of 1787 struggled at length with the fundamental tension between freedom and equality. This value conflict formed the very basis of initial party formation — between Federalists, who favored the ideal of liberty and the provisions of the new federal constitution, and Jeffersonians, who openly expressed fear that the Philadelphia drafters had sacrificed equality for the liberty of privileged upper classes. U.S. citizens have since, like many of their brethren elsewhere, claimed a simultaneous commitment to each of these values while making ad hoc adjustments as their particular interests required and opportunity permitted. The search for resolution of the equality-liberty problem has been one of the great humanistic quests.[16] For the last two hundred years, especially, the effort to place the distributional genie into a theoretically adequate bottle has taken on an almost religious mystique among secular thinkers.

Rousseau held that the greatest sin that could be committed by civil society is the creation and perpetuation of social inequality, the sin responsible for most social evil. "The greatest evil has already come about when there are poor men to be protected and rich men to be restrained."[17] Among our contemporaries, Melvin Tumin has taken up Rousseau's position by contending:

No society can expect or demand from any individual any more than that of which he is capable. Differences in social development and capabilities are due to two sources: (1) the inherited capacities, and (2) the trained and patterned utilization of these capacities. Among people of equal natural capacity, differences in their socially relevant talents are functions of training and learning over which the average society has dominant control. Thus to reward them differently, assuming equal conscientiousness, is to reward differences in opportunity which were socially generated in the first place.[18]

For Tumin, therefore, good social policy requires a strong conception of equality in resource distributions. However, most liberal thinkers have rejected such a strong version of egalitarianism on the grounds that it would destroy too much liberty. For these, the proper antidotes for a local inegalitarian evil are the liberty to move, the opportunity to rise, and the freedom to buy, sell, and invest.

However, reply the strong egalitarians, property protects those who own it, and minorities of property owners can gain control over majorities who are unpropertied — a fundamental insight that Karl Marx grasped much to the embarrassment of the liberal political economists. What one can do to protect oneself in the marketplace depends on what one owns and can offer to potential exchange partners. When livelihood is at stake in marketplace exchange, personal coercion is not only possible but highly probable. All this makes a mockery of the marketplace as a protector of liberty unless there is a substantial degree of equality in distribution. Those who control water in the desert can extract exorbitant prices from the thirsty who do not possess the freedom to decline the offer. So, it is argued, hundreds of millions of people cannot refuse exploitive offers because their livelihood is at stake, and they do not command the assets that would allow them to drive better bargains. Therefore, the advantaged will perpetuate their advantage at the expense of the less well endowed. Replying to this egalitarian attack upon their libertarian free-market conceptions, most liberals in the weak egalitarian tradition will simply point out that good social policy should not be taken to mean imposing a crude egalitarian sameness upon all that crushes out individuality and freedom.

Advocates of both broad views, however, would agree in general that liberty and equality stand best when they stand together in mutual support.[19] But what does such a statement mean? It is obviously nothing but a platitude. In deciding where to draw the theoretical line between illegitimate and legitimate inequalities, different thinkers have assumed radically different positions for the assessment of public policy. A brief examination of the major positions is now in order.

Distribution and Basic Needs

Basic needs theorists posit lists of material human requirements, the fulfillment of which is a sine qua non for the reproduction and sustenance of humankind.[20] The general idea is to quantify "basic" needs for food, clothing, shelter, medical care, and educational opportunity and then to determine minimum quantities and qualities required. Amounts in addition to such minimums are viewed as luxuries or at least as being nonbasic. This line of distributional reasoning typically advocates that the policy analyst establish the number of calories (or other good) required for people by age, sex, and occupational categories in various climatic zones. Then one selects that policy that would fulfill these requirements. A policy that would fulfill nonbasic needs while outstanding basic requirements remain unfulfilled would be rejected.

The problem with all of this, of course, is that if one views basic needs in raw physical terms, the approach suggests a very low priority for consumption on the part of the worst off. The cheapest medically balanced diet, which might well be an improvement from a strict nutritional viewpoint over what rich people eat, could consist of soybean curd, orange juice, and beef liver — all edible but not high on the preference list of most poor people or anybody else.[21] Are we prepared to compel people to consume such a diet in the name of fulfilling basic needs? Or take shelter, another of the "basic" needs. How much housing space is absolutely required to ensure that people live out a normal life span? Calculations would vary from region to region, but the answer is that very little square footage is physically required for survival in even the harshest climate, as any Eskimo will tell us. People have lived long lives in appalling prison conditions. The very flexibility, toughness, and capacity of human beings to endure make one wary of basic needs criteria stated in minimum physical terms.

On the other hand, if one wishes to reject strictly physical requirements as adequate to the specification of basic needs, one would define them relative to what other people in the socioeconomic system would prescribe as necessary. The problem with this approach, of course, is that such requirements are socially defined and culturally conditioned and become impossibly blurred with taste and preference. Individual needs, as defined in relation to extant cultural norms, are a product of socialization. One learns to need, not mashed soybeans, but hamburger and pasta. One learns to need electricity, tap water, central heating, books, paper for school, letter jackets, music and stereophonic reproduction of it. Need in a socially relative sense becomes unlimited. Art historians have a basic need to travel, athletes learn to need large gymnasiums, physicists have basic needs for cyclotrons, and sociology professors have certifiable needs for computers, expensive journals, and support for field work in faraway places. Which needs are truly basic, and which should be sacrificed on the grounds that they are less so? At what point does luxury begin?

Norms defining basic need by calculating average requirements are meaningless because few people are average or live and work in average conditions.[22] Averages are abstracted constructs removed from the actual experience of life and work. One person may not need medical services throughout an entire lifetime; another might not survive without constant medical care of the most intensive and expensive variety. One student might whip through basic reading instruction with the greatest of ease while a dyslexic child struggles and consumes far greater educational resources.

Putting aside the horrendous computational problems to be faced in the course of trying to implement such a distributional theory, the basic needs approach does not help with the distribution of power, hot water heaters, automobiles, books, sailboats, lettuce, skis, or hamburger because none of these things, strictly speaking in the physical sense, fulfills basic needs. As soon as we depart from minimum physical standards defining need, we are left with no criteria for distribution among competing constituencies. Should Mutt receive the books he desires, or should Jeff get that sewing machine so basic to his tailoring ambitions?

Nor does basic needs theory distribute resources among time periods in the life cycle. Should one invest in youth job training or in housing for the aged? Nor does it distribute among individuals vis-à-vis groups — should Bakke have been admitted to medical school at the expense of disenrolling an Afro-American? The problem with basic need theories of distribution, then, is that rules will be necessary to determine how to weigh competing needs, but each rule will raise perplexing issues as to which needs should have priority. Rules will be required for weighing rules. One must expect complete consensus at some point, or one must be prepared to arbitrarily impose an interpretation backed by coercion to squelch the loser.

The problem is, then, if basic needs are defined by physical minimums, the analysis would permit rather extreme deprivation because of the inherent robustness of humans who can endure so much and still live out considerable life spans. If basic needs are defined beyond physical minimums, they become a hopeless tangle of culturally conditioned noncommensurable preferences.

This discussion, however, does suggest the importance of reiterating a distinction that has been advanced throughout the argument of this book — the difference between micro-individualistic conceptions rooted in personal preferences and needs and macro-structural conceptions rooted in the shape of society. The basic needs theory as discussed in this section requires the service of a nonexistent micro theory that could weigh and balance individual characteristics. Macro theories, however, refer not to individual attributes and correspondences to merited reward but to attributes of the social web. At the structural level, the value logic advanced in Chapter 5, and summarized in Figure 5.4, represents something of a structural "needs" theory. It is asserted that people "need" to live in nonpolarized social networks; that they "need" equality of condition and of opportunity; that there is a "need" for taking losses in the structural context of choice where they can be most afforded as defined by scope, intensity, and duration of projected losses; that people "need" the freedom to choose — something that rising incomes can confer in marketplaces disciplined by the higher-order value criteria. In a macro-structural sense, then, the value theory advanced in Chapter 5 is a basic needs theory. But the sense in which basic needs are conceived and analyzed is altogether different from the micro-needs theory reviewed in the preceding paragraphs.

Distribution and Utilitarian Theory

A good utilitarian would argue that resources should be distributed to maximize satisfaction. More particularly, the utilitarian would contend that reduction of extreme inequalities will add to the community's welfare, because an additional increment given to the least advantaged at the expense of the most advantaged will grant more utility to the former than its loss subtracts from the latter. A dollar transferred from the house of J. Pierpont Morgan to someone on the brink of starvation will add to the aggregate utility of community members because of the diminishing marginal utility of the dollar as income increases. But the matter becomes complex. At what point should dollar flow from the richer to the poorer halt? This is much the same question as that posed in the basic needs discussion.

Is perfect equality in dollar distribution a value worth seeking? Equality is as satisfied with the equality of nothing as with the equality of plenty. Furthermore, given Robbins's attack on interpersonal comparisons of utility, one simply cannot know if the satisfaction sacrificed by Mutt in giving up filet mignon for dinner is less than Jeff receives by virtue of obtaining a new shirt. If we assume that the marginal income utility schedules for all people at all times in all places are absolutely identical and that all people are equally productive, then an equal distribution of income would be called for. But we cannot know if the schedules are the same, nor do we know, if they differ, how they differ. Furthermore, we sense that some people discipline themselves to produce more than do others and that their greater sacrifice is a relevant consideration. This makes it impossible to compare utility schedules of persons A and B in any meaningful manner, and even if we could do so the process would be so horribly complex at the macro-analytical level that we would be forever bound up in computations for the simplest policy assessments.

Furthermore, viewing the problem of maximum welfare (total or average) is most artificial. Society is experienced by individuals bound up in networks of social interaction. The fundamental sociological truth is that, in the absence of social interaction, one never knows what one's own preferences are. We only come to know ourselves, and our preferences, as we to some degree fulfill others' expectations of us; as we move from role-status position to role-status position our preferences change. There simply is no consistent structure of utility schedules for any given individual or for persons in the aggregate. There is no meaningful sum of individual welfare, or sensible conception of average individual welfare, computed as though individuals are separate and perfectly independent social atoms. However people perceive their well-being, or lack thereof, those perceptions emerge in multiple processes of interaction with others in interdependent networks and they are in constant flux. Why should reasonable analysts want to maximize a perfectly fictional sum of individual atomistic utility or average it? The utilitarian position is deeply problematic.

Distribution and Libertarian Theory

Libertarians argue that merit, as determined by individual performance, gives proper entitlement to reward. Resources should be distributed according to how well one performs. All inequalities rooted in differential performance are legitimate, and public policy should in no way interfere by transferring resources from the meritorious to the less fortunate.

The libertarian case has been forcefully articulated by Robert Nozick.[23] Nozick straightforwardly tells us that individuals have rights and that there are things no person or group may do to others without violating their rights. Unfettered use of private property is basic to any meaningful conception of liberty. To Nozick, imposition of resource redistributions necessarily constitutes a loss of rights for both the "haves" and the "have nots." Public policy with the objective of increasing equality of distributions would by definition have to interfere with the liberty of the advantaged. Furthermore, even the "have nots" would have to be restrained after redistribution has occurred so as to prevent them from entering into any exchanges that would reintroduce inequality. The tension between freedom and equality is resolved on the side of individual freedom and fundamental rights to make contracts as one sees fit.

Nozick posits that each individual has a set of natural rights that entitles the individual to make the best possible personal use of his or her resources. No involuntary resource transfers in the name of increased social equality shall be permitted. The degree of inequality that prevails in a given situation is simply irrelevant. Equality of resource distribution as a value criterion for policy assessment must be rejected because to accept it would mean unacceptable abridgement of individual liberty. Nozick has taken the atomistic view of the individual to an extreme. For him, the individual stands alone in the world, equipped with a fixed and competitive utility-hungry nature, centered on the pursuit of rational self-interest to maximize individual preference disconnected from any responsibility to the social whole.

The cornerstone of libertarian theory is the notion of free people making uncoerced mutually beneficial exchanges in free marketplaces. Markets in this world, however, deviate considerably from the ideal visions of the neoclassical economists. They suffer most significantly from the unfortunate defects discussed in Chapter 3 — technological externalities, erosion of consumer sovereignty, public-goods problems, distortions in bargaining due to grossly unequal distributions of resources, the tyranny of small decisions, and the accompanying freezing of decision-makers. Each of these defects undercuts the libertarian argument because each market breakdown assures that "free" exchange will lead to less than minimally satisfactory results for many parties and for society as a whole. Reflection upon the nature of each of these marketplace defects reminds us that markets are the collective products of people in interaction and that there is no natural law that ensures that such histories of interaction conform to rules of individual merit and justice, however defined.

Most particularly, free-market libertarians must assume that the existing resource distributions have been noncoercively established by merit and merit alone. Only then can the case be made that, if one is in a position of holding few resources of value and is thereby unable to drive advantageous bargains, one has received just deserts for personal failure. Can the libertarian assure us that the rich are rich only by dint of their superior merit? Are the poor in their unhappy state only because of their deficient personal past performances? One who sees in history happenstance of natural disaster, the luck of being in the right place at the right time to enjoy a windfall, the coercion of group by group, of class by class, of nation by nation, individual by individual — anyone who sees in human history anything other than reward earned by personal merit alone — must appreciate that resource transfers are often justified. One must find serious fault with the hidden libertarian premise that all deserts secured in the marketplace are just deserts — fairly earned and noncoercively sustained.

Distribution and Rawlsian Maximin Theory

John Rawls, pursuing a tack opposite to that of Nozick, has drawn a very different theoretical line between legitimate and illegitimate inequality.[24] Rawls's citizen is much more socialized than is Nozick's; the structure of society, rather than individual pursuit of utility, takes center stage. Rawls sees the problem of social justice as involving both freedom and equality. To provide genuine equality of opportunity, agents of the public household must give attention to those with fewer assets. Rawls sees clearly that "fair equality of opportunity" must mean similar chances to obtain comparable educational and cultural competence that will keep public offices potentially open to all. Without this, political liberty loses its value. Rawls concludes that those inequalities in resource distributions are justified that work to the benefit of the least advantaged.[25]

Rawls rejects libertarian notions of meritocracy because, even if there is equality of opportunity at a given time, it will lead to inequalities of outcomes. Those advantaged in the outcomes of early rounds of competition will cash in their winnings to create conditions perpetuating their advantage. The structure of the social game created by the most successful will lead to future competitions that will be unfair to the earlier losers. Nevertheless, Rawls blends a liberal concern for liberty with equality under two principles. First, each person is to have an equal right to the most extensive basic liberty compatible with similar liberty for others.[26] Rawls goes on, furthermore, to place a higher value on liberty than upon equality. Liberty, for Rawls, is to be restricted only for the sake of promoting the overall "total" system of liberty. Second, social and economic inequalities are to be organized such that they are to the greatest benefit to the least advantaged and are attached to offices and positions open to all under conditions of equality of opportunity.[27] The maximin feature of the second principle goes into effect after the first principle has guaranteed equality of opportunity. The priority of the first principle ensures that basic liberal freedoms — the right to vote; liberty of speech, assembly, press, and conscience; private personal property; and freedom from arbitrary arrest — are not sacrificed to the demands of the second principle. Liberty is not to be traded off for other social goods.[28]

It is far beyond the scope of this effort to examine Rawls's conception of justice in refined detail and to fully render the range and richness of the critical literature that has emerged around the Rawlsian argument. For a full discourse on this rewarding topic, one must look elsewhere.[29] Beyond the fact that the Rawlsian conception of maximin can lead to implausible results, as discussed in Chapter 4, other problems emerge that can be briefly articulated.

First, what is the sense of talking about a "total system" of equal basic liberties? Rawls seems to hold that various liberties occur independently of each other and that, if maximizing one variety of liberty is shown to be inconsistent with maximizing another, different proportions of the several liberties can be adjusted and combined to make for something called maximum possible total liberty. Somehow, in an undefined way that defies analysis, the decision-maker would play a role analogous to that of a cook mixing a variety of foodstuffs in a broth so as to maximize the total nutritional value of dinner. Unfortunately, Rawls provides little usable guidance about how the total conceptual broth is to be constituted. There is simply no known recipe for calculating and aggregating the different liberties so as to determine whether policy directions are increasing or diminishing the "total liberty" that the system can afford equally to all.[30]

Second, to what extent, and in what ways, are we prepared to make infringements upon the advantaged to implement maximin? Would this principle be compatible with the rough and tumble of liberal politics? It would seem to require a political system in which the authority of the state could be employed to hold in check those individuals and groups that by virtue of luck, skill, or sheer dogged work stake claims to disproportionate resource shares. Such a state must be able to conduct detailed surveillance of the population to determine when shares are "unfair." It must then possess police power to enforce the maximin rule and to deny to the advantaged the capacity of organizing politically to defend their disproportionate shares. Could such a state be trusted to maintain liberty as specified by Rawls under principle one?[31] Whereas Nozick is willing to move in the direction of liberty at the expense of equality, Rawls appears to move in the direction of maximin equality at the expense of liberty, even though he goes to great lengths to avoid the charge. Robert Nisbet has reflected that "the mind boggles at the thought of the political apparatus necessary to give expression to and enforce such a principle."[32]

Third, it has been already established that inequality is anything but a simple concept.[33] Inequality can vary on many dimensions at once; the dimensions may or may not be divisible; inequality can vary over time and take on a radically different complexion as it shifts from individual to group conceptions. How much of which kind of inequality is to be permitted? That which provides great advantage for the ethnically disadvantaged may simultaneously violate the maximin criterion relative to gender categories. Rawls is not able to provide assurance, even in the abstract, that the maximin principle can cope with such complexities.

A SCIENCE OF FACT AND LOGIC OF VALUE IN DISTRIBUTION

To search for a single distributional principle is to misunderstand the problem; namely, (1) that there is no single set of basic goods that have the same meanings for life and choice across all moral and material worlds and (2) that different distributional domains require different distributive rules. Piety may be critical to allocations within the church but is not defensible as a consideration in distributing legal services to the poor. To achieve an egalitarian society in any defensible meaning of that concept, one must employ multiple egalitarian criteria.[34] Yet one cannot hope to measure everything, or even many things, for policy assessment is conducted in a world of limited time and money. One must isolate a few dimensions that are strategic in that they are theoretically significant and small differences with regard to them can be expected to have important consequences for affected people and the shape of the social structure. Analysis can be focused upon such dimensions, leaving other complexities of rich social worlds to escape us. To proceed, one must develop a position on at least three questions:

1. What kinds of equality will be legitimate for public household concern and intervention? Since equality is a multidimensional concept, one must choose with care from among its many aspects.

2. What will agents of the public household legitimately redistribute — income, wealth, votes, golf clubs, schools, grand pianos?

3. How are redistributions to be justified? How can one know whether a proposed policy is to gain or lose merit?

What Kinds of Inequalities Are of Legitimate Public Concern?

One central meaning of equality is that which emerged under the umbrella of classic eighteenth-century liberal thought — equality of condition before the law, or equality of citizenship rights.[35] Equality of condition has been associated with universal suffrage on the basis of one person/one vote, freedom of assembly, liberty to form voluntary associations and to engage in free speech, a right to bodily security and to the protection of due process under the law, equal access to public spaces and public organizations, and freedom of movement that makes possible escape from unacceptable situations.[36] The rule of law establishes the rules of the social game, which apply to all players subject to the conditions that the law should require only possible behavior ("ought" implies "can"), that similar cases should be treated similarly, that there can be no legal offense without a law, that laws be clearly established and known to the community, that judges must be fair and impartial as defined by rules of evidence, and that no person should be able to judge his or her own case. Equal right to political participation means that all competent citizens are to be guaranteed an equal right to take part in the political-constitutional process that establishes the law.

The emphasis on the rule of law, the cluster of civil liberties, and equal opportunity for political participation are of strategic concern because they are essential to hold the power of physical force and of money to their proper limited spheres. Physical force needs to be constrained by the community to prevent tyranny of the strong over the weak. A developed society must be a society that crushes the dictum "Because I am in control of brute force, I should win the prize for having the best policy idea." The power of money must also be constrained to its proper sphere. A developed society must reject the dictum, "Because I am rich I should command obedience to my policy wishes." It may be legitimate to use money to hire star athletes, but it is not legitimate to purchase victories on the playing field. Money or brute force should not allocate the National Book Award, purchase an acquittal in a fair trial, or determine outcomes of policy assessment — things not for sale on the economic marketplace.

Equality of condition before the law, then, is absolutely essential to constrain the power of money and brute force. There can be no developmentally meaningful prospect for choice context expansion except insofar as the rule of law has been established for all citizens. Within the rule of law, individuals can be free to strike their own bargains, join voluntary associations, flee unsatisfactory circumstances, make their own choices — subject to community constraints operating to promote justifiable visions of social development.

A second major meaning of equality that has emerged is of legitimate concern to the public household — equality of opportunity. This variety has generally meant equality of access to means of developing personal potential — equality of opportunity to become educated, to compete for employment, and to seek other prizes of interest. Equality of opportunity, however, may be open to multiple meanings.[37] In particular, Douglas Rae and his associates remind us to distinguish between equality of opportunity as "prospect-regarding" and as "means-regarding."[38] Prospect-regarding equality of opportunity is associated with the logic of lotteries and coin flipping, wherein a certain probability exists for an event to occur that has nothing to do with skill or effort. One has a certain prospect-regarding equal chance to win a bingo game, but such an outcome is not associated with personal merit. Equality of opportunity in the means-regarding sense, however, ensures that each individual has an equal opportunity to employ means to pursue personal goals.

Most important, equality of opportunity stands against use of ascriptive criteria for allocating choices. Ascriptive criteria relate to distinctions among people over which individuals have no control — most particularly ethnic or racial background, gender, or age. Individuals do not control their own year of birth as male or female, their skin color, or the shape of their eyes, lips, or nose. To allocate opportunity according to such ascriptive distinctions is to stand opposed to allocations based on merit or achievement. Equality of opportunity, in the means-regarding sense, is denied insofar as ascriptive criteria are employed in distributing advantage. Equality of opportunity in the means-regarding sense is what legitimates unequal outcomes — different prizes — and is the meaning adopted here. Equality of opportunity implies, at its core, inequality of outcome or result; it is rendered meaningless if it does not yield unequal payoffs that can be further converted into additional means of success the next day, the next round, the next generation. What would be the purpose of striving to seek prizes by merit if such prizes could not be cashed in for further advantage?

Could equality of opportunity be expected to yield at least a rough equality of results? Probably not at the individual level. Given that winnings in any one competition can be converted to advantage in other future competitions, unequal outcomes can be expected to cumulate unless absolutely draconian measures are enforced to ensure that no advantage gained at time one, race A, can be converted into advantage at time two, race B. Such measures would imply a virtual police state that, in the extreme, would have to exercise specific control over genetic endowment of the newborn; determine family child-rearing practices; enforce absolutely equal school conditions, curricula, and teaching approaches and standardized testing for the genetically standardized children who would live in families receiving standardized incomes with parents who would spend those incomes so as to provide standardized environments, and then graduate to jobs wherein authorities enforced standardized behavior yielding equal performances. In other words, equality of opportunity cannot be expected to produce equality of outcomes except under gross tyranny. Unequal outcomes are not so much something to be eliminated as something to be harnessed to the service of equality of opportunity in the name of developmentally expanding structures of choice.

Whereas conservatives have seen equality of condition as sufficient to the definition of the good society, and liberals have added an emphasis on equality of opportunity, equality of outcome has been a major part of the socialist long-range promise.[39] Any number of strong socialist egalitarians, committed to equality of result, have attacked the principle of reward according to work, performance, or merit.[40] They hold that people should obtain equal prizes for running in life's race, and they attack any justification for income stratification and any factor associated with preventing equality of educational outcomes by occupational or family group. Yet the debate between proponents of equal opportunity and outcomes goes on among socialists, given that "pragmatists" faced with practical requirements of economic growth have justified merit and performance as principles for distributing unequal rewards.[41] They contend that the industrious worker needs to be disproportionately rewarded as compared to the lazy. Socialism will, at least in the near term, be better served if productivity is enhanced through application of performance-oriented reward systems that yield inequalities of outcome. Equality of outcome means little when the outcomes are uniformly meager. Later, when scarcity is eliminated — a happy thought — the performance principle can be dropped, say the pragmatic revisionist planners.

By way of counterattack, strict outcome egalitarians reject the performance principle by contending that "success" depends mainly on luck, happenstance, and the imponderables of personality.[42] Being the product of life's bingo game in which talent, skill, or effort plays little or no part, unequal rewards are rarely justified. Eliminating luck, the chance of the draw, is not usually possible, but it is possible to abolish unequal results. These thinkers see equality of opportunity in the prospect-regarding sense and judge the presence of meaningful equality of opportunity in the means-regarding sense by the extent to which outcomes are equal.

In sum, then, at least three basic meanings of equality can be distinguished — each with different implications for policy assessment. The question is not: Shall we pursue equality? Rather, the question is: Which variety of equality will be pursued under which rules about what things? This discussion has advanced the view that agents of the public household should defend equality of condition and promote inequality of outcomes insofar as they serve equality of means-regarding opportunity.

What Shall Be Distributed?

One thing to be equalized by agents of the public household is equality of condition under the law, but developmental expansion of choice contexts requires one to examine other types of goods. At least two major kinds of goods are candidates for legitimate concern and distributional intervention.

1. The first kind is basic infrastructural goods and services provided by the public sector that are prerequisite to the free and productive use of civic liberties secured under equality of condition and for the use of private income and wealth. Infrastructural goods and services are those collective public goods not exchangeable on private markets and not directly productive in the immediate sense of producing collectable profits, but essential to the productive use of private

income and wealth — clean air and water, public health services, police and fire protection, education, roads, power grids, and legal services. Access to such goods and services is considered essential to first-class citizenship. They are characterized by three common attributes:

1. lumpiness, meaning that they are not divisible, so that private persons cannot provide them for themselves by individual effort;

2. nonexcludability, meaning that it is easy to extend benefits to the next individual at low marginal cost; and

3. nonrivalness of consumption, meaning that consumption by one individual does not appreciably diminish the amount available to others.

Because of these properties, ideologists across the spectrum have agreed that governments must ensure that appropriate infrastructure is provided.

2. The second kind of goods is those private goods that can be purchased and maintained through individual effort with private income and wealth — bicycles, automobiles, shelter, food. Such private goods give satisfaction directly to the investor, but they typically must be used in conjunction with publicly provided infrastructure. Autos and bicycles do not perform well on ploughed fields but provide their service by rolling along community-provided streets, lanes, and highways. A privately owned electric sewing machine requires community production and transmission of electricity. Housing may qualify as a private good, but its potential for yielding satisfaction is attained only insofar as the community has made certain that it is built to specified construction codes on land that is properly graded and protected from the ravages of floods and served by electrical grids, fuel networks, water and sewer facilities, transportation, and fire and police protection.

The structure of choice is severely eroded when the means of survival, as represented by basic infrastructural services, are heavily concentrated among the upper classes or within particular regions to the exclusion of others, such that numbers of people die of slow poisoning due to poor waste disposal; are victims of random or organized violence; must contend with unbreathable air and undrinkable water, lack of education, and the denial of essential legal and public health services; and have little hope of making successful exit from such a situation. One can legitimately argue that management of the public household must make it a priority to select policies that (1) facilitate ease of exit and thereby signal abandonment of development in the given geographical and/or sectoral domain, or (2) extend infrastructural services into such situations so that choice-threatening conditions are corrected.

There has been much debate about investment in infrastructure. Some have asserted that it is the key to development and human progress; if only governments would invest in infrastructure, economic growth and prosperity would be certain to follow, as individual entrepreneurs would make best use of the opportunities to expand production.[43] Others have doubted the inherently productive impacts of infrastructural investment and have advocated stimulation of private production so as to generate the wealth for support of infrastructure.[44] Looked at in this perspective, infrastructure is seen to be the product of private investment — a result as opposed to cause. The old chicken and egg question is probably unanswerable in these terms. Which comes first, private income or public expenditure on public infrastructure? We need not answer. Surplus infrastructure may not attract private investment in certain instances, but it is equally true that lags in infrastructure must retard the many thousands of small private investments that are inhibited by shortage of basic means of survival and choice.

The argument for some kind of egalitarian ethic becomes strong for infrastructural goods and services in the name of equality of means-regarding opportunity. Given these, then and only then can one speak of the differential willingness of people to discipline themselves to achieve, to sink, or to rise on the basis of personal merit. Those forms of infrastructure that provide such basic "merit" goods are desirable in their own right, for in their absence, any discussion of equality of means-regarding opportunity is a blatant sham.

The distribution of private income and wealth is also of interest to agents of the public household. Here one speaks of the capacity to offer goods or services in exchange for others available in the marketplace — the purchase and use of the bicycle that will be ridden on the public path, the private acquisition of a refrigerator that will be plugged into the electrical grid, the private enjoyment of a book made possible by compulsory public education. Private incomes are of critical importance because incomes, combined with resources of public infrastructure, make possible creation and exploitation of choice opportunities.

229

Electrical grids made available to people with no income to purchase basic shelter, let alone a refrigerator, are not realizing their purposes. Some kind of egalitarian ethic is required in the distribution of private income and wealth to guarantee that equality of opportunity to make choice is served. It is the combination of private incomes, wealth, and public infrastructure that makes individual and collective choice possible when equality of condition has been secured.

Income (flow per time period) is, of course, to be distinguished from wealth (stock). Private wealth consists of the value of property and material possessions — for example, real estate, machinery, stocks, bank assets. In principle, there is every reason to focus attention of the public household on the distribution of wealth as well as on income flows. Extreme concentration of wealth in the hands of the few can be as potentially damaging to choice context as the concentration of income. Much wealth, typically, is not counted as income because it exists in the form of unrealized capital gains — increases in the value of assets that have not been converted to cash. It is perfectly possible to have extensive wealth — for example, in the form of agricultural land and machinery — but receive low income in a given year. The reverse is also possible. An individual can have a high income flow in a given period of time but convert little to wealth. Different proposed policies will differentially affect income flows as compared to wealth. In principle, the policy that reduces gaps in wealth could increase inequality of incomes as wealth is capitalized so as to promote enhanced income flows for those who release their grip on wealth. The point is that wealth, like income, is a generalized medium of choice to be viewed as a key dimension strategic to the structure of choice in the company of infrastructure. Agents of the public household should assess proposed technological and natural resource policies on both income and wealth dimensions while recognizing that it is quite possible that these two dimensions of generalized choice will be differently impacted by the same policy.

The Distributional Value Logic

From whom should agents of the public household subtract which kinds of resources in order to redistribute things to other people? What line of reasoning, rooted in a concern to developmentally expand choice contexts, can be advanced to make legitimate such transfers?

Given the distinction between ascriptive and achievement (merit) criteria, and given an appreciation of three distinct kinds of equality (condition, opportunity in the means-regarding sense, and outcome) and the distinctions between three kinds of generalized media of choice (access to infrastructure, income flows, and stocks of wealth), it is now possible to formulate a sequence of distributional value criteria. Proposed policies that shall gain merit in policy assessment are these:

1. Policies that do not abridge equality of condition. Equality of condition represents a set of basic rights that each person can insistently assert with full knowledge that it shall not be compromised by agents of the public household. Equality of condition is not a gift or favor to be withdrawn when policy convenience would have it so.

2. Policies that produce inequalities of policy outcome that reduce inequality in access to any variety of infrastructural good or service or reduce any inequality in income or wealth distribution along any one or more ascriptive distinctions (that is, age, gender, or ethnicity). A proposed policy estimated to move a Lorenz curve toward the line of perfect equality by any amount in any pattern shall pass this distributional test and be advanced for assessment on lower-order value criteria in the developmental logic of value.

Several points are in order. First, different proposed policies, each with a unique pattern of gain and loss, could pass the test in item 2 above. Policy X, which narrows income gaps as between females and males, would pass along with policy Y, which reduces wealth gaps among ethnic groups. The only operative requirement, assuming no violation of equality of condition, is that each proposed policy reduce the gap in access to infrastructure, income, and/or wealth on one or more ascriptive dimensions. The fundamental, and unhappy, fact of life is that there is no known method for comparing the gains and losses experienced by different individuals or groups along various dimensions of inequality. Gains for females cannot be meaningfully aggregated and compared with gains or losses for Hispanics, blacks, or southeast Asian refugees to determine which shift toward greater equality nets out the greatest human progress. Therefore, a proposed policy will pass assessment that redistributes in the direction of equality by any amount in any pattern for any of the three types of generalized media of choice (access to infrastructure, income or wealth) on any ascriptive (age, gender, ethnicity) dimension.[45]

Second, the distributional criterion, as formulated, does not reveal which policies, in the name of reducing a gap somewhere, would contribute to a greater inequality elsewhere. It is conceivable that a policy that reduces income gaps for females relative to males may enlarge gaps between blacks and whites. It is tempting to argue for a distributional criterion that would only accept reduction in inequality on one or more dimensions while not enlarging inequalities on any other. There would be at least two problems with such an attempt. First, it is not logically possible to establish that no gaps are increasing anywhere; it is only possible to contend that no inequalities are being enlarged on those dimensions of which we are aware and for which we have created reasonably valid measurements. Second, any assessment system that requires that one promise beyond reasonable doubt that no inequality will be increased on any dimension for which measurements could conceivably be constructed would be data hungry and theory consuming in the extreme. We simply have little prospect of showing in most policy-relevant situations that a measured increase in inequality in dimension X (for example, ethnicity, gender) is or is not directly and causally related to a reduction in inequality on dimension Y. Furthermore, even if one knows that all possible inequalities have been accounted for, one would not know how much gain in equality on dimension X would be required to compensate a given amount of loss to equality on dimensions Y and Z. Therefore, one is forced to settle for the less demanding criterion that a policy, to pass assessment, reduce an inequality in income, wealth, or access to infrastructure somewhere along some ascriptive dimension.

Third, it is tempting to insert a qualification to the effect that the shift in the Lorenz curve grant the most benefit to the least advantaged. This Rawlsian notion would entail little more than stating a preference for policy X, if X generated a Lorenz curve line closer to the line of perfect equality in the lower left sector as compared to Y (see Fig. 7.4). Obviously, the rationale would be that under policy X the least advantaged are better off and therefore X should be preferred. Problems arise with such a notion, as has been discussed. It suffices here to note that, as shown in Figure 7.5, policy X treats the least well off better than Y but imposes much greater costs on all other impacted people except the very best off. Would one really be willing to impose such great costs on the middle groups to achieve a modest gain for the least well off? How much would the least advantaged have to gain to justify the losses to the better off in the middle or higher ranges?

This raises the problem of distributional efficiency, defined as that

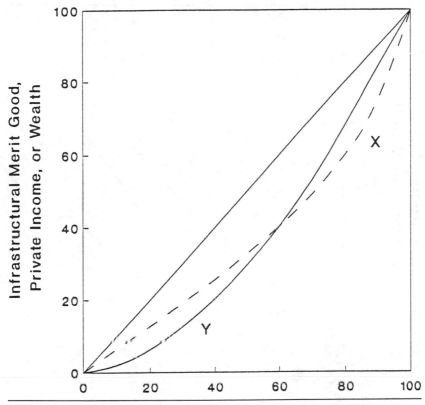

Figure 7.4. Illustration of Distributional Criterion Under Proposed Policies X and Y

redistribution that would obtain a given amount of gain for the less advantaged at the least possible cost to the more advantaged from whom the resources are shifted.[46] For any given loss to the better off, those less well off should gain the most. Distributional efficiency is an important concept; rational analysts would wish to attain it as much as possible, but the Rawlsian logic is blind to it. But even if blinders are removed from our eyes and we learn to seek distributional efficiency, doing so makes for difficulty. Gainers and losers can be highly dispersed and difficult to identify. Trying to determine just exactly who would lose how much under each proposed policy can be a problematic exercise subject to much error — especially when the losers are a broad spectrum of people representing many dimensions upon which inequality may be measured. The meaning of monetary and non-

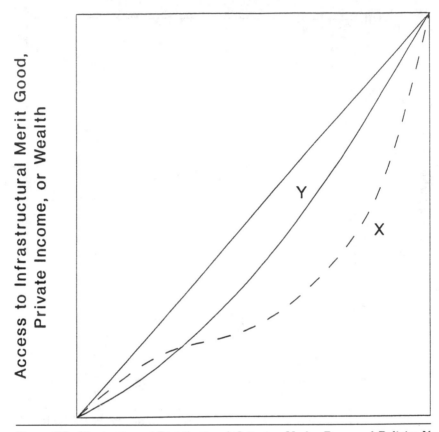

Figure 7.5. Illustration of Distributional Criterion Under Proposed Policies X and Y if Increased Benefit to Least Advantaged Were an Assessment Norm

monetary losses can be expected to shift widely from group to group, category to category, place to place, time to time. The measuring rod reflecting "least cost" bends, flexes, and changes shape as it is transferred across such dimensions and categories. A lost dollar or recreation day simply does not remain constant in meaning. The metrics are not common, and arguments about distributional efficiency would be unending.

The distributional criteria, as formulated, are egalitarian in the sense that they will require rejection of proposed policies that are estimated to violate equality of condition or, if securing that equality, enlarge gaps between less and more advantaged in the distribution of income, wealth, or access to infrastructure without reducing a gap on one or more ascriptive dimensions. If these kinds of generalized choice media are distributed by policy X across gender and ethnic ascriptive dimensions in such a manner that a gap is narrowed, policy X shall survive to be assessed on lower nondistributional criteria in the value logic. The distributional values set forth, however, cannot identify the "most equal" proposal, unless only one option should pass, because such a concept is meaningless given the conceptual ambiguities that surface in the analysis of equality.

Additional value criteria of a nondistributional nature must be employed to sort out those policies that survive the distributional assessment. There are, at bottom, many kinds of distributional patterns that can increase equality along some ascriptive dimension. In the final analysis, no equality criterion can be employed to choose from among them.

DISTRIBUTIONAL ASSESSMENT:
A CASE OF WATERCOURSE IMPROVEMENT IN PAKISTAN

The forty Pakistani farmers of Thikapur irrigation command cultivate a total area of 556 cropped acres in the Punjab province.[47] The social system shares the same characteristics described in the introduction to the Jalarabad village discussed in the section "Conflict Analysis in Pakistan" in Chapter 6. As elsewhere in the Punjab, an excellent climate makes yearround cultivation possible on deep alluvial soils of high potential productivity, but irrigation is essential to intensive agriculture in the arid region. Unfortunately, agricultural production is severely constrained by failure to deliver irrigation water to crop root zones at the time, and in the amount, required.[48]

Although important water losses are traceable to problems with major conveyance canals and large storage facilities, most irrigation water losses occur on poorly maintained local community-level watercourses such as Thikapur channel. On the average it has been estimated that about half of the water entering local watercourses, such as Thikapur's, is lost before reaching farmers' fields.[49] It might be contended that the "lost" water is simply a resource to be pumped from the ground upon demand and that it is therefore misleading to characterize it as a problem. In many circumstances this can be a most valid point. However, pumping water that has spilled or leaked from poorly constructed earthen watercourses can have serious implications. Pumping incurs high costs for equipment and energy — especially high-cost hydrocarbon energy. Moreover, if watercourses are excessively leaky, one must pump water back into the channel bed several times to secure delivery to remote field outlets, and at each pumping point one must pump several times as much water as is eventually delivered. Furthermore, pumping "lost" water can impose the additional cost of degraded water quality, given that many command areas confront severe salinity problems. In the Thikapur area, the pumped water is considerably more saline than the fresh water that directly flows down the canals. Insofar as water is reclaimed through use of private wells, there will be a welfare transfer from the poorer smaller farmer whose water share has disappeared into the ground to the larger operator who has the means to claim it by employing expensive capital equipment, thereby increasing a gap between poor and rich without creating a compensating reduction in inequality elsewhere.

In the Punjab and Sindh provinces, there are an estimated 78,000 local level community-maintained watercourses serving approximately 31,700,000 acres of cultivated area. Given an estimated 50 percent average loss, a significant national problem has come into focus. Poor watercourses contribute to waterlogging and associated salinity problems and fail to deliver minimally adequate quantities of water to farmers struggling at the tail ends.

In 1925, the first waterlogging inquiry commission was established by British colonial authorities to examine a problem that, by then, was recognized as most serious. By 1947, the problem was recognized as sufficiently acute for the new nation to justify technical assistance from the United Nations Food and Agriculture Organization. In 1954, Pakistan received Colombo Plan assistance to conduct an aerial survey of the problem, and in 1958, a report of that study estimated that 11 million acres of land were waterlogged and an additional 16 million acres were affected by salinity. Of those, 5 million were judged to be severely affected.[50] Waterlogging and salinity were soon thereafter defined by the government of Pakistan as one of the greatest threats to the nation.

One portion of the attack on constraints to increased agricultural production has been a program to reconstruct local watercourses with local labor and materials. The objectives would be reduction of waterlogging and salinity and production of greater supplies to farmers located at tail ends so as to increase cropping intensities and make possible the growing of improved plant varieties. High-yielding hybrid seed varieties — the heart of the "green revolution" — when combined with ample fertilizer and proper amounts of irrigation water can double and triple yields as compared to those attainable with the traditional technologies. The older technology, of course, required but a fraction of the fertilizer and water. Rational farmers, faced with uncertain and inadequate water supplies at the tails of watercourses or those faced with salinity and waterlogging problems at any location, will not go into debt to buy the improved seeds, the chemical fertilizers, the herbicides and pesticides. Water is the critical link in the technological complex. The seeds and fertilizers are highly responsive to adequate water delivered at the proper time in plant growth cycles. The matter of water supply takes us to the heart of the story, because water is delivered to fields through community-maintained watercourses — public infrastructure — that must be maintained to a relatively high standard if they are to hold water losses to a minimum. Furthermore, those watercourses must be run according to rules such that the allocation of water becomes predictable and controllable. Water at the wrong time and in the wrong amount is unproductive.

The Watercourse, the Environment,
and the Need for Social Organization

Earthen watercourses exist as vulnerable structures in a hostile environment. Typically in the Punjab there is little gradient to the land surface. Running irrigation water efficiently over flat surfaces in earthen structures is not a matter to be taken lightly. The upper portion of watercourse walls, the freeboard immediately above the waterline, is one of the parts of the ecosystem providing a relatively undisturbed habitat for insects, rodents, and snakes (see Fig. 7.6). Much of the surrounding area is periodically flooded, plowed, planted, cultivated, and otherwise disturbed by farmers in such a way that the upper walls provide attractive refuge to burrowing creatures well suited to perforating freeboard areas. As a consequence, earthen watercourses perform well only within narrow limits. When the water runs too low in the watercourse profile, dead storage of water below field level results, and there is insufficient "head" to create the necessary pressure to conduct water to fields. If silt should be deposited in the bottom of the channel so as to elevate the floor, or if plants grow there, water will run high on the freeboard and lateral seepage through the labyrinth of rodent holes increases rapidly. Earthen watercourses, to deliver water with much efficiency, must therefore be carefully constructed and maintained. The lack of robustness in the technology necessarily means that disciplined, well-organized labor must be mobilized for

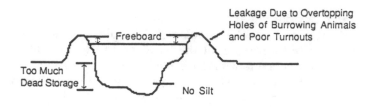

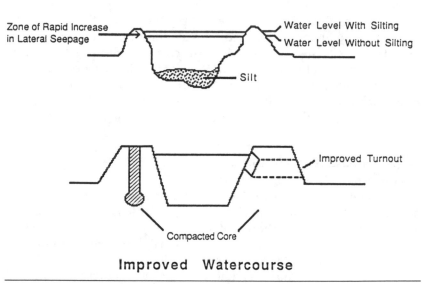

Figure 7.6. Unimproved and Improved Watercourse Cross Sections

maintenance and periodic reconstruction if such structures are to produce anything close to their potential conveyance efficiencies. This vulnerable earthen watercourse technology may be highly appropriate in a capital-short society that cannot import sufficient cement or secure adequate hydrocarbon energy to fire brick to line channels, but such technology requires disciplined social organization that can mobilize local resources and effectively sanction free riders who would otherwise attempt to draw benefits from a project to which they do not contribute a fair share of resources.

Distributional Equality in Watercourse Improvement Programs

Like people everywhere, the forty farmers of the Thikapur watercourse command can be examined for inequality on multiple dimensions. Two of the most significant variables about which valid data are available are the amount of cultivatable land (a key form of wealth in this agricultural community) and the extent to which the cultivatable land can be actually cropped over the annual double-cropping cycle — a central determinant of income.

First, Thikapur farmers can be examined from the perspective of the distribution of cultivatable land. The farmers, numbered consecutively, each possess acreage as listed on Table 7.1, in which farmers are ranked from smallest to largest. The associated farmer ranking is provided in column 4. Landholding data in Table 7.1, column 2, have been transferred to Figure 7.7 and from them a Lorenz curve has been constructed. A glance at Figure 7.7 reveals that cultivatable land ownership patterns in Thikapur command area are characterized by considerable inequality. The least advantaged 10 percent of the farmers together own one-half of 1 percent of the total cultivatable acreage, whereas the most advantaged 10 percent own 42 percent. Assuming that there is no reasonable prospect for successful exit from the situation, a policy that would improve access to cultivatable acreage for the least fortunate farmers would be more desirable than its opposite. However, ownership of cultivatable land per se is not the only defensible way to look at the distribution of advantage among Thikapur's forty farmers.

One might inquire about the extent to which acreage can actually be cultivated during the course of any given year. It is one thing to own land and quite another to exploit its potential for cultivation. The primary constraint upon cropping all of one's cultivatable acreage in this arid environment is the lack of sufficient irrigation water. Poorly constructed watercourses may run too low for certain fields or parts of fields at any location along the channel. More typically, however, farmers located at increasing distances from the inlet find that watercourse losses deprive them of supplies adequate to justify investment in seeds and fertilizer for some portion of their cultivatable land.

Given that, with existing technology, Punjabi farmers can expect to plant, cultivate, and harvest two full crops of most types per year, one seeks a concept that can express the proportion of potentially cultivatable land actually put into production for the two cropping seasons. That concept is "cropping intensity." A cropping intensity for farmer X of 100 percent would indicate that X has (1) placed one-half of his acreage under production during each of the two cropping

Table 7.1. Farmer Distributions on Ownership of Cultivable Land and Land Ownership Weighted by Cropping Intensity
(Listed from least to most)

	Raw Values			Rankings	
1	2	3	4	5
Farmer Number	Farmer Cult. Land (Acres)	Farmer Cult. Land Weighted by Cropping Intensity	Farmer Cult. Land (Acres)	Famer Cult. Land Weighted by Cropping Intensity
36	0.5	0.49	1.5	1
38	0.5	0.7	1.5	2
29	1	2.0	2.5	3.5
7	1	2.0	2.5	3.5
6	3	3.6	7	7.5
5	3	2.8	7	6
18	3	3.6	7	7.5
37	3	4.8	7	9
39	3	2.3	7	5
40	5	5.4	10	10
15	6	8.2	11	12
4	7	7.7	12	11
25	8	15.0	13	23
34	9	8.7	16	14
33	9	8.5	16	13
9	9	13.0	16	17
8	9	14.8	16	22
3	9	14.2	16	21
22	10	8.7	20.5	32
23	10	20.0	20.5	34
27	10	13.5	20.5	18
30	10	11.1	20.5	16
31	11	17.1	25	28
28	11	9.0	25	15
13	11	16.5	25	25

Table 7.1 (continued)

Raw Values			Rankings	
1	2	3	4	5
Farmer Number	Farmer Cult. Land (Acres)	Farmer Cult. Land Weighted by Cropping Intensity	Farmer Cult. Land (Acres)	Famer Cult. Land Weighted by Cropping Intensity
2	11	16.5	25	25
1	11	16.5	25	25
10	12	20.4	29	35
17	12	24.0	29	36.5
32	12	13.6	29	19
12	13	13.8	31	20
26	14	17.9	32	30
19	15	24.0	33	36.5
16	17	17.0	34	27
24	18	17.3	35	29
11	19	24.1	36	38
21	22	18.5	37	31
14	23	41.4	38	40
35	25	19.8	39	33
20	30	38.4	40	39

$$r_{2\times3} = .878$$

seasons (50 percent + 50 percent) or (2) placed all of the acreage into production during one season (for example, during summer monsoons) but has left it all fallow during another season (for example, the winter dry season). Farmer X may have taken this course if he is so poorly situated in the watercourse command area that he cannot expect to obtain minimally sufficient water during the dry season to justify investment in variable factors of production. A cropping intensity of 200 percent would indicate that X has placed all cultivatable land in production for both seasons.

Given that the command area consists of 556 cultivatable acres, there are, during the course of two seasons per year, potentially 1,112

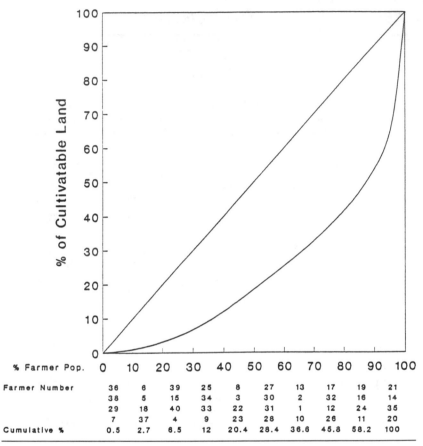

% Farmer Pop.	0	10	20	30	40	50	60	70	80	90	100
Farmer Number	36	6	39	25	8	27	13	17	19	21	
	38	5	15	34	3	30	2	32	16	14	
	29	18	40	33	22	31	1	12	24	35	
	7	37	4	9	23	28	10	26	11	20	
Cumulative %	0.5	2.7	6.5	12	20.4	28.4	36.6	45.8	58.2	100	

Figure 7.7. Distribution of Cultivatable Land in Thikapur

cropable acres. Farmers can be ranked according to these data, on a horizontal axis, and a Lorenz curve constructed displaying the cumulative proportions of cultivatable land weighted by cropping intensity values. Such a distribution is provided in Figure 7.8 employing data from Table 7.1. The cropping intensity distribution will vary from that of unweighted land acreage owned because farmer X with 4 acres and a cropping intensity of 100 percent would obtain a value of 4 acres, whereas farmer Y owning 3 acres, who enjoys a 200 percent cropping intensity, would obtain a weighted value of 6 acres. One immediately notes two things by examining Figure 7.8. First, when land distributions have been adjusted for cropping intensity, the de-

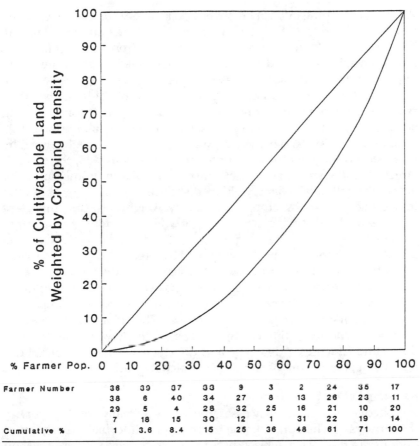

Farmer Number	36	33	37	33	9	3	2	24	35	17
	38	6	40	34	27	8	13	26	23	11
	29	5	4	28	32	25	16	21	10	20
	7	18	15	30	12	1	31	22	19	14
Cumulative %	1	3.6	8.4	15	25	36	48	61	71	100

Figure 7.8. Distribution of Cultivatable Land in Thikapur Weighted by Cropping Intensity

gree of inequality has been reduced in Thikapur — a most happy circumstance although not an inevitable one. The essence of the matter, obviously, is that many of those blessed with greater cultivatable acreage were not also favored with greater cropping intensities. Put another way, in the Thikapur instance, those farmers with smaller acreage have a slight tendency to be more advantaged by the water supply situation — a fact that shifts the Lorenz curve toward the line of perfect equality.

Table 7.1 also displays the acreage of cultivatable land weighted by cropping intensity values supplemented by farmer rankings. Examination of the ranking data reveals the second item of interest:

Although cropping intensity distribution is highly correlated with raw land ownership (r = .88), the two farmer rankings are not identical. There is a shift of farmer advantage as we move from unweighted farm land ownership to consider owned acres weighted by cropping intensity. For example, farmer 23 possessing ten cultivatable acres at a 200 percent intensity earns an adjusted value of twenty cultivatable acres per year, which places him in a more advantaged income earning situation than farmer 21, who places seventeen ranks above farmer 23 with regard to raw land owned. Farmer 23, exactly twentieth ranked by size, had even more production potential than farmer 35, the second-largest landowner. In sum, then, farmer inequality as measured by acreage of cultivatable land yields a distribution that is largely similar to the one yielded by cropping intensity weightings, but important changes in disadvantage come to light when one moves to another consideration such as cropping intensity. Should the unweighted acreage-owned distribution be thrown out to be replaced exclusively by the weighted distribution? Probably not. Even though it might not be as intensively cropped, an acre of land still has value. It can be employed for grazing or as security on loans, and it may have other important market and nonmarket values to the farmer. The point is that the world of equality and inequality changes shape when viewed from different distributional lenses. Advantage and disadvantage are distributed differently depending on the manner in which they are conceived.

Assessing Policy Alternatives

No distributional policy assessment was formally conducted with the farmers of Thikapur command, but much informal discussion of options did take place. A brief discussion can convey a feel for what an assessment would involve.

First and foremost, any proposed policy for operating an irrigation organization to reconstruct and maintain the improved watercourse must provide absolute equality of condition of all farmers. Such equality will typically rest upon an enforceable set of bylaws, backed by agents of the public household, that any farmer member can exercise when local money or brute force threatens to bend rules to the advantage of the few and thereby violate equality of condition. Beyond equality in this sense, local irrigation organizations must define policies for water distribution. There are many combinations of possibilities, but the primary options can be described and assessed.

Option One: Newly established farmer-operated irrigation organizations would construct, maintain, and operate improved watercourses on the operative principle that water shall be allocated on a time and locational basis as it runs from watercourse head to tail. The water would be allocated according to time shares based on acreage owned. Maintenance fees would be collected in direct proportion to land owned. Given that the larger canal system is designed to deliver one complete rotation along the local watercourse each 168-hour week, each farmer would be allocated a weekly time period during which to take whatever water flows. That time period, under this policy proposal, would be established by the formula:

$$\frac{\text{Farmer X hours / week}}{168 \text{ hours / week}} = \frac{\text{Farmer X acreage owned}}{\text{Total acreage in command}}$$

This policy option would pass the distributional assessment test because farmers toward the tail of the community channel would disproportionately bear the burdens of watercourse losses, and in this particular instance, larger farmers (weighted by cropping intensity) are located toward the tail. Table 7.1 and Figure 7.8 reveal that smaller farmers are somewhat advantaged by cropping intensity — a fact due to their superior access to canal water. The Lorenz curve is, therefore, pushed toward the line of equality on the dimension of land owned when weighted by cropping intensity. It must be noted, however, that larger operators are not always located disproportionately toward tail reaches of watercourses and that policy Option One might in such instances shift advantage toward the larger operators. In that case it would fail this assessment and be returned for reformulation before being advanced for further study on the lower-order value criteria.

Option Two: The organization would be based on the operative principle that irrigation water shall be allocated according to weekly time share rotation based on acreage conditioned by time of settlement — that is, the water will be delivered to the field outlet of the oldest settler who takes the full flow of water for the number of hours per week allocated as under Option One and then passes the "head" of water to the next senior settler, who repeats the procedure, and so on to the most junior settler. Although there may be some sympathy for a "first in time, first in right" rule among the irrigators who represent original colonists in the area, this option would fail the distributional test because, in this instance at least, older operations tend to be larger ones. Even though land has fragmented as fathers handed land to sons over three generations, newer settlers who came after the partition of the subcontinent tended to secure smaller acreage. Option Two would

245

increase resource disparity between larger and smaller operators whether or not landownership is weighted by cropping intensity, and the Lorenz curve would be shifted away from the line of equality. Option Two would fail the distributional test.

Option Three: The organization would be based on the principle that irrigation water would be allocated from tail to head and be apportioned on a volume share basis measured at each field outlet. Each volume share would deliver a quantity of the total weekly flow in proportion to the quantity of land owned. Maintenance fees would be assessed according to volume of water received. Given that one complete rotation to all watercourse farmers must occur in the weekly 168-hour period, this distributional principle would provide an incentive for the farmers located toward the head reaches to assure that the watercourse performed at peak delivery efficiency so that volume requirements toward the tail could be fulfilled and their turns more rapidly obtained within the weekly time limit. Such a policy would place a burden upon farmers toward the head — in this instance they tend to be the smaller operators — to employ resources so as to deliver water to the larger operators located disproportionately toward the tails. This would clearly drop the Lorenz curves away from the line of equality, and, therefore, Option Three would fail distributional assessment. Option Three, however, would pass in another command area wherein smaller operators were disproportionately located along tail reaches of the distribution system.

Option Four: The organization would eliminate the head-tail distinction by delivering measured volumes of water to each farm field or ditch per share owned. Because a measured volume of water is delivered to each shareholder without respect to location, the water "shrink" would be absorbed by all farmers in the irrigation community. A ditch loss to one at the tail must be made up to achieve the measured volume and becomes, therefore, a loss to all. Each farmer, therefore, has an interest in the performance of the channel. Farmers would pay an assessment per share equal to the share's fraction of the total seasonal cost of operations and maintenance on the watercourse. For example, if the total seasonal cost for a ditchtender and repairs were to equal 5,000 rupees, and if two hundred shares were outstanding, each share would obligate its owner to pay 25 rupees. In turn, each share in the irrigation organization would deliver 1/200 of the total water supply. Water shares could be leased on a local organizationally controlled water market. Prices for a seasonal lease could be expected to vary depending on seasonal demand for water, but leases would generally be expected to recoup at least the assessment cost.

Finally, and most importantly, shares would be initially equally distributed to all households without regard to amount of land owned. A new property right in water would have then been created. Those with more land than water would lease water from those with more water than required by their land holdings and production plans. Those with more water than profitably usable on their land-holdings would have an incentive to lease water out for at least enough to recoup the assessment cost that must be paid regardless of whether the water is employed productively. Because village landless and small landowners would have their resource positions improved by virtue of their new possession of a critical exchangeable resource, the Lorenz curve would reflect the move toward equality. This policy option would pass assessment.

Obviously, given the myriad forms that distributions of advantage and disadvantage can take, no specific organizational rule can be formulated for all of Pakistan's watercourse command areas any more than one can draw up one universal road map for all localities. Each unit has its unique features, and each unit can only be served by specific rules that will serve to fulfill the more general nomothetic distributional principle — shift a Lorenz curve toward the line of perfect equality on some significant dimension having to do with income, wealth, or access to infrastructure. The general principle can be employed from unit to unit, but each locality will require that rules be adapted to implement the general distributional value in specific circumstances. This fact necessitates that local organizations, fitted to the conditions of particular sites and providing an opportunity for local civic discourse about developmental directions, be present to conduct local policy assessment.[51]

Insofar as Options One and Four each reduce a gap in an important infrastructural good, but for different reasons, each will also pass to be compared on lower nondistributional assessment criteria. This analysis of distributional assessment will not identify the most egalitarian policy, an impossible task given the lack of coherent meaning of such a concept. It will, however, identify that set of policy proposals that narrow a gap somewhere and therefore survive for further scrutiny on lower-order value criteria — futures for choice opportunities forgone and economic efficiency.

247

CONCLUSION

> Equality is the simplest and most abstract of notions, yet the practices of the world are irremediably concrete and complex. How, imaginably, could the former govern the latter? It cannot. We are always confronted with more than one practical meaning for equality and equality itself cannot provide the basis for choosing among them. — Douglas Rae et al.[52]

There is real danger in formulating egalitarian value criteria. One wishes to serve expansion of contexts of choice according to a defensible developmental logic of value, but equality per se does not respect human choice. Equality is as well served by total desolation as by universal abundance. To quote Douglas Rae on this point, "Equality itself is as well pleased by graveyards as by vineyards."[53] No one valuing developmental expansion of choice structures can prefer the equality of nothing (A = 0, B = 0) to the inequality of something (A = 40,000, B = 12,000). One must proceed carefully with the concept of equality, or it will be employed to needlessly destroy human choice possibilities.

One begins by recognizing that equality splits into many distinct notions — equality of individuals, equality of groups, equality of means, equality of probabilistic prospect, equality of outcomes, equality of means-regarding opportunity, equality of condition, equality of absolute quantities, and equality of relative shares, to name a few. After distinguishing between specific types of equality, two specific varieties have been selected around which to build a distributional logic of value. The first is equality of condition before the law and of basic citizenship rights that constrain the power of money and of brute force. The second is equality of opportunity in the means-regarding sense, which is served by reducing inequalities in the distribution of infrastructural goods and services and by reduction of wealth and income inequalities. Distributions of these goods can be examined on at least three ascriptive dimensions — gender, age, and ethnicity. Ascriptive dimensions are selected because they reflect realities over which individuals have no control.

One then proceeds to state the value criteria for policy assessment:

1. No policy shall be found acceptable if it would abridge equality of condition.

2. Inequalities of policy outcome will be desirable insofar as they reduce an inequality of access to any variety of policy impacted

infrastructure or reduce an inequality of income or wealth distribution.

When one selects things to be allocated unequally to serve the distributional value logic, one must provide a rationale for the selection of the goods to be distributed. If agents of the public household are to examine the distribution of A, why only A? Why not B, C, and D? If access to the infrastructure represented by schools is to be increased for the poor relative to the rich, or females relative to males, or blacks relative to whites, why only schools? Why not golf courses, Cadillacs, and pianos? On what grounds should the public household stop intervening in the distributions of things? The answer, as formulated here, is that four kinds of goods are crucial to the development of choice contexts within which individuals can prescribe for themselves their own mixes of personal welfare — equality of condition, access to merit goods represented by infrastructure, stocks of wealth, and flows of income. Each of these represents a generalized medium of choice out of which private prescriptions can be meaningfully constructed. The public household is to be concerned with the distribution of these generalized choice media. Resources are to be allocated to ensure equality of condition and to narrow gaps in opportunity by selection of policies that appropriately manipulate wealth, incomes, and access to infrastructure. It is important to review what has not been done by way of this distributional assessment.

First, there is no argument that inequality should be reduced on grounds of any conception of "just desert." Notions of individual merit simply cannot apply in broad policy assessment across social units of any size.

Second, equality of outcome cannot be a defensible policy-assessment criterion. Intervention by authorities of the public household to secure equalities of outcome are, in the first instance, hopelessly doomed because that which would produce equality of results on dimension A (for example, gender) is quite likely to decrease it on dimension B (for example, ethnicity). But even misplaced attempts to secure outcome equality must inherently level down, must make people less autonomous, must destroy choice context. Individual autonomy must be restricted in all societies in the name of civil order, and the entire policy-assessment argument is dedicated to the proposition that such autonomy must be restricted in strategic ways required to sustain a reasoned conception of social development for all. However, restricted autonomy in the name of equality of result would restrict

249

individual choice in a fundamental and unjustifiable manner — unjustifiable if developmental expansion of choice networks is the objective. Some will choose to more productively employ their equal allotments of X at time 1 than will others, a fact that will lead to inequality of outcome by time 2. Agents of the public household would have to find ways to prohibit such behavior by placing significant restrictions on individual, organizational, or group autonomy. Equality, when it spreads to results, would necessarily shrivel the capacity of social networks to afford choice opportunities.

Additionally, equality of outcome becomes ridiculous when indivisible entities are involved. Crude equality of outcome destroys meaningful choice. Hope for choice springs from difference, not sameness, of outcomes. Finally, it is inequality of outcome that is employed to narrow inequalities in opportunity. Greater allotments must be directed to the less well off to narrow gaps and shift Lorenz curves in the desired direction.

Third, the distributional analysis advocated here cannot be expected to produce a strict equality of opportunity, although the policy assessment norms do support movement in this direction. Perfectly equal opportunity is extremely difficult to achieve.

Just as commissioners of professional sports leagues conduct player drafts according to rules that grant advantage to least successful teams in the name of a more viable league, so agents of the public household must reduce certain specified inequalities in the generalized media of social choice in the name of a more viable society. Individual team owners may not be advantaged by what is good for sustaining a competitive league, and particular individuals and organizations will not be advantaged by this policy-assessment argument for the wider society. Team owners, players, and coaches may miscalculate, exercise poor judgment, fall upon bad luck, or fail to make best use of the available resources, but leagues conduct new rounds of the draft each year in hopes that past disappointments will be overcome by better effort during the next season. The league must remain competitive so that outcomes of games are always uncertain and thereby sustain player and fan involvement. So it must be in the wider society. There will always be winners and losers, but agents of the public household must employ unequal outcomes in strategic allocations of generalized media of choice to maintain a viable society. Proposed technology policies that would fulfill the distributional criteria advanced here are to be advanced for inspection on lower-order value criteria, one of which is discussed in the next chapter.

VIII

Social Policy Assessment:
A Science of Fact and a Logic of Value
in the Domain of Futures Forgone

From a short-range, subjective perspective we can say that the value of
nature lies in its generation and support of human life and is therefore
only instrumental. But from a longer-range, objective perspective systematic nature is valuable intrinsically as a projective system, with
humans only one sort of its projects. — Holmes Rolston III[1]

When a tract of wildland is being considered for a use that irreversibly changes the landscape or ecology, the values which are lost by
foreclosing future options must be taken into account in the decision.
Neither traditional land economics nor the standard benefit cost
approach to resource management problems have done so. — John V.
Krutilla and Anthony C. Fisher[2]

People cannot pursue all choices because resources are scarce and
because exercise of one choice typically interferes with another. As
they choose to develop Boston's Logan Airport, they must forgo tranquility at Walden Pond. This bedrock notion of cost has undergirded
economics from the beginning, and all concepts of cost — long run,
short run, average, marginal, market, or nonmarket — refer to this
fundamental reality. In a world in which scarcity would be eliminated,
neither the concept of cost nor choice would have meaning.

Cost is that which the decision-maker must sacrifice when making
a choice.[3] The cost of a choice is equal to the highest-valued opportunity that must be forsaken. All costs are, therefore, in some sense
opportunity costs.[4] Traditionally, economists studying the firm have
used an opportunity cost approach to compare the receipts obtained from a given combination of factors of production with receipts projected from alternative arrangements. An economically

251

rational producer would not use an input to manufacture an item if the expected return of that input were greater in another use. When deciding to adjust levels of inputs, each resource unit carries its own cost according to the alternative opportunity forgone.

This view assumes, however, that all significant costs of choice are borne by the chooser and that none of the forsaken alternatives are sacrificed for anyone else, so that the choice opportunities available to the rest of the community are in no way diminished. Unfortunately, it is all too often the case that choice of option X will destroy possibilities for choosing Y by others not involved in the selection. Many costs are, therefore, not private — they impose important unpriced external costs upon contemporaries, upon future generations, and upon the ecosystem.

What is the value of a given natural resource? The traditional economic answer has been: exactly what it will bring in exchange on the pertinent market. However, the spotted owl is sitting on what some people estimate to be about $12 billion worth of old-growth Douglas-fir in Oregon and Washington.[5] Because the value of the spotted owl population and many other values associated with that ecological community are insufficiently reflected in marketplace exchange, the dollar value of the timber cannot be neatly traded off against the owl and its habitat. Many natural resources have attributes that make it impossible for market prices to capture important elements of their value. One simply does not judge the value of countless entities (for example, whales, elephants, black rhinos, tropical rainforests, the Grand Canyon of the Colorado River) in terms of market exchange. A key species or plant-animal-insect community — once exterminated — cannot contribute to the benefit of existing and future generations, or to local, regional, or global eco-dynamics. We have long recognized obligations to the future that go deeper than present market prices reveal, and many thinkers have recognized that communities of plants, soils, water, and animals have both instrumental and intrinsic values quite apart from current utility in market exchange.[6] At the instrumental level, a viable woodland ecosystem produces a range of valuable unpriced services — protecting soils, controlling erosion and downstream flooding, recycling wastes, cleansing air and water, providing habitat for valuable plant and animal species. Sustenance of such a ecological unit is the best and cheapest way to guarantee the continued supply of essential services for sustainable local, national, and international social development. At a deeper level, robust natural ecosystems are intrinsically valuable because human societies are not self-contained and sealed off from the past, present, and future of the natural world. Whatever is to become of us during the course of coming centuries will be importantly shaped by richness and diversity of our host natural ecosystems. Protecting biological and natural resources of the earth, and those human activities deeply intertwined with natural ecosystems, is therefore an imperative requiring some place in the sociology of policy assessment. What is required is a logic for assessing alternative mixes of losses — forgone futures — when those losses are beyond economic marketplace calculation. It is the purpose of this chapter to present such a logic.

BACKGROUND

Homo sapiens construct communities not only with other members of its species but also with plants, other animals, soil, water, and local atmospheres. In people's quest for expanded ranges, rates, and standards of choice, they have been busy altering landscapes in major ways for thousands of years. Through the conversion of grasslands to pasture for livestock, the use of mechanized equipment, the practice of plant husbandry, and the capacity to organize and apply concentrated forms of energy, all in the process of organizing human societies, people have eroded soils; changed vectors of disease; obliterated forests, wetlands, prairies, and fisheries; salinated land; promoted desertification; degraded air and water quality; and created unmanageable amounts of wastes. From the beginning of organized human society, social development projects have involved the modification of natural environments, and careless environmental policy has been associated with the demise of entire civilizations.

For the most part, however, social theorists have written about society and its socioeconomic development as though human beings were free *from* the environment; belatedly we are coming to incorporate the wisdom that humans are only able to be free *in* the natural world. With this realization, we have come to appreciate that loss of species and environmental quality is a *social* problem. Natural resource managers — whether bureaucrats, entrepreneurs, or peasant farmers — create ecosystem problems within their social orders that have in common a failure to sufficiently reconcile short-term individual-enterprise rationality with the requirements of longer-term collective rationality serving the idea of ecologically sustainable social development for the whole. Given the logics of technological externality and public goods and the tyranny of small decisions (see Chapter 3), what is rational for the individual actor may become most irrational for the collectivity. What stands between individual rationality and collective disaster is disciplined social organization to harness, constrain, and direct individual rationality into developmental directions.[7] The failure to adequately organize ourselves to properly assess and guide what passes for social development around the world in ecologically thoughtful ways has been the subject of a large and rapidly expanding literature.[8]

Recent environmental history is replete with examples of improperly constrained individual rationality directly destroying features of the environment in questionable ways and also generating destructive negative externalities.[9] To take a small example, the discharge of the pesticide Kepone into the James River of Virginia by a manufacturing plant during the course of a decade, 1966–1975, saved the plant managers approximately $200,000 in pollution control costs, but the result was destruction of both sport and commercial fishing opportunities on a ninety-mile stretch of river.[10] The measurable economic losses were estimated at over $20 million during the five-year period 1975–1980, but the dollars captured only an unknown, and unknowable, portion of the damage. In other cases, due to frontal assaults on the natural order, people have pursued their individual rationality at the expense of ecosystem viability. Madagascar has lost 93 percent of its forest cover, and the Atlantic coastal forest of Brazil that so attracted Charles Darwin upon his arrival in 1832 is now 99 percent gone.[11]

There will always be negative choice-destroying externalities of human action for many reasons, not the least of which is the inevitable playing out of the second law of thermodynamics, a statement that as technology captures energy to do work, energy must be degraded — that is, transformed from more to less useful forms. All movement, behavior, or work is founded on the availability of energy. The first law of thermodynamics stipulates that energy can neither be created nor destroyed. But energy takes on different forms, and it is only the total of energy in all forms that is required by the first law to be constant. The second law of thermodynamics specifies the direction of energy flow — always from more concentrated and useful forms toward dispersed, degraded, and less useful varieties.[12] Energy is most useful for work where it is more concentrated — for example, in highly structured chemical bonds or at high temperatures. Energy will always flow from the hotter to the colder; concentrates of anything tend to disperse; structure and organization tend to decay into disorder; order degrades to chaos. Any closed system, left to itself with no capability to import restoring energy, will decompose.

Entropy is the measure of a system's disorder: the more disorder, the less the capacity for work, the more entropy. Systems, in this universe as we know it, must import and process energy from beyond their boundaries to remain organized in the face of tendencies for entropy to increase. Organization, structure, and capacity to act can be built up through energy imports at one point in the universe only at the expense of creating disorder at other points. Refrigerators, for example, make the interior space colder by pumping more disorganized high entropy heat from the motor and compressor into the environment than is removed from the box.

Therefore, given the meaning of the second law, for every unit of wealth produced by a technology to sustain a pattern of human choice there must be production of the antiwealth that is popularly known as pollution — the degraded energy by-products. Residuals from production and consumption processes making up the context of choice of human social organization must be discharged into the environment; negative externalities are, therefore, built into the very structure of things.

Natural processes proceed in ways indifferent to human life and logics of value. The facts of the continual struggle among the living species of the natural world cannot define values. Each organism, operating within its particular web of life, attempts to promote its own survival. Flesh eaters feed upon plant eaters, who in turn consume grasses and insects. Natural ecosystems are intricate food webs within which individual living things are bound up in continuous struggle for survival. Within and among species, not much is consciously done by any one individual organism for the benefit of another, much less for human benefit. Nevertheless, human beings for better or worse must inevitably socially construct values regarding natural processes. We are sluggishly coming to realize that we ought to value healthy biotic communities because we are intimately tethered to them, and we ought not to impoverish the biotic pyramid on top of which we live. We construct values having to do with recreational opportunity, aesthetic experience, scientific understanding, new medicines, ecosystem services such as flood control and breakdown of pollutants, and historical meaning associated with past cultural episodes in the life of human communities.[13] These various types of value are incommensurable, yet we must possess some logic for considering them.

In sum, then, humans not only help and hurt aspects of the natural environment but are in turn helped and hurt by it. The social and natural worlds have interpenetrated and conditioned each other from the beginnings of organized human society. Natural areas are not necessarily made less natural by human presence — important aspects of them are what they are because of thousands of years of patterned human choice. We have come to know that because of the necessities of energy use and degradation, we cannot separate our social worlds from the natural ones, and we have come to appreciate that what people affect does not need to be destroyed or made ugly by human touch. The real issue has to do with how human structures of choice can be organized along with their energy bases in sustainable ways sensitive to requirements of plant and animal communities essential to a healthy physical environment within which all societies must sustain their development.

A LOGIC OF FACT AND VALUE
FOR ANALYSIS OF FUTURES FORGONE

Determining What Is

The analysis of futures forgone begins with the construction of an inventory of existing choice opportunities located in a particular geographical area and sector of activity. In the world of forest planning, for example, those opportunities might include such items as timber production (board feet), livestock grazing (animal unit months), wilderness experience (acres of qualified land and water), developed campground recreation (sites and visitor days), and game and nongame animal species (count). In each sector, the listing of choice opportunities will represent the range of choice options available in the structure of choice within the unit of analysis.

Although no simple recipe is available to guide analysts in the construction of choice opportunity inventories, several points are in order. First, one seeks to include choice opportunities without regard to their popularity among affected populations. A choice opportunity for an archaeological dig exists even if archaeologists are in a tiny minority and the scientific value of potential finds are uncertain. A choice opportunity for worship exists as soon as it becomes known that Native Americans of a given tribe possess sacred ground in the policy-assessment unit. Likewise, an opportunity for mineral extraction exists by virtue of known deposits in the area of a given quality, not by virtue of the presence of active mining. Or a choice opportunity for a species of plant or animal life exists by virtue of appropriate habitat and at least some minimally viable population. We typically employ a capstone or indicator species high on the food chain to represent ecological webs upon which they are dependent — for example, the panda, tiger, eagle, elk, elephant, whale, or dolphin.

Second, ecosystems are inextricably intertwined with human activities and choices. Short-grass rangeland in the western United States and stockmen are socially organized to go together, just as sawmills are fitted to timberland, miners to mineral deposits, fishermen to tuna, or kayakers to white water. It is not possible to view a lake, stream, river, mountain, or patch of prairie without seeing that it is a stage for a multiplicity of human as well as natural theaters. What happens, or does not happen, on a given patch is, at least in part, human social behavior and choice and requires social analysis.

Third, it must be further recognized that any given list of choice opportunities cannot be final but must be open to revision as more refined information becomes available. One makes the best initial inventory of choice opportunities possible and then proceeds with the analysis. As knowledgeable individuals enter into the estimation and review process, new insights about choice opportunities can be expected to emerge.

Determining What Ought

The concept of futures forgone is disaggregated into three measurable dimensions.

Scope of Loss. The scope of loss value expresses the proportion of any given choice opportunity estimated to be lost in the primary planning unit if the proposed policy alternative were to be implemented (see Fig. 8.1). Scope values for each listed choice opportunity range from zero — no reduction in the availability of the opportunity to engage in the activity — to unity, representing complete destruction of that choice opportunity in the primary planning area. For example, if it is estimated that policy X would generate a combination of direct and indirect effects that would destroy 10 percent of the winter habitat for an elk herd in the primary planning unit, the scope value relative to elk would equal .10. Scope values are generated for each choice opportunity in the planning unit under each proposed policy alternative by a modified Delphi procedure designed to integrate nomothetic knowledge of the several relevant disciplines and site-specific local idiographic knowledge (see Appendix II).

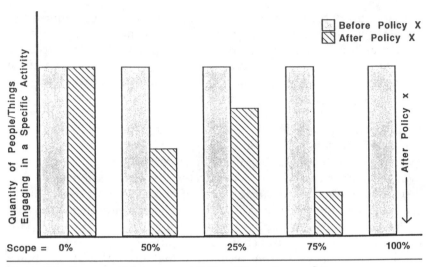

Figure 8.1. Impact of Management Policy Alternative on Scope

Intensity of Loss. The intensity of loss value expresses the extent to which a given scope of loss to a choice opportunity in the primary assessment unit can be afforded. The less that the fraction of loss can be compensated by remaining available choice opportunities of a like nature within the overall primary and secondary planning area, the greater the intensity of the loss (see Fig. 8.2). More specifically, intensity values vary inversely in an exponentially increasing manner with the decline in the number of other places at which the choice opportunity is afforded.

Intensity values indicate the significance of losses represented by reduced scope values. Intensity does not measure a psychological state of feeling with regard to lost or reduced choices; it has a structural meaning free of the tug of human wants, wishes, or desires as expressed by any particular interest group. If a choice opportunity suffers a given scope of loss, the intensity value will diminish according to the extent that the choice is available within the encompassing primary and secondary planning units. If available at many points in viable and sustainable ways, a given scope of loss to a choice within the primary unit will engender a lower intensity of loss than if available at few or no other points.

For example, 50 percent of the United States' original endowment of wetlands had, by the late 1980s, been destroyed by unbridled agricultural, industrial, and urban growth.[14] These ecosystems not only

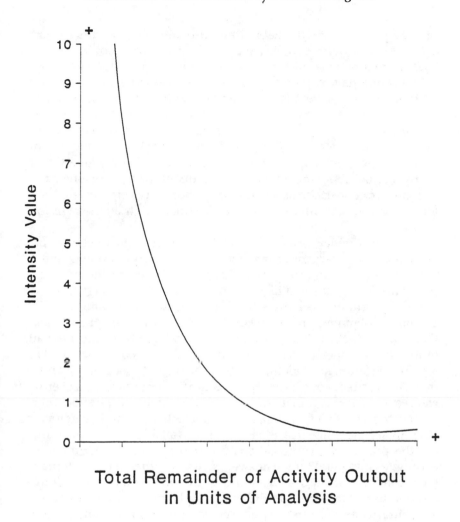

Figure 8.2. Intensity of Loss Curve

provide precious wildlife habitat but also, among other things, produce cleansed water supplies and flood protection. Looking at wetlands from a national historical perspective, a 1 percent loss (a scope value) would have earned a low intensity of loss prior to their earliest destruction. A 1 percent loss to a great quantity of high-quality wetlands could rather easily be afforded. However, now after decades of destructive activities that have much reduced their availability and quality, an additional 1 percent loss in the scope column would take on a much higher intensity value. Or, when there is only one Grand Canyon of the Colorado, one remaining free-flowing river, one Amazon forest, or one ozone layer, small depletions have big consequences for the present and future that earn extremely high intensity of loss scores.

A distinction has been added to the discussion: that between primary and secondary planning units. The primary planning unit is defined as that geographic area directly subjected to the proposed policy manipulations — a highway or river corridor, a neighborhood, town, city, county, forest, river basin, or irrigation command area. The secondary planning area is a larger encompassing geographic area that surrounds the primary planning unit and affords some, if not all, of the choice opportunities inventoried in the primary unit (see Fig. 8.3). The criterion for defining limits of the secondary planning area is that of accessibility of choices to the sectorial user groups who exercise choices in the primary planning unit. For example, the question might be: If commercially viable timber is of interest to sawmill operators in the primary planning area, is such timber available in areas surrounding the primary unit in locations accessible to the operators given existing technologies? If the answer is positive, then the line defining the secondary planning area should be drawn in a manner such that those timber stands outside the primary planning area are included. To arbitrarily exclude an accessible choice opportunity from a secondary planning area will unjustifiably inflate the intensity of losses sustained in the primary area. Unfortunately, there is no ultimate logic in science for defining boundaries of systems — such is certainly the case in policy assessment. The ultimate check on poorly drawn primary and secondary planning boundaries is review by knowledgeable people who, by participating in the estimation of futures-forgone scores, can suggest that a particular intensity of loss value appears to be unjustifiable given the demonstrable fact that substantial amounts of a particular choice opportunity are accessible beyond the secondary planning area as initially drawn. Such people would point out that a

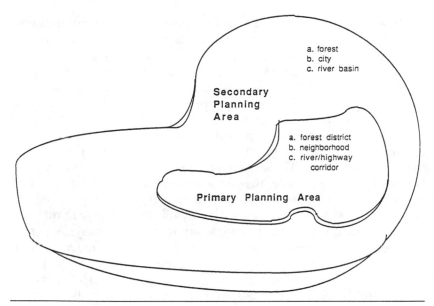

a. forest
b. city
c. river basin

**Secondary
Planning
Area**

a. forest district
b. neighborhood
c. river/highway
   corridor

Primary Planning Area

Figure 8.3. Primary and Secondary Planning Areas

boundary for the secondary planning area, redrawn to be more encompassing, would include accessible choice opportunities. This, in turn, would have the effect of lowering the intensity of loss score for the choice upon which discussion focused.

Why does the intensity value increase as an exponential function? Such a function has been selected because it best reflects the essence of the underlying argument. The rarer an environment, the more we resist loss to it, and we reflect that resistance in an increasing curvilinear fashion. Grasslands are relatively common as compared to desert springs, the natural bridge on the shores of Lake Powell, Old Faithful geyser, or cathedral groves of redwoods. Since some ecological webs are rare, whether or not they are essential to human life on the planet, they are planetary heirlooms to be preserved. At bottom, extinction of a species or destruction of an environmental heirloom is irreversible; we lose diversity, beauty, a genetic resource, a natural wonder, an irreplaceable souvenir of our common past and of our earth. Most of all, the exponentially increasing intensity value that goes off the chart prior to total destruction expresses the value that we should not destroy the last few units of something we can never re-create.

In addition to arguments about intrinsic worth of threatened eco-systems, there are instrumental arguments to bolster an exponentially increasing intensity value. By exponentially penalizing proposed policies that would threaten rarer, more intensely valued ecological phenomena, one is hedging against future unknowns. We are taking out socioecological insurance against unpredictable catastrophe. Agriculture, industry, science, and medicine are dependent upon sources of genetic materials for both improving existing products and for development of entirely new varieties as yet to be invented. Those stocks require preservation. The less such communities are reduced by careless human activity now, the more resilient they will be to future perturbations — for example, climate change, acid rain — and the greater the likelihood that they will be available for future human use in ways now quite unforeseeable. Many threatened ecosystems provide essential services to human well-being, such as the recycling of nutrients, the purifying of water, flood control, breakdown of pollutants, protection of soil, fixation of solar energy, waste treatment. As such useful biotic communities are reduced, their capacity to meaningfully render such services is threatened. Additionally, there may be nonconsumptive uses — for example, carefully designed tourism and recreation — of ecological communities that may well add to the wealth of the nation in ways which would be impossible if they were not preserved in robust condition. For all of these reasons, an exponentially increasing intensity curve is justified.

Scope and intensity values will vary independently. One might witness a small scope of loss with an associated high intensity value in situations where small fractions of choice depletion are estimated to occur on rare opportunities — for example, habitat for an endangered species of bird, animal, or plant; a unique scenic vista; a region especially suited to the production of a unique variety of agricultural crop; a rich vein of ore not to be found elsewhere; a small depletion of this planet's only ozone layer. On the other hand, high scope values do not necessarily imply significant intensity scores. One can lose all of a choice opportunity for timbering, hydroelectric power production, or wilderness recreation in the primary planning unit and still obtain low intensity of loss values if futures are being sustained for an abundance of those choice opportunities elsewhere in the primary and secondary planning units. Wilderness had a negative value for seventeenth-century Americans because they were faced with so much. Now, however, the situation is typically much reversed; given its relative scarcity and its highly uneven distribution, loss of a potential wilderness in many units of analysis would engender high intensity scores. The rarer a choice opportunity, the less desirable a depletion to it even if there is little or no popular support for that choice opportunity (wolves among cattle ranchers; snail darters among Tennessee dam builders) among the human population — such is the meaning of the intensity value.

Duration of Loss. Duration of loss values express the number of years required for a particular lost choice opportunity to be restored to its present standard, if decision-makers should wish to restore it, given present technology and current levels of budgetary resources. Making predictions about future social needs, technological capacities, and political priorities is hazardous, costly, and subject to much error. Panels of informed judges making futures-forgone calculations (see Appendix II) are not expected to estimate whether decision-making authorities would ever actually choose to modify or terminate the proposed policy under assessment. Analytical crystal balls for peering into the future with accuracy are simply not available. Instead, informed participants in a futures-forgone exercise, estimating duration values for particular choice opportunities, address an answerable question: If the proposed policy were to be implemented, and then be terminated by public household decision-makers, how many years would be required with current levels of technology and budget to restore the lost choice opportunity to its current standard?[15] Current technological and budgetary levels are employed to provide a common basis for comparing duration of impacts under each alternative. Duration values are illustrated in Figure 8.4.

To adopt a policy for the public household that yields consequences easily reversed or modified is to leave open choice possibilities that can be exercised in the future as new information generates a need for policy change. On the other hand, to adopt a policy which irreversibly sets into motion a chain of events that is not open to change except at high cost in time and money is to foreclose future opportunities. In an uncertain, dynamic, and complex world where knowledge is partial and hypotheses are tentative, decision-makers should value highly those courses of action that retain greatest latitudes for future corrective and adaptive action. Reversibility of action should be counted as a major benefit and irreversibility as a significant cost.[16] There is value in having the capacity to restore a lost choice quickly and at low cost should it be desirable to do so.

In sum, then, each non-zero scope of loss value is weighted by intensity and duration values. These three variables vary independently,

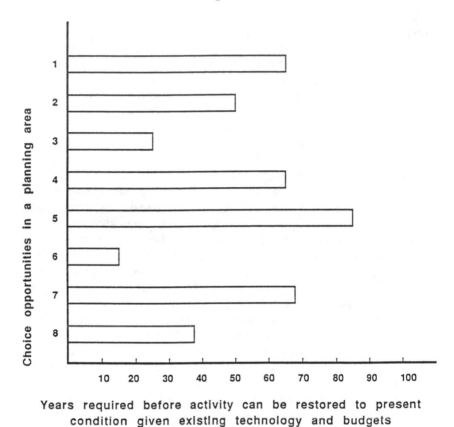

Figure 8.4. Duration of Loss Associated With Policy X

but together they are employed to compose profiles of harm that would be imposed by alternative policy proposals. That policy estimated to impose a profile of harm that can most be afforded (that is, the one that possesses the lowest intensity and shortest duration of losses) is judged superior as compared to those with higher futures-forgone scores.

Computing the Futures-Forgone Score

The three dimensions of futures for choice opportunities forgone yield values that can be combined into a summary value. How specifically are the dimensions to be combined and weighted? Illustrative futures-forgone data are displayed in Table 8.1.

Table 8.1. Futures-Forgone Scores for Policy Options — An Example

Choice Opportunity	Policy Option A			Policy Option B		
	Scope	Intensity	Duration	Scope	Intensity	Duration
Commercial timber	.03	2.0	.0	.50	6.3	2.0
Farming	.0	.0	.0	.0	.0	.0
Ranching	.05	1.5	.0	.18	3.3	.5
Food processing	.0	.0	.0	.0	.0	.0
Water-agricultural	.17	6.5	3.0	.0	.0	.0
Water-municipal	.0	.0	.0	.25	6.0	2.0
Mining	.25	2.0	.5	.50	2.0	1.0
Construction	.16	1.8	.5	.40	4.2	1.5
Retail sales	.05	.5	.5	.35	3.5	1.0
Motels-restaurants	.20	1.5	.5	.20	4.5	2.5
Dispersed recreation/non-motorized	.05	4.0	1.5	.0	.0	.0
Dispersed recreation/motorized	.15	3.5	1.3	.64	6.5	.5
TOTALS	1.11	23.3	7.8	3.02	36.3	11.0
Futures-Forgone Score =	10.69			24.70		

Looking down the columns of Table 8.1, one sees "scope" estimates for each listed choice opportunity under each of two policy options. Where scope values are 0, intensity and duration of loss values must also equal 0. There can be no meaningful intensity or duration of loss for a choice opportunity that is not suffering a scope of loss. Where scope is a non-zero value, however, one will find accompanying estimates for intensity and duration. The summary futures-forgone score is computed as follows:

$$FF = \sum S \left(\sum I / N \right) + \sum D$$

where:

FF = futures forgone for a given proposed policy alternative;

$\sum$ S = sum of scope of loss scores for each proposed policy alternative;

$\sum$ I = sum of intensity scores for each proposed policy alternative;

$\sum$ N = the number of choice opportunity items obtaining a non - zero intensity value;

$\sum$ D = sum of duration scores for each proposed policy alternative.

This formula weights intensity as a critical variable in the equation. Scope varies only between 0 and 1; intensity values are used as multipliers and consist of whole numbers that range across a potentially wide spectrum. Duration values, by being added to the product of scope and the adjusted intensity values, have a significant impact on the futures-forgone score but do not have as much impact as if the duration value were also employed as a multiplier.

The sum of intensity scores under each proposed alternative is divided by the number of intensity scores, to control for the number of intensity values contributing to the summary score. If the sum of intensity values equals sixteen by virtue of one very intense loss to one activity category, the sum of sixteen will be divided by one and the high intensity score will stand. If, on the other hand, the sum of intensity equals sixteen by virtue of sixteen activity categories each obtaining a score of one, the intensity value in the futures-forgone equation will equal one.

Examination of Table 8.1 reveals that policy option A is preferable, or less inferior, as compared to option B because A imposes losses where they can be more afforded.

Several points are in order. First, futures-forgone data consist of ordinal values that indicate direction of impacts in a manner that provides "greater than" and "less than" statements. When summing scope scores, therefore, it is essential to remember that a value of 3.6 is not exactly nine units less than 12.6, only that 3.6 is considerably less. Second, it is important to examine not only total futures-forgone scores that yield the policy ranking at the bottom of Table 8.1 but also to inspect distributions of scores along each dimension — scope, intensity, and duration. Two or more policy options may well generate identical summary scores, but there may be large differences in the distribution of losses to the choice context. However useful the summary scores, the analyst must not overlook the fact that the column totals may be a result of very different profiles of forgone choice opportunities.

Third, there is nothing inherent in the substance of environmental preservation proposals that necessarily gives them advantage as compared to economic growth proposals. Environmental preservation policies, in particular places, can forgo futures with high scope, great intensity, and extended duration just as other types of policy can. To place a river under wild and scenic designation in the name of environmental quality could forgo options for irrigation water development that would be of the most intensive and extended impact. Poorly constructed environmental protection policies can be expected to lose out to well-drawn economic development policies. There is no built-in bias toward environmental protection proposals, except insofar as the very purpose of the analysis is to protect against excessive loss of biodiversity and environmental robustness. It is not the policy label that counts; it is the nature of the estimated policy impact at a given time in a specific socioecological niche.

Last, one interest of policy assessment is to provide information that will serve as a foundation upon which to reformulate proposed options based on the estimated impact profiles of each. If policy alternatives are to be reformulated, and thereby made more developmentally defensible, they must be revised with a view toward reducing losses to scope that carry high intensities and durations of loss. It is, therefore, generally desirable to conduct a sequence of assessments, each successive one operating with improved policy options generated by prior efforts.

FUTURES-FORGONE ANALYSIS IN THE UNITED STATES: THE CASE OF "BIG VISTA DIVIDE"

The Big Vista Divide planning unit was introduced in Chapter 6.[17] In addition to the conflict polarization analysis reported in Chapter 6, a futures-forgone analysis was also conducted on the four forest policy options (briefly summarized again here).

Alternative A. Under this option protection and enhancement of wilderness, aesthetic, and air and water quality values would be the primary emphasis. Other resource uses and activities would be subordinated to the goal of environmental preservation and wilderness use. The maximum amount of wilderness within the definition of the wilderness act would be provided.

Alternative B. Long-term continuation of existing uses and activities is the focus of this alternative. Primary emphasis would be placed on maintaining endangered and threatened fish and wildlife habitat coupled with maintenance of historical and cultural sites. Dispersed recreational activities in a natural environment would be emphasized along with protection and use of unique natural areas. No wilderness would be made available, although opportunities for primitive non-motorized recreation would be provided.

Alternative C. This alternative promotes recreation diversity. Primary emphasis would be to provide maximum diversity of dispersed recreation activities within a tank of gasoline of "metroplex." Amenities and intangible values would be protected and enhanced in support of this policy — for example, developed campgrounds would be limited to the proposed highway corridor, and there would be no provision for the concentrated recreation represented by a ski area. The amount of wilderness provided would be less than that under alternative A but more than that provided by policy option D.

Alternative D. This option promotes tangible forest commodity production. Emphasis would be placed on stimulating local and regional economic growth through construction of highly concentrated recreation sites (for example, a ski area and numerous summer campground facilities), accelerated commercial timber production, and intensified utilization of forage, wildlife, and water. Policy emphasis would provide for maximizing economic values at minimum possible amenity costs. A lesser amount of wilderness would be available than provided by either options A or C, but it would provide a minimum wilderness designation as compared to option B, which would provide no designated wilderness.

Futures-forgone data generated by panels of informed citizens and technically trained people (see Appendix II) are displayed in Table 8.2. Looking down the left-hand column, one views the list of thirty-three choice opportunities as identified on the planning unit. Data reveal the estimated losses sustained under each of the four proposed policy alternatives. Inspection of Table 8.2 reveals that in this particular planning unit policy option A, environmental quality, emerged as being the least inferior. It is followed, at some distance, by alternative C — recreation diversity, which in turn is followed by the two remaining policy options nearly tied for third place. The economic development policy is the most inferior given the attributes of this particular planning unit.

FUTURES-FORGONE ANALYSIS IN PAKISTAN: THE HYPOTHETICAL CASE OF ZAFFABAB DISTRICT

The description of the Thikapur village[18] in Chapter 7 introduced the problem of waterlogging and salinity in Pakistan. Rising water tables have reduced agricultural production as a result of the increase of soil salinity in crop root zones. Salinity, beyond certain thresholds, can interfere with seed germination and with yields of mature plants. There are any number of possible policy options for confronting the threat, but for illustrative purposes, the following four are forwarded.

Alternative A: This policy would involve central government investment in large publicly owned and administered tubewells, each of which would have a capacity of pumping groundwater at a rate of up to three cubic feet per second. These wells, powered by electric motors wired into the central electrical grid, would typically be located near main canals so as to pump canal seepage water and be near the heads of local irrigation community watercourses so that the pumped water could be delivered to farmers' fields.

Alternative B. Government would promote, by subsidy, the purchase of small tubewells from local equipment dealers by small groups of farmers organized for sharing costs of purchase operations and maintenance. Such tubewells would pump groundwater at a fraction of a cubic foot per second and be powered by small diesel or solar engines. Farmers would locate the wells according to their estimate of groundwater levels; they would also set their own pumping schedules. In addition, in order to effectively conduct water from their wells to their fields and in order to make possible efficient water exchange among themselves, farmers would rehabilitate the existing earthen community watercourse by employing local labor and materials. Rehabilitation would involve reconstruction of the earthen ditch in a manner that would provide improved cross section, slope, and alignment. Earthen improvements would substantially reduce losses of both canal and tubewell water.

269

Table 8.2. Futures Forgone in Big Vista Divide

Choice Opportunity	Policy A Environmental Quality			Policy B Present Management			Policy C Recreational Diversity			Policy D Economic Development		
	S	I	D	S	I	D	S	I	D	S	I	D
Sawmills	1	6	4	.3	2	5	.5	4	5	0	0	0
Logging contractors	1	6	2	.3	2	3	.5	4	5	0	0	0
Cattle grazing	0	0	0	0	0	0	.2	4	3	0	0	0
Other livestock	0	0	0	0	0	0	.3	4	1	0	0	0
Food processing	1	2	3	0	0	0	.3	2	3	0	0	0
Wilderness recreation	0	0	0	.3	7	100	.3	6	50	.7	8	100
Dispersed recreation	0	0	0	0	0	0	0	0	0	.5	8	3
Wildlife recreation	0	0	0	0	0	0	0	0	0	.3	6	1
Developed recreation	.8	6	5	.3	4	2	.3	2	5	0	0	0
Minerals/mining	.9	7	3	.2	3	1	.5	4	5	0	0	0
Watershed	.4	6	3	.2	6	5	.3	6	5	.3	4	5
Gas stations/auto	.6	2	1	.2	2	1	.3	2	1	0	0	0
Restaurants/bars	.4	4	1	.2	2	1	.3	2	1	0	0	0
Transport-storage	.5	4	2	0	0	0	.3	2	3	0	0	0
Personal services	.5	4	2	0	0	0	0	0	0	0	0	0
Other retail	.4	4	2	0	0	0	.3	2	1	0	0	0
Hunting-birds	0	0	0	0	0	0	0	0	0	.4	3	2
Hunting-sm. game	.5	4	1	0	0	0	0	0	0	.4	3	2
Hunting-lg. game	.3	4	1	0	0	0	0	0	0	.3	4	5
Camping-remote	0	0	0	0	0	0	0	0	0	.7	7	2
Camping-developed	.5	6	2	.2	4	4	0	0	0	0	0	0
Hiking	0	0	0	0	0	0	0	0	0	0	0	0

Table 8.2 (continued)

Choice Opportunity	Policy A Environmental Quality			Policy B Present Management			Policy C Recreational Diversity			Policy D Economic Development		
	S	I	D	S	I	D	S	I	D	S	I	D
Auto touring	.5	4	5	.3	4	5	.4	2	1	0	0	0
Skiing-downhill	.5	0	0	0	0	0	0	0	0	0	0	0
Skiing–cross-country	0	0	0	0	0	0	0	0	0	.4	4	1
Fishing	0	0	0	0	0	0	0	0	0	.3	4	1
Boating-power	1	1	0	.5	2	1	.3	1	1	0	0	0
Boating-no power	0	0	0	0	0	0	0	0	0	.2	2	0
Housing	1	4	2	.3	2	2	.5	3	1	0	0	0
Business-indusrial	.8	2	3	.3	2	5	.8	2	5	0	0	0
Business-agricultural	0	0	0	0	0	0	.5	3	5	0	0	0
Totals	12.6	76	42	3.6	42	135	6.9	55	101	5	57	123

S = Scope, I = Intensity, D = Duration
Futures Forgone Ranking: A-Environmental Quality = 94.9
C-Recreation Diversity = 122.4
B-Continue Present Mgt. = 146.5
D-Economic Development = 149.0

271

Alternative C: Government would promote, by subsidy, farmer construction of concrete- or brick-lined watercourses. Such improvement could be expected to eliminate seepage from local watercourse channels and thereby reduce waterlogging while at the same time improving supplies of irrigation water at the tail reaches. Landowners on each watercourse would arrange to hire local contractors to construct the improved community watercourse from the main canal outlet to the farmers' earthen field ditches. The older watercourses would be destroyed to make way for the improved structures along existing rights-of-way. Local farmer organizations would be provided subsidized loans to pay contractors. Government inspectors would enforce construction standards upon farmers and contractors. Given the expense of lining materials, it is known that increased farm production due to diminished salinity and improved water supplies would not justify the expense of bathing pools and laundry areas along the new watercourses.

Alternative D. Agents of the public household will do nothing. In a planning unit already without public tubewells, without available small tubewells, and without lined watercourses, the status quo will continue.

No futures-forgone assessment was actually conducted; the analysis reported here is hypothetical. One would like to report data actually generated by a set of panels, consisting of locally knowledgeable citizens. Unfortunately, this was not possible. However, much informal discussion of policy options did take place among local informants, expatriates, and decision-makers, and it is possible, for illustrative purposes, to report a hypothetical analysis of futures for choice opportunities forgone under each of the four general policy alternatives.

Table 8.3 reports results of the hypothetical analysis. Proceeding down the table, one views sixteen choice opportunities likely to be impacted by the policy proposals. There are, of course, more choice possibilities exercised in Zaffabab district but choices for education, health care, worship, birth-control assistance, and marketing of farm products are not affected by the policies being assessed, so such items are not incorporated in the analysis. If, however, a case could be made that an unlisted choice opportunity would be affected by a proposed policy, that opportunity should be added.

The data deserve some inspection and explanation. The first striking fact about the data in Table 8.3 is that the last-ranked option — alternative C — earns its high futures-forgone score by virtue of heavy

Table 8.3 Futures Forgone in Zaffabab District

Choice Opportunity	Policy A Large Tubewells			Policy B Small Tubewells			Policy C W-C Lining			Policy D No Action		
	S	I	D	S	I	D	S	I	D	S	I	D
Cattle grazing	.4	4	6	0	●	0	0	0	0	.10	4	8
Goat grazing	.2	4	6	0	●	0	0	0	0	.04	4	8
Sheep grazing	.4	4	6	0	●	0	0	0	0	.04	4	8
Communal bathing/females	0	0	0	0	●	0	.33	8	15	0	0	0
Comunal bathing/males	0	0	0	0	●	0	.33	8	15	0	0	0
Shesham wood/crafts	0	0	0	0	●	0	.35	16	60	0	0	0
Mosque/worship	0	0	0	0	●	0	0	0	0	.20	2	8
Sacred sites	0	0	0	0	●	0	0	0	0	.40	16	5
Cottage textiles	0	0	0	0	●	0	0	0	0	0	0	0
Fodder production	.5	8	10	.2	●	2	0	0	0	.10	8	8
Sugarcane production	.1	1	3	.1	●	2	0	0	0	.05	1	3
Wheat production	0	0	0	0	●	0	0	0	0	.03	2	3
Cotton production	.1	1	3	0	●	0	0	0	0	.05	1	3
Vegetables/spinach, onions	.15	16	10	.5	●	2	0	0	0	.30	16	10
Fruit/oranges, melons	.10	16	10	.3	●	2	0	0	0	.25	16	10
Fuel-cow dung	0	0	0	0	●	0	0	0	0	.04	0	0
Fuel-bagasse	.1	1	3	0	●	0	0	0	0	.03	2	3
Totals	.43	55	57	.11	32	8	1.01	32	90	1.63	76	77

S = Scope, I = Intensity, D = Duration
Futures Forgone Ranking: B-Small Fractional Cusec Tubewells = 96.00
A-Large Government Tubewells = 319.73
D-No Action (status quo) = 1,108.79
C-Concrete Lining of Watercourses = 1,160.50

negative impacts on three choice opportunities. The number of choices affected are fewest as compared to the more successful alternatives, but the losses are relatively intense and the duration scores are considerable. The analysis reveals that about one-third of the community bathing opportunities would be destroyed, that the alternative bathing opportunities are quite limited, and that the concrete linings are expected to have a life of approximately fifteen years. Also, alternative C would be extremely destructive of the shesham trees upon which local craftsmen are dependent for raw material, upon which villagers are highly dependent for shade, and upon which several species of birds are dependent for nesting opportunities. Trees tend to grow on or near the canal banks where their roots find ample water and where they present little obstacle to the farmers' plows. Reconstruction of watercourses and concrete lining of them is estimated to destroy 35 percent of the shesham trees. The scope value is not greater because trees would be cut down only along main watercourse channels where reconstruction would take place. Sixty-five percent of the living trees would remain along smaller field ditches serving as off-takes from the watercourses.

The relatively high intensity scores associated with the loss of bathing and shesham wood reflect the lack of accessible alternatives to sustain them. Private bathing within the confines of the home is not available to any but the very rich. The new concrete watercourses are not amenable to this activity, and farmers' field ditches are too small. The existing earthen watercourses have been widened at select points over the years to provide bathing opportunities. To destroy them would impose a considerable cost. The destruction of shesham trees earns a high intensity score because there are simply no alternative sources for this valued commodity in the primary or secondary planning areas. It is estimated to require sixty years to restore the shesham stands to today's level with existing technology — if one should attempt to do so.

Doing nothing, policy proposal D, is also one that forgoes futures to a great extent. It spreads the costs around more than option C, but it is expected to impose high costs on several choice opportunities:

1. The opportunity to keep religious structures intact in the face of rising water tables leading to deterioration in foundations and walls. Some religious structures can be moved more easily than others, but no alternative locations are available for several religious sites.

2. Opportunities to grow vegetables and fruit that are highly sensitive to increases in soil and water salinity. A substantial proportion of district land is estimated to be lost to vegetable and fruit production if the status quo prevails, and the high intensity scores reflect the fact that, given the already highly intense use of the land, the lost production could not be made up elsewhere in the secondary planning unit.

Proposed Alternative A, second ranked, imposes small losses on grazing due to increased salinity associated with rapid pumping of fresh groundwater, which in turn sucks up a deeper layer of saline groundwater. This also imposes a small loss on fodder production, very little loss to sugarcane and cotton, no loss to wheat, but greater losses to vegetable crops, melons, and fruit production. The intensity scores associated with Alternative A reflect the lesser access to the diminished choice opportunities in the secondary planning area.

Proposed policy B is the first ranked. Small tubewells, purchased and managed by small groups of farmers sharing a given segment of the local watercourse system, do not draw up fresh groundwater at such a rate that the deeper layer of saline water is disturbed and intermixed so as to reduce water quality. This option does not provide for any watercourse rehabilitation. Therefore, it is estimated that some small losses would occur in opportunities to grow fodder, sugarcane, vegetables, fruit, and melons. These losses to production are as intensive as those expected to occur under Alternative A.

Given the profile of losses shown on Table 8.3, it is the task of policy assessment to investigate potentials for policy reformulation before adopting what appears to be the preferred approach on the basis of the initial analysis. If policy dialogue between farmers and analysts were to reveal ways to alter any one or more of the proposed options, different scores would be generated and different rankings of policy proposals would emerge. It is expected that proposed policy options will be reformulated and the more refined versions reassessed. Successive iterations of this analysis can result in creation of new policy proposals that are more sensitive to the conditions of the planning unit than any that could be devised by the most informed and creative analyst in a first round of policy formulation.

CONCLUSION

Selection of a given policy choice for the public household imposes costs in the form of choices forgone. Policy choices, moreover, must be exercised from among whole bundles of goods and bads. This chapter has contended that policies should be assessed according to the profile of nonmarket costs each imposes on the context of choice in a given sector of choice located in a particular geographical area divided into primary and secondary planning units. Those proposed policies that impose nonmarket costs where they can be most afforded (by earning low intensity and duration scores) are viewed as more developmental than those that impose a more corrosive profile of harm.

There are several implications. Because the analysis does not operate at the individual level of private preference, there is no need to weigh losses and gains according to attributes of individual users of choice opportunities. One knows that, for any given choice opportunity, there are those who directly exercise that choice — they actively enjoy wilderness, produce corn, or occupy a favorite spot on the trout stream. Other individuals take comfort in simply knowing that a choice opportunity exists without actively exploiting it. This analysis, structural as it is, values choice opportunities per se. It analyzes their respective merits according to their replaceability by measuring and combining intensity and duration. There is no defensible logic for weighing choices according to the attributes of the users — rich or poor, cosmopolitan or parochial, insider or outsider relative to the planning area, direct or indirect consumers of the opportunities. One can be a hunter for pleasure, out of concern for exercise, a desire to display status, or because one has a taste for game. There is no need, in the futures-forgone analysis to evaluate motives. This is a most fortunate implication of the analysis, as we do not, and in all likelihood cannot, know how to make interpersonal comparisons of motives or individual meaning for policy assessment purposes.

Another implication is that the analysis of natural resource policies cannot be confined to public lands per se but must be extended to all land and resource ownership categories. To exclude private resource holdings would be to unjustifiably inflate futures-forgone scores in ways that would badly skew analysis. For example, if private lands offered much commercially viable timber and that fact was overlooked by an analysis that excluded that timber because of its ownership category, the intensity of loss value to the timber choice opportunity would be inflated and the analysis distorted. Public household policy assessment must cope with choice opportunities emanating from all resources relevant to the sector in question.

It is also worth noting that this analysis is relevant to the vexed question of humankind's moral relation, if any, to other forms of animal and plant life — forms without the cerebral capacity to consciously develop sophisticated technologies capable of wreaking destruction upon us. There is much to be said about this relationship far beyond the scope of this analysis, but the futures-forgone logic suggests that a choice opportunity to sustain a habitat for a species of animal or plant life has value independent of current social fashion, political pressure, or economic motive.

In the larger social developmental logic of value (see Chapter 5), the futures-forgone analysis is the first criterion that can be expected to operate as a tie breaker for whatever variety of policy proposals succeed in passing higher-order assessments — that is, reduction of polarization, fulfillment of equality of condition, and reduction of gaps in the distribution of income, wealth, or access to infrastructure. To select from among the policy-induced distributions of advantage and disadvantage that have passed higher-order tests, and to choose those surviving proposals producing patterns of benefit and cost that forgo futures that will be least missed, is to leave a legacy of expanded choice opportunities that has been justified by a coherent logic of value. It is a critical dimension of what progress in social life is all about.

IX

Implications

The social function of social science is thus not simply to serve the interest of any particular class in a given period of history, nor is it to serve the interests of academics themselves. Rather, it is to provide guidance to society, through research, reasoned discourse, and education as to what interests should be served in particular circumstances and as to the means to do so. — Duncan MacRae[1]

A crucial failure in modern political thought and political practice has been an inability or unwillingness even to begin the project I am suggesting here: the critical evaluation and control of our society's technical constitution. The silence of liberalism on this issue is matched by an equally obvious neglect in Marxist theory. Both persuasions have enthusiastically sought freedom in sheer material plenitude, welcoming whatever technological means (or monstrosities) seemed to produce abundance the fastest. — Langdon Winner[2]

In 214 B.C. Syracuse was invaded by Rome. Archimedes, intent on a geometric problem, was tracing figures in sand when a hostile legionnaire appeared. Glancing up, the greatest mathematician of antiquity is said to have snapped, "Disturb not my circle." The Greek thinker perished — phased out by a sword. In our own time technological capacities remain unguided by minimally adequate values. Powerful technological potentials are at the service of imperfect marketplaces, politicians serving parochial interests back home, the warped visions of ideologues possessing revealed truths not to be questioned openly in free discussion. Technological potentials for action are so poorly assessed by agents of the public households around the world that many astute observers have agonized as to whether any social system can harness them to humane and ecologically sane purposes.

Yet, even though the need for improved policy assessment is beyond dispute, it is the essence of modernity to grasp that there is no ultimate fact or value on which to base the enterprise. What we are able to conclude about policy impacts depends upon the procedures we employ. The modern and postmodern world is provisional, methodologically contingent, and theoretically relative and has led us far from fixed certainties. When we ask ourselves the question, How long is the Alaskan coast? we know that the answer we obtain depends upon the procedures we employ. If we use a map constructed at a scale of a hundred miles to an inch, it smooths out the details of the bays, promontories, capes, and edges, and the factual answer we obtain is different than if we use a map drawn to a scale of ten miles to an inch wherein new features are recorded and new irregularities add to the distance. What if we use a scale of one mile per inch, or drop to a microscopic level where one would sum even the tiny irregularities on the surface of pebbles and sand? Enough! We can go on forever and there will be no ultimate fact regarding the distance of the Alaskan coast independent of our choice of procedures. We have little choice but to work at that level of measurement accuracy that suits our purpose and let the matter go.

This is, likewise, the case in valuation. There is no ultimate value upon which to rest a conception of the "more developed" society, no ultimately fixed foundation upon which to rest policy assessment. But it is still possible to do a job that much needs to be done — namely, to employ sociology and associated disciplines to assist agents of the public household in appraising the merit of policies advanced in the name of promoting social development. The idea of development must not continue to be a vague ill-defined conceptual cover-up for uncritical faith in evolutionary progress and aggregate economic growth. Whatever the inadequacies, and incompleteness, of the argument in foregoing chapters, a case has been made that sociological logics, open to interdisciplinary collaboration, can distinguish those policies that will increase polarization from those that will decrease it and choose the latter for good reasons. Furthermore, those logics can give merit to policies that honor equality of condition, can analyze distributional effects, and can then identify those proposals that promise to reduce one or more inequalities of opportunity for good reasons and rank proposed policies according to the scope, intensity, and duration of futures to be forgone for good reasons. Finally, there are good reasons for selecting the policy that, after satisfying the higher-order structural criteria, promises best economic efficiencies. It is, therefore, possible to pursue a coherent conception of social development in which nomothetic generalizable principle can be blended with site-specific circumstance, in which judgments of fact and value become compelling in guiding us toward a "better society" in a relativistic world.

This idea of development accepts, and copes with, a world wherein values are in conflict not only in the sense of good versus bad that is melodrama, but in the sense that good for some must be traded against good for others. Good must struggle with good, or more properly, good-bad must be assessed vis-à-vis good-bad. All of this is to guide us and give meaningful direction to the onslaught of modern technological instrumental rationality that addresses no normative ends and that shrivels common communication by imposing its specialized languages. Viable public discourse is possible about policy assessment.

The old consensus within the house of social science has been both moral and political. Social science was guaranteed a beneficial role by virtue of the implicit assumption that the means and ends of liberal society, especially in the United States, were progressive. The basic sciences would be protected from political attack by separation of facts from values and the associated separation of roles of scientist and citizen. The applied sciences took defensive precaution by talking a language of service to clients. Throughout, valuative considerations were shoved aside — left to philosophers and politicians.[3] Both pure and applied scientists went beyond the justifiable distinction between statements of fact and value to the unjustifiable elimination of reasoned valuative discourse. Such discourse has been thoughtlessly relegated to the status of amateur activity admitting of no cumulative knowledge.

It is much too simple to say that scientists trade in facts and politicians deal in values. Political authorities left to themselves cannot adequately analyze the value problems of our age, and the facts of science can possess meaning only within valuative frameworks. Like Max Weber, social scientists must see the necessity of valuation in an otherwise meaningless world.[4] Unlike Weber, social scientists must place valuation on a firm, logically viable basis open to inspection by rational individuals with freedom to conduct critical factual and valuative discourse. A policy-assessing sociology must speak, in Walter Lippmann's apt phrase, to the choice of "mastery over drift."[5] Such mastery involves constant labor on two kinds of analysis: (1) the best possible scientific analysis of "what is" in a factually uncertain world, and (2) the best possible valuative analysis of "what ought" in a normatively uncertain world.

All the while we must keep in mind Karl Popper's admonition not to fall victim to grand designs that enslave. A concern with public household management and civic discourse about impacts of technology must not dissolve conceptions of "man," "woman," or "self" into the background, to view people as incapable of free, purposive, responsible, and creative action. The idea of people as "shapers" of social structure, as active subjects, is the conception that has undergirded the values of freedom, autonomy, dignity, and rights that came out of the optimism of Enlightenment thought. When human beings are denied this vision, when they are regarded as a recalcitrant mass to be molded by faceless bureaucratic elites — what Hannah Arendt has called the "rule of nobody"[6] — the idea of meaningful policy assessment is destroyed. Utopias are necessarily illiberal because only elites possess the grand design, and they leave no meaningful room for error, open discussion of error, and the consequent never-ending need for correction. Value proposals must be approached with a skeptical eye just as statements of factual hypotheses, knowing that normative theory cannot be rounded off and made tidy.

POLICY ASSESSMENT AND THE LIBERAL POLITY

Liberalism is, essentially, government by free reasoned discussion. It implies a structure of political institutions to accomplish that discussion — constitutional rule of law to minimize arbitrariness so as to create stable expectations for individual life planning and to ensure respect for privacy based on the recognition that not everything of importance occurs in the public sphere. Liberalism divides powers and insists upon checks and balances among the legislatures, executives, and courts; it recognizes legitimate oppositions and the existence of multiple interests expressed through free flow of information, an informed electorate, and universal adult suffrage. Liberal politics rests on the Faustian vision of individual lives of self-mastery, self-expression, active pursuit of knowledge, and acceptance of moral responsibility. The liberal conception holds that there can be progress not only in terms of prevailing value criteria but also in terms of the value criteria themselves. It is within such political orders that the policy-assessment logic articulated in these pages can hope to flourish.[7]

Not every regime must be organized along the lines of the liberal democracies of Western Europe or North America, but there must be a democratically responsive political system characterized by checks on political authorities and balances of powers that will encourage open debate about policy options, questioning of data, and deep interest in competing value criteria. Citizens must know that it is their right and duty to engage in discussion of matters pertaining to the public household, and they must have legal rights to participate in public decision-making. Furthermore, citizens must have both the rights and the political capacity to place agents of the state in the dock and have the potential to win. The realm of debate must be inclusive, and no party to it can be exempt from challenge. In regimes where due process is thin, where checks and balances are few, there can be no effective institutionalization of procedures for policy assessment, nor can there be enthusiasm for refining policy-assessment concepts and procedures.

Critical means the quality of being able to render meaningful criticism of the status quo and of alternatives to it without respect to which social powers endorse which positions. This quality cannot be selective as both the conservative-authoritarian and the totalitarian ideologue would have it. Critical policy assessment in the service of social development must be implemented over and against the claims of party dogma, religious fiat, blood ties, majority impulse, or minority threat. Valuation for policy assessment cannot be made safe for the powers that be. It is something to be worked at continuously, and a liberal democratic political and constitutional environment is essential to sustain the necessary labor.

POLICY ASSESSMENT AND SUBSTANTIVE VALUE CRITERIA

The often unexamined assumption that only "undeserving" policy options lose out in a liberal society is unworthy of serious consideration. The liberal polity must commit itself to some specific definition of development; pure neutrality on the issue of progress is not justifiable. Citizens and agents of the public household, in liberal societies, must possess a theory of policy assessment with substantive value content. Walter Lippmann saw this clearly when he wrote: "The public philosophy is addressed to the government of our appetites and passions by reason of a second, civilized, and therefore acquired nature. Therefore the public philosophy cannot be popular. For it aims to resist and negate those very desires and opinions which are most popular."[8]

The experience of the present century has starkly revealed the limits of instrumental reason and the barbarity that comes with its undisciplined use. The terrors of authoritarian and totalitarian regimes are well known, but it is also the case that valuational concerns too often escape careful deliberation in liberal society; appeals to public interest and development are powerless given the thoughtless conceptions of each. The modern world has its polytheism; the gods, however, are no longer Jupiter, Apollo, and Neptune but consist of a hodgepodge of inconsistent and uninterpretable value criteria. Clichés such as quality of life, liberty, equality, social justice, appropriate technology, public involvement, felt needs, and basic needs cannot pass in serious intellectual discourse as if they had interpretable meaning and did not each involve the interests of some groups over others.

Liberal politics have been placed under severe strain by two global wars in this century, the great international depression of the 1930s, the emergence of the nuclear arms race in the 1950s, the erosion of legitimacy of public authority in the 1960s, the worldwide stagflation of the 1970s, economic depression of the early 1980s, and the valuatively blind economic growth of the later 1980s. Public elections have become a time of national ritual for politicians and cynicism for many citizens. The citizen of liberal regimes today, when asked about his or her larger vision for future directions, is either negative or embarrassed. Liberal governments, with no conception of proper ends for the public household, become arenas for interest group clash and resolve those clashes by parceling out power to the better-organized interests, which do not acknowledge coherent values for public life and social development.

The withdrawal from views of social development is founded upon a misreading of the lesson of value relativism, which most citizens correctly see to be associated with different cultural meaning systems and incorrectly see to necessitate a resigned value-empty toleration. It is a fallacy that relativism necessarily implies tolerance.[9] If Mutt should impose his way of life on Jeff, Jeff protests that Mutt has no rational justification for that oppressive action. Mutt simply replies "so what." His way of life requires that Jeff defer to him. There is nothing more to be said. If there is no logical method for reaching agreement about the superiority of policy options in public discourse, then one opinion of "ought" is as unworthy as any other. If this is the case, why should one accede to another? Failure to define *development* for the community at large by addressing specific substantive policy-assessment value criteria leads not to tolerance but to cynical struggle in which power unhinged from reason is the final arbitrator. Public life becomes no more than a game in which "clubs are trump."

Liberalism has erred in seeing freedom too much as simply the absence of restraint, by melding in a view that normative issues are beyond reason, and by asserting a radically individualist view of choice that has held all decisions to be exclusively individual and has asserted that only the individual's interest can count. All this has led to a situation in which autonomy of person and corporation is reconciled with the authority of the public household on terms that favor politically and economically advantaged groups, making liberty for the disadvantaged a civil sham.

The disintegration of substantive policy-assessment criteria, serving a viable conception of social development, has been the open wound of liberal politics. Liberal regimes can, however, contain a conception of social development that is neither valuatively empty nor culturally dogmatic. The liberal state does not have to exist just to preside benignly over various groups with different life-styles while the strong smash the weak.

POLICY ASSESSMENT AND STRUCTURAL ANALYSIS

Value criteria forwarded here do not rest on counting and aggregating attributes of individual human beings. Rather, they are rooted in structural relationships — patterns of social conflict; equality of condition; patterns of distribution of wealth, income, and access to infrastructure; and profiles of forgone choice possibilities. Proper management of the public household to promote social development has been viewed as having to do with manipulation of structural parameters within which people choose for themselves.

The message of Arrow's Impossibility Theorem, public-goods problems, technological externality, the tyranny of small decisions, market imperfections, problems of resource distribution, and failed utilitarian individualism is that logically defensible value criteria for policy assessment cannot be derived from aggregations of individual attributes. Listings of private preferences for policy-assessment purposes are both uninteresting and unproductive. Just as one cannot make good hamburger from spoiled beef, one cannot construct defensible public policy-assessment criteria from aggregations of personal preferences or wants. Defensible reasons for public policy choice cannot be based on counting or summing such attributes of people, however democratic it may appear to do so. The logic of good reasons is nonadditive for the same reason that it would be absurd to determine a legal outcome by counting the number of earlier pro and con decisions on an issue.[10] The reason to choose policy A rather than B is a rational appeal for all to accept policy A, and that reason cannot be reducible to a property of individuals singly or in the aggregate. The defensible appeal must be made in terms of the structure of some relation. This is not to argue against governments being responsive to voters; it is to argue for voters who are able to conduct structural developmental discourse.

Does the distinction between the individual and the structural level mean dehumanizing manipulation of people by social engineers? No. A structural logic grants dignity to the individual by not insisting that individual psyches be probed for private definitions of personal preference, welfare, or other meanings. Individual prescriptions are left to individuals while at the same time people are actively involved in employing structural value criteria to assess policy proposals for the community at large. Private meaning systems are left to people to shape for themselves so long as they remain within community parameters. Herein lies reverence for the dignity of the individual. Dignity is best served by not probing individual preferences and by avoiding normative manipulations of those preferences in bogus methods of aggregation.

Within the logic of policy assessment there is room for a diversity of cultural content and structural forms. Let phenomenologists, ethnomethodologists, and citizens at large convey meaning systems to us and let agents of the public household be sensitive to them, but let us not view in such systems the need to manipulate them for policy purposes. Advanced technological societies, especially, have created the structural foundations for the flourishing of a rich diversity of cultural and subcultural meaning. Amidst this, the discourse of the public household has descended into a terrible enfeebling confusion of self-interests battling matters out in inappropriate languages of individual preference aggregation and cultural assertion. The response must be to create a structural language of policy assessment available to all subgroups and designed to serve developmental expansion of choice contexts. But this structural language for policy assessment does not imply global homogeneity of taste or a universal culture or aesthetics.

Policies do not have impact common to all in large populations — they vary from time to time and site to site. Real people are never impacted nationally or globally — always locally. In their literature, Samuel Clemens and Sholem Aleichem each confronted large human truths in local patches particular to the Mississippi and to Eastern Europe. They have made us homesick for places we have never been and times we have never lived, by finding the universal in the local. Nomothetic social science, too, synthesizes large propositional abstractions of fact and value from the observation of particular patterns of local behavior, and the abstracted propositions must be activated in local sites by citizen and scientist. If the principles are not to be too remote from life as lived in particular places, if they are not to aridly and woodenly dangle beyond all special places and times, they must be energized by people locally associating for the purpose of policy assessment. Only then are the abstractions given life in specific contexts by inquiring people conducting reasoned civic discourse.

A word about the social units upon which policy assessment centers is important in at least two senses. First, people are virtually never affected by policy impacts as individual atoms, but always as members of social organizations. Whether organized within relatively small informal kinship groups in the Indus valley or within large timber corporations that work the forests drained by the Columbia, people are embedded in organizational networks that are much more than simple aggregates of individual persons. Much democratic theory has it that the representative state obtains its legitimacy from, is guided by, and is responsive to people who have entered into a covenant with it as atomistic citizens and who keep it on track by expressing their personal desires through electoral processes counting individual votes. This is, of course, largely myth. From early times of state formation, people have approached the business of state policy as members of organized corporate actors — guilds, priesthoods, soldiers, and companies of trappers, loggers, or contractors — and it is important to keep in mind that all this has greatly intensified over the last few centuries as formal organizations pursuing corporate interests have become the central stuff of modern public life in all contemporary nation-states. The policy-assessment logic advanced in these pages adapts well to this reality.

Second, it is important to note that policies must be assessed and fitted to a rich variety of local environments far beyond the effective control of any central manager. A central area for organizational innovation, therefore, must be the sustenance, revitalization, or creation of policy-assessment structures scaled to geographic and sectoral units real to technological and natural resource problems.[11] Many will be intermediate between the larger agencies of the public household and local citizens. Some will cross the usual regional, state, provincial, or national boundaries. In a society committed to rational policy discourse, there must be freedom to associate according to policy-assessment needs. Only in this manner can large-scale centralized public and private bureaucracies be compelled to allow room for the fitting of particular policies to the developmental requirements of specific locales and sectors. One must rely on a variety of intermediate organizations to do the best possible policy assessments by involving the most knowledgeable people in units real to a sectoral problem, questioning these assessments, and pressuring decision-makers to adapt to results. Valid assessment information and analysis is a source of such pressure.

Policies must, therefore, be assessed within units real to technological and natural resource impacts. Formal units of government — cities, counties, districts, states, and nation-states — may not most usefully bound the affected phenomena. Policy assessment must be specific to real units — neighborhoods, transportation corridors, irrigation command areas, forests, river basins, ecological habitat zones. Yet much development administration currently takes place in formal political units inappropriate to the affected natural and social processes; this has tended to remove bureaucratic units of the public household from any meaningful empirical base.[12]

There is typically too much variability from locale to locale to make national averages of assessment data meaningful. The idea of national development is utterly meaningless when taken as an average of many contexts of choice in many sectors across many geographic units. We cannot, in most instances, speak of national development in any logically defensible manner. In an age of nationalism, this realization may seem awkward, but we must learn to speak of development of choice contexts in terms of specific sectors of activity located in particular geographic units that may or may not follow formal lines of governmental authority domestically or internationally. As we do this, we may well find greater within-nation variability on relevant dimensions of development than among nations. Analysts and the citizens who work in policy assessment will no longer be blinded to the vast differences of choice contexts afforded within nations, and they may see greater similarities in choice contexts among peoples across national borders. Dropping the illusion of national development as an analytically meaningful concept may seem strange, but it may prove to be most constructive now that we have come to appreciate that national tribalism and human safety do not mix.

POLICY ASSESSMENT AND APPLIED INTERDISCIPLINARY ANALYSIS

Each scientific discipline is tightly organized around its selective principles so as to abstract a slice of life in ways most amenable to construction of its nomothetic propositions. Each policy for the public household is freighted with impacts that we struggle clumsily to divide under the rubrics of sociology, political science, economics, engineering, physics, chemistry, biology, zoology, agronomy, and so on. No one can deny that the need for nomothetic abstraction is an essential condition of any science — essential to reduce the complexity of the world to manageable propositions. Yet no one can deny that real people and other living things do not experience the world through the abstract categories and concepts of any single science, nor can any one discipline reflect more than a small portion of the strategic parameters impacted by policy. Social and ecological processes are experienced as unitary and indivisible. Twentieth-century science has become a myriad of competing theoretical lenses by which to abstract pieces of problems. Disciplinary boundaries may serve the promotion and tenure requirements of the ivory tower, but they do not well serve the needs of policy assessment.

Proliferation of disconnected disciplinary research about complex social and ecological phenomena creates not intellectual excitement, but deep frustration. Yet no science of a whole society can exist, and specialized disciplines must continue to make torturous progress in the fight for nomothetic knowledge in a tumultuous theory-defying world. But the disciplines, each in nomothetic command of a few strategic processes reflecting certain slices of life, must collaborate in common policy-assessment enterprise, and disciplinary work can be brought into interdisciplinary focus through thoughtful policy assessment. If, for example, few trustworthy data are available about the effects of strip mining on subsurface water quality, and therefore upon the choice opportunities associated with water in the impacted area, then our limited disciplinary research resources can be directed at this problem. As a case in point, the Fort Union coal formation — a natural unit encompassing portions of southeastern Montana, northeastern Wyoming, and western North Dakota — contains coal seams that serve as aquifers. Groundwater is contained and purified by the coal. If those aquifers are broken by strip mining at low points of a particular basin, water can be expected to flow downward and outward leaving wells and streams to go dry along higher reaches. Water tables might drop so that roots of prairie grass could not reach it, and human communities, livestock, and wildlife might thereby be affected. We do not know enough about the structure of these aquifers to know the location of critical low points so as to avoid strip mining at such vulnerable places.[13] A reasonably careful analysis of policy options affecting this area could be expected to expose this problem, and given discovery of the deficiencies of existing knowledge, it would be possible to direct research of the several relevant disciplines in appropriate avenues. Upon completion of such research, a round of policy assessment could take place employing the improved data.

The policy-assessment logic, therefore, organizes research questions around strategic policy-relevant concerns. It can be expected to unparalyze the disciplinary mind at critical research decision-making junctures. It may suggest heretofore unperceived questions and may place each piece of research in interdisciplinary frameworks in such a way that the hard-won data and theory will be better understood in themselves and in their policy implications.

CONCLUSION

The logic of fact and value that has been advanced here is, and must be, incomplete. However inadequate it may be, nevertheless a case has been made that a sociological science of fact can be connected to a structural logic of value for policy assessment that serves a coherent cross-cultural conception of social development. A logic of social policy assessment for a society of free, conflicting, diverse, reasonable men and women has been advanced; it is "good reasons" that must prevail in policy discourse, and sociology can centrally participate in the production of "good reasons" for policy acceptance and rejection. This is the faith in which this argument is put forth, and it is not to be lightly discarded in view of the alternatives.

What is proposed is that social science in general, and sociology in particular, provide a significant place on the working agenda for valuation and policy assessment in the service of social development. A vision has been advanced of a theoretically viable, socially responsible, cross-culturally applicable, ecologically aware, policy-assessing sociology compatible with the essential requirements of an open liberal society. The objective has been to bring clarity to valuational investigations in order to bring reason to conflict. I have done no more than articulate what I have been able to see and have it judged along with what others see. The possibilities that inhere in this effort may be of more value than whatever has been accomplished. Possibility may be our most precious possession. To travel may be better than to arrive. I make my best formulations and hold ready for amendment.

Appendix I

Valuational Meta-Criteria:
How to Judge a Value Logic

If reasoned discourse about value logics for policy assessment is to proceed, it must do so with respect for rules. Duncan MacRae, Jr., has advanced rules for conduct of such discourse.[1] The "norms of science" advanced by MacRae that are applicable to valuational argument are:

1. The norm of generality: Does the proposed value system apply, or fail to apply, to the choice situation of central interest to the discussants?

2. The norm of internal consistency: Does one value system have fundamental principles that cannot all be true, or does it yield contradictory recommendations in a situation suggested by a critic in which the critic's system is self-consistent?

3. The norm of consistency with shared convictions: Does the proposed value system lead to conclusions at odds with presumably widely shared moral commitments?

4. The norm of responsibility to received tradition: Does each contributor to the valuative discourse take into account what has gone on before and not capriciously distort previous contributions?

Discussants, keeping these rules for normative discourse in mind, are to specify in advance and in writing their value criteria. Each discussant shall have equal opportunity to argue for his or her valuative system, and against the opposing one, by pointing out shortcomings of the opponents' formulation. After each opportunity to present problems with a particular value formulation, the proponent of the ethical system under criticism shall decide whether s/he wishes to alter the valuative system or make the choice dictated by it. Each party to ethical discourse must postulate a valuative system — a fact that insures that no single opponent gains an unfair advantage by being able to attack one system on an ad hoc basis without having to reconcile the inconsistencies between value criteria employed in the critical attack.

Norms governing scientific communication are necessary to the process of giving consideration to both meta-values and substantive values, but they do not themselves constitute either. Discussants are requested to observe the norms of scientific communication specified above, but they additionally require an operational conception of how to judge a value judgment. My formulation of six meta-criteria for judging the adequacy of logics of value is repeated here in somewhat expanded form.[2]

1. Value criteria must be clear. Clarity refers to the capacity of a verbal or written expression to indicate precisely its meaning and to note those observations to which it would and would not apply independently of the speaker, listener, or subsequent qualification. The opposite of clarity is dependence on context. Opposing politicians might agree that they wish to pursue "peace," but such a criterion is so vacuous that it can justify virtually any kind of policy choice. One requires a value criterion sufficiently clear such that any two or more observers would independently produce identical rankings of policy alternatives when employing the criterion. To be clear, in the sense of avoiding context dependence, value criteria must be nomothetic statements of generalizable form as opposed to idiographic statements of particular cultural content.[3]

Value criteria formulated around conceptions of efficiency or equality, for example, are nomothetic. Efficiency relates input to output without respect to the particular cultural content of the input or output. Equality may refer to the notion of reducing a difference in resource holding by parties without regard to the particular cultural content of that which is to be distributed. Idiographic cultural value criteria for policy assessment have meaning only within their cultural settings and do not travel with clarity across cultural boundaries, a fact that damages their use in policy assessment. Any aggrieved party under a policy option can contend that his or her culture is not being sufficiently recognized and request appropriate bending of meaning. This may appeal to some observers if the cultural meaning system in question is associated with a deprived underdog, but it is not so appealing when the cultural system being supported by the reshaping of valuative meaning is associated with the boardrooms of the rich or the dictates of the tyrant. The fundamental reality is that some cultural idiographic meaning systems must be damaged as others are advanced, and an idiographic value criterion so sensible in one cultural or subcultural unit may be insensible in another. If there is to be a defensible logic of policy assessment in the service of a coherent notion of social development, choices among idiographic realities cannot be made by idiographic criteria. Policy assessment requires use of nomothetic criteria within the scope of which idiographic realities can have their play.

2. Value criteria must be hierarchically ranked. Multiple criteria must be ordered in priority so that conflicts among them can be resolved in the same direction by analysts working independently, who will know how each criterion is to be ranked relative to all other criteria. If an efficiency criterion is to be used in the valuative logic along with an equality criterion, which is to take precedence? The analyst must formulate and justify a hierarchy to resolve this question.

3. Value criteria must be operationally measurable. One must be able to tell when each criterion has been fulfilled. Measures of fulfillment must be

capable of independent replication. Value criteria must be logically justified in terms of some empirically knowable, methodologically replicable, conception of human welfare rooted in the experience of actual human beings. People, and other living things, experience the consequences of policy choice. Value criteria defining social development are not to be defined in terms of God's will, historical necessity, class interest, imperial glory, or perception of ancestral wish. Such nonoperational abstractions defy logical and empirical check. Defensible abstractions must be rooted in experience open to examination in this world.

4. Value criteria must deal with the problem of forced choice. Not to decide is, in fact, a policy choice in favor of the status quo and its attendant pattern of benefit and misery. To choose to do nothing, therefore, is to choose the existing policy situation, and that choice has immediate consequences in the form of benefit and harm just as do other options. To hold that one will do nothing unless an alternative to the status quo reaches some given standard of goodness not also applied to the status quo is to give privileged position to the existing state of affairs. The status quo should not have a privileged position in the valuative system for any a priori and unexamined reason. The valuative system must be capable of examining the "do nothing" status quo policy action and permitting examination of policy alternatives to it.

5. The valuative system must acknowledge the omnipresence of risk and uncertainty. One cannot say with certainty that a given policy option will actually fulfill the value standards when implemented. Very seldom, in complex dynamic social and ecological situations, can consequences of policy choice be established in advance with certainty. Most policy choices involve (1) risk — by which is meant that a known probabilistic relationship can be established between a policy and its expected consequences, and (2) uncertainty — by which is meant that one does not possess any probability distribution to connect a policy action to its effects. Formulation of value criteria must not assume the absence of risk and uncertainty in policy implementation.

6. Value criteria must acknowledge the relevance of time. One must think of policy outcomes as temporal sequences of events; analysts performing a policy assessment must be able to see trade-offs between short- and long-run effects. Policies have both proximate and distant consequences, and a valuative system that focuses on only one or the other would be seriously deficient. In a risky and uncertain world, the policy-assessment logics must be capable of iteration. One might make a five-, seven-, or ten-year estimate, but it will be necessary to remake frequent corrected estimates.

If valuation for policy assessment is a rational procedure governed by norms that have become associated with scientific reason, there is an implication that requires explicit recognition. No single valuational logic can serve all domains of collective choice. No single valuative logic will apply to all possible decision situations any more than any single statistical procedure can apply to all data and all questions that can be properly put to those data. "Good reasons" for constraining self-interest vary from domain to domain. There is no reason to expect that a logic of "good reasons" that makes sense in one domain of human activity necessarily applies to all. The definition of, and rationale for, "good reasons" for overriding self-interest in the doctor-patient relationship might well be expected to vary from those that can be justified for international diplomacy. Logicians such as Stephen Toulmin (following upon Ludwig Wittgenstein, *Philosophical Investigations*, 1953) have argued that the problem of telling sound arguments from untrustworthy ones depends on the characteristics of the arena of discourse.[4] Others have agreed with Friedrich Waismann's contention that known relationships of logic can only hold between statements belonging to a homogeneous field of discourse.[5] There is nothing binding about the norms of science unless one is doing science. Likewise, there is nothing binding about the value criteria for governing self-interest in medicine unless one is doing medicine. The search for improved valuational logics is a search for value criteria that are ever more discriminating and justifiable in particular policy domains.

The policy-assessment logic advanced in Chapter 5, and specific elements of it discussed in greater detail in Chapters 6, 7, and 8, are intended for use in the domain of technology and natural resource planning. This arena for discourse, although broad in scope, is not inclusive of everything with which citizens must deal in the public household. It remains to be determined by analysts and citizens confronting valuation in other domains whether value criteria advanced here have applicability.

APPENDIX II

Methodology for Obtaining Conflict and Futures-Forgone Data

Data for conflict and futures-forgone analyses can be generated from informed and methodologically disciplined estimates of local people, familiar with the resource unit in question and in possession of information regarding actions to be conducted under each policy alternative. A method is required that will fuse the abstract nomothetic principles central to each analysis with local realities in a manner open to inspection and replication. The method must inform the application of nomothetic principle with local knowledge, it must preserve the integrity of the conceptual logics, and it must not be corrupted by conceptions of individual welfare. To accomplish this task a modified version of the Delphi has been constructed and employed.[1]

The Delphi method, named after the seat of the ancient Greek temple and famous oracle of Apollo, originated in attempts to allow people with specialized knowledge to interactively and nonjudgmentally share their best estimates of future states of affairs. It quickly became a popular, but not always credible, technique in technological and social forecasting.[2] One familiar with the variety of Delphi procedures used over the last thirty years will quickly appreciate that what is advanced here constitutes an important set of modifications; these are described in the following paragraphs.

1. The method is not based upon a sequence of mailed questionnaires tapping into some amalgam of personal opinion and preference. Rather, data are generated under tightly controlled conditions extracting estimates of factual conditions that will likely obtain under policy options.

2. Participants are selected because of their local social, ecological, geographical, and technical knowledge. Technical knowledge beyond that available to panelists is available in at least two forms: (1) availability of technically competent consultants to panelists during the exercise, and (2) technical consulting between iterations of exercises.

3. Participants are not expected to do long-range forecasting of futures. Panelists are only expected to make and evaluate if-then statements, such as (1) if option X were to be implemented (or continued) in land-water unit u, then activity a in that unit will suffer a given scope, duration, or intensity of

loss; or (2) if policy option X were to be implemented, then actor a will take a position for, against, or neutral to it with a specified salience.

4. Participants do not assert individual preferences or welfare prescriptions. They are not asked to make value judgments. Rather, each panelist reviews the facts of the case and then proceeds to make estimates about positions of actors relative to conflict cleavages or about scope, intensity, and duration of impacts. Value judgments are arrived at via a logic of value that has no basis in individual preferences or welfare. Whereas it would be expected that strong environmentalists, for example, would differ in their private valuations from those who favor commercial commodity production, it is reasonable to expect that such opponents can agree on which group takes which position on a conflict cleavage or about which choices will be forgone with given scope, intensity, or durations.

Use of modified Delphi procedures as described here provides an opportunity for significant and authentic involvement of informed publics in the assessment of proposed policy. However, since panelists may be subject to hidden biases, distorted or incomplete information, fear of ridicule, or concern for postassessment political repercussions, it is important that the process of obtaining estimates minimizes distorting factors and maximizes the flow of useful information to members of panels. To accomplish the task of creating a social environment for informed "free speech" and mutually informative discussion from which valid estimates are made and to fuse local idiographic knowledge with nomothetic principle certain steps are taken.

1. Judges are briefed about the specific nature of the proposed policy alternatives; estimates under the proposal are specified by location and scale (for example, a ski area of specified size on the southwest slope of Bald Mountain).

2. A list of activities (or conflict groups) significant to the affected area is formulated and presented to each participant.

3. Participants working independently make a best estimate of losses to activities (or conflict positions) under each proposed alternative and pass their estimates back to the coordinator.

4. The coordinator sets aside those items on which agreement easily occurs and passes back items on which disagreement has been revealed.

5. Protecting anonymity, each panelist examines comments given as reasons for estimates made by the others and then proceeds to render once again a best estimate, possibly revised, based on the anonymous judgments of the others.

6. Within the course of two to four rounds, there typically is a convergence of judgment; where judgments fail to converge, reasons for differences emerge.

7. There is no pressure to compromise any panelist's best estimate or reasoning process. Reasons provided for differing estimates are examined and evaluated. When reasons for differences in estimates are probed, one of three things can occur: (1) a line of reasoning is found to be inapplicable or not

compelling and is therefore discarded; (2) both diverging lines of reasoning, and estimates, are found to be convincing but are applicable to differing subsets of activities or conflict groups, thereby necessitating further refinement in treatment of the choice activity or group; each line of reasoning is then applied to an estimate for that more discriminating understanding of the subset; or (3) both diverging lines of reasoning are found to be convincing, both are applicable to the same activity or group, and further investigation must be conducted to determine respective validity of arguments. This, then, leads to a sensitivity analysis. If the outcome of the assessment is not sensitive to the difference in estimates — that is, the analysis produces the same ranking of policy options either way — then no further investigation is required for immediate assessment purposes. However, if the outcome of policy assessment is sensitive to the divergent lines of reasoning, appropriate investigation — possibly systematic research — must be undertaken to clarify validity of the respective arguments.

It is not the purpose here to convey the full range of detail involved in the successful conduct of assessment of conflict polarization or choice opportunities forgone. Interested parties may obtain a manual, available at low cost, that provides a detailed guide to the conduct of the modified Delphi exercises.[3] However, a general overview of a few considerations involved in the conduct of such assessments is in order.

SPECIFY AND CLARIFY POLICY ALTERNATIVES

1. Written summaries of proposed policy alternatives are essential; lack of clarity as to the meaning of a policy constitutes the greatest single threat to reliability and validity of panel estimates. A well-constructed statement of a policy alternative will include a description of what will be done (for example, ski area, power plant, transmountain road and utility corridor, irrigation project construction), the location where the planned activity will take place, the scale of the proposed activity, and the timing of policy actions.

2. Substantive names for proposed policy alternatives are not designated, since this might create negative or positive bias (for example, wilderness, intensive timber cut, and so on.). Alternatives are identified only by letter and/or color (for example, Alternatives A-Blue, B-Orange, C-Green, D-White).

3. The same proposed alternatives are employed for both analyses — social conflict and futures forgone. Failure to hold the proposed alternatives constant for both dimensions of the exercise means that results cannot be integrated in a meaningful fashion at the conclusion of the analysis.

4. Although, in theory, there is no upper limit to the number of alternatives that can be subjected to analysis, practical limits are real. The number of policy alternatives that can be assessed by panelists will depend upon the complexity of the proposed policies, the availability of relevant data about the planning unit, and the amount of time panelists can devote to the exercise. I

have successfully run assessments of four reasonably complex alternatives, given the prearranged availability of good data on the planning area, in one day for each of the analyses — futures forgone and conflict polarization.

DETERMINE BOUNDARIES OF PLANNING AREA

Careful delineation of the relevant unit for analysis of local choice contexts is critical. Boundaries must be drawn to reflect impact upon socio-ecologic units. A larger secondary planning area containing the smaller primary planning area must be delineated. The primary planning area is that which is subjected to direct policy manipulation and impact. The secondary planning area encompasses the primary area and places it in a policy-relevant context.

Primary and secondary planning areas, with policy-induced activities clearly indicated, are presented on wall maps so all participants can view them.

DEFINE EXISTING CHOICE CONTEXT

Coordinators of the policy assessment must list and describe significant activities in the affected sector of the policy-impacted primary unit. Each list of choice opportunities must be constructed to reflect important occupational, recreational, and cultural activities. Theoretically, any number of activities can be employed. However, practical experience has demonstrated that panelists — given existing techniques of information sharing — have difficulty handling more than about thirty items per day when making judgments on four policy options. The same list is employed in both the social conflict and futures-foregone exercise.

Construction of the list of choice opportunities is important and must be performed with care. The list should be devised with the help of local informants and pretested with local knowledgeables prior to initiation of an assessment exercise. One must not overlook activities beyond the local social mainstream — for example, historical sites, archaeological diggings, or activities of importance to minorities. A general heading (farming), suitable for one area, may need to be more specific in another area if dryland wheat farmers need to be distinguished from irrigated vegetable truck farmers and cattle ranchers. In certain instances where the coordinator is uncertain of the adequacy of any a priori list, a Delphi exercise can be run to create the description of the existing choice context. In such a case, two or more panels of judges review a preliminary list of local choice opportunities, reconstruct it, and thereby create a description adequate for initiation of futures-forgone and conflict analyses.

Appendix II

SELECT PANEL(S) FOR THE EXERCISE

Panels should include at least four and no more than seven members. Problems of information sharing become a serious constraint if panels are too large, and panels require the diversity of knowledge and experience of a minimum number of informants. Additional people are accommodated by constituting additional panels employed as reliability and validity checks.

Panel members should be selected on the basis of experience in, and knowledge of, primary and secondary planning areas. In addition, they must have serious interest in the proposed policy options. Relative proportions of agency personnel and citizens can be adjusted given the purposes at hand. If the purpose is to formulate policy options, or to increase their level of refinement and clarity for assessment in a subsequent phase, one may place a heavy emphasis on inclusion of agents of the public household. If the purpose is assessment of policy options, the analyst will wish to increase the proportions of locally knowledgeable people. Recruitment of locally knowledgeable citizens constitutes a major and constructive way for a planning organization to authentically involve publics in agency policy processes.

All participants should respond, prior to the exercise, to a questionnaire documenting demographic characteristics such as age, sex, education, occupation, ideological commitments, and type of experience in the planning unit. Such information allows panels to be constituted in ways that allow the conduct of reliability checks. It may be desirable, for example, to place highly committed environmentalists on a given panel and commodity producers on another to determine if they "bake the same analytical cake" over the course of the exercise. If the method has been properly implemented, emergent policy rankings should be the same regardless of panel composition. The demonstration that panels of significantly different composition, working independently, arrived at the same policy rankings is evidence that the assessment outcome is not sensitive to the presence or absence of any particular individual or any particular set of private preferences.

It is always desirable to use two or more panels for any given policy-assessment exercise. Some assurance of reliability exists if multiple panels arrive at the same ranking of proposed policy alternatives. (See Table A.1 for illustration of reliable and unreliable panel designs.)

CONCLUSION

A methodological procedure for constructing estimates that inform the analysis of futures forgone and social conflict must provide at least three kinds of integration:

1. the defensible integration of specialized nomothetic knowledge with local idiographic knowledge whereby the abstracted scientific slices are connected to site-specific wholes apprehended as "uni-verses";

299

Table A.1. Reliability of Panel Designs

Residence	Idealogical Orientation		
	Environmental	Commodity Production	
Urban	4-7 members Panel-1	4-7 members Panel-2	A six-panel exercise provides a strong check on reliability.
Rural	4-7 members Panel-3	4-7 members Panel-4	
Urban/rural	4-7 members Panel-5	4-7 members Panel-6	
Urban	4-7 members Panel-1	4-7 members Panel-2	A four-panel exercise provides an adequate check on reliability.
Rural	4-7 members Panel-3	4-7 members Panel-4	
Urban/rural	4-7 members Panel-1	4-7 members Panel-2	A two-panel exercise provides a weak check on reliability.
Urban/rural Single panel		4-7 members	With a single panel there can be no check on reliability.

2. the defensible integration of procedures that produce statements of fact with those that produce statements of value;

3. the defensible integration of the policy scientist with the citizen in which both share what they know about phenomena critical to social choice; "objective" knowledge is not to be divorced from what citizens know about.

An ideal speech situation presupposes the construction of an ideal community. Critical theorists have been less than clear about how to achieve such an ideal, but one can establish an approximation via the employment of the procedures for exchange and assessment in the assessment panels. Lines of reasoning justifying policy choice emanating from such disciplined exchange can never be totally compelling. Such "softness" is not peculiar to the normative dimension. The science of fact is not "hard" because it has an unassailable foundation of "objective fact" upon which it rests; rather, the sciences of fact are credible because they are self-correcting enterprises organized to place all claims in jeopardy. Lines of normative policy reasoning, disciplined by carefully honed valuational logics articulated to local arrangements of fact, open to constant critical inspection, can also place before the community of investigators — citizens and scientists — claims capable of sustaining reasoned support and refutation.

NOTES

CHAPTER I

1. Ralf Dahrendorf, *The New Liberty: Survival and Justice in a Changing World* (Stanford, Calif.: Stanford University Press, 1975) 69.

2. Nathan Rosenberg, "Technology, Economy, and Values," in *The History and Philosophy of Technology*, ed. George Bugliarello and Dean B. Doner (Urbana: University of Illinois Press, 1979) 98.

3. Quoted by Samuel Eliot Morison, *The Great Explorers: The European Discovery of America* (New York: Oxford University Press, 1978) xii.

4. Henry Teune, *Growth* (Newbury Park, Calif.: Sage, 1988) 15, 44.

5. See, for overviews of the debate about the meaning of development, Fred W. Riggs, "Development," in *Social Science Concepts: A Systematic Analysis*, ed. Giovanni Sartori (Beverly Hills, Calif.: Sage, 1984) 125–204. See also David E. Apter, *Rethinking Development: Modernization, Dependency, and Post-Modern Politics* (Newbury Park, Calif.: Sage, 1987); Herbert Blumer, "The Idea of Social Development," *Studies in Comparative International Development* 2, no. 1 (1966); Szymon Chodak, *Societal Development: Five Approaches with Conclusions from Comparative Analysis* (New York: Oxford University Press, 1973); Willard A. Beling and George O. Totten (eds.), *Developing Nations: Quest for a Model* (New York: Van Nostrand, 1970); and Sandra Wallman (ed.), *Perceptions of Development* (London: Cambridge University Press, 1977).

6. Teune, *Growth*, 111.

7. See Corinne Lathrop Gilb, "Public and Private Governments?" in *Handbook of Organizational Design*, ed. Paul C. Nystrom and William H. Starbuck (New York: Oxford University Press, 1981) vol. 2., 464–491. See also: Barry Bozeman, *All Organizations Are Public: Bridging Public and Private Organizational Theories* (San Francisco: Jossey-Bass, 1987); and Charles S. Maier (ed.), *Changing Boundaries of the Political: Essays on the Evolving Balance Between the State and Society, Public and Private in Europe* (Cambridge: Cambridge University Press, 1987).

8. Harry C. Boyte, *Commonwealth: A Return to Citizen Politics* (New York: Free Press, 1989); and Michael Novak, *Free Persons and the Common Good* (Lanham, Md.: Madison Press, 1989).

303

9. For an excellent discussion of the concept of public household, see Daniel Bell, *The Cultural Contradictions of Capitalism* (New York: Basic Books, 1976) 220–282. Richard Musgrave centered his analysis on the public household in his *The Theory of Public Finance* (New York: McGraw-Hill, 1959). See also Richard Musgrave and B. Musgrave, *Public Finance in Theory and Practice,* 3d ed. (New York: McGraw-Hill, 1980); and P. O. Steiner, "The Public Sector and the Public Interest," in *Public Expenditure and Policy Analysis,* 2d ed., ed. R. H. Haveman and J. Margolis (Chicago: Rand McNally, 1977) 27–66.

10. William M. Sullivan, *Reconstructing Public Philosophy* (Berkeley: University of California Press, 1986) 157.

11. Karl Polanyi, for example, saw clearly that the economy was only one aspect of society and that it must be "embedded" in a successful encompassing social structure. Polanyi deplored a "market society" in which all other relationships would be subordinated to the marketplace. More recently Arthur Okun, among others, has spoken plainly to the effect that the market requires a place as an efficient allocator of scarce resources and as a protector of individual freedom of expression, but Okun holds that it needs to be kept in its place. Okun's position distinguishes him from the extremists who would abolish marketplace capitalism and also from exponents of laissez-faire exchange who would broaden its role to more fully encompass the public household. See Karl Polanyi, "Our Obsolete Market Mentality," in *Primitive Archaic and Modern Economies,* ed. George Dalton (Boston: Beacon Press, 1971) 59–77; and Arthur M. Okun, *Equality and Efficiency: The Big Trade-Off* (Washington, D.C.: Brookings Institution, 1975). Charles E. Lindblom makes the control of markets one of his central points in *Politics and Markets* (New York: Basic Books, 1976) esp. 156. Market failures may provide the rationale for public intervention, but the question becomes what nonmarket public choice mechanisms are to be substituted for market mechanisms. Political intervention requires a coherent theory of development, or the political cures may be worse than the market diseases. This point is made by Kenneth A. Shepsle and Barry R. Weingast, "Political Solutions to Market Problems," *American Political Science Review* 78, no. 2 (June 1984) 417–434.

12. Robert A. Dahl, *A Preface to Economic Democracy* (Berkeley: University of California Press, 1985); Lester B. Lave, *The Strategy of Social Regulation: Decision Frameworks for Policy* (Washington, D.C.: Brookings Institution, 1981); and Charles L. Schultze, *The Public Use of Private Interest* (Washington, D.C.: Brookings Institution, 1977).

13. A compelling discussion of this point is provided by Arthur J. Vidich and Stanford M. Lyman, *American Sociology: Worldly Rejections of Religion and Their Directions* (New Haven: Yale University Press, 1985).

14. Ibid. 283.

15. For a review of the thought of the Frankfurt School, see Paul Connerton, *The Tragedy of Enlightenment* (New York: Cambridge University Press, 1980).

16. Jürgen Habermas, *The Theory of Communicative Action: Of Reason and the Rationalization of Society,* trans. Thomas McCarthy (Boston: Beacon Press, 1981). See also his *Toward a Rational Society* (London: Heineman, 1971) and *Legitimation Crisis* (Boston: Beacon Press, 1975). Fred R. Dallmayr provides most insightful discourse on the issues raised by Habermas in his *Polis and Praxis: Exercises in Contemporary Political Theory* (Cambridge, Mass.: MIT Press, 1984) esp. chapts. 6, 7.

17. David Easton, "The New Revolution in Political Science," *American Political Science Review* 63, no. 4 (December 1969), 1051–1061.

18. See, for example, Thomas R. Dye, *Understanding Public Policy,* 2d ed. (Englewood Cliffs, N.J.: Prentice-Hall, 1975) 1–7.

19. For example, Eugene Meehan, *Value Judgment and Social Science* (Homewood, Ill.: Dorsey, 1969).

20. Duncan MacRae, *The Social Function of Social Science* (New Haven: Yale University Press, 1976).

21. Robert Nisbet, *The Present Age: Progress and Anarchy in Modern America* (New York: Harper and Row, 1988) 128–129.

22. For a discussion of the distributional consequences of the clean air amendments of 1970 and a case that policies affect various people differently, see Henry M. Peskin, "Environmental Policy and the Distribution of Benefits and Costs," in *Policy Studies Review Annual,* vol. 3., ed. Robert H. Haveman and Bruce Zellner (Beverly Hills, Calif.: Sage, 1979) 291–310. For a discussion of technological redistribution in the agricultural sector, see Cheryl Payer, "The World Bank and the Small Farmers," *Journal of Peace Research* 16, no. 4 (1979) 293–312.

23. See, for example, Peter F. Drucker, *Technology, Management, and Society* (New York: Alfred A. Knopf, 1964).

24. For one widely read textbook presentation of this point, see Everett Hagen, *The Economics of Development* (Homewood, Ill.: Richard D. Irwin, 1968) 201.

25. Rosenberg, "Technology, Economy, and Values," 81–111, esp. 82. For an excellent effort in tracing how the values of U.S. inventors, engineers, and system builders were built into U.S. technology, see Thomas P. Hughes, *American Genesis: A Century of Invention and Technological Enthusiasm, 1870–1970* (New York: Viking, 1989).

26. Langdon Winner, "Do Artifacts Have Politics?" in *Technology and Politics,* ed. Norman J. Vig and Michael E. Kraft (Durham, N.C.: Duke University Press, 1988) 33–53. Excellent discussions of the political implications of technology are also found in Daniel R. Headrick's *The Tools of Empire: Technology and Imperialism in the Nineteenth Century* (New York: Oxford

University Press, 1981) and *The Tentacles of Progress: Technology Transfer in the Age of Imperialism, 1850–1940* (New York: Oxford University Press, 1988).

27. For an extensive set of discussions of railroad technology in its social and political aspects, see Bruce Mazlish (ed.), *The Railroad and the Space Program: An Exploration in Historical Analogy* (Cambridge, Mass.: MIT Press, 1965).

28. On the concept of social role, see Bruce J. Biddle, *The Present Status of Role Theory* (Columbia: University of Missouri, Social Psychology Laboratory, 1961). See also Bruce J. Biddle and Edwin J. Thomas, *Role Theory: Concepts and Research* (New York: John Wiley, 1966); and Jerald Hage and Gerald Marwell, "Toward the Development of an Empirically Based Theory of Role Relationships," *Sociometry* 31 (1968) 200–212.

29. The notion that technology is a social phenomenon by virtue of its implications for social roles does not originate here. James K. Feibleman makes a case for viewing technology as a role-producing phenomenon in his "Technology as Skills," *Technology and Culture* 7, no. 3 (Summer 1966) 318–328.

30. Martin Meissner viewed the demands of industrial technology as central to roles and social organization in his *Technology and the Worker* (San Francisco: Chandler, 1969). Robert K. Merton defined the idea of role-set in "The Role-Set: Problems in Sociological Theory," *British Journal of Sociology* 8 (1957) 106–120. William M. Evan developed the concept into the next higher level of analysis in his "The Organization Set — Toward a Theory of Inter-organizational Relationships," in *Approaches to Organizational Design*, ed. James D. Thompson (Pittsburgh: University of Pittsburgh Press, 1966).

31. Jim Hightower, *Hard Tomatoes, Hard Times: The Failure of the Land Grant College Complex* (Cambridge, Mass.: Shenkman, 1978).

32. Bruce Mazlish argued for the view that there is no discontinuity between technology and social life in his "The Fourth Discontinuity," *Technology and Culture* 8, no. 1 (January 1967) 1–15. Furthermore, the point is illustrated by the collection of papers assembled by Wiebe E. Bijker, Thomas P. Hughes, and Trevor J. Pinch (eds.), *The Social Construction of Technological Systems: New Directions in the Sociology and History of Technology* (Cambridge, Mass.: MIT Press, 1987). A movement is also underway in sociology to place social behavior in its technological-ecological nexus, as evidenced by environmental sociology. See William R. Catton, Jr., and Riley E. Dunlap, "Environmental Sociology: A New Paradigm," *The American Sociologist* 13 (February 1978) 41–49. Reprinted in *Theoretical Perspectives in Sociology*, ed. Scott G. McNall (New York: St. Martin's Press, 1979) 265–278.

33. Ernest Nagel reported that the nomothetic-idiographic distinction was first stated in this manner by Wilhelm Windelband in "Geschichte und

Naturwissenschaft," reprinted in a collection of his essays entitled *Praludien,* 5th ed. (Tubingen: Siebeck, 1915). See Ernest Nagel, *The Structure of Science: Problems in the Logic of Scientific Explanation* (New York: Harcourt, Brace, and World, 1961) 548. The idea that only idiographic interpretation of the world was possible for the social sciences was rejected by Max Weber. See his "Objectivity of Knowledge in Social Science and Social Policy," in *The Methodology of the Social Sciences,* trans. and ed. Edward A. Shils and Henry A. Finch (New York: The Free Press of Glencoe, 1949) 50–112, esp. 57.

34. Georg Simmel, *Soziologie* (Leipzig: Duncker und Humblot, 1908). See also Jeffrey T. Bergner, *The Origin of Formalism in Social Science* (Chicago: University of Chicago Press, 1981) esp. 89. Peter T. Manicas provides a most insightful discussion of issues related to the nomothetic-idiographic distinction in his *A History and Philosophy of the Social Sciences* (New York: Basil Blackwell, 1987) esp. 127–135.

35. Ernest Nagel noted that it would be an error to conclude that idiographic statements do not interact with nomothetic ones. They make use of each other, as pure nomothetic science must refer to concrete evidence at particular sites, and discussions of the unique are frequently motivated by some apprehension of the universal. See Nagel, *The Structure of Science,* 550.

36. Larry W. Isaac and Larry J. Griffin, "Ahistoricism in Time-Series Analysis of Historical Process: Critique, Redirection, and Illustrations From U.S. Labor History," *American Sociological Review* 54, no. 6 (December 1989) 873–890.

37. Karl R. Popper, *The Poverty of Historicism* (New York: Harper and Row, 1964) 115.

38. For discussions of the growth of science and its relationship to technology, see Daniel J. Boorstein, *The Discoverers* (New York: Vintage, 1985); J. Bernard Cohen, *Revolution in Science* (Cambridge: The Belknap Press of Harvard University Press, 1985); and Melvin Kranzberg and Carroll W. Pursell (eds.), *Technology in Western Civilization* (New York: Oxford University Press, 1967).

39. The need for a standard of social value to supplement the market exchange value for development has been clearly seen by many. For one review, see John M. Clark, "Toward a Concept of Social Value," chap. 2 in John M. Clark, *Preface to Social Economics* (New York: A. Kelley, 1936) 44–65. For a recent set of essays that recognize that value neutrality is impossible but that we do not know how to articulate value commitments to the social sciences, see Norma Haan, Robert N. Bellah, Paul Rabinow, and William M. Sullivan (eds.), *Social Science as Moral Inquiry* (New York: Columbia University Press, 1983).

40. For elaboration on this point, see MacRae, *The Social Function of Social Science,* 5. Randall Collins noted that the applied fields will have to free

themselves of the quackery that presently prevails as value commitments are hidden under collections of facts — facts that never actually speak for themselves independently of values. See Randall Collins, *Conflict Sociology* (New York: Academic Press, 1975) 547. See also Jan Drewnowski, "Valuation Systems Implied in Planning Decisions: Shall We Try to Reveal Them?" *Co-existence* 6, no. 1 (January 1969) 39–41. Robert Merton brought values in the back door by stating that a socially oriented scientist will explore only policy alternatives that do not violate his own values. See Robert K. Merton's statements in *The Policy Sciences: Recent Developments in Scope and Method*, ed. Daniel Lerner and Harold D. Lasswell (Stanford, Calif.: Stanford University Press, 1951) 5, 302.

41. Bellah, Rabinow, and Sullivan, *Social Science as Moral Inquiry*. McRae, *The Social Function of Social Science;* and Eugene J. Meehan, *Value Judgment and Social Science: Structures and Processes* (Homewood, Ill.: Dorsey Press, 1969).

42. David Hume, *A Treatise of Human Nature*, bk. 3, pt. I, sec. 1.

43. G. E. Moore, *Principia Ethica* (Cambridge: Cambridge University Press, 1903). For a more recent discussion of the naturalistic fallacy, see Paul W. Taylor, *Normative Discourse* (Englewood Cliffs, N.J.: Prentice-Hall, 1961). Hasan Ozbekhan argued that in much technological planning, considerations of technical feasibility — the "is" — have tended to dominate the "ought." Hasan Ozbekhan, "The Triumph of Technology: 'Can Implies Ought,'" in *Planning for Diversity and Choice*, ed. Stanford Anderson (Cambridge, Mass.: MIT Press, 1968) 204–233. Important general treatments of the is/ought distinction are found in Max Weber, "The Meaning Of Ethical Neutrality," in *The Methodology of the Social Sciences*, trans. and ed. Edward A. Shils and Henry A. Finch (New York: The Free Press of Glencoe, 1949) 1–49; and Ernest Nagel, *The Structure of Science* (New York: Harcourt Brace, 1958) esp. chapts. 13 and 14.

44. For a discussion of value relativism, see Abraham Edel, *Ethical Judgement: The Use of Science in Ethics* (New York: Free Press, 1955); and Abraham and May Edel, *Anthropology and Ethics: The Quest for Moral Understanding* (Cleveland: Press Of Case Western Reserve University, 1968). Although these works provide excellent discussions of the value relativist position, Abraham Edel has been concerned to develop a position that moves beyond it. See his *Exploring Fact and Value: Science, Ideology, and Value* (New Brunswick, N.J.: Transaction Books, 1979).

45. Phrase from Edel, *Ethical Judgment;* 16.

46. Clifford Geertz has addressed, at length, uncertainties encountered by ethnographers as they attempt to comprehend cultures they study. See his *Works and Lives: The Anthropologist as Author* (Stanford, Calif.: Stanford University Press, 1988) esp. 71.

47. Central pieces in this literature include Kurt Baier, *The Moral Point of View: A Rational Basis for Ethics* (Ithaca: Cornell University Press, 1958);

Leslie Sklair, "Moral Progress and Social Theory," *Ethics* 79 (April 1969) 229–234; MacRae, *The Social Function of Social Science;* and James S. Fishkin, *Beyond Subjective Morality: Ethical Reasoning and Political Philosophy* (New Haven: Yale University Press, 1984). William N. Dunn has complied a group of papers focusing heavily on valuation for policy analysis in his edited collection, *Policy Analysis: Perspectives, Concepts, and Methods* (Greenwich, Conn.: JAI Press, 1986).

CHAPTER II

1. Duncan MacRae, *The Social Function of Social Science* (New Haven: Yale University Press, 1976) 54.

2. Abraham Edel, "Social Science and Value: A Study in Interrelations," in *The New Sociology: Essays in Social Science and Social Theory in Honor of C. Wright Mills,* ed. Irving L. Horowitz (New York: Oxford University Press, 1964) 218.

3. Jack L. Roach, "The Radical Sociology Movement: A Short History and Commentary," *The American Sociologist* 5 (August 1970) 224–232. See also the several pieces included in "Varieties of Political Expression in Sociology," *American Journal of Sociology* 78, no. 1 (July 1972) entire issue; and see Andrew J. Weigert, "The Immoral Rhetoric of Scientific Sociology," *The American Sociologist* 5 (May 1970) 111–119.

4. L. Braude, "Ethical Neutrality and the Perspective of the Sociologist," *Sociological Quarterly* 5 (1964) 396–399.

5. J. B. Bury, *The Idea of Progress* (New York: Macmillan, 1932). Bury held the view that the idea of progress did not become fully formulated until the eighteenth-century Enlightenment. Bury's view of this matter was adopted by W. Warren Wagar in Warren Wagar (ed.), *The Idea of Progress Since the Renaissance* (New York: John Wiley, 1969). Morris Ginsberg employed Bury's definition of progress. See Morris Ginsberg, *The Idea of Progress: A Reevaluation* (London: Metheun, 1953). However, recent scholarship takes the view that the idea of progress was well formulated by the classical Greeks and Romans. See Robert Nisbet, *History of the Idea of Progress* (New York: Basic Books, 1980). Nisbet in turn has built upon the work of Ludwig Edelstein, *The Idea of Progress in Classical Antiquity* (Baltimore: Johns Hopkins University Press, 1967). An excellent set of essays that critique the modern idea of progress and relate it to central problems of sociological theory is provided by Jeffrey C. Alexander and Piotr Sztompka (eds.), *Rethinking Progress: Movements, Forces and Ideas at the End of the Twentieth Century* (Boston: Unwin Hyman, 1990).

6. For an excellent review of moral thought and its relationship to science from the Middle Ages to present times, see Ernest Becker, *The Structure Of Evil: An Essay on the Unification of the Science of Man* (New York: Free

Press, 1968). A most complete history of value theory is provided by W. H. Werkmeister, *The German Language Group*, vol. I, and *The Anglo-American Group*, vol. II of *Historical Spectrum of Value Theories* (Lincoln, Neb.: Johnson Publishing Company, 1970 and 1973). Alasdair MacIntyre identifies the moral discussions of the past and evaluates the various claims to moral objectivity and authority. His central thesis is that the breakdown of the Enlightenment project of providing a rational justification for morality is the historical background against which our own late twentieth century predicaments become intelligible. See Alasdair MacIntyre, *After Virtue: A Study in Moral Theory* (Notre Dame, Ind.: University of Notre Dame Press, 1981).

7. Becker, *The Structure of Evil*, 19–20.

8. T. G. Bergin and M. H. Fisch (ed. and trans.), *New Science of Giambattista Vico* (New York: Doubleday Anchor, 1961); and Isaiah Berlin, *Vico and Herder: Two Studies in the History of Ideas* (New York: Viking Press, 1976).

9. See William Donald Hudson (ed.), *The Is-Ought Question: A Collection of Papers on the Central Problem in Moral Philosophy* (New York: St. Martin's Press, 1969).

10. John Chavvet, *The Social Problem in the Philosophy of Rousseau* (Cambridge: Cambridge University Press, 1974); and Frederick Charles Green, *Rousseau and the Idea of Progress* (Folcroft, Pa.: Folcroft Press, 1969).

11. John E. Smith, "The Question of Man," in *The Philosophy of Kant and Our Modern World*, ed. C. W. Hendel (New York: Liberal Press, 1957) 18–19.

12. Sidney Pollard, *The Idea of Progress* (New York: Basic Books, 1968) 18–19, 91–95. See also Becker, *The Structure of Evil*, 14–18.

13. Adam Smith, *An Inquiry into the Nature and Causes of the Wealth of Nations* (1776), ed. Edwin Cannon (New York: The Modern Library, 1937). For the benchmark textbook treatment of the thought of both Adam Smith and Thomas Malthus, see chapts. 4 and 5 of Eric Roll, *A History of Economic Thought*, 3d ed. (Englewood Cliffs, N.J.: Prentice Hall, 1956).

14. John H. Randal, Jr., *The Making of the Modern Mind* (Boston: Houghton Mifflin, 1940) esp. 328.

15. Warren W. Wagar, *Good Tidings: The Belief in Progress from Darwin to Marcuse* (Bloomington: Indiana University Press, 1972) 19–20.

16. See, for a discussion of the history of this stream of thought, Sidney Pollard, *The Idea of Progress*, esp. chap. 3, 96–144.

17. Wagar, *Good Tidings*, 19–20.

18. Quoted by Becker, *The Structure of Evil*, 41.

19. Frank E. Manvel, *The New World of Henri Saint Simon* (Cambridge: Harvard University Press, 1956) 248.

20. Alvin Gouldner made this argument in much more detail in *The Coming Crisis of Western Sociology* (New York: Basic Books, 1970) 108–116.

21. Ibid. 113.

22. Auguste Comte, *A General View of Positivism* (New York: Speller, 1848) 420. Positivism rests on the heritage of the seventeenth-century political arithemeticians and later moral statisticians who believed quantification would provide the basis for a dispassionate analysis of social affairs. For an excellent history and review of the various meanings of positivism, see Peter Halfpenny, *Positivism and Sociology: Explaining Social Life* (Winchester Terrace, Mass.: Allen and Unwin, 1982).

23. Auguste Comte, *Cours de Philosophe Positive*, 6 vols. (Paris: Schlecher Edition, 1908). See vol. 4, esp. 274.

24. Becker, *The Structure of Evil*, 63–64.

25. Albion Small, "Socialism in the Light of Social Science," *American Journal of Sociology* 17 (1911–1912) 804–819, esp. 810. In general Marx contended that moral conceptions rise and fall with different systems of production and that concepts of social justice differ from period to period and class to class. Some have found Marx and Engels to eschew all moral concepts, but others have found them to be moral realists in the sense that they saw justice as objectively increasing in an advancing political-economic community. For a discussion of this topic, see Alan Gilbert, "An Ambiguity in Marx's and Engels's Account of Justice and Equality," *American Political Science Review* 76, no. 2 (June 1982) 328–346.

26. Ernest Becker, *The Structure of Evil*, 67.

27. See, on this point, L. E. Easton, "Alienation and History in the Early Marx," *Philosophy and Phenomenological Research* 22 (1961–1962) 193–205.

28. Herbert Spencer, *The Evolution of Society: Selections from Herbert Spencer's Principles of Sociology*, ed. Robert L. Carneiro (Chicago: University of Chicago Press, 1967).

29. Becker, *The Structure of Evil*, 61.

30. Nicholas S. Timasheff, *Sociological Theory: Its Nature and Growth*, rev. ed. (New York: Random House, 1957) 124–127.

31. Wagar, *Good Tidings*, 20.

32. Ibid. 9; Daniel Bell, *The Cultural Contradictions of Capitalism* (New York: Basic Books, 1976); and Robert Nisbet, *The Twilight of Authority* (New York: Oxford, 1975).

33. Emile Durkheim, *The Elementary Forms of Religious Life* (New York: Macmillan, 1915; New York: Macmillan Company, 1954). See also Emile Durkheim, *The Division of Labor in Society*, trans. George Simpson (1893; New York: Macmillan Co., 1933).

34. This point is developed by Alasdair MacIntyre, *After Virtue*, 107–111.

35. The story of early sociology and its commitments to social betterment has been ably told by Luther L. Bernard and Jessie Bernard, *Origins of American Sociology: The Social Science Movement in the United States* (New York:

Crowell, 1943). See also Anthony Oberschall, *The Establishment of Empirical Sociology: Studies in Continuity, Discontinuity, and Institutionalization* (New York: Harper and Row, 1973).

36. Lester F. Ward, *Dynamic Sociology,* 2 vols. (1883; New York: Appleton, 1902) xxvii.

37. Lester F. Ward, "Contemporary Sociology, Part II," *American Journal of Sociology* 7 (1902) 629–658. For a good discussion of what happened to Ward's thinking on this matter, see Bernard and Bernard, *Origins of American Sociology.*

38. Thomas Henry Huxley, *Evolution and Ethics* (New York: D. Appleton and Co., 1902).

39. Albion Small, "The Era of Sociology," *American Journal of Sociology* 1 (July 1895) 1–15, esp. 3.

40. Ibid. 14.

41. Albion Small, *General Sociology* (Chicago: University of Chicago Press, 1905) 655. William Graham Sumner, the most vociferous advocate of Spencerian social Darwinism, opposed planning in "The Absurd Effort to Make the World Over" (1894) in his *War and Other Essays* (New Haven: Yale University Press, 1911) 195–210.

42. Robert A. Scott and Arnold R. Shore, *Why Sociology Does Not Apply: A Study of the Use of Sociology in Public Policy* (New York: Elsevier, 1979) 9.

43. George Mowry, *The Era of Theodore Roosevelt* (New York: Harper and Brothers, 1958).

44. This story, and its implications for social planning, was well told by Richard Hofstader, *The Progressive Movement: 1900–1915* (Englewood Cliffs, N.J.: Prentice-Hall, 1963) and by Robert H. Wiebe, *The Search for Order: 1877–1920* (New York: Hill and Wong, 1967).

45. Scott and Shore, *Why Sociology Does Not Apply,* 99.

46. Mary O. Furner traced the disputes between the social reformers and those edging toward a value-free position in her *Advocacy and Objectivity: A Crisis in the Professionalization of American Social Science: 1865–1905* (Lexington: University of Kentucky Press, 1975). An academic freedom case of particular note discussed by Furner was that engendered after E. A. Ross of Stanford University openly attacked Leland Stanford for exploiting Chinese workers in amassing his fortune. See esp. 143, 204.

47. Peter Caws, *Science and the Theory of Value* (New York: Random House, 1967) 23.

48. Franz Boas, *Race, Language, and Culture* (New York: Macmillan, 1940; New York: Macmillan, 1955).

49. Boas taught at Columbia University and trained many anthropologists in cultural relativist thinking — Ruth Benedict, Alfred Kroeber, Margaret Mead, and Robert Lowie to name a few. Nevertheless, many came to

have serious misgivings about the valuative implications of cultural relativism. For example, by the 1950s Margaret Mead became an unblushing spokeswoman for the concept of progress and for the swift transformation of primitive societies into modern ones. After revisiting the New Guinea village where she conducted fieldwork in 1928–1929, she wrote that anthropologists, once so fearful of ethnocentrism, should no longer necessarily "protect" primitive societies from Western encroachment. In her New Guinea village, social change had occurred rapidly, and it had been, in her judgment, for the better. People were happier, more affectionate, healthier, and more fulfilled than under the traditional life pattern. She frankly looked to an open world fertilized by the genius of American civilization. See *Margaret Mead, New Lives for Old* (New York: Morrow, 1966) 5–6, 458. Chicago anthropologist Robert Redfield confronted the problem of cultural relativism and ethical neutrality and came down unequivocally on the side of "progress." See Robert Redfield, *The Primitive World and Its Transformations* (Ithaca, N.Y.: Cornell University Press, 1953).

50. For one of the best discussions of the value judgment question as formulated by Weber and his contemporaries, see Arnold Brecht, *Political Theory: Foundations of Twentieth Century Thought* (Princeton: Princeton University Press, 1959) esp. Chapters 5 and 6. Max Weber would have been the first to admit that he did not originate the doctrine of value relativism and that he was indebted to many others who saw the problems of fusing the "is" and the "ought." Among the most notable of those who preceded Weber was Georg Simmel, who scattered his discussions of the subject across two volumes of his *Einleitung in Die Moralwissenschaft* (Berlin: W. Hertz, vol. 1, 1892, and vol. 2, 1893). See especially his comments in vol. 1, 8, 72, 98, 99.

51. Max Weber, "Objectivity of Knowledge in Social Science and Social Policy," (1904) in *The Methodology of the Social Sciences*, trans. and ed. Edward A. Shils and Henry A. Finch (New York: The Free Press of Glencoe, 1949). For commentary on this article, see Arnold Brecht, *Political Theory*, 221–31.

52. Weber, "Objectivity of Knowledge in Social Science and Social Policy," 1, 3, 4, 9.

53. Max Weber, "Politics as Vocation" and "Science as Vocation" in *From Max Weber: Essays in Sociology*, trans. and ed. Hans H. Gerth and C. Wright Mills (New York: Oxford University Press, 1946). For insightful commentary on "Science as Vocation," see Robert Nisbet, "Max Weber and the Roots of Academic Freedom," in *Controversies and Decisions: The Social Sciences and Public Policy*, ed. Charles Frankel (New York: Russell Sage Foundation, 1976) 103–122.

54. Brecht, *Political Theory*, 223–224.

55. Weber, "Objectivity of Knowledge in Social Science and Social Policy," 14.

56. Stuart Rice, "What Is Sociology?" *Social Forces,* 10 (1931–1932) 319–326.

57. Ibid., 325.

58. See Robert C. Bannister, *Sociology and Scientism: The American Quest for Objectivity, 1880–1940* (Chapel Hill: University of North Carolina Press, 1987).

59. Ibid. 6.

60. Ibid. 6, 121–125.

61. For a summary discussion of the logical positivism emergent out of the Vienna circle in the 1920s, see MacRae, *The Social Function of Social Science,* 64–68.

62. The distinction between the value skeptic and the value relativist is made by Dennis C. Foss, *The Value Controversy in Sociology: A New Orientation for the Profession* (San Francisco: Jossey-Bass, 1977) 53.

63. For an example of a value-free approach to the study of values, see Milton Rokeach, *The Nature of Human Values* (New York: Free Press, 1973).

64. P. H. Hauser, "On Actionism in the Craft of Sociology," *Sociological Inquiry* 39 (1969) 139–147. See also Walter R. Gove, "Should the Sociology Profession Take Moral Stands on Political Issues?" *American Sociologist* 5 (August 1970) 221–223.

65. Robert K. Merton, "Basic Research and Potentials of Relevance," *American Behavioral Scientist* 6 (1963) 86–90; and Lewis Coser, "Letter to a Young Sociologist," *Sociological Inquiry* 39 (1969) 131–138.

66. Carol H. Weiss, "Introduction," in *Using Social Research in Public Policy Making,* ed. Carol H. Weiss (Lexington, Mass.: Lexington–D. C. Heath, 1977) 2.

67. Quoted in John C. Burnham, *Lester Ward in American Thought* (Washington, D.C.: Public Affairs Press, 1956) 10–11.

68. Quoted in Becker, *The Structure of Evil,* 78–79.

69. Robert Bierstedt, "Social Science and Social Policy," *American Association of University Professors Bulletin* 34 (1948) 310–319.

70. Robert S. Lynd, *Knowledge for What? The Place of Social Science in American Culture* (Princeton: Princeton University Press, 1939) 2. See also John D. Bernal, *The Social Function of Science* (London: G. Routledge, 1939).

71. Julian Huxley, "Evolutionary Ethics," in T. H. Huxley and Julian Huxley, *Touchstone for Ethics,* (New York: Harper and Row, 1947) 114.

72. Redfield, *The Primitive World and Its Transformations.*

73. This effort has been traced in a monumental work by Jeffrey C. Alexander, who clearly sees the valuational aspects of Parsonian theory in his *Theoretical Logic in Sociology,* vol. 4 of *The Modern Reconstruction of Classical Thought: Talcott Parsons* (Berkeley: University of California Press, 1983). The reader who wishes to obtain a more succinct summary of what is

valuationally at stake in the Parsonian project will find most useful Jeffrey C. Alexander's chapter entitled "Lecture Two: Parson's First Synthesis," in his *Twenty Lectures: Sociological Theory Since World War II* (New York: Columbia University Press, 1987) 22–35. Parsons provided his own synopsis of his valuational reasoning in his "Evolutionary Universals in Society," *American Sociological Review* 29 (June 1964) 339–357.

74. For major expressions of this view, see Alvin W. Gouldner, "Anti-Minotaur: The Myth of a Value-free Sociology," in *The New Sociology: Essays in Social Science and Social Theory in Honor of C. Wright Mills,* ed. Irving L. Horowitz (New York: Oxford University Press, 1964) 196–217; Heinz Eulau, "Values and Behavioral Science, Neutrality Revisited," in Heinz Eulau, *Micro-Macro Political Analysis,* (Chicago: Aldine, 1969) 364–369. David J. Gray, "Value-free Sociology: A Doctrine of Hypocrisy and Irresponsibility," *The Sociological Quarterly* 9, no. 2 (Spring 1968) 176–185. Ralf Dahrendorf, "Values in Social Science," in Ralf Dahrendorf, *Essays in the Theory of Society,* (Stanford, Calif.: Stanford University Press, 1968) 1–18; and Richard A. Berk, "How Applied Sociology Can Save Basic Sociology," in *The Future of Sociology,* ed. Edgar F. Borgatta and Karen S. Cook (Newbury Park, Calif.: Sage, 1988) 57–72.

75. John Dewey, *The Quest for Certainty: A Study of the Relation of Knowledge and Action* (New York: Putnam, 1929). Also see John Dewey, "Theory of Valuation," in *International Encyclopedia of Unified Science,* vol. 2, no. 4 (Chicago: University of Chicago Press, 1939).

76. John Ladd employs Dewey's valuational arguments in his "Policy Studies and Ethics," in *Policy Studies and the Social Sciences,* ed. Stuart S. Nagel (Lexington, Mass.: D. C. Heath, 1975) 127–184.

77. Lynd, "Knowledge for What?" 183.

78. Morris Janowitz, "Sociological Models and Social Policy," in *Political Conflict,* ed. Morris Janowitz (Chicago: Quadrangle Books, 1970) 247. Janowitz prefers the Enlightenment model. David P. Street and Eugene A. Weinstein discussed models of applied science in "Problems and Prospects of Applied Sociology," *American Sociologist* 10, no. 2 (May 1975) 65–72.

79. Edward A. Shils, "The Calling of Sociology," in *Theories of Society,* ed. Talcott Parsons, Edward A. Shils, Kaspar Naegele, and Jesse R. Pitts (New York: Free Press, 1961). See also MacRae, *The Social Function of Social Science,* 40–41.

80. For textbook treatments of applied sociology, see Paul Lazarsfeld and Jeffry G. Reitz, *An Introduction to Applied Sociology* (New York: Elsevier, 1975); A. B. Shostak (ed.), *Putting Sociology to Work* (New York: David McKay, 1974); and Alvin W. Gouldner and S. M. Miller, *Applied Sociology: Opportunities and Problems* (New York: Free Press, 1965).

81. Daniel Lerner and Harold H. Lasswell (eds.), *The Policy Sciences: Recent Developments in Scope and Method* (Stanford, Calif.: Stanford University Press, 1951). For Lasswell's later thought, see his *A Pre-View of Policy Science* (New York: American Elsevier, 1971). Lasswell's seminal thinking launched the policy science book series that advances the perspectives of members of the Policy Studies Organization. See, for an example of offerings in this series, Stuart S. Nagel (ed.), *Policy Studies and the Social Sciences* (Lexington, Mass.: D. C. Heath, 1975).

82. Daniel Lerner, "From Social Science to Policy Science: An Introductory Note," in *Policy Studies and the Social Sciences*, ed. Stuart S. Nagel (Lexington, Mass.: D. C. Heath, 1975) 3–8. For another view of Lasswell's developmental vision, see David G. Garson, "From Policy Science to Policy Analysis: A Quarter Century of Progress," in *Policy Analysis: Perspectives, Concepts, and Methods*, ed. William Dunn (Greenwich, Conn.: JAI Press, 1986) 3–32.

83. For a review of policy research during the 1950s and 1960s, see: James Fennessey, "Some Problems and Possibilities in Policy-Oriented Social Research," *Social Science Research* 1, no. 4 (December 1972) 359–383.

84. For a discussion of the report and the negative assessment of its implications, see Yehezkel Dror, *Design for Policy Sciences* (New York: American Elsevier, 1971).

85. Scott and Shore, *Why Sociology Does Not Apply*; Carol H. Weiss, "Policy Research in the University: Practical Aid or Academic Exercise," *Policy Studies Journal* 4, no. 3 (1976) 224–229; Charles E. Lindblom and David K. Cohen, *Usable Knowledge: Social Science and Social Problem Solving* (New Haven: Yale University Press, 1979); Rita Mae Kelly, "Trends in the Logic of Policy Inquiry: A Comparison of Approaches and a Commentary," *Policy Studies Review* 5, no. 3 (February 1986) 520–528; Charles E. Lindblom, *Inquiry and Change: The Troubled Attempts to Understand and Shape Society* (New Haven: Yale University Press, 1990); and Bernard Barber, *Effective Social Science: Eight Cases in Economics, Political Science, and Sociology* (New York: Russell Sage Foundation, 1987).

86. W. Keith Warner and J. Lynn England, "The Dual Aspirations of Rural Sociology," *The Rural Sociologist* 8, no. 6 (December 1988) 516. James A. Christenson calls for sociologists to address questions of what "ought" as well as "what is" in his "Social Research and Rural Sociology," *Rural Sociology* 53, no. 1 (Spring 1988) 1–24.

87. Patrick C. Jobes, "Natural and Relativistic Perspectives in Social Science: A Quandary From the Warner and England Paper," *The Rural Sociologist* 8, no. 6 (December 1988) 549–550. For good examples of applied sociologists reflecting on the fact that valuation is central to their efforts in theory building, see *The Rural Sociologist* 9, no. 2 (Spring 1989).

88. MacRae, *The Social Function of Social Science*, 10; and Irving L. Horowitz (ed.), *The Use and Abuse of Social Science*, 2d ed. (New Brunswick, N.J.: Transaction Press, 1975).

89. Scott and Shore, *Why Sociology Does Not Apply*. See also Clare Wenger (ed.), *The Research Relationship: Practice and Politics in Social Policy Research* (London: Allyn and Unwin, 1987).

90. Scott and Shore, *Why Sociology Does Not Apply*. 222.

91. Henry Rieken, "Social Science and Social Problems," *Social Science Information* (February 1969) 101–109.

92. Scott and Shore, *Why Sociology Does Not Apply*. 230.

93. Lindblom and Cohen, *Usable Knowledge*.

94. Scott and Shore, *Why Sociology Does Not Apply*. 234–238. Lindblom and Cohen, *Usable Knowledge*, passim.

95. Edgar F. Borgatta and Karen S. Cook, "Sociology and Its Future," in *The Future of Sociology*, ed. Edgar F. Borgatta and Karen S. Cook (Newbury Park, Calif.: Sage, 1988) 14. Walter Wallace has also kept the faith by arguing that sociology " . . . is by far the most reliable known strategy for doing something about the world . . . and, potentially, thereby improving the quality of human life." See his "Toward a Disciplinary Matrix in Sociology," in *Handbook of Sociology*, ed. Neil Smelser (Newbury Park, Calif.: Sage, 1988) 24.

96. For reviews of the content of radical critical sociology, see Michael Lessnoff, "Technique, Critique, and Social Science," in *Philosophical Disputes in the Social Sciences*, ed. S. C. Brown (Sussex: The Harvester Press, 1979) 89–116; Richard Flacks and Gerald Turkel, "Radical Sociology: The Emergence of Neo-Marxian Perspectives in U.S. Sociology," in *Annual Review of Sociology*, ed. Ralph H. Turner et al., vol. 4 (Palo Alto, Calif.: Annual Reviews, Inc., 1978) 193–238; Franco Ferrorotti, *An Alternative Sociology*, trans. Pasqualino and Barbara Columbaro (New York: Irvington Publishers, 1979); and Fred R. Dallmayer, "Critical Theory and Public Policy," in *Policy Analysis: Perspectives, Concepts, Methods*, ed. William N. Dunn (Greenwich, Conn.: JAI Press, 1986) 41–68.

97. Flacks and Turkel, "Radical Sociology," 193.

98. C. Wright Mills, "On Knowledge and Power," in *Power, Politics and People*, ed. Irving Louis Horowitz (New York: Ballantine Books, 1963).

99. Radical sociology has been expanded by the work of many. One notable example is James O'Conner, *The Fiscal Crisis of the State* (New York: St. Martin's Press, 1973). See also his *Accumulation Crisis* (London: Basil Blackwell, 1986).

100. Jack L. Roach, "The Radical Sociology Movement: A Short History and Commentary," *The American Sociologist* 5 (August 1970) 224–232. Within political science there emerged the Caucus for a New Political Science,

the position of which is articulated in Marvin Surkin and Alan Wolf (eds.), *An End to Political Science: The Caucus Papers* (New York: Basic Books, 1970). Radicals in economics have organized the Association for Evolutionary Economics, founded in 1958, which has published the *Journal of Economic Issues* since 1967.

101. Alvin W. Gouldner, *The Coming Crisis of Western Sociology* (New York: Basic Books, 1970).

102. Ibid. 333.

103. Ibid. 107

104. Ibid. 488–500.

105. Ibid. 499. Gouldner is criticized by other radical sociologists for his tendency to study sociology rather than to judge a situation and take a clear stand on it. See Ferrorotti, *An Alternative Sociology*, 34–35.

106. For a collection of papers reflecting the tradition of the Frankfurt group, see Paul Connorton (ed.), *Critical Sociology* (New York: Penguin Books, 1976).

107. For a comprehensive treatment of the early phases of the Frankfurt School (1923–1950), see M. Jay, *The Dialectical Imagination* (London: Heineman, 1973).

108. Herbert Marcuse, *One Dimensional Man: Studies in the Ideology of Advanced Industrial Society* (Boston: Beacon Press, 1964).

109. Jürgen Habermas, *Theory and Practice*, trans. John Viestel (Boston: Beacon Press, 1973). See also his *Toward a Rational Society* (London: Heineman, 1971) and *Legitimation Crisis* (Boston: Beacon Press, 1975). For a sympathetic, but not wholly uncritical, explication of Habermas's thought, see Thomas McCarthy, *The Critical Theory of Jürgen Habermas* (Cambridge, Mass.: MIT Press, 1978). See also Stephen K. White, "Reason and Authority in Habermas: A Critique of the Critics," *American Political Science Review* 74, no. 4 (December 1980) 1007–1017; and Stephen K. White, *The Recent Work of Jürgen Habermas: Reason, Justice, and Modernity* (Cambridge: Cambridge University Press, 1988).

110. Jürgen Habermas, *Knowledge and Human Interests*, trans. Jeremy J. Shapiro (Boston: Beacon Press, 1971) 162. Max Horkheimer and Theodore Adorno wrote that in positivist science "the everlastingness of the factual is confirmed." See their *Dialectic of Enlightenment*, trans. John Cumming (New York: Herder and Herder, 1972) 23.

111. Michael Lessnoff, "Technique, Critique, and Social Science," in *Philosophical Disputes in the Social Sciences*, ed. S. C. Brown (Sussex: The Harvester Press, 1979) 93.

112. Marcuse, *One Dimensional Man*, 170, 175, 181–83, 185–86.

113. Habermas, *Knowledge and Human Interests*, 191–98, 212, 308ff.

114. Lessnoff, "Technique, Critique, and Social Science," 111.

115. Fred R. Dallmayr, "Toward a Critical Reconstruction of Ethics and Politics," *Journal of Politics* 36, no. 4 (November 1974) 926–957.

116. McCarthy, *The Critical Theory of Jürgen Habermas* 272–282, 310–111, 325; Karl-Otto Apel, "The Apriori of Communication and the Foundation of Ethics," in Karl-Otto Apel, *Transformation der Philosophie*, 2 vols. (Frankfurt-Main: Suhrkamp, 1973) see vol. 2 and Jürgen Habermas, "Toward a Theory of Communicative Competence," in *Recent Sociology, No. 2: Patterns of Communicative Behavior*, ed. Hans P. Dreitzel (New York: Macmillan, 1970) 115–130.

117. McCarthy, *The Critical Theory of Jürgen Habermas*, 325.

118. Dallmayr, "Toward a Critical Reconstruction of Ethics and Politics," 953–954.

CHAPTER III

1. John Maynard Keynes, *General Theory of Employment, Interest, and Money* (London: Macmillan, 1936).

2. For discussion of market problems, social welfare, and development values, see Robert A. Dahl and Charles E. Lindblom, *Politics, Economics, and Welfare* (New York: Harper and Brothers, 1953); James M. Buchanan and Gordon Tullock, *Calculus of Consent* (Ann Arbor: Ann Arbor Paperbacks, 1965); Kurt Baier, "What Is Value? An Analysis of the Concept," in *Values and the Future*, ed. Kurt Baier and Nicholas Rescher (New York: Free Press, 1969) 33–67; and Duncan MacRae, *The Social Function of Social Science* (New Haven: Yale University Press, 1976). J. Ron Stanfield, in his *Economic Thought and Social Change* (Carbondale: Southern Illinois University Press, 1979), saw the crisis of current economic theory as centering on the fact that economic growth does not serve development values. Richard Zeckhauser and Elmer Schaefer provided one of the best overviews of the attempts of economists to deal with market failure in their "Public Policy and Normative Economic Theory," in *The Study of Policy Formulation*, ed. Raymond A. Bauer and Kenneth J. Gergen (New York: The Free Press, 1968) 27–102. For a critique and extension of economic logic as it applies to the problem of defining welfare in the domain of natural resources, see John V. Krutilla and Anthony C. Fisher, *The Economics of Natural Environments: Studies in the Valuation of Commodity and Amenity Resources* (Baltimore: Published for Resources for the Future by Johns Hopkins University Press, 1975).

3. MacRae, *The Social Function of Social Science*, esp. 160–161.

4. Karl Polanyi, "Our Obsolete Market Mentality," in *Primitive Archaic and Modern Economies*, ed. George Dalton (Boston: Beacon Press, 1971) 59–77; Arthur M. Okun, *Equality and Efficiency: The Big Trade-Off* (Washington,

D.C.: Brookings Institution, 1975) 12–13; Amartya Sen, *On Ethics and Economics* (New York: Basil Blackwell, 1987).

5. For a useful discussion of Pareto optimality, see Zeckhauser and Schaefer, "Public Policy and Normative Economic Theory," 43–48.

6. Discussions of conditions of pure market competition and its variants abound in the economic literature. For an introductory textbook treatment, see William J. Baumol and Alan S. Blinder, *Economic Principles and Policy* (New York: Harcourt Brace Jovanovich, 1979) 418–419.

7. Thorstein Veblen, *Imperial Germany and the Industrial Revolution* (New York: Viking Press, 1915). Wesley C. Mitchell (ed.), *What Veblen Taught* (New York: Viking Press, 1936); John R. Commons, *Institutional Economics: Its Place in Political Economy* (Madison: University of Wisconsin Press, 1934). Clarence Edwin Ayers, *The Industrial Economy: Its Technological Basis and Institutional Destiny* (Boston: Houghton Mifflin, 1952); Gunnar Myrdal, *Against the Stream: Critical Essays on Economics* (New York: Pantheon, 1973); Robert L. Heilbroner, *In the Name of Profit* (Garden City, N.Y.: Doubleday, 1972); Robert Lekachman, *National Income and the Public Welfare* (New York: Random House, 1972); Stanfield, *Economic Thought and Social Change;* John Kenneth Galbraith, *Economics and the Public Purpose* (Boston: Houghton Mifflin, 1973).

8. John Kenneth Galbraith, *The New Industrial State* (Boston: Houghton Mifflin, 1967).

9. Charles E. Lindblom, *Politics and Markets: The World's Political-Economic Systems* (New York: Basic Books, 1977) 356. Also this argument has been extended by James S. Coleman, *The Asymmetric Society* (Syracuse: Syracuse University Press, 1982) and by Alan Neustadt and Dan Clausen, "Corporate Political Groupings: Does Ideology Unify Business Political Behavior?" *American Sociological Review* 53 (April 1988) 172–190. Also see Bennett Harrison and Barry Bluestone, *The Great U-Turn: Corporate Restructuring and the Polarizing of America* (New York: Basic Books, 1988). Alfred D. Choudler, Jr., the dean of U.S. business historians, has traced the growth of large-scale private corporations and has examined their capacity to manage prices, manipulate supplies, fix product standards, and influence consumer demands. See his *The Visible Hand: The Managerial Revolution in American Business* (Cambridge: Harvard University Press, 1978) and *Scale and Scope: The Dynamics of Industrial Capitalism* (Cambridge: Belknap Press, 1990).

10. For extended analysis of the problems in neoclassical economic theory induced by corporate power, see Stanfield, *Economic Thought and Social Change;* Carl Kaysen, "Corporations: How Much Power? What Scope?" and Eugene V. Rostow, "To Whom and for What Ends Is Corporate Power Responsible?" both in *The Corporation in Modern Society*, ed. Edward S. Mason (Cambridge: Harvard University Press, 1959).

11. The fountainhead for analysis of externality is Arthur C. Pigou, *The Economics of Welfare*, 4th ed. (London: Macmillan and Company, 1950). A useful review is provided by E. J. Mishan, "The Postwar Literature on Externalities; An Interpretative Essay," *Journal of Economic Literature* 9 (March 1971) 1–28. See also F. M. Bator, "The Anatomy of Market Failure," *The Quarterly Journal of Economics* 72, no. 3 (August 1958) 351–379; Kenneth J. Arrow, "Political and Economic Evaluation of Social Effects and Externalities," in *The Analysis of Public Output*, ed. Julius Margolis (New York: Columbia University Press and the National Bureau of Economic Research, 1970); and K. William Kapp, *The Social Costs of Private Enterprise* (New York: Schocken Books, 1971). The problem of externality is by no means limited to capitalist systems, as demonstrated by Marshall I. Goldman, "Externalities and the Race for Economic Growth in the USSR: Will the Environment Ever Win?" *Journal of Political Economy* 80, no. 2 (March–April 1972) 314–327.

12. V. Smil, *The Bad Earth* (New York: Sharpe, 1983); B. Komavov, *The Destruction of Nature in the Soviet Union* (White Plains, N.Y.: Sharpe, 1980); Philip R. Pryde, "The 'Decade of the Environment' in the U.S.S.R.," *Science* 220, no. 4594 (April 15, 1983) 274–279; and Paul Wallich, "Dark Days: Eastern Europe Brings to Mind the West's Polluted Past," *Scientific American* 263, no. 2 (August 1990) 16–20.

13. J. R. Vincent and J. D. Russell, "Alternatives for Salinity Management in the Colorado River Basin," *Water Resources Bulletin* 7, no. 4 (1971) 856–867; *Arizona Daily Star* (Tucson) "Salinization Concern to Echeverria," May 30, 1972; *Arizona Daily Star* (Tucson), "Americans Make Colorado River Three Times Too Salty for Drinking," June 21, 1972.

14. The problem of "public goods" received its original formulation at the hands of Paul Samuelson. See his "The Pure Theory of Public Expenditure," *Review of Economics and Statistics* 36 (November 1954) 387–389. For extensions and critique of the concept, see Mancur Olson, *The Logic of Collective Action* (New York: Schocken Books, 1970); John Chamberlain, "Provision of Collective Goods as a Function of Group Size," *American Political Science Review* 68, no. 2 (June 1974) 707–735; and O. A. Davis and A. B. Whinston, "On the Distinction Between Public and Private Goods," *American Economic Review* 57, no. 2 (1967) 360–373.

15. Because goods are owned by public authorities does not necessarily mean that they can be classified as public goods. For example, publicly owned timber stands or grasslands are not public goods because access to the timber or grass resources is a privilege obtained only by payment of a proper fee (excludability), and one party's consumption does reduce that which is available to another (rivalness).

16. The discrepancy between individual and community logics has been forcefully argued by Garrett Hardin, "The Tragedy of the Commons," *Science* 162 (1968) 1243–1248. Reprinted in *Managing the Commons*, ed.

Garrett Hardin and John Baden (San Francisco: W. H. Freeman and Co., 1977) 16–30. Specific case studies of the manner in which people have organized to protect public goods are presented by Bonnie M. McCay and James M. Acheson (eds.), *The Question of the Commons: The Culture and Ecology of Communal Resources* (Tucson: University of Arizona Press, 1987).

17. See Michael Taylor, "The Theory of Collective Choice," in *Macropolitical Theory*, ed. Fred I. Greenstein and Nelson W. Polsby (Reading, Mass.: Addison-Wesley Publishing Company, 1975) 413–481, esp. 466. See also Robert Axelrod and William D. Hamilton, "The Evolution of Cooperation," *Science* 211, no. 4489 (March 27, 1981) 1390–1396.

18. Alfred E. Kahn, "The Tyranny of Small Decisions: Market Failures, Imperfections, and the Limits of Economics," *Kyklos: International Review for Social Scientists* 19 (Fasc. 1, 1966) 23–47.

19. Ibid. 24.

20. The problem of "freezing" was treated more broadly in David M. Freeman, *Technology, Culture, and Society: Issues in Assessment, Conflict, and Choice* (Chicago: Rand McNally, 1974) 29–31, 116–118.

21. This was identified as a major problem confronting technology assessment in U.S. Congress, House Committee on Science and Astronautics, Subcommittee on Science, Research, and Development, *Hearings. Technology Assessment* 91st Cong. 1st sess., no. 13.(Washington, D.C.: Government Printing Office, 1970) 229.

22. Lindblom, *Politics and Markets,* 45–49.

23. Richard G. Lipsey and Kelvin Lancaster, "The General Theory of Second Best," *Review of Economic Studies* 24 (1956) 11–32.

24. For discussion of this point by one sympathetic to socialist ideals, see Radoslov Selucky, *Marxism, Socialism, Freedom* (New York: St. Martin's Press, 1979). See also John P. Burke, Lawrence Crocker, and Lyman Legters (eds.), *Marxism and the Good Society* (Cambridge: Cambridge University Press, 1981). The classic statement by one less sympathetic was, of course, Friedrich A. Hayek, *The Road to Serfdom* (Chicago: University of Chicago Press, 1944). See also Igor Sahforevich, *The Socialist Phenomenon* (New York: Harper and Row, 1980). The reader wishing to pursue the deficiencies of Marxist value criteria for policy-making and assessment will also want to read Tom Campbell, *The Left and Rights* (London: Routledge & Kegan Paul, 1983); Allen E. Buchanan, *Marx and Justice: The Radical Critique of Liberalism* (Totawa, N.J.: Rowman and Littlefield, 1982); and David A. Crocker, *Praxis and Democratic Socialism: The Critical Theory Of Markovic and Stojanovic* (Atlantic Highlands, N.J.: Humanities Press, 1983); and Steven Lukes, *Marxism and Morality* (New York: Oxford University Press, 1985).

25. Two textbook writers who contended that socialism is the answer are Charles H. Anderson, *The Sociology of Survival: Social Problems of Growth* (Homewood, Ill.: Dorsey Press, 1976) and Joan Smith, *Social Issues and the Social Order: The Contradictions of Capitalism* (Cambridge, Mass.: Winthrop Publishers, 1981). Peter Berger debunked both the capitalist myth of growth and the socialist myth of revolution in his *Pyramids of Sacrifice: Political Ethics and Social Change* (Garden City, N.Y.: Doubleday Anchor, 1976).

26. See, on this point, Allen Buchanan, *Ethics, Efficiency and the Market* (Totowa, N.J.: Rowman and Allenheld, 1985).

27. For discussion of this point, see Lawrence Crocker, "Marx, Liberty, and Democracy," in *Marxism and the Good Society*, ed. John P. Burke, Lawrence Crocker, and Lyman Legters (Cambridge: Cambridge University Press, 1981) 32–58. The crisis in Marxist theory since de-Stalinization is insightfully addressed by Vladimir Tismaneanu, *The Crisis of Marxist Ideology in Eastern Europe* (New York: Routledge, 1988). A most lucid critique demonstrating the failure of Marxist intellectuals to come to grips with valuation is advanced by Axel van den Berg, *The Immanent Utopia: From Marxism on the State to the State of Marxism* (Princeton: Princeton University Press, 1989) passim and esp. 500–519.

28. Roger S. Gottlieb, *History and Subjectivity: The Transformation of Marxist Theory* (Philadelphia: Temple University Press, 1987). See also David A. Crocker, *Praxis and Democratic Socialism*.

29. Alasdair MacIntyre, *After Virtue* (Notre Dame, Ind.: University of Notre Dame Press, 1981) 293.

30. Marshall J. Goldman, *The Spoils of Progress* (Cambridge, Mass.: MIT Press, 1972); Malcolm Pryde, *Conservation in the Soviet Union* (Cambridge: Cambridge University Press, 1972). For a most penetrating discussion of how forced industrialization doomed the conservation movement in the U.S.S.R. in the early years of Soviet planning up to 1933 and led to reckless waste of resources, see Douglas R. Weiner, *Models of Nature: Ecology, Conservation, and Cultural Revolution in Soviet Russia* (Bloomington: Indiana University Press, 1988). Also, Hilary F. French provides an overview of the environmental calamity socialism has created in the U.S.S.R. and Eastern Europe in "Restoring the East European and Soviet Environments," in *State of the World, 1991*, ed. Lester R. Brown (New York: W. W. Norton, 1991) 93–112.

31. Buchanan, *Ethics, Efficiency and the Market*, 106–108.

32. Szymon Chodak, *Societal Development: Five Approaches with Conclusions from Comparative Analysis* (New York: Oxford University Press, 1973) 3–13.

33. Immanuel Wallerstein, "The Development of the Concept of Development," in *Sociological Theory, 1984*, ed. Randall Collins (San Francisco: Jossey-Bass, 1984) 102–103.

34. Fred W. Riggs, "Development," in *Social Science Concepts: A Systematic Analysis*, ed. Giovanni Sartori (Beverly Hills, Calif.: Sage, 1984) 125–204, esp. 126.

35. Ankie M. Hoogvelt provided an excellent summary of modernization theory in the first part of her *The Sociology of Developing Countries* 2d ed. (London: The Macmillan Press, 1978) 9–62. Influential pieces of the modernization literature included Bert F. Hoselitz, "Noneconomic Barriers to Economic Development." *Economic Development and Cultural Change* 1, no. 1 (1952–1953) 14–15; David C. McClelland, *The Achieving Society* (New York: Free Press, 1961); Wilbert Moore, *Social Change* (Englewood Cliffs, N.J.: Prentice-Hall, 1963) esp. Chapter 5; Bert F. Hoselitz and Wilbert E. Moore, (eds.), *Industrialization and Society* (The Hague: UNESCO-Mouton, 1966); Alex Inkeles, "Making Men Modern: On the Causes and Consequences of Individual Change in Six Developing Countries," *American Journal of Sociology* 75, no. 2 (1969) esp. 210–211; and Chodak, *Societal Development*.

36. Joseph R. Gusfield, "Tradition and Modernity: Misplaced Polarities in the Study of Social Change," *American Journal of Sociology* 7 (January 1967) 351–362. See also Reinhard Bendix, "Tradition and Modernity Reconsidered," *Comparative Studies in History and Society* 9, no. 3 (1967) 292–346; Henry Bernstein, "Modernization Theory and the Sociological Study of Development," *Journal of Development Studies* 7, no. 2 (1971) 141–160. David E. Apter, *Rethinking Development* (Beverly Hills, Calif.: Sage, 1987) 27; and Jan Berting and W. Blackman (eds.), *Beyond Progress and Development* (Brookfield, Mass.: Avebury, 1987).

37. For recent reviews of the literature, see Joel S. Migdal, "Studying the Politics of Development and Change: The State of the Art," in *Political Science: The State of the Discipline*, ed. Ada W. Finifter (Washington, D.C.: The American Political Science Association, 1983) 309–338; and Peter B. Evans and John D. Stephens, "Development and the World Economy," in *The Handbook of Sociology*, ed. Neil J. Smelser (Beverly Hills, Calif.: Sage, 1988) 739–773.

38. Gunnar Myrdal, *Asian Drama: An Inquiry into the Poverty of Nations* (New York: The Twentieth Century Fund, 1968) vol. 1, 49–70; and Peter L. Berger, *Pyramids of Sacrifice: Political Ethics and Social Change* (Garden City, N.Y.: Doubleday Anchor, 1976). Berger updated his analysis of development values in *The Capitalist Revolution: Fifty Propositions About Prosperity, Equality and Liberty* (New York: Basic Books, 1986). Unfortunately, in my view Berger has rather uncritically jumped on the aggregate economic growth bandwagon in this later effort. See Denis Goulet, *The Cruel Choice*

(New York: Atheneum, 1973) esp. 215–235. See also Goulet's, "Tasks and Methods in Development Ethics," *Cross Currents* 28, no. 2 (1988) 146–172.

39. Myrdal, *Asian Drama*, 71

40. Denis Goulet, "Development for What?" *Comparative Political Studies* 1, no. 2 (July 1968) 295–312. See also his *The Cruel Choice*, esp. preface and chap. 6.

41. Kyong-Dong Kim, "Toward A Sociological Theory of Development: A Structural Perspective," *Rural Sociology* 38 (Winter 1973) 468–476.

42. Dudley Seers, "The Meaning of Development," *International Development Review* 11, no. 4 (December 1969) 2–6.

43. J. A. Hobson, *Imperialism: A Study* (London: Allen and Unwin, 1902); and Nikolai Lenin, *Imperialism: The Highest Stage of Capitalism* (London: Lawrence and Wishart, 1916). This perspective was elaborated by Paul Baran, *The Political Economy of Growth* (New York: Monthly Review Press, 1957) and by Harry Magdoff, *The Age of Imperialism: The Economics of U.S. Foreign Policy* (New York: Monthly Review Press, 1969). Ankie Hoogvelt summarizes the essence of dependency theory in *The Sociology of Developing Countries*.

44. See, for example, Ranjit Sau, *Unequal Exchange, Imperialism and Underdevelopment: An Essay on the Political Economy of World Capitalism* (Calcutta: Oxford University Press, 1978); and Ian Roxborough, *Theories of Underdevelopment* (Atlantic Highlands, N.J.: Humanities Press, 1979). For a recent review of the literature, see Evans and Stephens, "Development and the World Economy," 739–773.

45. Herbert Blumer, "The Idea of Social Development," *Studies in Comparative International Development* 2, no. 1 (1966).

46. Fred W. Riggs, "Development," 133–134.

47. Ibid. 150

48. Ibid.

49. Warren F. Ilchman and Norman Thomas Uphoff, *The Political Economy of Change* (Berkeley: University of California Press, 1971).

50. Ibid. 5.

51. Amitai Etzioni, *The Moral Dimension: Toward a New Economics* (New York: The Free Press, 1988).

52. Ibid. 181–186.

53. Ibid. 205–208.

CHAPTER IV

1. Yehezkel Dror, "On Becoming More of a Policy Scientist," *Policy Studies Review* 4, no. 1 (August 1984) 16.

2. For a clear presentation of the main elements of welfare economics, see Peter Bohm, *Social Efficiency: A Concise Introduction to Welfare Economics* (New York: John Wiley and Sons, 1973). For a historical treatment, see Maurice Dobb, *Theories of Value and Distribution Since Adam Smith: Ideology and Economic Theory* (Cambridge: Cambridge University Press, 1973).

3. Joseph Cropsey, "What Is Welfare Economics?" *Ethics* 55 (January 1955) 116–125, esp. 116. For a discussion as to why "preference" must be a normative concept, see Ian Malcolm and David Little, *A Critique of Welfare Economics* (Oxford: Clarendon Press, 1950).

4. Charles W. Anderson, "The Place of Principles in Policy Analysis," *American Political Science Review* 73, no. 3 (September 1979) 713.

5. Mary Peter Mack, "Jeremy Bentham," in *International Encyclopedia of the Social Sciences*, ed. David L. Sills (New York: The Macmillan Company and the Free Press, 1968) vol. 2, 55.

6. Jeremy Bentham, *An Introduction to Principles of Morals and Legislation* (1780; London: Pickering, new ed., 1823; New York: Hafner, 1948).

7. For a discussion and bibliography on utilitarianism, see Dan W. Brock, "Recent Work in Utilitarianism," *American Philosophical Quarterly* 10, no. 4 (October 1973). For an excellent review of the content of utilitarian thought and critique, see Stuart Hampshire (ed.), *Public and Private Morality* (New York: Cambridge University Press, 1978). See also Duncan MacRae's critique in *The Social Function of Social Science* (New Haven: Yale University Press, 1976) esp. 58–59; and see Richard Posner, *The Economics of Justice* (Cambridge: Harvard University Press, 1983), esp. chap. 3, 48–87; and J.J.C. Smart and Bernard Williams, *Utilitarianism: For and Against* (New York: Cambridge University Press, 1973).

8. F. Y. Edgeworth, *Mathematical Psychics* (London: C. Kegan Paul and Company, 1881) 56–82, esp. 57; and Alfred Marshall, *Principles of Economics*, 8th ed. (New York: The Macmillan Company, 1949) 130–134; 467–476.

9. Lionel Robbins, "Interpersonal Comparisons of Utility: A Comment," *Economic Journal* 48, no. 192 (1938) 637.

10. Lionel Robbins, *An Essay on the Nature and Significance of Economic Science* (London: Macmillan, 1937) 140.

11. See, for a review of the implications of Robbins's insight and for the normative problems faced by the welfare economist, Kenneth J. Arrow, *Social Choice and Individual Values*, 2d ed. (New York: John Wiley, 1963) 9, 59–66.

12. Vilfredo Pareto, *Manual of Political Economy*, trans. Ann S. Schwier (Geneva: Droz, 1909; New York: Kelley, 1971). For a discussion and critique

of the principle of Pareto optimality, see Brian Barry and Douglas W. Rae, "Political Evaluation," *Handbook of Political Science*, vol. 1, ed. Fred I. Greenstein and Nelson W. Polsby (Reading, Mass.: Addison-Wesley, 1975) 337–401.

13. N. Kaldor, "Welfare Propositions of Economics and Interpersonal Comparisons of Utility," *Economic Journal* 49 (September 1939) 549–552; and J. R. Hicks, "The Foundations of Welfare Economics," *Economic Journal* 49 (December 1939) 696–700, 711–712.

14. The Kaldor-Hicks compensation principle has been criticized by W. J. Baumol, "Community Indifference," *Review of Economic Studies* 14, no. 1 (1946–1947) 44–48.

15. See, for an extension of this argument, Alan T. Peacock and Charles K. Rowley, "Pareto Optimality and the Political Economy of Liberalism," *Journal of Political Economy* 80, no. 3 (May–June 1972) 476–490.

16. For description and critique of cost-benefit analysis, see MacRae, *The Social Function of Social Science*, 129–135; Aaron Wildavsky, "The Political Economy of Efficiency," *Public Administration Review* 26, no. 4 (1966) 292–310; and E. S. Mishan, *Economics for Social Decisions: Elements of Cost Benefit Analysis* (New York: Praeger, 1973).

17. MacRae, *The Social Function of Social Science*, 133.

18. Robert A. Dahl and Edward R. Tufte, *Size and Democracy* (Stanford, Calif.: Stanford University Press, 1973) 7, 10–11.

19. Kenneth J. Arrow, *Social Choice and Individual Values*, 2d ed. (New York: John Wiley, 1963). See also Michael Taylor, "The Theory of Collective Choice," in *Macropolitical Theory*, ed. Fred I. Greenstein and Nelson W. Polsby (Reading, Mass.: Addison-Wesley, 1975) 413–481. A complete summary of the problem of aggregating individual choices into collective decisions is provided by W. Riker, "Voting and the Summation of Preferences: An Interpretive Bibliographic Review of Selected Developments During the Last Decade," *American Political Science Review* 55 (December 1961) 900–911. A more recent review of the problem of aggregating individual preferences into collective choice, with special focus on Arrow's Impossibility Theorem, is Douglas Blair and Robert A. Pollak, "Rational Collective Choice," *Scientific American* 249, no. 2 (August 1983) 88–95.

20. Herbert J. Gans, *More Equality* (New York: Pantheon Books, 1973). David G. Gil set up a model for policy analysis centering on the value of equality. See his *Unraveling Social Policy*, rev. ed. (Cambridge, Mass.: Schenkman, 1976). See also N. Birnbaum, "Sociology: Discontent Present and Perennial," *Social Research* 38 (1971) 732–750; and Alvin Gouldner, "The Sociologist as Partisan: Sociology and the Welfare State," *American Sociologist* 3 (1968) 103–116.

21. For distinctions between equality of initial position, equality of opportunity, and equality of outcome, see Daniel Bell, *The Cultural Contradictions*

of Capitalism (New York: Basic Books, 1976) 260–274. See also Mark V. Pauly and Thomas D. Willett, "Two Concepts of Equity and Their Implications for Public Policy," *Social Science Quarterly* 53 (1972) 8–19. An excellent discussion of the varieties of equality is found in Douglas Rae et al., *Equalities* (Cambridge: Harvard University Press, 1981).

22. Walter Buckley, "On Equitable Inequality," *American Sociological Review* 28 (October 1963) 799–801.

23. John Rawls, *A Theory of Justice* (Cambridge: The Belknap Press of Harvard University Press, 1971). The first exposition appeared in his "Justice as Fairness," *Philosophical Review* 67 (1958) 164–194. For a summary and critique, see Brian Barry, *The Liberal Theory of Justice: A Critical Examination of the Principal Doctrines in* A Theory of Justice *by John Rawls* (New York: Oxford University Press, 1973). See also Robert Paul Wolff, *Understanding Rawls* (Princeton: Princeton University Press, 1977); and Norman Daniels (ed.), *Reading Rawls: Critical Studies of* A Theory of Justice (New York: Basic Books, 1976).

24. Barry and Rae, "Political Evaluation," 365.

25. Ibid. 357. James S. Fishkin, in his *Tyranny and Legitimacy: A Critique of Political Theories* (Baltimore: Johns Hopkins University Press, 1979), also made a powerful argument that extant value premises suffer from dehabilitating defects.

26. See, for this history, Luther L. Bernard and Jessie Bernard, *Origins of American Sociology: The Social Science Movement in the United States* (New York: Crowell, 1943).

27. Marshall B. Clinard, "The Sociologist and Social Change in Underdeveloped Countries," *Social Problems* 10, no. 3 (Winter 1963) 207–219; and Arthur K. Davis, "Social Theory and Social Problems: Fragments of a Philosophy of Social Science," *Philosophy and Phenomenological Research* 18 (1957) 190–208.

28. See, for statements of this commitment, Irwin Deutscher, "Words and Deeds: Social Science and Social Policy," *Social Problems* 13, no. 3 (Winter 1966) 235–254; and Clinard, "The Sociologist and Social Change in Underdeveloped Countries."

29. See, for an example, Stanley D. Eitzen, *Social Problems* (Boston: Allyn & Bacon, 1983) esp. 4–7.

30. The political and valuative nature of social problems has been addressed and left unresolved by many students of the subject. One may wish to consult Howard S. Becker, "Whose Side Are We On?" *Social Problems* 14 (Winter 1967) 239–247; Henry Etzkowitz and Gerald M. Schaflander, "A Manifesto for Sociologists," *Social Problems* 14, no. 4 (Spring 1968) 399–408; Jerome G. Manis, "The Concept of Social Problems: Vox Populi and Sociological Analysis," *Social Problems* 21 (Winter 1974) 305–315; Francis E. Merrill, "The Study of Social Problems," *American Sociological Review*

13, (1948) 251–259; and John R. Seeley, "The Making and Taking of Problems: Toward an Ethical Stance," *Social Problems* 14, no. 4 (Spring 1967) 382–389.

31. Donnella H. Meadows et al., *The Limits to Growth* (New York: Universe Books, 1972).

32. For a view that economic growth can no longer serve as a development ideal, see Edward J. Woodhouse, "Revisioning the Future of the Third World: An Ecological Perspective on Development," *World Politics* 25, no. 1 (October 1972) 1–33. For an opposing view, see Walter Heller, "Economic Growth and Ecology — An Economist's View," *Monthly Labor Review* 9 (November 1971) 14–21. For additional perspective on the debate, see William D. Nordhaus, "World Dynamics: Measurement Without Data," *Economic Journal* 83 (December 1973) 1156–1183; Robert M. Solow, "Is the End of the World at Hand?" in *The Economic Growth Controversy*, ed. Andrew Weintraub, Eli Schwartz, and J. Richard Aronson (White Plains, N.Y.: International Arts and Sciences Press, 1973) 39–61. Mancur Olson and Hans H. Landsberg (eds.) *The No Growth Society* (New York: W. W. Norton, 1973); Herman Kahn, *The Next 200 Years: A Scenario for America and the World* (New York: William Morrow, 1976); and Peter W. House and Edward Williams, *The Carrying Capacity of a Nation: Growth and Quality of Life* (Lexington, Mass.: D. C. Heath, 1976).

33. H.S.D. Cole et al., *Models of Doom: A Critique of the Limits to Growth* (New York: Universe Books, 1973).

34. Duncan MacRae, Jr., "Democratic Information Systems: Policy Indicators and Public Statistics," in *Policy Analysis: Perspectives, Concepts, Methods*, ed. William N. Dunn (Greenwich, Conn.: JAI Press, 1986) 131–168. See also Duncan MacRae, Jr., *Policy Indicators: Links Between Social Science and Public Debate* (Chapel Hill: University of North Carolina Press, 1985). The valuative nature of the social indicator movement was clearly recognized in a document helping to launch the effort. See U.S. Department of Health, Education, and Welfare, *Toward a Social Report* (Washington, D.C.: Government Printing Office, 1969) esp. 97.

35. MacRae, "Democratic Information Systems," 132.

36. Ibid. 134.

37. President's Research Committee on Social Trends, *Recent Social Trends in the United States*, 2 vols. (New York: McGraw-Hill, 1933). William F. Ogburn took a leading role in the planning and execution of this study, and it represents a landmark in the history of applied sociology in the United States.

38. Eleanor B. Sheldon and Wilbert E. Moore (eds.), *Indicators of Social Change: Concepts and Measurements* (New York: Russell Sage Foundation, 1968); David M. Smith, *The Geography of Social Well-Being in the United States: An Introduction to Territorial Social Indicators* (New York: McGraw

Hill, 1973); Philip M. Hauser, *Social Statistics in Use* (New York: Russell Sage Foundation, 1975); and Angus Campbell, Philip E. Converse, and Willard Rodgers, *The Quality of American Life: Perceptions, Evaluations, and Satisfactions* (New York: Russell Sage Foundation and Basic Books, 1976).

39. Daniel Bell, *The Coming of Post-Industrial Society: A Venture in Social Forecasting* (New York: Basic Books, 1973); and George Chaplin and Glenn D. Paige (eds.), *Hawaii 2000* (Honolulu: University Press of Hawaii, 1973).

40. Richard A. Liroff, *A National Policy for the Environment: NEPA and Its Aftermath* (Bloomington: Indiana University Press, 1976). See also Lynton K. Caldwell, "Environmental Impact Analysis (EIA): Origins, Evolution, and Future Directions," *Policy Studies Review* 8, no. 1 (Autumn 1988) 75–83.

41. U.S. Water Resources Council, "Principles and Standards for Planning Water and Related Land Resources," *Federal Register*, 38, pt. 3, no. 174 (September 10, 1973) 24778–24869.

42. For an overview of the variety of social indicators used by sociologists in community impact studies, see: Rabel J. Burdge and Sue Johnson, "Sociocultural Aspects of the Effects of Resource Development," in *Handbook for Environmental Planning: The Social Consequences of Environmental Change* (New York: John Wiley and Sons, 1977) 243–278. See also Kurt Finsterbusch and Charles P. Wolf (eds.), *Methodology of Social Impact Assessment* (Stroudsburg, Pa.: Dowden, Hutchenson, and Ross, 1977); Kurt Finsterbusch, *Understanding Social Impacts* (Beverly Hills, Calif.: Sage, 1980); F. Larry Leistritz and Steven H. Murdock, *The Socioeconomic Impact of Resource Development: Methods for Assessment* (Boulder, Colo.: Westview Press, 1981); Kristi Branch, et al., *Guide to Social Assessment: A Framework for Assessing Change* (Boulder, Colo.: Westview Press, 1984); and William R. Freudenburg, "Social Impact Assessment," *Annual Review of Sociology*, ed. Ralph H. Turner and James F. Short, Jr., vol. 12 (Palo Alto, Calif.: Annual Reviews, Inc. 1986) 451–478. For explicit acknowledgement of the need for reasoned valuation in this arena of work, see Eric L. Hyman and Bruce Stiftel, *Combining Facts and Values in Environmental Impact Assessment* (Boulder, Colo.: Westview Press, 1988).

43. Bertram Gross, "A Model of Society," in *A Great Society*, ed. Bertram Gross (New York: Basic Books, 1966) 32–57; and Raymond A. Bauer (ed.), *Social Indicators* (Cambridge, Mass.: The MIT Press, 1966).

44. See, on this point, Werner J. Danhauser, "What Constitutes 'Quality' in Life?" in *Qualities of Life: Critical Choices for Americans* 7. (Lexington, Mass.: D. C. Heath, 1976).

45. Caplan reports that nine out of ten respondents to a survey agreed that an index of social well-being would be a good idea, but when pressed to explain what use might be made of such social indicator data, their responses were so obscure and heterogeneous as to be unusable. Nathan

Caplan, "Factors Associated with Knowledge Use Among Federal Executives," *Policy Studies Journal* 4, no. 3 (1976) 229–234.

46. U.S. Congress, House Committee on Science and Astronautics, Subcommittee On Science, Research, and Development Hearings Technology Assessment, 90th Cong. 1st sess., serial 1, (Washington, D.C.: Government Printing Office, 1967) 6–10.

47. For a collection of articles discussing the technology assessment efforts of several nations, see Marvin J. Cetron and Bodo Bartocha, (eds.), *Technology Assessment in a Dynamic Environment* (New York: Gordon and Breach Science Publishers, 1973).

48. For discussions of technology assessment, see Sherry R. Arnstein and Alexander N. Christokis, *Perspectives on Technology Assessment* (Jerusalem: Science and Technology Publishers, 1975); and David M. Freeman, *Technology and Society: Issues in Assessment, Conflict, and Choice* (Chicago: Rand McNally, 1974).

49. E. F. Schumacher, *Small Is Beautiful: Economics as if People Mattered* (New York: Harper and Row, 1973).

50. Richard C. Dorf and Yvonne L. Hunter (eds.), *Appropriate Visions: Technology, the Environment, and the Individual* (San Francisco: Boyd and Fraser, 1978); and Austin Robinson (ed.), *Appropriate Technologies for Third World Development* (New York: St. Martin's, 1979). See also Marilyn Carr, *Economically Appropriate Technologies for Developing Countries: An Annotated Bibliography* (Nottingham: The Russell Press Ltd., 1976); and David French, *Appropriate Technology in Social Context: An Annotated Bibliography* (Washington, D.C.: U.S. Agency For International Development, 1977).

51. L. F. Nelson, and W. C. Burrows "The U.S. Agricultural Energy Picture," *Agricultural Engineering* 55 (1974) 17–20. See also J. S. Steinhart and C. E. Steinhart, "Energy Use in the U.S. Food System," *Science* 184 (1974) 307–316.

52. Amory B. Lovins, *Soft Energy Paths: Toward a Durable Peace* (New York: Harper Colophon Books, 1977); and Barry Commoner, *The Poverty of Power: Energy and the Economic Crisis* (New York: Alfred A. Knopf, 1976).

53. Claude G. Barnes, *Jefferson and Hamilton: The Struggle for Democracy in America* (Boston: Houghton Mifflin, 1925).

54. Peter Woll, *Public Policy* (Cambridge, Mass.: Winthrop, 1974) esp. 7–8.

55. Important contributions to this literature include Stuart Langton (ed.), *Citizen Participation in America* (Lexington, Mass.: Lexington Books, 1978); Bernard van Heck, *Participation of the Poor in Rural Organizations* (Rome: Food and Agriculture Organization of The United Nations, 1979); and L. Irland, "Citizen Participation: A Tool for Conflict Management on the Public Lands," *Public Administration Review* 39 (1975) 263–269.

56. Peter L. Berger, *Pyramids of Sacrifice: Political Ethics and Social Change* (Garden City, N.Y.: Doubleday Anchor Press, 1976) 184–188, 201–202.

57. Martin S. Baker, Joseph S. Kaming, and Richard E. Morrison, *Environmental Impact Statements: A Guide to Preparation and Review* (New York: Practicing Law Institute, 1977) 156–158; and Hyman and Stiftel, *Combining Facts and Values in Environmental Impact Assessment*, esp. chaps. 3 and 8.

CHAPTER V

1. Abraham Edel, "Social Science and Value: A Study in Interrelations," in *The New Sociology: Essays in Social Science and Social Theory in Honor of C. Wright Mills*, ed. Irving Louis Horowitz (New York: Oxford University Press, 1969) 238.

2. Irving Louis Horowitz, "Science and Revolution in Contemporary Sociology: Remarks to an International Gathering," *American Sociologist* 10, no. 2 (May 1975) 75.

3. For a discussion of the distinction between "hard" and "soft" justification of value criteria, see David A. Crocker, *Praxis and Democratic Socialism* (Atlantic Highlands, N.J.: Humanities Press, 1983) 179–185. Hard justificationists have included such notables as Plato, Descartes, and Kant. For an argument of a contemporary hard justificationist, see Alan Gewirth, *Reason and Morality* (Chicago: University of Chicago Press, 1978). Another is Roger D. Masters, who has advanced a hard justificationist argument in his "Evolutionary Biology and Political Theory," *American Political Science Review* 84, no. 1 (March 1990) 195–210, esp. 204–205. Difficulties in arriving at meaningful hard justifications have been convincingly probed by Alasdair MacIntyre in *Whose Justice? Which Rationality?* (South Bend, Ind.: Notre Dame University Press, 1988). MacIntyre has produced a careful examination of the claims of rival and incompatible accounts of social justice and rationality in four traditions of thought: Aristotelian, Augustinian, Humian, and post-Enlightenment liberalism.

4. Crocker, *Praxis and Democratic Socialism*, 384–385. See also Charles Taylor, "Neutrality in Political Science," in *Philosophy, Politics, and Society* (3d ser.), ed. Peter Laslett and W. C. Runciman (London: Basil Blackwell, 1978).

5. For discussions of the sense in which "ought" propositions can be subjected to criticism and revision on rational grounds by scientists qua scientists, see Charles W. Anderson, "The Place of Principles in Policy Analysis," *American Political Science Review* 73, no. 3 (September 1979) 711–723. See also Duncan MacRae, *The Social Function of Social Science* (New Haven: Yale University Press, 1976); Eugene J. Meehan, *Value Judgment and Social Science* (Homewood, Ill.: Dorsey Press, 1969). Stephen G. Salkever, "'Cool Reflexion' and the Criticism of Values: Is, Ought, and Objectivity in Hume's Social Science," *American Political Science Review*

74, no. 1 (March 1980) 70–77; and James K. Feibleman, "Introduction to an Objective, Empirical Ethics," *Ethics* 65, no. 2 (January 1955) 102–115. Jürgen Habermas also argued that practical questions of ethics can be decided rationally. See, for a summary discussion, Thomas McCarthy, *The Critical Theory of Jürgen Habermas* (Cambridge, Mass.: MIT Press, 1978) 310–311; and Gunnar Myrdal, "What Is Political Economy?" in *Value Judgment and Income Distribution,* ed. Robert A. Solo and Charles W. Anderson (New York: Praeger, 1981) 41–53. Myrdal made a plea for opening the social sciences up to explicit evaluation of moral choices.

6. Crocker, *Praxis and Democratic Socialism,* 184.

7. The presentation of the meta-ethical tests owes much to MacRae, *The Social Function of Social Science;* to Charles W. Anderson, "The Place of Principles in Policy Analysis," esp. 715; and to Brian Barry and Douglas W. Rae, "Political Evaluation," in *Handbook of Political Science,* vol. 1., ed. Fred I. Greenstein and Nelson W. Polsby (Reading, Mass.: Addison Wesley, 1975) 340–348.

8. The reader will recall presentation of the Arrow Impossibility Theorem in Chapter 4 (also Note 11 to Chapter 4), the critique of utilitarianism in Chapter 4 (also Note 7 in Chapter 4), and the discussion of the concepts of externality and public goods in Chapter 3 (also Notes 11 through 17 in Chapter 3).

9. James K. Feibleman, "Introduction to an Objective, Empirical Ethics," 102–115, esp. 103.

10. The idea of social structure thoroughly permeates sociology, and no adequate review of the concept can be undertaken in these pages. Central pieces include Peter M. Blau, *Inequality and Heterogeneity: A Primitive Theory of Social Structure* (New York: Free Press, 1977); Robert K. Merton, *Social Theory and Social Structure* (New York: Free Press, 1968), S. D. Berkowitz, *An Introduction To Structural Analysis* (Toronto: Butterworths, 1987); Douglas V. Popora, *The Concept of Social Structure* (Westport, Conn.: Greenwood Press, 1987); Frederick L. Bates and Walter Gillis Peacock, "Conceptualizing Social Structure: The Misuse of Classification in Structural Modeling," *American Sociological Review* 54 (August 1989) 565–577; and Neil J. Smelser, "Social Structure," in *Handbook of Sociology,* ed. Neil Smelser (Newbury Park, Calif.: Sage, 1988) 103–129.

11. The context of choice concept formulated here, although related to the concept of life chances offered by others, is not identical. Ralf Dahrendorf speaks of life chances as being options (choice possibilities) and ligatures (bonds, allegiances, and linkages that are the source of meaning). Dahrendorf sees progress for human societies as materializing in the form of greater life chances. The problem is that Dahrendorf fails to specify particular operational normative criteria by which to assess whether life chance A ought or ought not to be promoted vis-à-vis life chance B when A and B are in conflict. See Ralf Dahrendorf, *Life Chances:*

Approaches to Social and Political Theory (Chicago: University of Chicago Press, 1979). Foss made a similar argument and floundered for the same lack of specificity. See Dennis C. Foss, *The Value Controversy in Sociology* (San Francisco: Jossey-Bass, 1977) esp. 60–61. See also Edward J. Logue, "The Idea of America Is Choice," in *Qualities of Life: Critical Choices for Americans*, vol. 3 (Lexington, Mass.: D. C. Heath, 1976). W. Keith Warner also employed the concept of life chances to define the meaning of social development. Life chances are viewed as the product of social organization; he asked how much increase in which life chances had been produced by organizations at what costs to people relative to alternatives. This is in much the same spirit that informs the notion of choice context here, but like Dahrendorf, Warner did not specify a logic of value for assessing which trade-offs among competing life chances should be made. See W. Keith Warner, "The Structural Matrix of Development," in *Sociological Perspectives of Domestic Development*, ed. George M. Beal, Ronald C. Powers, and Walter E. Coward (Ames: Iowa State University Press, 1971) 94–115, esp. 98–99.

12. For a discussion of lexicographic value ordering, see Richard Zeckhauser and Elmer Shaefer, "Public Policy and Normative Economic Theory," in *The Study of Policy Formation*, ed. Raymond A. Bauer and Kenneth J. Gergen (New York: Free Press, 1968) 37–38.

13. Charles W. Anderson saw the economic efficiency criterion in the same way as it is used here — i.e., as a tie breaker for policies that successfully pass higher-order tests. See Charles W. Anderson, "The Place of Principles in Policy Analysis," 720. Robert L. Heilbroner also made a case that the economic efficiency value must be subordinated to higher-order social values in his *Between Capitalism and Socialism: Essays in Political Economics* (New York: Vintage Books, 1970).

14. Quoted by Robert A. Kocia, "Reason, Development, and the Conflicts of Human Ends: Sir Isaiah Berlin's Vision of Politics," *American Political Science Review* 74, no. 1 (March 1980) 44.

15. Karl Popper, *The Open Society and Its Enemies*, rev. ed. (Princeton, N.J.: Princeton University Press, 1950).

16. Isaiah Berlin, *Four Essays on Liberty* (New York: Oxford University Press, 1969). For an excellent historical treatment of the concept of freedom, see Herbert J. Muller, *Freedom in the Modern World* (New York: Harper and Row, 1966). For a discussion of the concepts of negative and positive liberty, see also Charles Taylor, "What's Wrong with Negative Liberty?" in *The Idea of Freedom: Essays in Honor of Isaiah Berlin*, ed. Alan Ryan (New York: Oxford University Press, 1979) 175–193.

17. Joel Feinberg, *Rights, Justice, and the Bounds of Liberty* (Princeton, N. J.: Princeton University Press, 1980) 7.

18. Berlin, *Four Essays on Liberty,* xiii.

19. See Feinberg, *Rights, Justice, and the Bounds of Liberty,* esp. 7.

CHAPTER VI

1. For reviews of definitions of social conflict, see Clinton F. Fink, "Some Conceptual Difficulties in the Theory of Social Conflict," *Journal of Conflict Resolution* 12, no. 4 (1968) 413–458; Raymond W. Mack and Richard C. Snyder, "The Analysis Of Social Conflict — Toward an Overview and Synthesis," in *Conflict Resolution: Contributions of the Behavioral Sciences,* ed. Claget Smith (Notre Dame, Ind.: Notre Dame University Press, 1971) 3–35; Stuart M. Schmidt and Thomas A. Kochan, "Conflict: Toward Conceptual Clarity," *Administrative Science Quarterly* 17, no. 3 (September 1972) 359–370; and Anthony Obershall, "Theories of Social Conflict," in *Annual Review of Sociology,* vol. 4, ed. Ralph H. Turner et al., (Palo Alto, Calif.: Annual Reviews, Inc., 1978) 291–316.

2. Lewis Coser, *The Functions of Social Conflict* (Glencoe, Ill.: Free Press, 1956); and Georg Simmel, *Conflict and the Web of Group-Affiliations,* trans. Kurt H. Wolff and Reinhard Bendix (Glencoe, Ill.: Free Press, 1955).

3. From a critique of Marxian conflict theory, Ralf Dahrendorf proceeded to outline a general theory of conflict that supports this point of view. He argued that conflict is a necessary element in all imperatively coordi nated associations — i.e., the distribution of authority in such associations is a "cause" of conflict group formation. Since imperatively coordinated associations are a necessary feature of society, conflict was viewed as being universal. See Ralf Dahrendorf, *Class and Class Conflict in Industrial Society* (Stanford, Calif.: Stanford University Press, 1959).

4. Simmel, *Conflict and the Web of Group-Affiliations,* 26, 35. Coser, *The Functions of Social Conflict* .

5. This argument I have made elsewhere. See David M. Freeman, *Technology and Society: Issues in Assessment, Conflict, and Choice* (Chicago: Rand McNally, 1974); and David M. Freeman, JoAnne Tremaine, and Patti Madson, "Social Well-Being — A Conflict Approach," *Journal Of Environmental Management* 5 (1977) 319–333.

6. The literature employing the conflict cleavage concept is too vast to be fully reviewed here, but the reader should consult Douglas L. Rae and Michael Taylor, *The Analysis of Political Cleavages* (New Haven: Yale University Press, 1970) and Bruce Bueno de Mesquita, "Theories of International Conflict: An Analysis and an Appraisal," in *Handbook of Political Conflict: Theory and Research,* ed. Ted Robert Gurr (New York: Free Press, 1980) 361–398.

7. The concept of polarization has been examined by any number of authors. Anthony Oberschall, in his *Social Conflict and Social Movements* (Englewood Cliffs, N.J.: Prentice-Hall, 1973) 287, defines polarization as the breaking up of a community, group, or society into two internally mobilized and mutually hostile camps. James S. Coleman views polarization as "the division of the community into two socially and attitudinally separate camps, each convinced it is absolutely right." See his *Community Conflict* (New York: Free Press, 1957) 13. These views are compatible with those forwarded by Jeffrey Hart, "Symmetry and Polarization in the European International System, 1870–1879: A Methodological Study," *Journal Of Peace Research* 11, no. 3 (1974) 232. Kenneth Boulding has provided a detailed account of the polarizing process, which he connects to destructive conflict, in his *Conflict and Defense* (New York: Harper Torchbooks, 1962) esp. chap. 2.

8. Karl Marx, *Das Kapital: A Critique of Political Economy*, ed. Friedrich Engels and condensed by Serge L. Levitsky (Chicago: Henry Regnery Company, n.d.).

9. Dahrendorf, *Class and Class Conflict in Industrial Society*, esp. 268. Judith Marsh employs the concepts of polarizing and crosscutting conflict in the manner employed herein, and she has concluded that from 1952 to 1968, polarization increased in U.S. society, at least with regard to two issues — school integration and guaranteed jobs. See Judith Marsh, "Patterns of Conflict in American Society, 1952–1968," *Sociology and Social Research* 57, no. 3 (April 1973) 315–334.

10. Peter M. Blau, *Inequality and Heterogeneity: A Primitive Theory of Social Structure* (New York: The Free Press, 1977) 86.

11. Rudolph J. Rummel, *Conflict in Perspective*, vol. 3 of *Understanding Conflict and War* (Beverly Hills, Calif.: Sage, 1977) 140.

12. Clifford Geertz, "The Integrative Revolution: Primordial Loyalties and Civil Politics in the New States," in *Old Societies and New States: The Quest for Modernity in Asia and Africa*, ed. Clifford Geertz (New York: Free Press, 1963) 105–157.

13. Max Gluckman, *Custom and Conflict in Africa* (New York: Barnes and Noble, 1964) 1–4. Gay Elizabeth Kang examined Gluckman's data and qualified his analysis in her "Conflicting Loyalties Theory: A Cross-Cultural Test," *Ethnology* 15, no. 2 (April 1976) 210 ff.

14. See, for example, Karl W. Deutsch, "Social Mobilization and Political Development," *American Political Science Review* 55 (September 1961) 493–514; Cyril E. Black, *The Dynamics of Modernization: A Study in Comparative History* (New York: Harper and Row, 1966); S. N. Eisenstadt, *Modernization: Protest and Change* (Englewood Cliffs, N.J.: Prentice-Hall, 1966); and Mancur Olsen, Jr., "Rapid Growth — A Destabilizing Force," *Journal Of Economic History* 23 (December 1963) 529–552.

15. For example, Ekkehart Krippendorff, "Minorities, Violence, and Peace Research," *Journal of Peace Research* 16, no. 1 (1979) 26–40.

16. Coleman, *Community Conflict*. Also, the negative dynamics of conflict polarization in the case of a Chicago community organization are examined by Eric L. Hirsch, "The Creation of Political Solidarity in Social Movement Organizations," *The Sociological Quarterly* 27, no. 3 (1986) 373–387.

17. Ibid. 14.

18. William Gamson, "Rancorous Conflict in Community Politics," *American Sociological Review* 31 (1966) 71–81.

19. Louis Kriesburg, *The Sociology of Social Conflict* (Englewood Cliffs, N.J.: Prentice-Hall, 1973) 158–161.

20. Quoted in ibid., 161. Crane Brinton described this process of squeezing moderates in revolutions. See *The Anatomy of Revolution* (New York: W. W. Norton, 1938; New York: Vintage Books, 1952). Lynn Eden provided a case study of how a minister who was a civil rights activist polarized a small Wisconsin town. See his *Crisis in Watertown: The Polarization of an American Community* (Ann Arbor: University of Michigan Press, 1972).

21. Muzafer Sherif, "Experiments in Group Conflict," *Scientific American* 195, no. 5 (November 1956) 54–58. See also his *Intergroup Conflict and Cooperation: The Robbers' Cave Experiment* (Norman, Okla.: University Book Exchange, 1961) and *In Common Predicament: The Social Psychology of Intergroup Conflict and Cooperation* (Boston: Houghton Mifflin, 1966).

22. Sherif, *In Common Predicament*, 90.

23. Morton Deutsch, "Conflicts: Productive and Destructive," *Journal of Social Issues* 25 (January 1969) 7–42. See also his *The Resolution of Conflict: Constructive and Destructive Processes* (New Haven: Yale University Press, 1973).

24. Arthur F. Bentley, *The Process of Government: A Study of Social Pressures* (Bloomington, Ind.: Principia Press, 1908; Bloomington, Ind.: Principia Press, 1949); David B. Truman, *The Governmental Process* (New York: Knopf, 1951); William J. Kornhauser, *The Politics of Mass Society* (Glencoe, Ill.: Free Press, 1959); S. M. Lipset, *Political Man* (New York: Doubleday, 1960); S. M. Lipset and Stein Rokkan (eds.), *Party Systems and Voter Alignments: Cross National Perspectives* (New York: Free Press, 1967). Mack and Snyder, "The Analysis of Social Conflict," 3–35, esp. 33; Ernest B. Haas, "International Integration, the European and the Universal Process," in *International Political Communities: An Anthology* (Garden City, N.Y.: Doubleday Anchor, 1966); and Claude Ake, *A Theory of Political Integration* (Homewood, Ill.: Dorsey Press, 1967) 10.

25. Thomas Sterns Elliot, *Notes Toward the Definition of Culture* (New York: Harcourt Brace, 1949) 58–59.

26. Gluckman, *Custom and Conflict in Africa*, 17.

27. For example, Charles R. Nixon, "The Adaptation of Cultural Ties to Economic Development," *The American Behavioral Scientist* 18, no. 1 (September-October 1974) 36–58.

28. Richard Sandbrook, "Patrons, Clients, and Factions: New Dimensions of Conflict Analysis in Africa," *Canadian Journal of Political Science* 5, no. 1 (March 1972) 104–119.

29. Simmel, *Conflict and the Web of Group-Affiliations.*

30. E. A. Ross, *The Principles of Sociology* (New York: The Century Company, 1920) 164–165.

31. Coser, *The Function of Social Conflict*, 72–80.

32. Dahrendorf, *Class and Class Conflict in Industrial Society*, 213–223. Sherif, *In Common Predicament*, esp. 93; and Amtai Etzioni, "Strategic Models for a De-Polarizing World," in *Conflict Resolution: Contributions of the Behavioral Sciences*, ed. Claget Smith (Notre Dame, Ind.: Notre Dame University Press, 1971) 542–550.

33. See, for a discussion of legitimacy; Max Weber, *The Theory of Social and Economic Organization*, trans. A. M. Henderson and Talcott Parsons (New York: The Free Press, 1947) 124–132; 324–329. See also Richard M. Merelman, "Learning and Legitimacy," *The American Political Science Review* 60, no. 3 (September 1966) 548–561.

34. William H. Riker, *The Theory of Political Coalitions* (New Haven: Yale University Press, 1962) esp. 47; Karl Deutsch, *Communication Theory and Political Communities* (Philadelphia: J. B. Lippincott, 1964) 53; and Anatol Rapoport, "Game Theory and Human Conflict," in *The Nature of Human Conflict*, ed. Elton McNeil (Englewood Cliffs, N.J.: Prentice-Hall, 1965).

35. Thomas C. Schelling, *The Strategy of Conflict* (New York: Galaxy Books, 1963) 83; and Lester Thurow, *The Zero Sum Society: Distribution and the Possibilities for Economic Change* (New York: Basic Books, 1980).

36. I. William Zartman, "Negotiation as a Joint Decision-Making Process," *Journal of Conflict Resolution* 21, no. 4 (December 1977) 619–638.

37. Simmel, *Conflict and the Web of Group-Affiliations*, esp. 130. Sherif, *In Common Predicament*, 137.

38. Simmel, *Conflict and the Web of Group-Affiliations*, 87.

39. This point has been made by Eric A. Nordlinger in his *Conflict Regulation in Divided Societies* (Cambridge: Harvard University Center for International Affairs, 1972) 3, 93–96. For an explicit test of the hypothesis that as polarization increases, negotiability decreases, see David M. Freeman and David Hittle, "Conflict Polarization and Negotiability of Issues — An Empirical Assessment with Reference to Natural Resource Cleavages in a Western River Basin," *The Social Science Journal* 22, no. 2 (April 1985) 1–15.

40. One who has correctly distinguished between power and conflict, and who has contended that the two concepts should be considered as theoretically and empirically distinct, is Jeffery Hart in his "Symmetry and Polarization in the European International System, 1870–1879," 229–244.

41. See, for example, Murray Edelman, "Escalation and Ritualization of Political Conflict," *American Behavioral Scientist* 13, no. 2 (November-December 1969) 231–247. Raymond Tanter, issue ed., "Why Fight? Conflict Models for Strategists and Managers," *American Behavioral Scientist* 15, no. 6 (July-August, 1972) entire issue; Jeffrey Paige, *Agrarian Revolution: Social Movements and Export Agriculture in the Underdeveloped World* (New York: The Free Press, 1975); Charles Tilly, Louise Tilly, and Richard Tilly, *The Rebellious Century, 1830–1930* (Cambridge: Harvard University Press, 1975); and William A. Gamson, *The Strategy of Social Protest* (Homewood, Ill.: Dorsey Press, 1975). Hubert M. Blalock, Jr., has advanced a theory that incorporates both conflict and power variables in an explanation of decisions to commit violence. See his *Power and Conflict: Toward a General Theory* (Newbury Park, Calif.: Sage, 1989). For an excellent review and critique of sociological thought about violence, along with insightful reflections on problems of theory construction in the social sciences, see James B. Rule, *Theories of Civil Violence* (Berkeley: University of California Press, 1988).

42. Charner Perry, "Violence — Visible and Invisible," *Ethics* 81, no. 1 (October 1970) 1–21. James C. Dick, *Violence and Oppression* (Athens: University of Georgia Press, 1979); and Sheldon G. Levy, "Political Violence: A Critical Evaluation," *The Handbook of Political Behavior*, vol. 2, ed. Samuel L. Long, (New York: Plenum Press, 1981) 163–224.

43. See, on this point, Terry Nardin, "Theories of Conflict Management," *Peace Research Review* 4, no. 2 (1971) 1–93.

44. Charner Perry, *Violence — Visible and Invisible*, 15.

45. Michael Walzer, *Just and Unjust Wars: A Moral Argument with Historical Illustrations* (New York: Basic Books, 1977). Walzer showed that a profound justification of "just wars" can be generated from two most basic and widely recognized rights of human beings — not be robbed of life or liberty. See also James T. Johnson, *Ideology, Reason, and Limitation of War* (Princeton: Princeton University Press, 1975); and James T. Johnson, *The Just War Tradition and the Restraint of War: A Moral and Historical Inquiry* (Princeton: Princeton University Press. 1981). For a view that argues that war in the modern world cannot be justified, see Robert L. Holmes, *On War and Morality* (Princeton: Princeton University Press, 1989). Holmes centers his case against the justifiability of war on the unjustifiability of killing innocents that must necessarily accompany modern war. I find that Holmes does not give sufficient attention to the killing of innocents that may accompany structures of oppression found in conditions of "peace."

46. R. P. Turco et al., "Nuclear Winter: Global Consequences of Multiple Nuclear Explosions," *Science* 222, no. 4630 (December 23, 1983) 1283–1292; P. R. Ehrlich, "Long-Term Biological Consequences of Nuclear War," *Science* 222, no. 4630 (December 23, 1983) 1293–1300; and Jonathan Schell, "Nuclear Arms — Parts 1 & 2," *New Yorker* (January 2, 9, 1984) 36–75, 43–94.

47. A useful discussion of polarization measurement is that of Rae and Taylor, *The Analysis of Political Cleavages*. See also Lawrence S. Mayer, "An Analysis of Measures of Crosscutting and Fragmentation," *Comparative Politics* 4, no. 3 (April 1972) 405–415. William Schneider, "Issues, Voting, and Cleavages: A Methodology and Some Tests," *American Behavioral Scientist* 18, no. 1 (September-October 1974) 111–146; G. Bingham Powell, Jr., "Political Cleavage Structure, Cross-Pressure Processes, and Partisanship: An Empirical Test of the Theory," *American Journal of Political Science* 20, no. 1 (February 1976) 1–23; and Edward O. Laumann and Peter V. Marsden, "The Analysis of Oppositional Structures in Political Elites: Identifying Collective Actors," *American Sociological Review* 44, no. 5 (October 1979) 713–732.

48. David M. Freeman with assistance of Jan Quint and R. Scott Frey, *Social Analysis of Proposed Natural Resource Management Alternatives: Concepts and Procedures for Policy Evaluation*, Colorado State University Experiment Station Bulletins, special series no. 18 (Fort Collins, Colo: Colorado State University, May 1981).

49. The problem of choosing a base group is a bit more complex than it has been made to appear. Polarization scores can be expected to vary depending on which conflict group is defined as a base group. Each conflict cleavage provides space in which actors can ally or oppose or from which they can withdraw into neutrality. The question becomes: From the perspective of which one cleavage space should the analyst compare the positions of alliance and opposition generated in all spaces? I have not determined a way to successfully compare all positions to all positions simultaneously, but it is possible to compare all conflict positions on all cleavages to any one actor's positions on all cleavage spaces. Given a distribution of conflict positions in a multispaced figure, from which direction should the analyst approach and enter to compare positions of conflict groups? The solution employed here is as follows: (1) Take each conflict group in consecutive order and compute the positions and salience scores for all other actors relative to each base group, (2) determine which base group comparison has yielded the highest polarization score, and (3) select for policy ranking the computation that yields the highest polarization score. In other words, compute polarization scores against all possible base groups and choose for policy assessment the base group that generates the greatest polarization score. For economy of presentation, the examples employed in this chapter do not display a calculation of polarization scores on all possible base groups. David F. Hittle has

examined this approach and has offered a refinement that, for reasons of economy in presentation, will not be discussed here. A serious student of cleavage theory and measurement is advised to read David F. Hittle, "Theory and Measurement of Crosscutting Conflict in Sociological Research" (Ph.D. diss., Dept. of Sociology, Colorado State University, 1989).

50. This was argued by Robert A. Dahl, "Some Explanations," in *Political Oppositions in Western Democracies*, ed. Robert A. Dahl (New Haven: Yale University Press, 1966) 348–387, esp. 378.

51. When a policy-induced cleavage is introduced into the analysis, the potentially highest deviation score increases. However, the policy cleavages are introduced into the analysis one at a time, so the potential shift in the denominator is the same in all instances. It is possible to compare each policy-induced shift in the numerator to the base deviation potential without adjusting the latter value for the additional deviation potential. Therefore, only numerator values are adjusted with insertion of the policy cleavage. Given that each proposed policy cleavage will shift the denominator in exactly the same amount, the conflict polarization ranking will not be affected.

52. The data reported in this section were generated in a conflict analysis applied to the study area under the auspices of the U.S. Forest Service in 1976. However, the name has been changed for purposes of this presentation. Furthermore, in the interest of brevity, important details have been omitted from the discussion of the unit and from the presentation of the proposed policy options.

53. For a detailed presentation specifying procedures for panel selection and operation for generation of conflict data see: Freeman, *Social Analysis of Proposed Natural Resource Management Alternatives*.

54. The sixteen social conflict groups were identified as those reflecting the kinds of organizations important to life on the Big Vista Divide unit. There is no theoretical or practical obstacle to alternative lists to reflect local realities on any given unit.

55. Although the village irrigation command area designated here as Jalarabad was the subject of study as one of sixteen villages in a sample for research on irrigation water management in Pakistan, the name has been changed for purposes of this presentation. The larger study from which this presentation is drawn has been reported by Max K. Lowdermilk, David M. Freeman, and Alan C. Early, *Farm Irrigation Constraints and Farmers' Responses: Comprehensive Field Survey in Pakistan*, 6 vols., Water Management Technical Report No. 48A-F (Fort Collins, Colo.: Colorado State University Pakistan Project, 1978). See esp. vols. 2 and 4. As in the case of the Forest Service planning unit in Colorado no attempt is made to present the full richness of the social situation from which the conflict analysis has been abstracted.

56. For an excellent historical examination of the river and associated irrigation system, see Aloys Arthur Michael, *The Indus River* (New Haven: Yale University Press, 1967).

57. Ibid, and David M. Freeman et al., *Local Organization for Social Development: Concepts and Cases of Irrigation Organization* (Boulder, Colo.: Westview Press, 1989) chap. 5.

58. Zekige Elgar, *A Punjabi Village in Pakistan* (New York: Columbia University Press, 1960); and Muhammad Rafique Raza, *Two Pakistani Villages: A Study in Social Stratification* (Lahore: University of the Punjab, 1969).

59. The most detailed treatment of caste in Pakistan is that of Sir Denzil Ibbetson, *Punjab Castes* (Lahore: Superintendent, Government Printing, Punjab, 1916; Lahore: Mubarak Ali Publishers, 1974). It must be noted that there are distinct differences between Pakistani and traditional Indian caste patterns. To qualify as a caste system, social networks must display at least three properties: (1) status hierarchy, (2) ascribed position in the status hierarchy for life, and (3) graduated levels of ritual purity along the hierarchy. In Pakistan, where urbanization and industrialization have not destroyed traditional patterns, the first two of these criteria tend to be fulfilled, but the third is largely absent. Although many employ the term *caste* in Pakistan, castes in the fullest sense are not likely to be found there.

60. Water losses of this magnitude in watercourses are common in Pakistan — and probably in most other countries. Whether such losses are problematic depends on a variety of factors such as costs of pumping lost water from the ground, degradation of such pumped water, and distributional effects of the losses. See Lowdermilk, Freeman, and Early, *Farm Irrigation Constraints and Farmers' Responses,* esp. vol. 1.

61. Although the episodes roughly summarized in this case occurred, they were never adequately documented. Brief mention is made in ibid., vol. 4, 197.

CHAPTER VII

1. Quoted in *The Great Quotations,* ed. George Seldes (New York: Pocket Books, 1972) 320.

2. Quoted by Max Lerner, *America as a Civilization: Life and Thought in the United States Today* (New York: Simon and Schuster, 1957) 362.

3. Francis M. Wilhoit, *Quest for Equality in Freedom* (New Brunswick, N.J.: Transaction Books, 1979) 53.

4. Quoted by Amy Gutmann, *Liberal Equality* (Cambridge: Cambridge University Press, 1980) ix.

5. Martin Bronfenbrenner has questioned whether anything called a mal-distribution can be properly said to exist, given the great conceptual difficulties in defining one. See his "Equality and Equity," *Annals of the American Academy of Political and Social Science* 409 (September 1973) 9–23, esp. 10. Amy Gutmann and Lester Thurow also agree that there is no apparent solution to the problem of defining a just distribution despite the many efforts to do so. See Gutmann, *Liberal Equality;* and Lester C. Thurow, *Generating Inequality* (New York: Basic Books, 1975). Ryan C. Amacher, Robert D. Tollison, and Thomas D. Willett explore the complexities of the problem in their "A Menu of Distributional Considerations," in *The Economic Approach to Public Policy,* ed. Ryan C. Amacher, Robert D. Tollison, and Thomas D. Willett (Ithaca, N.Y.: Cornell University Press, 1976) 246–275. A most lucid account of the problems confronted in defining equality was also provided by Douglas Rae et al., *Equalities* (Cambridge: Harvard University Press, 1981).

6. Martin Bronfenbrenner, "Equality and Equity"; Wendell Bell, "A Conceptual Analysis of Equality and Equity in Evolutionary Perspective," *American Behavioral Scientist* 18, no. 1 (September-October 1974) 8–35, esp. 17–18; Thurow, *Generating Inequality,* 22; and Karen S. Cook and Karen A. Hegtvedt, "Distributive Justice, Equity, and Equality," in *Annual Review of Sociology,* vol. 9, ed. Ralph H. Turner (Palo Alto, Calif: Annual Reviews, Inc., August 1983).

7. Amy Gutmann made this point in her *Liberal Equality,* 163–164.

8. Measures of inequality have been widely discussed. The best synthesis of materials has been provided by Philip B. Coulter, *Measuring Inequality: A Methodological Handbook* (Boulder, Colo.: Westview Press, 1989). See also Hayward R. Alker, Jr., and Bruce M. Russett, "Indices for Comparing Inequality," *Comparing Nations: The Use of Quantitative Data in Cross National Research,* ed. Richard L. Merritt and Stein Rokkan (New Haven: Yale University Press, 1966) 349–372; Paul D. Allison, "Measures of Inequality," *American Sociological Review* 43, no. 6 (December 1978) 865–880; and Joseph Schwartz and Christopher Winship, "The Welfare Approach to Measuring Inequality," *Sociological Methodology, 1980,* ed. Karl F. Schussler (San Francisco: Jossey-Bass, 1977) 1–36.

9. For the distinction between divisible and indivisible goods and the implications for equality measurement, I am indebted to Tord Hoivik, "Social Inequality — The Main Issues," *Journal of Peace Research* 8, no. 2 (1971) 120.

10. For a more thorough treatment of approaches to the measurement of inequality, consult materials cited in Note 8.

11. Tord Hoivik has introduced the concept of relative mean deviation (RMD) to further distinguish between degrees of inequality in a way left untouched by the Gini coefficient and the Lorenz curve. See Hoivik, "Social Inequality," 121. See also Coulter *Measuring Inequality,* and

Schwartz and Winship, "The Welfare Approach to Measuring Inequality," for a discussion of alternatives to the Lorenz curve and Gini coefficient. The Gini index and the associated Lorenz curve rest on the assumption that equal importance may be attached to equal absolute differences in the good being distributed even though one of the differences is taken between two low-value positions and another difference is taken between two high-value points on the curve. The assumption of equal absolute differences is open to attack on the grounds that an additional acre of land or an additional dollar may be of more value to the relatively deprived than to the more advantaged. Rae and Fessler have demonstrated the "moral gerrymandering" that can occur with Gini coefficients because they plainly cannot always demonstrate which distribution is most equal. See Douglas W. Rae and Carol Fessler, "The Varieties of Equality," in *Value Judgment and Income Distribution,* ed. Robert A. Solo and Charles W. Anderson (New York: Praeger, 1981) 201–226.

12. Philip B. Coulter, "Measuring the Inequity of Urban Public Services: A Methodological Discussion with Applications," *Policy Studies Journal* 8, no. 5 (Spring 1980) 683–698; L. E. Brouthers, "Measuring Inequality in the Distribution of Urban Public Services: A Simplification," *Policy Studies Journal* 9 (Summer 1981) 999–1000; and Philip B. Coulter, "Measuring Distributional Equity," *Policy Studies Journal* 10, no. 2 (December 1981) 396–405.

13. Timothy J. O'Neill, "The Language of Equality in a Constitutional Order," *American Political Science Review* 75, no. 3 (September 1981) 626–635.

14. Ibid. passim.

15. See, for example, Bronfenbrenner, "Equality and Equity," esp. 23; and Thurow, *Generating Inequality,* 50. Michael Walzer has argued that a society in which any single distributive principle is dominant cannot be a truly egalitarian society. Equality requires a diversity of principles that mirrors the diversity of goods and arenas for the use of those goods. See Michael Walzer, *Radical Principles* (New York: Basic Books, 1980) 243. For a charting of the many ways in which equality can be split, see Rae et al., *Equalities.*

16. For good reviews of the issues to be faced, see Wilhoit, *Quest for Equality in Freedom;* Isaiah Berlin, "Equality as an Ideal," *Justice and Social Policy,* ed. Frederick A. Olafson (Englewood Cliffs, N.J.: Prentice-Hall, 1961) 128–150; and Sanford A. Lakeoff, *Equality in Political Philosophy* (Cambridge: Harvard University Press, 1964). A compelling and principled argument for more equality has been provided by Burton Zwieback, *The Common Life: Ambiguity, Agreement, and the Structure of Morals* (Philadelphia: Temple University Press, 1988).

17. Jean Jacques Rousseau, "A Discourse on Political Economy," in *The Social Contract and the Discourses*, trans. G.D.H. Cole (New York: E. P. Dutton, 1950) 306.

18. Melvin Tumin, "On Equality," *American Sociological Review* 28, no. 1 (February 1963) 26. Tumin was responding to Wilbert Moore's functionalist argument that equity does not require equality of reward. See Wilbert E. Moore, "But Some Are More Equal Than Others," *American Sociological Review* 28, no. 1 (February 1963) 13–18.

19. This position has been persuasively argued by several thinkers. In particular, see R. H. Tawney, *Equality* (New York: Barnes and Noble, 1964) esp. 164. See also Gutmann, *Liberal Equality*, 7–9.

20. Hans Singer, *Technology for Basic Needs* (Geneva: International Labor Office, 1977); Guy Standing and Richard Szal, *Poverty and Basic Needs: Evidence from Guyana and the Philippines* (Geneva: International Labor Office, 1979); and Steven H. Arnold, *Implementing Development Assistance: European Approaches to Basic Needs* (Boulder, Colo.: Westview Press, 1982). Ralf Dahrendorf discussed the concept of survival chances as distinguished from chances for the good life and luxury chances. See his *Life Chances* (Chicago: University of Chicago Press, 1979) 77. A most serious attempt to come to grips with the problem of defining basic needs in a rights framework is Henry Shue, *Basic Rights: Subsistence, Affluence, and U.S. Foreign Policy* (Princeton: Princeton University Press, 1980). Adequate consideration of Shue's important argument is precluded by the limits of this effort, but a brief comment is in order. Shue contends that everyone has a basic right to subsistence and physical security and that these basic rights must be fulfilled at all costs to those above the subsistence and security minimums subject to the constraint that basic rights of the people bearing the burden not be diminished. An unfulfilled basic right for A must be met at any cost to other citizens' enjoyment of nonbasic rights, cultural enrichment, or preferences (see 118). Shue's argument stumbles on the problem of distributional efficiency. This is to say, it cannot cope with the fact that small gains in equality might come at very great cost to the well-being of others. Furthermore, the basic rights theory presupposes the existence of a coherent basic needs theory that would inform the decision-maker as to when basic needs have been fulfilled. The awful fact of life is that we possess no minimally adequate theory of basic needs to serve a theory of basic rights as defined by Shue. Another who has thought long and carefully about basic needs is David Braybrooke, in *Meeting Needs* (Princeton: Princeton University Press, 1987). Braybrooke centers his argument upon a conception of basic needs organized around four strategic social roles: parent, householder, worker, and citizen. People "need" those resources required to carry out tasks associated with these roles (see 48–51) over the course of the mean life expectancy of people in the most favored occupations — i.e., all those occupations in which the mean life expectancy is greater than the median

life expectancy over all occupations. Something counts as a need if failure to provide it leads to a life shorter than this minimum. Braybrooke's argument is sophisticated and subtle. However, I am much persuaded by his own critique of his concept of basic needs, a critique that establishes that we are not likely to implement it with existing or foreseeable moral and political capacities.

21. Victor E. Smith calculated that such a diet would cost less than $154 per year, in his *Electronic Computation of Human Diets*, M.S.U. Business Studies (East Lansing: Michigan State University, 1964) chap. 2, 20.

22. Radoslav Selucky provided an excellent discussion of the problems of analyzing basic needs from a socialist perspective in his *Marxism, Socialism, and Freedom* (New York: St. Martin's Press, 1979) 159–165.

23. Robert Nozick, *State, Anarchy, and Utopia* (New York: Basic Books, 1974).

24. John Rawls, *A Theory of Justice* (Cambridge: The Belknap Press of Harvard University Press, 1971).

25. Ibid. 75. The Rawlsian conception of justice is related to the one earlier and less systematically forwarded by Christian Bay, who argued that a society is free only to the extent that its least privileged and its least tolerated members are free. See Christian Bay *The Structure of Freedom* (Stanford, Calif.: Stanford University Press, 1958) 7.

26. Ibid. 60.

27. Ibid. 60–61, 302.

28. This point becomes a bit murky. H.L.A. Hart questioned whether Rawls really means this in Hart's essay, "Rawls on Liberty and Its Priority," in *Reading Rawls: Critical Studies of* A Theory of Justice, ed. Norman Daniels (New York: Basic Books, 1976) 230–252.

29. For excellent critiques of Rawls's theory of justice, see Brian M. Barry, *The Liberal Theory of Justice: A Critical Examination of the Principal Doctrines of* A Theory of Justice *by John Rawls* (Cambridge: Oxford University Press, 1973); Norman Daniels (ed.), *Reading Rawls: Critical Studies of* A Theory of Justice (New York: Basic Books, 1976); Robert Paul Wolff, *Understanding Rawls: A Reconstruction and Critique of* A Theory of Justice (Princeton: Princeton University Press, 1977).

30. Barry, *The Liberal Theory of Justice*, 34.

31. Walter D. Connor raised this issue in his *Socialism, Politics, and Equality: Hierarchy and Change in Eastern Europe and the U.S.S.R.* (New York: Columbia University Press, 1979) 337.

32. Robert A. Nisbet, "The New Despotism," *Commentary* (June 1975) 38.

33. Rae et al., *Equalities*. Rae shows how equality breaks out into at least 108 different varieties. See esp. 133.

34. For an argument that equality analyses require a diversity of principles, each relevant to its sphere, see Bernard Williams, "The Idea of Equality,"

in *Philosophy, Politics, and Society,* 2d ser., ed. Peter Laslett and W. G. Runcinan (Oxford: Basil Blackwell, 1962) 110-131. A most important recent statement of this position is: Michael Walzer, *Spheres of Justice* (New York: Basic Books, 1983).

35. For a general discussion of equality of condition as well as the other two varieties, see Felix E. Oppenheim, "The Concept of Equality," in *The International Encyclopedia of the Social Sciences* (New York: Macmillan and Free Press, 1968) vol. 5, 102–108. See also Larry Gostin (ed.), *Civil Liberties in Conflict* (New York: Routledge, 1988).

36. T. H. Marshall provided an unrivaled analysis of the process by which such basic rights were gradually extended in the course of Western history. See his *Class, Citizenship, and Social Development* (Garden City, N.Y.: Doubleday, 1964).

37. Norman E. Bowie (ed.), *Equal Opportunity* (Boulder, Colo.: Westview Press, 1988). In this volume see especially the James S. Fishkin piece, "Do We Need a Systematic Theory of Equal Opportunity?" 15–21, and that of Brian Barry, "Equal Opportunity and Moral Arbitrariness," 23–44. See also James S. Coleman, "The Concept of Equality of Educational Opportunity," *Harvard Educational Review* 38 (Winter 1968) 7–22; and Mark Pauly and Thomas Willett, "Two Concepts of Equity and Their Implications for Public Policy," *Social Science Quarterly* 53 (June 1973) 8–19.

38. Rae et al., *Equalities,* 65–66.

39. Walter D. Connor, *Socialism, Politics, and Equality: Hierarchy and Change in Eastern Europe and the U.S.S.R.* (New York: Columbia University Press, 1979) esp. 17–19.

40. Ibid. 19–22. Also see Susan Ferge, "Some Relations Between Social Structure and the School System," *Hungarian Sociological Studies, The Sociological Review Monograph,* no. 17, ed. Paul Halmos (North Staffordshire, England: University of Keele, February, 1972) esp. 217.

41. Ota Sik, "Czechoslovakia's New System Of Economic Planning and Management," *Eastern European Economics* (Fall 1965) esp. 22; and Frank Parkin, *Class Inequality and Political Order* (New York: Praeger, 1971) esp. 177.

42. Christopher Jencks et al., *Inequality: A Reassessment of the Effects of Family and Schooling in America* (New York: Basic Books, 1972). Jencks and his collaborators argued that no one, by and large, really has earned his or her greater rewards. Herbert Gans argued that equality of opportunity is not a truly egalitarian principle, that only equality of result can qualify as such. See his *More Equality* (New York: Random House Vintage Books, 1974) esp. 63–64, 78.

43. W. Arthur Lewis, *Development Planning: The Essentials of Economic Policy* (New York: Harper and Row, 1966) 97–102; and Michael P. Todaro, *Economic Development in the Third World* 2d ed. (New York: Longman, 1981) 87, 526.

44. Lewis, *Development Planning*, 97–98. The question of optimum supply of infrastructure has been addressed by economists. See, for example, Jesse Burkhead and Jerry Miner, *Public Expenditure*, 2d ed. (Hawthorne, N.Y.: Aldine Press, 1971).

45. Lieberson's Index of Diversity is a measure highly appropriate to computing inequality among gender and ethnic categories. It can be employed to measure the diversity between two populations for any number of nominal categories. It compares a social category's proportions within each of two populations; higher index values indicate greater diversity or less concentration. A set of category proportions from one population is compared to the equivalent set of category proportions from another population, one intercategory pair at a time. See Philip B. Coulter, *Measuring Inequality: A Methodological Handbook* (Boulder, Colo.: Westview Press, 1989) 146–149.

46. The concept of distributive efficiency is discussed by Richard A. Musgrave and Peggy B. Musgrave, *Public Finance in Theory and Practice*, 3d ed. (New York: McGraw-Hill, 1980) 91.

47. The four watercourses aggregated together here were the subject of study as part of research on forty watercourse command areas in Pakistan. The name has been changed for purposes of this discussion. The larger study from which this presentation is drawn has been reported by Max K. Lowdermilk, David M. Freeman, and Alan C. Early, *Farm Irrigation Constraints and Farmer's Responses: Comprehensive Field Survey in Pakistan*, 6 vols., Water Management Technical Report No. 48A-F (Fort Collins, Colo.: Colorado State University Pakistan Project, 1978).

48. Ibid., vols. 1, 2, 3. For an updated analysis of the failure of irrigation organization in Pakistan, see David M. Freeman and Edwin Shinn, "Irrigation Organization on the Niazbeg Distributary in Punjab, Pakistan," in David M. Freeman, *Local Organizations for Social Development: Concepts and Cases of Irrigation Organization* (Boulder, Colo.: Westview Press, 1989) 63–132.

49. Lowdermilk, Freeman, and Early, Farm Irrigation Constraints and Farmers' Responses, vol. 1, 4; vol. 3, 89–99.

50. For a discussion of the waterlogging and salinity problem in Pakistan, see Aloys Arthur Michael, *The Indus Rivers* (New Haven: Yale University Press, 1967).

51. See, for a discussion of the design of local organizations that can sustain civic discourse about social development and that can adapt central government policy to site-specific circumstances, David M. Freeman, *Local Organizations for Social Development: Concepts and Cases of Irrigation Organization* (Boulder, Colo.: Westview Press, 1989).

52. Rae et al. *Equalities*, 150.

53. Ibid. 129.

Notes

CHAPTER VIII

1. Holmes Rolston III, *Environmental Ethics: Duties to and Values in the Natural World* (Philadelphia: Temple University Press, 1988) 198.

2. John V. Krutilla and Anthony C. Fisher, *The Economics of Natural Environments: Studies in the Valuation of Commodity and Amenity Resources* (Baltimore: Published for Resources for the Future by Johns Hopkins University Press, 1975) 15.

3. For treatments linking cost to choices forgone, I recommend J. M. Buchanan, *Cost and Choice: An Inquiry in Economic Theory* (Chicago: Markham, 1969) esp. 7, 42–43. See also R. H. Coose, "The Problem of Social Cost," *Journal of Law and Economics* 3 (October 1960) 1–44; Robert Dahl and Charles E. Lindblom, *Politics, Economics, and Welfare* (New York: Harper and Row, 1953) 164; Kenneth E. Boulding, *Economic Analysis*, 4th ed. (New York: Harper and Row, 1966) 76–77; and Armen Alchian, "Cost," in *International Encyclopedia of the Social Sciences*, ed. David L. Sills (New York: Macmillan Company and the Free Press, 1968) vol. 3, 404–415.

4. The cost notion in classical economics referred to something quite different — required outlay of labor, disutility, and physical and psychological pain. This conception of cost had no connection with sacrificed alternatives. The distinction between these two kinds of cost was not recognized by the classical economists or by many of their successors. An excellent review of this distinction is found in Buchanan, *Cost and Choice.*

5. Michael E. Gilpin, "Minimum Viable Populations: A Restoration Ecology Perspective," in *Restoration Ecology: A Systematic Approach to Ecological Research*, ed. William R. Jordan, Michael Gilpin, and John D. Aber (Cambridge: Cambridge University Press, 1987) 303.

6. See, for example, Rolston, *Environmental Ethics.*

7. David M. Freeman, *Local Organizations for Social Development: Concepts and Cases of Irrigation Organization* (Boulder, Colo.: Westview Press, 1989). See also Bonnie M. McCay and James M. Acheson (eds.), *The Question of the Commons: The Culture and Ecology of Communal Resources* (Tucson: The University of Arizona Press, 1987).

8. This literature is much too vast to be reviewed here. Key pieces include M. Taghi Farvar and John P. Milton (eds.), *The Careless Technology: Ecology and International Development* (Garden City, N.Y.: The Natural History Press, 1972); World Commission on Environment and Development, *Our Common Future* (New York: Oxford University Press, 1987); The Conservation Foundation, *The State of the Environment: A View Toward the Nineties* (Washington, D.C.: The Conservation Foundation, 1987); E. O. Wilson (ed.), *Biodiversity* (Washington, D.C.: National Academy Press, 1988); and Lester R. Brown et al., *State of the World, 1991* (New York: W. W. Norton, 1991). This is the most recent of a continuing series of annual volumes by

that same senior author and title that was initiated in 1984. Another central piece is that produced by the World Resources Institute and the International Institute for Environment and Development, *World Resources 1990–91* (New York: Oxford University Press, 1990). Earlier editions were produced in 1986 and 1987. Another excellent overview has been provided by the editors of *Scientific American* in their special issue entitled "Managing Planet Earth," 261, no. 3 (September 1989). Piers Blaikie and Harold Brookfield clearly see the problem of land degradation in a social and political context in their *Land Degradation and Society* (London: Methuen, 1987).

9. See, for example, Farvar and Milton, *The Careless Technology;* James P. Lester and Ann Bowman, *The Politics of Hazardous Waste Management* (Durham, N.C.: Duke University Press, 1983); James A. Lee, *The Environment, Public Health, and Human Ecology: Considerations for Economic Development* (Baltimore: Johns Hopkins University Press, 1985); and Charles E. Davis and James P. Lester (eds.), *Dimensions of Hazardous Waste Politics and Policy* (Westport, Conn.: Greenwood, 1988).

10. Walter E. Westman, *Ecology, Impact Assessment, and Environmental Planning* (New York: Wiley Inter-Science, 1985) 5.

11. Wilson, *Biodiversity,* 10.

12. Many discussions of the first and second laws of thermodynamics have been forthcoming in the popular literature in recent years. One of the most widely read is Jeremy Rifkin's *Entropy: A New World View* (New York: Viking, 1980), which was followed by his: *Entropy: Into the Greenhouse World* (New York: Bantam, 1989). A more technically adequate exposition, still accessible to the general reader, is that by P. W. Atkins, *The Second Law* (New York: Scientific American Books, 1984).

13. See, for a discussion of the values of a healthy natural world, The Conservation Foundation, *The State of the Environment,* 539–542.

14. Ibid. 290–291.

15. Impacted phenomena require different amounts of time to restore themselves and do so in different patterns. For example, two fifty-year impacts may have altogether different response curves as shown.

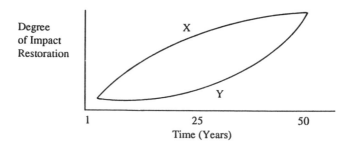

Impact X rejuvenates quickly in the early years and by year 25 has been largely restored to initial condition, whereas impact Y requires twenty-five years before the lost choice begins restoration to former condition. Each impact would be fifty years in duration, but from a choice perspective, clearly one should prefer impact profile X to Y. It must become the task of policy assessment to employ available knowledge to draw impact profiles for the phenomena associated with particular impacted choice opportunities. Such data would then be used to weight the duration value in the futures-forgone equation.

16. The concept of reversibility has been addressed by several analysts, most notably John V. Krutilla and Anthony Fisher in *The Economics of Natural Environments,* esp. 14, 39–59. See also K. J. Arrow and Anthony C. Fisher, "Environmental Preservation, Uncertainty, and Irreversibility," *Quarterly Journal of Economics* 88, no. 2 (May 1974) 312–319.

17. The name of the forest unit has been changed for the purposes of this presentation. The data reported in this section were generated in an analytical workshop conducted by the author under the auspices of the U.S. Forest Service in 1976.

18. Zaffabab District does not exist. Whereas Thikapur is a name selected to protect the identity of an actual command area for which data were reported in Chapter 6, Zaffabab district is an artifact of my imagination. However, the problems of waterlogging and salinity, the several policy options, and the list of choice opportunities are constructed so as to reflect something of conditions found in actual districts in Pakistan.

CHAPTER IX

1. Duncan MacRae, *The Social Function of Social Science* (New Haven: Yale University Press, 1976) 306.

2. Langdon Winner, *The Whale and the Reactor: The Search for Limits in an Age of High Technology* (Chicago: University of Chicago Press, 1986) 57–58.

3. There were those who resisted this tendency. See Leo Strauss, *Natural Right and History* (Chicago: University of Chicago Press, 1953); Leonard Goodwin, "The Historical Philosophical Basis for Unitary Social Science with Social Problem Solving," *Philosophy of Science* 29, no. 4 (October 1962) 377–392; and MacRae, *The Social Function of Social Science.*

4. Max Weber, "Objectivity of Knowledge in Social Science and Social Policy," in *The Methodology of the Social Sciences,* trans. and ed. Edward A. Shils and Henry A. Finch (New York: The Free Press of Glencoe, 1949) 57.

5. Walter Lippmann, *Drift and Mastery: An Attempt to Diagnose the Current Unrest* (Englewood Cliffs, N.J.: Prentice-Hall, 1961).

6. Hannah Arendt, *On Violence* (New York: Harcourt, Brace, and World, 1969) 81.

7. Much literature examines the requirements of a polity in which liberal dialogue can discipline and direct public policy. See in particular, James M. Buchanan and Gordon Tullock, *The Calculus of Consent: Logical Foundations of Constitutional Democracy* (Ann Arbor: University of Michigan Press, 1962). This analysis shows how the structure of a state having many features contained in the U.S. constitution can be derived from an individualistic calculus, but no set of policy-assessment value criteria could be derived from that calculus. See esp. 7. See also Bruce A. Ackerman, *Social Justice in a Liberal State* (New Haven: Yale University Press, 1980).

8. Quoted by Daniel Bell, *The Cultural Contradictions of Capitalism* (New York: Basic Books, 1976) 279. John Dewey also wrote a good deal about the public community devoted to aspects of life that all share and the threat represented by warring special interests unconstrained by a viable public philosophy. See John Dewey, *The Public and Its Problems* (Chicago: Swallow Press, 1954).

9. William Galston discusses this point at length in his "Defending Liberalism," *American Political Science Review* 76, no. 3 (September 1982) 621–629, esp. 625.

10. This is a point discussed by Fred M. Frohock, "Rationality, Morality, and Impossibility Theorems," *American Political Science Review* 74, no. 2 (June 1980) 373–384.

11. I have examined properties of local organizations that can successfully provide interfaces between large-scale bureaucracies and local people in specific niches in the realm of public goods generally and irrigation water management specifically. See David M. Freeman, *Local Organizations for Social Development: Concepts and Cases of Irrigation Organization* (Boulder, Colo.: Westview Press, 1989). It is my view that such local organizations, linking specific people in particular niches with central authorities, provide a primary social base for conduct of policy assessment.

12. This implication has been discussed by Lynton K. Caldwell, "The Ecosystem as a Criterion for Public Lands Policy," *Natural Resources Journal* 10, no. 2 (April 1970) 203–211, esp. 206. See also Amtai Etzioni and Edward W. Lehman, "Some Dangers in 'Valid' Social Measurement," in *Social Intelligence for America's Future,* ed. Bertram M. Gross (Boston: Allyn and Bacon, 1969) 45–62, esp. 59–60.

13. K. Ross Toole discusses this problem in "The Energy Crisis and the Northern Great Plains," in *The Future of Agriculture in the Rocky Mountains,* ed. E. Richard Hart (Salt Lake City: Westminster Press, 1980) 34.

Notes

APPENDIX I

1. Duncan MacRae, *The Social Function of Social Science* (New Haven: Yale University Press, 1976) 88–92. MacRae acknowledged that he based his specification of these rules for ethical discourse upon Talcott Parsons's formulation of the norms for scientific communication, as postulated in Talcott Parsons, *The Social System* (Glencoe, Ill.: The Free Press, 1951) 335.

2. As I indicate in Note 7, Chapter 5, I have drawn heavily from the work of Duncan MacRae, Charles Anderson, Brian Barry, and Douglas Rae in arriving at this formulation of meta-ethical criteria.

3. The use of the nomothetic-idiographic distinction is not a notion advanced by MacRae, *The Social Function of Social Science* or Charles W. Anderson, "The Place of Principles in Policy Analysis," *American Political Science Review* 73, no. 3 (September 1979) 711–723. I advance it here as a strategic consideration in the matter of clarity.

4. Stephen Toulmin, *The Uses of Argument* (Cambridge: Cambridge University Press, 1969) 188.

5. Friedrich Weismann, "Verifiability," in *Logic and Language*, ed. G. N. Flew (Oxford: Oxford University Press, 1951) 117.

APPENDIX II

1. David M. Freeman with assistance of Jan Quint and R. Scott Frey, *Social Analysis of Proposed Natural Resource Management Alternatives: Concepts and Procedures for Policy Evaluation*, Colorado State University Experiment Station Bulletins, special series, no. 18 (Fort Collins: Colorado State University, May 1981). This report describes the procedures in detail and provides references to specific applications of the methodology in applied policy assessment settings.

2. For discussions of the Delphi technique as it has been employed by others, see R. H. Ament, "Comparison of Delphi Forecasting Studies," *Futures* 2 (1970) 35–44; K. Q. Hill and J. Fowles, "The Methodological Worth of the Delphi Forecasting Technique." *Technological Forecasting and Social Change* 7 (1975) 179–92; V. E. Huckfeldt and R. C. Judd, "Issues in Large Scale Delphi Studies," *Technological Forecasting and Social Change* 6 (1974) 75–88; H. Linestone and M. Turoff (eds.), *The Delphi Method: Techniques and Applications* (New York: Addison-Wesley, 1975); Juri Pill, "The Delphi Method: Substance and Context: A Critique and Annotated Bibliography," *Socio-Economic Planning Science* 5 (1971) 57–71; and Alan L. Porter et al., *A Guidebook for Technology Assessment and Impact Analysis* (New York: North Holland, 1980), 122–127.

3. See Freeman, Quint, and Frey, *Social Analysis of Proposed Natural Resource Management Alternatives*. The report may be ordered by contacting the Bulletin Room, Experiment Station, 101 Aylesworth Hall, Colorado State University, Fort Collins, Colorado 80523.

INDEX

Index

Index

Index